SUPER EXTRA DELUXE ESSENTIAL HANDBOOK

The need-to-know stats and facts on over 875 characters!

SCHOLASTIC INC.

All rights reserved. Published by Scholastic Inc., *Publishers since
1920*. Scholastic and associated logos are trademarks and/or
registered trademarks of Scholastic Inc.

The publisher does not have any control over and does not assume
any responsibility for author or third-party websites or their content.

This book is a work of fiction. Names, characters, places, and
incidents are either the product of the author's imagination or are
used fictitiously, and any resemblance to actual persons, living
or dead, business establishments, events, or locales is entirely
coincidental.

ISBN 978-1-338-71412-8

10 9 8 7 6 5 4 3 2 1   21 22 23 24 25

Interior designed by Kay Petronio
Cover designed by Cheung Tai

Printed in the U.S.A.   40

First printing 2021

WELCOME TO THE WORLD OF POKÉMON!

Kanto . . . Johto . . . Hoenn . . . Sinnoh . . . Unova . . . Kalos . . . Alola . . . and now, Galar!

There are eight known Pokémon regions bursting with fascinating Pokémon—creatures that come in all shapes, sizes, and personalities. They live in oceans, caves, old towers, rivers, tall grass, and many other areas.

Trainers can find, capture, train, trade, collect, and use Pokémon in battle against their rivals in the quest to become the best.

The key to success with Pokémon is staying informed. Information about each Pokémon's type, category, height, and weight can make all the difference in catching, raising, battling, and evolving your Pokémon.

In this book, you'll get all the stats and facts you need about more than 875 Pokémon. You'll discover how each Pokémon evolves and which moves it uses.

So get ready, Trainers: With this *Super Extra Deluxe Essential Handbook*, you'll be prepared to master almost any Pokémon challenge!

HOW TO USE THIS BOOK

This book provides the basic stats and facts you need to know to start your Pokémon journey. Here's what you'll discover about each Pokémon:

NAME

CATEGORY

All Pokémon belong to a certain category.

TYPE

Each Pokémon has a type, and some even have two. (Pokémon with two types are called dual-type Pokémon.) Every Pokémon type comes with advantages and disadvantages. We'll break them all down for you here.

DESCRIPTION

Knowledge is power. Pokémon Trainers have to know their stuff. Find out everything you need to know about your Pokémon here.

HOW TO SAY IT

When it comes to Pokémon pronunciation, it's easy to get tongue-tied! There are many Pokémon with unusual names, so we'll help you sound them out. Soon you'll be saying Pokémon names so perfectly, you'll sound like a professor.

HEIGHT AND WEIGHT

How does each Pokémon measure up? Find out by checking its height and weight stats. And remember, good things come in all shapes and sizes. It's up to every Trainer to work with their Pokémon and play up its strengths.

POSSIBLE MOVES

Every Pokémon has its own unique combination of moves. Before you hit the battlefield, we'll tell you all about each Pokémon's awesome attacks. And don't forget—with a good Trainer, they can always learn more!

EVOLUTION

If your Pokémon has an evolved form or pre-evolved form, we'll show you its place in the chain and how it evolves.

PIKACHU

Mouse Pokémon

REGIONS:
ALOLA
GALAR
KALOS
(CENTRAL)
KANTO

TYPE: ELECTRIC

Pikachu that can generate powerful electricity have cheek sacs that are extra soft and super stretchy.

When Pikachu meet, they'll touch their tails together and exchange electricity through them as a form of greeting.

HOW TO SAY IT: PEE-ka-choo
IMPERIAL HEIGHT: 1'04"
IMPERIAL WEIGHT: 13.2 lbs.

METRIC HEIGHT: 0.4 m
METRIC WEIGHT: 6.0 kg

POSSIBLE MOVES: Agility, Charm, Discharge, Double Team, Electro Ball, Feint, Growl, Light Screen, Nasty Plot, Nuzzle, Play Nice, Quick Attack, Slam, Spark, Sweet Kiss, Tail Whip, Thunder, Thunder Shock, Thunder Wave, Thunderbolt

PICHU

PIKACHU

RAICHU

ALOLAN RAICHU

Curious about what Pokémon types you'll spot on your journey? Find out more about all eighteen known types on the next page . . .

GUIDE TO POKÉMON TYPES

A Pokémon's type can tell you a lot about it—from where to find it in the wild to the moves it'll be able to use on the battlefield. Type is the key to unlocking a Pokémon's power.

A clever Trainer should always consider type when picking a Pokémon for a match, because each type shows a Pokémon's strengths and weaknesses. For example, a Fire-type may melt an Ice-type, but against a Water-type, it might find it's the one in hot water. And while a Water-type usually has the upper hand in battle with a Fire-type, a Water-type move would act like a sprinkler on a Grass-type Pokémon. But when that same Grass-type is battling a Fire-type, it just might get scorched.

HERE ARE THE EIGHTEEN KNOWN POKÉMON TYPES:

FIRE

GRASS

WATER

NORMAL

ELECTRIC

BUG

GHOST

FLYING

FIGHTING

PSYCHIC

STEEL

ROCK

GROUND

ICE

POISON

DARK

DRAGON

FAIRY

BATTLE BASICS

WHY BATTLE?

There are two basic reasons for a Pokémon to battle. One is for sport. You can battle another Trainer in a friendly competition. Your Pokémon do the fighting, but you decide which Pokémon and which moves to use.

The second reason is to catch wild Pokémon. Wild Pokémon have no training and no owners. They can be found pretty much anywhere. Battle is one of the main ways to catch a Pokémon. But other Trainers' Pokémon are off-limits. You can't capture their Pokémon, even if you win a competition.

CHOOSING THE BEST POKÉMON FOR THE JOB

As you prepare for your first battle, you may have several Pokémon to choose from. Use the resources in this book to help you decide which Pokémon would be best. If you're facing a Fire-type Pokémon, like Scorbunny, you can put out its sparks with a Water-type Pokémon, like Sobble.

THE FACE-OFF

You and your Pokémon will have to face, and hopefully defeat, each and every Pokémon on the other Trainer's team. You win when your Pokémon have defeated all the other Trainer's Pokémon. But Pokémon do not get seriously hurt in battle. If they are defeated, they faint and then return to their Poké Balls to rest and be healed. An important part of a Trainer's job is to take good care of their Pokémon.

MEGA EVOLUTION

A select group of Pokémon possesses the ability to Mega Evolve. A Pokémon can only Mega Evolve during battle, and Mega Evolution increases its strength in ways no Trainer could imagine.

But Mega Evolution requires more than just capturing a Pokémon of a specific species. First, there must be an incredibly strong bond of trust and friendship between the Trainer and Pokémon. They must be unified on and off the battlefield.

Second, the Trainer must possess both a Key Stone and the right Mega Stone. Each Pokémon species has a specific Mega Stone. A Trainer must quest for the perfect one and prove themself worthy of its power.

LUCARIO   LUCARIONITE   MEGA LUCARIO

GIGANTAMAX POKÉMON

In the Galar region, some Pokémon have a Gigantamax form. It's a special kind of Dynamax that both increases their size and changes their appearance! Gigantamax Pokémon are extremely rare—not every Pokémon of a given species can Gigantamax—and each has access to a special G-Max Move.

ALOLAN AND GALARIAN FORMS

Alolan and Galarian Pokémon can look very different and be of a different type than their regular forms. When Pokémon develop a distinct appearance based on the region in which they live, it's called a regional variant. For example, the reason Alolan Exeggutor have grown taller is Alola's warm and sunny climate. It's perfect for Exeggcute and Exeggutor to thrive. Some believe that Alolan Exeggutor looks exactly the way it's supposed to because of Alola's environment.

ULTRA BEASTS

Ultra Beasts possess mighty powers. These mysterious creatures come from Ultra Wormholes.

LEGENDARY AND MYTHICAL POKÉMON

These extremely rare and powerful Pokémon are a bit of a mystery. They are unusually strong, and many have had incredible influence. Some have used their power to shape history and the world. And they are so rare that few people ever glimpse them. Trainers who have spotted a Legendary or Mythical Pokémon count themselves among the lucky.

Ready to discover more about each Pokémon? Then let's begin!

ABOMASNOW

Frost Tree Pokémon

REGIONS:
GALAR
KALOS
(MOUNTAIN)
SINNOH

TYPE: GRASS-ICE

If it sees any packs of Darumaka going after Snover, it chases them off, swinging its sizable arms like hammers.

This Pokémon is known to bring blizzards. A shake of its massive body is enough to cause whiteout conditions.

HOW TO SAY IT: ah-BOM-ah-snow
IMPERIAL HEIGHT: 7'03"
IMPERIAL WEIGHT: 298.7 lbs.
METRIC HEIGHT: 2.2 m
METRIC WEIGHT: 135.5 kg

POSSIBLE MOVES: Ice Punch, Powder Snow, Leer, Razor Leaf, Icy Wind, Grass Whistle, Swagger, Mist, Ice Shard, Ingrain, Wood Hammer, Blizzard, Sheer Cold

MEGA ABOMASNOW

Frost Tree Pokémon

TYPE: GRASS-ICE

IMPERIAL HEIGHT: 8'10"
IMPERIAL WEIGHT: 407.9 lbs.
METRIC HEIGHT: 2.7 m
METRIC WEIGHT: 185.0 kg

SNOVER   ABOMASNOW   MEGA ABOMASNOW

TYPE: PSYCHIC

REGIONS:
ALOLA
KALOS
(CENTRAL)
KANTO

ABRA

Psi Pokémon

This Pokémon uses its psychic powers while it sleeps. The contents of Abra's dreams affect the powers that the Pokémon wields.

Abra can teleport in its sleep. Apparently the more deeply Abra sleeps, the farther its teleportations go.

HOW TO SAY IT: AB-ra
IMPERIAL HEIGHT: 2'11"
IMPERIAL WEIGHT: 43.0 lbs.
METRIC HEIGHT: 0.9 m
METRIC WEIGHT: 19.5 kg

POSSIBLE MOVE:
Teleport

ABRA

KADABRA

ALAKAZAM

MEGA ALAKAZAM

ABSOL

Disaster Pokémon

TYPE: DARK

The only thing unlucky about Absol is its appearance. It protects fields and warns people of disaster, so one ought to be grateful for it.

The elderly call it the disaster Pokémon and detest it, but interest in its power to predict disasters is on the rise.

HOW TO SAY IT: AB-sahl
IMPERIAL HEIGHT: 3'11"
IMPERIAL WEIGHT: 103.6 lbs.
METRIC HEIGHT: 1.2 m
METRIC WEIGHT: 47.0 kg

POSSIBLE MOVES: Perish Song, Future Sight, Scratch, Feint, Leer, Quick Attack, Pursuit, Taunt, Bite, Double Team, Slash, Swords Dance, Night Slash, Detect, Psycho Cut, Me First, Sucker Punch, Razor Wind

MEGA ABSOL

Disaster Pokémon

TYPE: DARK

IMPERIAL HEIGHT: 3'11"
IMPERIAL WEIGHT: 108.0 lbs.
METRIC HEIGHT: 1.2 m
METRIC WEIGHT: 49.0 kg

ABSOL   MEGA ABSOL

ACCELGOR
Shell Out Pokémon

TYPE: BUG

It moves with blinding speed and lobs poison at foes. Featuring Accelgor as a main character is a surefire way to make a movie or comic popular.

Discarding its shell made it nimble. To keep itself from dehydrating, it wraps its body in bands of membrane.

HOW TO SAY IT: ak-SELL-gohr
IMPERIAL HEIGHT: 2'07"
IMPERIAL WEIGHT: 55.8 lbs.
METRIC HEIGHT: 0.8 m
METRIC WEIGHT: 25.3 kg

POSSIBLE MOVES: Absorb, Acid, Acid Armor, Acid Spray, Agility, Body Slam, Bug Buzz, Curse, Double Team, Final Gambit, Giga Drain, Guard Swap, Mega Drain, Power Swap, Quick Attack, Recover, Struggle Bug, Swift, Toxic, U-turn, Water Shuriken, Yawn

SHELMET ⇒ ACCELGOR

SHIELD FORME

BLADE FORME

AEGISLASH
Royal Sword Pokémon

TYPE: STEEL-GHOST

In this defensive stance, Aegislash uses its steel body and a force field of spectral power to reduce the damage of any attack.

Its potent spectral powers allow it to manipulate others. It once used its powers to force people and Pokémon to build a kingdom to its liking.

HOW TO SAY IT: EE-jih-SLASH
IMPERIAL HEIGHT: 5'07"
IMPERIAL WEIGHT: 116.8 lbs.
METRIC HEIGHT: 1.7 m
METRIC WEIGHT: 53.0 kg

POSSIBLE MOVES: Aerial Ace, Autotomize, Fury Cutter, Head Smash, Iron Defense, Iron Head, King's Shield, Metal Sound, Night Slash, Power Trick, Retaliate, Sacred Sword, Shadow Sneak, Slash, Swords Dance, Tackle

HONEDGE ⇒ DOUBLADE ⇒ AEGISLASH

AERODACTYL

Fossil Pokémon

TYPE: ROCK-FLYING

A savage Pokémon that died out in ancient times. It was resurrected using DNA taken from amber.

HOW TO SAY IT: AIR-row-DACK-tull

METRIC HEIGHT: 1.8 m

IMPERIAL HEIGHT: 5'11"

METRIC WEIGHT: 59.0 kg

IMPERIAL WEIGHT: 130.1 lbs.

POSSIBLE MOVES: Iron Head, Ice Fang, Fire Fang, Thunder Fang, Wing Attack, Supersonic, Bite, Scary Face, Roar, Agility, Ancient Power, Crunch, Take Down, Sky Drop, Hyper Beam, Rock Slide, Giga Impact

MEGA AERODACTYL

Fossil Pokémon

TYPE: ROCK-FLYING

IMPERIAL HEIGHT: 6'11"

IMPERIAL WEIGHT: 174.2 lbs.

METRIC HEIGHT: 2.1 m

METRIC WEIGHT: 79.0 kg

AERODACTYL   MEGA AERODACTYL

AGGRON
Iron Armor Pokémon

TYPE: STEEL-ROCK

Aggron claims an entire mountain as its own territory. It mercilessly beats up anything that violates its environment. This Pokémon vigilantly patrols its territory at all times.

Aggron is protective of its environment. If its mountain is ravaged by a landslide or a fire, this Pokémon will haul topsoil to the area, plant trees, and beautifully restore its own territory.

HOW TO SAY IT: AGG-ron
IMPERIAL HEIGHT: 6'11"
IMPERIAL WEIGHT: 793.7 lbs.
METRIC HEIGHT: 2.1 m
METRIC WEIGHT: 360.0 kg

POSSIBLE MOVES: Tackle, Harden, Mud-Slap, Headbutt, Metal Claw, Rock Tomb, Protect, Roar, Iron Head, Rock Slide, Take Down, Metal Sound, Iron Tail, Iron Defense, Double-Edge, Autotomize, Heavy Slam, Metal Burst

MEGA AGGRON
Iron Armor Pokémon

TYPE: STEEL

IMPERIAL HEIGHT: 7'03"
IMPERIAL WEIGHT: 870.8 lbs.
METRIC HEIGHT: 2.2 m
METRIC WEIGHT: 395.0 kg

ARON   LAIRON   AGGRON   MEGA AGGRON

AIPOM

Long Tail Pokémon

REGIONS:
ALOLA
JOHTO

TYPE: NORMAL

As it did more and more with its tail, its hands became clumsy. It makes its nest high in the treetops.

It searches for prey from the tops of trees. When it spots its favorite food, Bounsweet, Aipom gets excited and pounces.

HOW TO SAY IT: AY-pom
IMPERIAL HEIGHT: 2'07"
IMPERIAL WEIGHT: 25.4 lbs.
METRIC HEIGHT: 0.8 m
METRIC WEIGHT: 11.5 kg

POSSIBLE MOVES: Scratch, Tail Whip, Sand Attack, Astonish, Baton Pass, Tickle, Fury Swipes, Swift, Screech, Agility, Double Hit, Fling, Nasty Plot, Last Resort

AIPOM ▸ AMBIPOM

ALAKAZAM
Psi Pokémon

TYPE: PSYCHIC

It has an incredibly high level of intelligence. Some say that Alakazam remembers everything that ever happens to it, from birth till death.

Alakazam wields potent psychic powers. It's said that this Pokémon used these powers to create the spoons it holds.

HOW TO SAY IT: AL-a-kuh-ZAM
IMPERIAL HEIGHT: 4'11"
IMPERIAL WEIGHT: 105.8 lbs.
METRIC HEIGHT: 1.5 m
METRIC WEIGHT: 48.0 kg

POSSIBLE MOVES: Kinesis, Teleport, Confusion, Disable, Psybeam, Miracle Eye, Reflect, Psycho Cut, Recover, Telekinesis, Ally Switch, Psychic, Calm Mind, Future Sight, Trick

MEGA ALAKAZAM
Psi Pokémon

TYPE: PSYCHIC

IMPERIAL HEIGHT: 3'11"
IMPERIAL WEIGHT: 105.8 lbs.
METRIC HEIGHT: 1.2 m
METRIC WEIGHT: 48.0 kg

ABRA → **KADABRA** → **ALAKAZAM** → **MEGA ALAKAZAM**

ALCREMIE

Cream Pokémon

REGION: GALAR

TYPE: FAIRY

When it trusts a Trainer, it will treat them to berries it's decorated with cream.

When Alcremie is content, the cream it secretes from its hands becomes sweeter and richer.

HOW TO SAY IT: AL-kruh-mee
IMPERIAL HEIGHT: 1'00"
IMPERIAL WEIGHT: 1.1 lbs.
METRIC HEIGHT: 0.3 m
METRIC WEIGHT: 0.5 kg

POSSIBLE MOVES: Acid Armor, Aromatherapy, Aromatic Mist, Attract, Dazzling Gleam, Decorate, Draining Kiss, Entrainment, Misty Terrain, Recover, Sweet Kiss, Sweet Scent, Tackle

MILCERY   ALCREMIE

Alternate Form:
GIGANTAMAX ALCREMIE

Cream pours endlessly from this Pokémon's body. The cream stiffens when compressed by an impact. A harder impact results in harder cream.

It launches swarms of missiles, each made of cream and loaded with 100,000 kilocalories. Get hit by one of these, and your head will swim.

IMPERIAL HEIGHT: 98'05"+
IMPERIAL WEIGHT: ????.? lbs.
METRIC HEIGHT: 30.0+ m
METRIC WEIGHT: ???.? kg

ALOMOMOLA
Caring Pokémon

TYPE: WATER

Fishermen take them along on long voyages, because if you have an Alomomola with you, there'll be no need for a doctor or medicine.

The reason it helps Pokémon in a weakened condition is that any Pokémon coming after them may also attack Alomomola.

HOW TO SAY IT: uh-LOH-muh-MOH-luh
IMPERIAL HEIGHT: 3'11"
IMPERIAL WEIGHT: 69.7 lbs.

METRIC HEIGHT: 1.2 m
METRIC WEIGHT: 31.6 kg

POSSIBLE MOVES: Play Nice, Hydro Pump, Wide Guard, Healing Wish, Helping Hand, Pound, Water Sport, Aqua Ring, Aqua Jet, Double Slap, Heal Pulse, Protect, Water Pulse, Wake-Up Slap, Soak, Wish, Brine, Safeguard, Whirlpool

ALTARIA

Humming Pokémon

TYPE: DRAGON-FLYING

Altaria dances and wheels through the sky among billowing, cotton-like clouds. By singing melodies in its crystal-clear voice, this Pokémon makes its listeners experience dreamy wonderment.

Altaria sings in a gorgeous soprano. Its wings are like cotton clouds. This Pokémon catches updrafts with its buoyant wings and soars way up into the wild blue yonder.

HOW TO SAY IT: ahl-TAR-ee-uh
IMPERIAL HEIGHT: 3'07"
IMPERIAL WEIGHT: 45.4 lbs.
METRIC HEIGHT: 1.1 m
METRIC WEIGHT: 20.6 kg

POSSIBLE MOVES: Sky Attack, Pluck, Peck, Growl, Astonish, Sing, Fury Attack, Safeguard, Disarming Voice, Mist, Round, Natural Gift, Take Down, Refresh, Dragon Dance, Dragon Breath, Cotton Guard, Dragon Pulse, Perish Song, Moonblast

MEGA ALTARIA

Humming Pokémon

TYPE: DRAGON-FAIRY

IMPERIAL HEIGHT: 4'11"
IMPERIAL WEIGHT: 45.4 lbs.
METRIC HEIGHT: 1.5 m
METRIC WEIGHT: 20.6 kg

SWABLU → ALTARIA → MEGA ALTARIA

AMAURA
Tundra Pokémon

TYPE: ROCK-ICE

It lived in cold areas in ancient times. It's said that when Amaura whinnies, auroras appear in the night sky.

Amaura was restored successfully, but it's not expected to live long because of the heat of the current environment.

HOW TO SAY IT: ah-MORE-uh
IMPERIAL HEIGHT: 4'03"
IMPERIAL WEIGHT: 55.6 lbs.
METRIC HEIGHT: 1.3 m
METRIC WEIGHT: 25.2 kg

POSSIBLE MOVES: Growl, Powder Snow, Thunder Wave, Rock Throw, Icy Wind, Take Down, Mist, Aurora Beam, Ancient Power, Round, Avalanche, Hail, Nature Power, Encore, Light Screen, Ice Beam, Hyper Beam, Blizzard

AMAURA   AURORUS

AMBIPOM
Long Tail Pokémon

TYPE: NORMAL

In their search for comfortable trees, they get into territorial disputes with groups of Passimian. They win about half the time.

It uses its tails for everything. If it wraps both of its tails around you and gives you a squeeze, that's proof it really likes you.

HOW TO SAY IT: AM-bee-pom
IMPERIAL HEIGHT: 3'11"
IMPERIAL WEIGHT: 44.8 lbs.
METRIC HEIGHT: 1.2 m
METRIC WEIGHT: 20.3 kg

POSSIBLE MOVES: Dual Chop, Scratch, Tail Whip, Sand Attack, Astonish, Baton Pass, Tickle, Fury Swipes, Swift, Screech, Agility, Double Hit, Fling, Nasty Plot, Last Resort

AIPOM   AMBIPOM

AMOONGUSS
Mushroom Pokémon

TYPE: GRASS-POISON

This Pokémon puffs poisonous spores at its foes. If the spores aren't washed off quickly, they'll grow into mushrooms wherever they land.

Amoonguss generally doesn't move much. It tends to stand still near Poké Balls that have been dropped on the ground.

HOW TO SAY IT: uh-MOON-gus
IMPERIAL HEIGHT: 2'00"
IMPERIAL WEIGHT: 23.1 lbs.
METRIC HEIGHT: 0.6 m
METRIC WEIGHT: 10.5 kg

POSSIBLE MOVES: Absorb, Growth, Astonish, Bide, Mega Drain, Ingrain, Feint Attack, Sweet Scent, Giga Drain, Toxic, Synthesis, Clear Smog, Solar Beam, Rage Powder, Spore

FOONGUS

AMOONGUSS

AMPHAROS
Light Pokémon

TYPE: ELECTRIC

The light from its tail can be seen from space. This is why you can always tell exactly where it is, which is why it usually keeps the light off.

Its tail shines bright and strong. It has been prized since long ago as a beacon for sailors.

HOW TO SAY IT: AMF-fah-rahs
IMPERIAL HEIGHT: 4'07"
IMPERIAL WEIGHT: 135.6 lbs.
METRIC HEIGHT: 1.4 m
METRIC WEIGHT: 61.5 kg

POSSIBLE MOVES: Zap Cannon, Magnetic Flux, Ion Deluge, Dragon Pulse, Fire Punch, Tackle, Growl, Thunder Wave, Thunder Shock, Cotton Spore, Charge, Take Down, Electro Ball, Confuse Ray, Thunder Punch, Power Gem, Discharge, Cotton Guard, Signal Beam, Light Screen, Thunder

MEGA AMPHAROS
Light Pokémon

TYPE: ELECTRIC-DRAGON

IMPERIAL HEIGHT: 4'07"
IMPERIAL WEIGHT: 135.6 lbs.
METRIC HEIGHT: 1.4 m
METRIC WEIGHT: 61.5 kg

MAREEP   **FLAAFFY**   **AMPHAROS**   **MEGA AMPHAROS**

ANORITH
Old Shrimp Pokémon

TYPE: ROCK-BUG

When restored Anorith are released into the ocean, they don't thrive because the water composition has changed since their era.

This is one kind of primeval bug Pokémon. With eight wings, it could apparently swim a lot faster than you'd expect.

HOW TO SAY IT: AN-no-rith
IMPERIAL HEIGHT: 2'04"
IMPERIAL WEIGHT: 27.6 lbs.
METRIC HEIGHT: 0.7 m
METRIC WEIGHT: 12.5 kg

POSSIBLE MOVES: Scratch, Harden, Mud Sport, Water Gun, Fury Cutter, Smack Down, Metal Claw, Ancient Power, Bug Bite, Brine, Slash, Crush Claw, X-Scissor, Protect, Rock Blast

ANORITH

ARMALDO

APPLETUN
Apple Nectar Pokémon

TYPE: GRASS-DRAGON

Eating a sweet apple caused its evolution. A nectarous scent wafts from its body, luring in the bug Pokémon it preys on.

Its body is covered in sweet nectar, and the skin on its back is especially yummy. Children used to have it as a snack.

HOW TO SAY IT: AP-pell-tun
IMPERIAL HEIGHT: 1'04"
IMPERIAL WEIGHT: 28.7 lbs.
METRIC HEIGHT: 0.4 m
METRIC WEIGHT: 13.0 kg

POSSIBLE MOVES: Apple Acid, Astonish, Body Slam, Bullet Seed, Curse, Dragon Pulse, Energy Ball, Growth, Headbutt, Iron Defense, Leech Seed, Protect, Recover, Recycle, Stomp, Sweet Scent, Withdraw

APPLIN   **APPLETUN**

Alternate Form:
GIGANTAMAX APPLETUN

It blasts its opponents with massive amounts of sweet, sticky nectar, drowning them under the deluge.

Due to Gigantamax energy, this Pokémon's nectar has thickened. The increased viscosity lets the nectar absorb more damage than before.

IMPERIAL HEIGHT: 78'09"+
Imperial Weight: ????.? lbs.
METRIC HEIGHT: 24.0+ m
METRIC WEIGHT: ???.? kg

APPLIN

Apple Core Pokémon

TYPE: GRASS-DRAGON

It spends its entire life inside an apple. It hides from its natural enemies, bird Pokémon, by pretending it's just an apple and nothing more.

As soon as it's born, it burrows into an apple. Not only does the apple serve as its food source, but the flavor of the fruit determines its evolution.

HOW TO SAY IT: AP-lin
IMPERIAL HEIGHT: 0'08"
IMPERIAL WEIGHT: 1.1 lbs.
METRIC HEIGHT: 0.2 m
METRIC WEIGHT: 0.5 kg

POSSIBLE MOVES: Astonish, Withdraw

APPLETUN

APPLIN

FLAPPLE

ARAQUANID

Water Bubble Pokémon

TYPE: WATER-BUG

It launches water bubbles with its legs, drowning prey within the bubbles. This Pokémon can then take its time to savor its meal.

It acts as a caretaker for Dewpider, putting them inside its bubble and letting them eat any leftover food.

HOW TO SAY IT: uh-RACK-wuh-nid
IMPERIAL HEIGHT: 5'11"
IMPERIAL WEIGHT: 180.8 lbs.
METRIC HEIGHT: 1.8 m
METRIC WEIGHT: 82.0 kg

POSSIBLE MOVES: Aqua Ring, Bite, Bubble Beam, Bug Bite, Crunch, Entrainment, Headbutt, Infestation, Leech Life, Liquidation, Lunge, Mirror Coat, Soak, Water Gun, Wide Guard

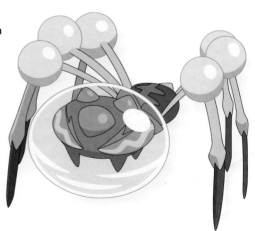

DEWPIDER   ARAQUANID

ARBOK
Cobra Pokémon

TYPE: POISON

The frightening patterns on its belly have been studied. Six variations have been confirmed.

HOW TO SAY IT: ARE-bock
IMPERIAL HEIGHT: 11'06"
IMPERIAL WEIGHT: 143.3 lbs.
METRIC HEIGHT: 3.5 m
METRIC WEIGHT: 65.0 kg

POSSIBLE MOVES: Ice Fang, Thunder Fang, Fire Fang, Wrap, Leer, Poison Sting, Bite, Glare, Screech, Acid, Crunch, Stockpile, Swallow, Spit Up, Acid Spray, Mud Bomb, Gastro Acid, Belch, Haze, Coil, Gunk Shot

EKANS **ARBOK**

ARCANINE
Legendary Pokémon

TYPE: FIRE

The sight of it running over 6,200 miles in a single day and night has captivated many people.

A Pokémon that has long been admired for its beauty. It runs agilely as if on wings.

HOW TO SAY IT: ARE-ka-nine
IMPERIAL HEIGHT: 6'03"
IMPERIAL WEIGHT: 341.7 lbs.
METRIC HEIGHT: 1.9 m
METRIC WEIGHT: 155.0 kg

POSSIBLE MOVES: Agility, Bite, Burn Up, Crunch, Ember, Extreme Speed, Fire Fang, Flame Wheel, Flamethrower, Flare Blitz, Helping Hand, Howl, Leer, Play Rough, Retaliate, Reversal, Roar, Take Down

GROWLITHE **ARCANINE**

ARCEUS

Alpha Pokémon

REGION: SINNOH

MYTHICAL POKÉMON

TYPE: NORMAL

According to the legends of Sinnoh, this Pokémon emerged from an egg and shaped all there is in this world.

It is told in mythology that this Pokémon was born before the universe even existed.

HOW TO SAY IT: ARK-ee-us
IMPERIAL HEIGHT: 10'06"
IMPERIAL WEIGHT: 705.5 lbs.
METRIC HEIGHT: 3.2 m
METRIC WEIGHT: 320.0 kg

POSSIBLE MOVES: Seismic Toss, Cosmic Power, Natural Gift, Punishment, Gravity, Earth Power, Hyper Voice, Extreme Speed, Refresh, Future Sight, Recover, Hyper Beam, Perish Song, Judgment

DOES NOT EVOLVE

ARCHEN

First Bird Pokémon

REGIONS: ALOLA UNOVA

TYPE: ROCK-FLYING

Once thought to be the ancestor of all bird Pokémon, some of the latest research suggests that may not be the case.

Restored from a fossil, this ancient bird Pokémon has wings but can't yet fly.

HOW TO SAY IT: AR-ken
IMPERIAL HEIGHT: 1'08"
IMPERIAL WEIGHT: 20.9 lbs.
METRIC HEIGHT: 0.5 m
METRIC WEIGHT: 9.5 kg

POSSIBLE MOVES: Quick Attack, Leer, Wing Attack, Rock Throw, Double Team, Scary Face, Pluck, Ancient Power, Agility, Quick Guard, Acrobatics, Dragon Breath, Crunch, Endeavor, U-turn, Rock Slide, Dragon Claw, Thrash

ARCHEN   ARCHEOPS

ARCHEOPS

First Bird Pokémon

TYPE: ROCK-FLYING

This ancient Pokémon's plumage is delicate, so if anyone other than an experienced professional tries to restore it, they will fail.

Said to be an ancestor of bird Pokémon, the muscles it uses to flap its wings are still weak, so it needs a long runway in order to take off.

HOW TO SAY IT: AR-kee-ops
IMPERIAL HEIGHT: 4'07"
IMPERIAL WEIGHT: 70.5 lbs.

METRIC HEIGHT: 1.4 m
METRIC WEIGHT: 32.0 kg

POSSIBLE MOVES: Quick Attack, Leer, Wing Attack, Rock Throw, Double Team, Scary Face, Pluck, Ancient Power, Agility, Quick Guard, Acrobatics, Dragon Breath, Crunch, Endeavor, U-turn, Rock Slide, Dragon Claw, Thrash

ARCHEN   **ARCHEOPS**

ARCTOVISH

REGION:
GALAR

Fossil Pokémon

TYPE: WATER-ICE

Though it's able to capture prey by freezing its surroundings, it has trouble eating the prey afterward because its mouth is on top of its head.

The skin on its face is impervious to attack, but breathing difficulties made this Pokémon go extinct anyway.

HOW TO SAY IT: ARK-toh-vish
IMPERIAL HEIGHT: 6'07"
IMPERIAL WEIGHT: 385.8 lbs.
METRIC HEIGHT: 2.0 m
METRIC WEIGHT: 175.0 kg

POSSIBLE MOVES: Ancient Power, Aurora Veil, Bite, Blizzard, Crunch, Fishious Rend, Freeze-Dry, Icicle Crash, Icy Wind, Powder Snow, Protect, Super Fang, Water Gun

DOES NOT EVOLVE

ARCTOZOLT

Fossil Pokémon

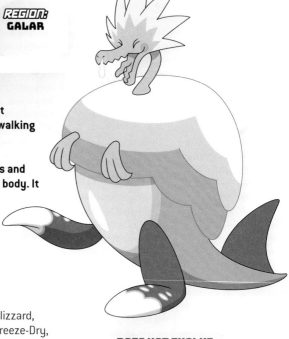

TYPE: ELECTRIC-ICE

The shaking of its freezing upper half is what generates its electricity. It has a hard time walking around.

This Pokémon lived on prehistoric seashores and was able to preserve food with the ice on its body. It went extinct because it moved so slowly.

HOW TO SAY IT: ARK-toh-zohlt
IMPERIAL HEIGHT: 7'07"
IMPERIAL WEIGHT: 330.7 lbs.
METRIC HEIGHT: 2.3 m
METRIC WEIGHT: 150.0 kg

POSSIBLE MOVES: Ancient Power, Avalanche, Blizzard, Bolt Beak, Charge, Discharge, Echoed Voice, Freeze-Dry, Icicle Crash, Pluck, Powder Snow, Slam, Thunder Shock

DOES NOT EVOLVE

ARIADOS

Long Leg Pokémon

TYPE: BUG-POISON

Every night, it wanders around in search of prey, whose movements it restrains by spewing threads before it bites into them with its fangs.

It spews threads from its mouth to catch its prey. When night falls, it leaves its web to go hunt aggressively.

HOW TO SAY IT: AIR-ree-uh-dose
IMPERIAL HEIGHT: 3'07"
IMPERIAL WEIGHT: 73.9 lbs.
METRIC HEIGHT: 1.1 m
METRIC WEIGHT: 33.5 kg

POSSIBLE MOVES: Swords Dance, Focus Energy, Venom, Drench, Fell Stinger, Bug Bite, Poison Sting, String Shot, Constrict, Absorb, Infestation, Scary Face, Night Shade, Shadow Sneak, Fury Swipes, Sucker Punch, Spider Web, Agility, Pin Missile, Psychic, Poison Jab, Cross Poison, Sticky Web, Toxic Thread

SPINARAK   ARIADOS

ARMALDO
Plate Pokémon

TYPE: ROCK-BUG

It lived on land and went out into the sea to hunt for prey. Its sharp claws were its greatest weapon.

Armaldo adapted from living in water to living on land. It has been determined that it is the ancestor of some bug Pokémon.

HOW TO SAY IT: ar-MAL-do **METRIC HEIGHT:** 1.5 m
IMPERIAL HEIGHT: 4'11" **METRIC WEIGHT:** 68.2 kg
IMPERIAL WEIGHT: 150.4 lbs.

POSSIBLE MOVES: Scratch, Harden, Mud Sport, Water Gun, Fury Cutter, Smack Down, Metal Claw, Protect, Ancient Power, Bug Bite, Brine, Slash, Rock Blast, Crush Claw, X-Scissor

ANORITH   ARMALDO

REGIONS:
GALAR
KALOS
(CENTRAL)

AROMATISSE
Fragrance Pokémon

TYPE: FAIRY

The scent that constantly emits from its fur is so powerful that this Pokémon's companions will eventually lose their sense of smell.

The scents Aromatisse can produce range from sweet smells that bolster allies to foul smells that sap an opponent's will to fight.

HOW TO SAY IT: uh-ROME-uh-teece
IMPERIAL HEIGHT: 2'07"
IMPERIAL WEIGHT: 34.2 lbs.
METRIC HEIGHT: 0.8 m
METRIC WEIGHT: 15.5 kg

POSSIBLE MOVES: Aromatherapy, Aromatic Mist, Attract, Calm Mind, Charm, Disarming Voice, Draining Kiss, Echoed Voice, Fairy Wind, Flail, Heal Pulse, Misty Terrain, Moonblast, Psych Up, Psychic, Skill Swap, Sweet Kiss, Sweet Scent

SPRITZEE   AROMATISSE

ARON

Iron Armor Pokémon

REGIONS:
HOENN
KALOS
(MOUNTAIN)

TYPE: STEEL-ROCK

This Pokémon has a body of steel. To make its body, Aron feeds on iron ore that it digs from mountains. Occasionally, it causes major trouble by eating bridges and rails.

Aron has a body of steel. With one all-out charge, this Pokémon can demolish even a heavy dump truck. The destroyed dump truck then becomes a handy meal for the Pokémon.

HOW TO SAY IT: AIR-ron
IMPERIAL HEIGHT: 1'04"
IMPERIAL WEIGHT: 132.3 lbs.
METRIC HEIGHT: 0.4 m
METRIC WEIGHT: 60.0 kg

POSSIBLE MOVES: Tackle, Harden, Mud-Slap, Headbutt, Metal Claw, Rock Tomb, Protect, Roar, Iron Head, Rock Slide, Take Down, Metal Sound, Iron Tail, Iron Defense, Double-Edge, Autotomize, Heavy Slam, Metal Burst

ARON   **LAIRON**   **AGGRON**   **MEGA AGGRON**

ARROKUDA

Rush Pokémon

REGION:
GALAR

TYPE: WATER

If it sees any movement around it, this Pokémon charges for it straightaway, leading with its sharply pointed jaw. It's very proud of that jaw.

After it's eaten its fill, its movements become extremely sluggish. That's when Cramorant swallows it up.

HOW TO SAY IT: AIR-oh-KOO-duh
IMPERIAL HEIGHT: 1'08"
IMPERIAL WEIGHT: 2.2 lbs.
METRIC HEIGHT: 0.5 m
METRIC WEIGHT: 1.0 kg

POSSIBLE MOVES: Agility, Aqua Jet, Bite, Crunch, Dive, Double-Edge, Fury Attack, Laser Focus, Liquidation, Peck

ARROKUDA   **BARRASKEWDA**

LEGENDARY POKÉMON

ARTICUNO
Freeze Pokémon

TYPE: ICE-FLYING

A legendary bird Pokémon. It freezes water that is contained in winter air and makes it snow.

HOW TO SAY IT: ART-tick-COO-no
IMPERIAL HEIGHT: 5'07"
IMPERIAL WEIGHT: 122.1 lbs.
METRIC HEIGHT: 1.7 m
METRIC WEIGHT: 55.4 kg

POSSIBLE MOVES: Roost, Hurricane, Freeze-Dry, Tailwind, Sheer Cold, Gust, Powder Snow, Mist, Ice Shard, Mind Reader, Ancient Power, Agility, Ice Beam, Reflect, Hail, Blizzard

DOES NOT EVOLVE

AUDINO
Hearing Pokémon

REGIONS:
KALOS
(CENTRAL)
UNOVA

TYPE: NORMAL

Using the feelers on its ears, it can tell how someone is feeling or when an egg might hatch.

It touches others with the feelers on its ears, using the sound of their heartbeats to tell how they are feeling.

HOW TO SAY IT: AW-dih-noh
IMPERIAL HEIGHT: 3'07"
IMPERIAL WEIGHT: 68.3 lbs.
METRIC HEIGHT: 1.1 m
METRIC WEIGHT: 31.0 kg

POSSIBLE MOVES: Last Resort, Play Nice, Pound, Growl, Helping Hand, Refresh, Double Slap, Attract, Secret Power, Entrainment, Take Down, Heal Pulse, After You, Simple Beam, Double-Edge, Hyper Voice, Misty Terrain, Baby-Doll Eyes, Disarming

MEGA AUDINO
Hearing Pokémon

TYPE: NORMAL-FAIRY

IMPERIAL HEIGHT: 4'11"
IMPERIAL WEIGHT: 70.5 lbs.
METRIC HEIGHT: 1.5 m
METRIC WEIGHT: 32.0 kg

AUDINO **MEGA AUDINO**

TYPE: ROCK-ICE

An Aurorus was found frozen solid within a glacier, just as it appeared long ago, which became quite a big event in the news.

This usually quiet and kindly Pokémon has a surface temperature of around −240 degrees Fahrenheit.

HOW TO SAY IT: ah-ROAR-us
IMPERIAL HEIGHT: 8'10"
IMPERIAL WEIGHT: 496.0 lbs.
METRIC HEIGHT: 2.7 m
METRIC WEIGHT: 225.0 kg

POSSIBLE MOVES: Freeze-Dry, Growl, Powder Snow, Thunder Wave, Rock Throw, Icy Wind, Take Down, Mist, Aurora Beam, Ancient Power, Round, Avalanche, Hail, Nature Power, Encore, Light Screen, Ice Beam, Hyper Beam, Blizzard

REGIONS:
ALOLA
KALOS
(COASTAL)

AURORUS
Tundra Pokémon

AMAURA   AURORUS

REGIONS:
GALAR
KALOS
(MOUNTAIN)

AVALUGG
Iceberg Pokémon

TYPE: ICE

At high latitudes, this Pokémon can be found with clusters of Bergmite on its back as it swims among the icebergs.

As Avalugg moves about during the day, the cracks in its body deepen. The Pokémon's body returns to a pristine state overnight.

HOW TO SAY IT: AV-uh-lug
IMPERIAL HEIGHT: 6'07"
IMPERIAL WEIGHT: 1,113.3 lbs.
METRIC HEIGHT: 2.0 m
METRIC WEIGHT: 505.0 kg

POSSIBLE MOVES: Avalanche, Bite, Blizzard, Body Slam, Crunch, Curse, Double-Edge, Harden, Ice Fang, Icy Wind, Iron Defense, Powder Snow, Protect, Rapid Spin, Recover, Skull Bash, Tackle, Take Down, Wide Guard

BERGMITE   AVALUGG

AXEW
Tusk Pokémon

TYPE: DRAGON

These Pokémon nest in the ground and use their tusks to crush hard berries. Crushing berries is also how they test each other's strength.

They play with each other by knocking their large tusks together. Their tusks break sometimes, but they grow back so quickly that it isn't a concern.

HOW TO SAY IT: AKS-yoo
IMPERIAL HEIGHT: 2'00"
IMPERIAL WEIGHT: 39.7 lbs.
METRIC HEIGHT: 0.6 m
METRIC WEIGHT: 18.0 kg

POSSIBLE MOVES: Assurance, Bite, Crunch, Dragon Claw, Dragon Dance, Dragon Pulse, Dual Chop, False Swipe, Giga Impact, Guillotine, Laser Focus, Leer, Outrage, Scary Face, Scratch, Slash, Swords Dance, Taunt

AXEW　　　FRAXURE　　　HAXORUS

AZELF
Willpower Pokémon

REGION:
SINNOH

LEGENDARY POKÉMON

TYPE: PSYCHIC

Known as "The Being of Willpower." It sleeps at the bottom of a lake to keep the world in balance.

It is thought that Uxie, Mesprit, and Azelf all came from the same egg.

HOW TO SAY IT: AZ-elf
IMPERIAL HEIGHT: 1'00"
IMPERIAL WEIGHT: 0.7 lbs.
METRIC HEIGHT: 0.3 m
METRIC WEIGHT: 0.3 kg

POSSIBLE MOVES: Rest, Confusion, Imprison, Detect, Swift, Uproar, Future Sight, Nasty Plot, Extrasensory, Last Resort, Natural Gift, Explosion

DOES NOT EVOLVE

AZUMARILL

Aqua Rabbit Pokémon

TYPE: WATER-FAIRY

It spends most of its time in the water. On sunny days, Azumarill floats on the surface of the water and sunbathes.

These Pokémon create air-filled bubbles. When Azurill play in rivers, Azumarill will cover them with these bubbles.

HOW TO SAY IT: ah-ZU-mare-rill
IMPERIAL HEIGHT: 2'07"
IMPERIAL WEIGHT: 62.8 lbs.
METRIC HEIGHT: 0.8 m
METRIC WEIGHT: 28.5 kg

POSSIBLE MOVES: Tackle, Water Gun, Tail Whip, Water Sport, Bubble, Defense Curl, Rollout, Bubble Beam, Helping Hand, Aqua Tail, Play Rough, Double-Edge, Aqua Ring, Rain Dance, Superpower, Hydro Pump

AZURILL   MARILL   AZUMARILL

AZURILL

Polka Dot Pokémon

TYPE: NORMAL-FAIRY

The ball on Azurill's tail bounces like a rubber ball, and it's full of the nutrients the Pokémon needs to grow.

Although Azurill are normally docile, an angry one will swing around the big ball on its tail and try to smash its opponents.

HOW TO SAY IT: uh-ZOO-rill
IMPERIAL HEIGHT: 0'08"
IMPERIAL WEIGHT: 4.4 lbs.
METRIC HEIGHT: 0.2 m
METRIC WEIGHT: 2.0 kg

POSSIBLE MOVES: Splash, Water Gun, Tail Whip, Water Sport, Bubble, Charm, Bubble Beam, Helping Hand, Slam, Bounce

AZURILL   MARILL   AZUMARILL

BAGON

Rock Head Pokémon

REGIONS:
ALOLA
HOENN
KALOS
(COASTAL)

TYPE: DRAGON

Whenever it sees bird Pokémon flying through the sky, it becomes envious and smashes its surroundings to bits with headbutts.

Some theories suggest that its behavior of forcefully bashing its head into things stimulates cells that affect its evolution.

HOW TO SAY IT: BAY-gon
IMPERIAL HEIGHT: 2'00"
IMPERIAL WEIGHT: 92.8 lbs.

METRIC HEIGHT: 0.6 m
METRIC WEIGHT: 42.1 kg

POSSIBLE MOVES: Rage, Ember, Leer, Bite, Dragon Breath, Headbutt, Focus Energy, Crunch, Dragon Claw, Zen Headbutt, Scary Face, Flamethrower, Double-Edge

| BAGON | SHELGON | SALAMENCE | MEGA SALAMENCE |

BALTOY

Clay Doll Pokémon

REGIONS:
ALOLA
GALAR
HOENN

TYPE: GROUND-PSYCHIC

It moves while spinning around on its single foot. Some Baltoy have been seen spinning on their heads.

It was discovered in ancient ruins. While moving, it constantly spins. It stands on one foot even when asleep.

HOW TO SAY IT: BAL-toy
IMPERIAL HEIGHT: 1'08"
IMPERIAL WEIGHT: 47.4 lbs.

METRIC HEIGHT: 0.5 m
METRIC WEIGHT: 21.5 kg

POSSIBLE MOVES: Ancient Power, Confusion, Cosmic Power, Earth Power, Explosion, Extrasensory, Guard Split, Harden, Imprison, Mud-Slap, Power Split, Power Trick, Psybeam, Rapid Spin, Rock Tomb, Sandstorm, Self-Destruct

| BALTOY | CLAYDOL |

BANETTE
Marionette Pokémon

TYPE: GHOST

It's a stuffed toy that was thrown away and became possessed, ever searching for the one who threw it away so it can exact its revenge.

Resentment at being cast off made it spring into being. Some say that treating it well will satisfy it, and it will once more become a stuffed toy.

HOW TO SAY IT: bane-NETT
IMPERIAL HEIGHT: 3'07"
IMPERIAL WEIGHT: 27.6 lbs.
METRIC HEIGHT: 1.1 m
METRIC WEIGHT: 12.5 kg

POSSIBLE MOVES: Phantom Force, Knock Off, Screech, Night Shade, Curse, Spite, Will-O-Wisp, Shadow Sneak, Feint Attack, Hex, Shadow Ball, Sucker Punch, Embargo, Snatch, Grudge, Trick

MEGA BANETTE
Marionette Pokémon

TYPE: GHOST

IMPERIAL HEIGHT: 3'11"
IMPERIAL WEIGHT: 28.7 lbs.
METRIC HEIGHT: 1.2 m
METRIC WEIGHT: 13.0 kg

SHUPPET **BANETTE** **MEGA BANETTE**

BARBARACLE

Collective Pokémon

TYPE: ROCK-WATER

Seven Binacle come together to form one Barbaracle. The Binacle that serves as the head gives orders to those serving as the limbs.

Having an eye on each palm allows it to keep watch in all directions. In a pinch, its limbs start to act on their own to ensure the enemy's defeat.

HOW TO SAY IT: bar-BARE-uh-kull
IMPERIAL HEIGHT: 4'03"
IMPERIAL WEIGHT: 211.6 lbs.
METRIC HEIGHT: 1.3 m
METRIC WEIGHT: 96.0 kg

POSSIBLE MOVES: Ancient Power, Cross Chop, Fury Cutter, Fury Swipes, Hone Claws, Mud-Slap, Razor Shell, Rock Polish, Scratch, Shell Smash, Skull Bash, Slash, Stone Edge, Water Gun, Withdraw

BINACLE   BARBARACLE

BARBOACH

Whiskers Pokémon

REGIONS:
ALOLA
GALAR
HOENN
KALOS
(MOUNTAIN)

TYPE: WATER-GROUND

Its slimy body is hard to grasp. In one region, it is said to have been born from hardened mud.

It probes muddy riverbeds with its two long whiskers. A slimy film protects its body.

HOW TO SAY IT: bar-BOACH
IMPERIAL HEIGHT: 1'04"
IMPERIAL WEIGHT: 4.2 lbs.
METRIC HEIGHT: 0.4 m
METRIC WEIGHT: 1.9 kg

POSSIBLE MOVES: Amnesia, Aqua Tail, Earthquake, Fissure, Future Sight, Muddy Water, Mud-Slap, Rest, Snore, Water Gun, Water Pulse

BARBOACH   WHISCASH

BARRASKEWDA

Skewer Pokémon

TYPE: WATER

This Pokémon has a jaw that's as sharp as a spear and as strong as steel. Apparently Barraskewda's flesh is surprisingly tasty, too.

It spins its tail fins to propel itself, surging forward at speeds of over 100 knots before ramming prey and spearing into them.

HOW TO SAY IT: BAIR-uh-SKYOO-duh
IMPERIAL HEIGHT: 4'03"
IMPERIAL WEIGHT: 66.1 lbs.
METRIC HEIGHT: 1.3 m
METRIC WEIGHT: 30.0 kg

POSSIBLE MOVES: Agility, Aqua Jet, Bite, Crunch, Dive, Double-Edge, Fury Attack, Laser Focus, Liquidation, Peck, Throat Chop

ARROKUDA   BARRASKEWDA

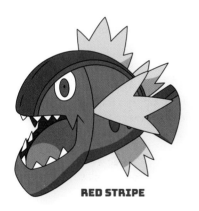
RED STRIPE

REGIONS:
ALOLA
GALAR
KALOS
(MOUNTAIN)
UNOVA

BASCULIN

Hostile Pokémon

TYPE: WATER

Anglers love the fight this Pokémon puts up on the hook. And there are always more to catch—many people release them into lakes illicitly.

In the past, it often appeared on the dinner table. The meat of red-striped Basculin is on the fatty side, and it's more popular with the youth.

HOW TO SAY IT: BASS-kyoo-lin
IMPERIAL HEIGHT: 3'03"
IMPERIAL WEIGHT: 39.7 lbs.
METRIC HEIGHT: 1.0 m
METRIC WEIGHT: 18.0 kg

POSSIBLE MOVES: Aqua Jet, Aqua Tail, Bite, Crunch, Double-Edge, Final Gambit, Flail, Head Smash, Headbutt, Scary Face, Soak, Tackle, Tail Whip, Take Down, Thrash, Water Gun

BLUE STRIPE

DOES NOT EVOLVE

BASTIODON

Shield Pokémon

TYPE: ROCK-STEEL

The bones of its face are huge and hard, so they were mistaken for its spine until after this Pokémon was successfully restored.

This Pokémon is from roughly 100 million years ago. Its terrifyingly tough face is harder than steel.

HOW TO SAY IT: BAS-tee-oh-DON
IMPERIAL HEIGHT: 4'03"
IMPERIAL WEIGHT: 329.6 lbs.
METRIC HEIGHT: 1.3 m
METRIC WEIGHT: 149.5 kg

POSSIBLE MOVES: Block, Tackle, Protect, Taunt, Metal Sound, Take Down, Iron Defense, Swagger, Ancient Power, Endure, Metal Burst, Iron Head, Heavy Slam

SHIELDON   BASTIODON

BAYLEEF

Leaf Pokémon

TYPE: GRASS

Bayleef's neck is ringed by curled-up leaves. Inside each tubular leaf is a small shoot of a tree. The fragrance of this shoot makes people peppy.

HOW TO SAY IT: BAY-leaf
IMPERIAL HEIGHT: 3'11"
IMPERIAL WEIGHT: 34.8 lbs.
METRIC HEIGHT: 1.2 m
METRIC WEIGHT: 15.8 kg

POSSIBLE MOVES: Tackle, Growl, Razor Leaf, Poison Powder, Synthesis, Reflect, Magical Leaf, Natural Gift, Sweet Scent, Light Screen, Body Slam, Safeguard, Aromatherapy, Solar Beam

CHIKORITA   BAYLEEF   MEGANIUM

BEARTIC
Freezing Pokémon

TYPE: ICE

It swims through frigid seas, searching for prey. From its frozen breath, it forms icy fangs that are harder than steel.

It swims energetically through frigid seas. When it gets tired, it freezes the seawater with its breath so it can rest on the ice.

HOW TO SAY IT: BAIR-tick
IMPERIAL HEIGHT: 8'06"
IMPERIAL WEIGHT: 573.2 lbs.
METRIC HEIGHT: 2.6 m
METRIC WEIGHT: 260.0 kg

POSSIBLE MOVES: Aqua Jet, Blizzard, Brine, Charm, Endure, Flail, Frost Breath, Fury Swipes, Growl, Hail, Icicle Crash, Icy Wind, Play Nice, Powder Snow, Rest, Sheer Cold, Slash, Superpower, Swagger, Thrash

CUBCHOO **BEARTIC**

BEAUTIFLY
Butterfly Pokémon

TYPE: BUG-FLYING

Beautifly's favorite food is the sweet pollen of flowers. If you want to see this Pokémon, just leave a potted flower by an open window. Beautifly is sure to come looking for pollen.

Beautifly has a long mouth like a coiled needle, which is very convenient for collecting pollen from flowers. This Pokémon rides the spring winds as it flits around gathering pollen.

HOW TO SAY IT: BUE-tee-fly
IMPERIAL HEIGHT: 3'03"
IMPERIAL WEIGHT: 62.6 lbs.
METRIC HEIGHT: 1.0 m
METRIC WEIGHT: 28.4 kg

POSSIBLE MOVES: Absorb, Gust, Stun Spore, Morning Sun, Air Cutter, Mega Drain, Whirlwind, Attract, Silver Wind, Giga Drain, Bug Buzz, Rage, Quiver Dance

WURMPLE **SILCOON** **BEAUTIFLY**

BEEDRILL
Poison Bee Pokémon

REGIONS:
KALOS
(CENTRAL)
KANTO

TYPE: BUG-POISON

It has three poisonous stingers on its forelegs and its tail. They are used to jab its enemy repeatedly.

HOW TO SAY IT: BEE-dril
IMPERIAL HEIGHT: 3'03"
IMPERIAL WEIGHT: 65.0 lbs.
METRIC HEIGHT: 1.0 m
METRIC WEIGHT: 29.5 kg

POSSIBLE MOVES: Fury Attack, Focus Energy, Twineedle, Rage, Pursuit, Toxic Spikes, Pin Missile, Agility, Assurance, Poison Jab, Endeavor, Fell Stinger, Venoshock

MEGA BEEDRILL
Poison Bee Pokémon

TYPE: BUG-POISON

IMPERIAL HEIGHT: 4'07"
IMPERIAL WEIGHT: 89.3 lbs.
METRIC HEIGHT: 1.4 m
METRIC WEIGHT: 40.5 kg

WEEDLE   KAKUNA   BEEDRILL   MEGA BEEDRILL

BEHEEYEM
Cerebral Pokémon

TYPE: PSYCHIC

Whenever a Beheeyem visits a farm, a Dubwool mysteriously disappears.

Sometimes found drifting above wheat fields, this Pokémon can control the memories of its opponents.

HOW TO SAY IT: BEE-hee-ehm
IMPERIAL HEIGHT: 3'03"
IMPERIAL WEIGHT: 76.1 lbs.
METRIC HEIGHT: 1.0 m
METRIC WEIGHT: 34.5 kg

POSSIBLE MOVES: Calm Mind, Confusion, Growl, Guard Split, Headbutt, Imprison, Power Split, Psybeam, Psychic, Psychic Terrain, Recover, Teleport, Wonder Room, Zen Headbutt

ELGYEM **BEHEEYEM**

TYPE: STEEL-PSYCHIC

Instead of blood, magnetism flows through its body. When it's feeling bad, try giving it a magnet.

If you anger it, it will do more than rampage. It will also burst out strong magnetism, causing nearby machines to break.

HOW TO SAY IT: BELL-dum
IMPERIAL HEIGHT: 2'00"
IMPERIAL WEIGHT: 209.9 lbs.
METRIC HEIGHT: 0.6 m
METRIC WEIGHT: 95.2 kg

POSSIBLE MOVE: Take Down

REGIONS:
ALOLA
HOENN

BELDUM
Iron Ball Pokémon

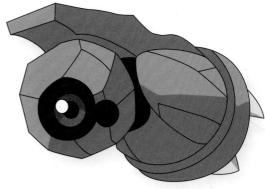

BELDUM **METANG** **METAGROSS** **MEGA METAGROSS**

BELLOSSOM

Flower Pokémon

REGIONS:
GALAR
JOHTO
KALOS
(CENTRAL)

TYPE: GRASS

Plentiful in the tropics. When it dances, its petals rub together and make a pleasant ringing sound.

Bellossom gather at times and appear to dance. They say that the dance is a ritual to summon the sun.

HOW TO SAY IT: bell-LAHS-um
IMPERIAL HEIGHT: 1'04"
IMPERIAL WEIGHT: 12.8 lbs.
METRIC HEIGHT: 0.4 m
METRIC WEIGHT: 5.8 kg

POSSIBLE MOVES: Absorb, Acid, Giga Drain, Grassy Terrain, Growth, Mega Drain, Moonblast, Moonlight, Petal Blizzard, Petal Dance, Poison Powder, Quiver Dance, Sleep Powder, Stun Spore, Sweet Scent, Toxic

ODDISH   **GLOOM**   **BELLOSSOM**

BELLSPROUT

Flower Pokémon

REGIONS:
KALOS
(MOUNTAIN)
KANTO

TYPE: GRASS-POISON

Prefers hot and humid places. It ensnares tiny bugs with its vines and devours them.

HOW TO SAY IT: BELL-sprout
IMPERIAL HEIGHT: 2'04"
IMPERIAL WEIGHT: 8.8 lbs.
METRIC HEIGHT: 0.7 m
METRIC WEIGHT: 4.0 kg

POSSIBLE MOVES: Vine Whip, Growth, Wrap, Sleep Powder, Poison Powder, Stun Spore, Acid, Knock Off, Sweet Scent, Gastro Acid, Razor Leaf, Poison Jab, Slam, Wring Out

BELLSPROUT   **WEEPINBELL**   **VICTREEBEL**

TYPE: ICE

They chill the air around them to −150 degrees Fahrenheit, freezing the water in the air into ice that they use as armor.

This Pokémon lives in areas of frigid cold. It secures itself to the back of an Avalugg by freezing its feet in place.

HOW TO SAY IT: BERG-mite
IMPERIAL HEIGHT: 3'03"
IMPERIAL WEIGHT: 219.4 lbs.
METRIC HEIGHT: 1.0 m
METRIC WEIGHT: 99.5 kg

POSSIBLE MOVES: Avalanche, Bite, Blizzard, Crunch, Curse, Double-Edge, Harden, Ice Fang, Icy Wind, Iron Defense, Powder Snow, Protect, Rapid Spin, Recover, Tackle, Take Down

REGIONS:
GALAR
KALOS
(MOUNTAIN)

BERGMITE
Ice Chunk Pokémon

BERGMITE   AVALUGG

TYPE: NORMAL-FIGHTING

Once it accepts you as a friend, it tries to show its affection with a hug. Letting it do that is dangerous—it could easily shatter your bones.

The moves it uses to take down its prey would make a martial artist jealous. It tucks subdued prey under its arms to carry them to its nest.

HOW TO SAY IT: beh-WARE
IMPERIAL HEIGHT: 6'11"
IMPERIAL WEIGHT: 297.6 lbs.
METRIC HEIGHT: 2.1 m
METRIC WEIGHT: 135.0 kg

POSSIBLE MOVES: Baby-Doll Eyes, Bind, Brutal Swing, Double-Edge, Endure, Flail, Hammer Arm, Leer, Pain Split, Payback, Strength, Superpower, Tackle, Take Down, Thrash

STUFFUL   BEWEAR

BIBAREL

Beaver Pokémon

REGIONS:
KALOS
(CENTRAL)
SINNOH

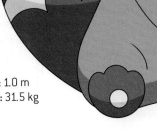

TYPE: NORMAL-WATER

It busily makes its nest with stacks of branches and roots it has cut up with its sharp incisors.

It makes its nest by damming streams with bark and mud. It is known as an industrious worker.

HOW TO SAY IT: bee-BER-rel
IMPERIAL HEIGHT: 3'03"
IMPERIAL WEIGHT: 69.4 lbs.
METRIC HEIGHT: 1.0 m
METRIC WEIGHT: 31.5 kg

POSSIBLE MOVES: Aqua Jet, Rototiller, Tackle, Growl, Defense Curl, Rollout, Water Gun, Headbutt, Hyper Fang, Yawn, Crunch, Take Down, Super Fang, Swords Dance, Amnesia, Superpower, Curse

BIDOOF   BIBAREL

BIDOOF

Plump Mouse Pokémon

REGIONS:
KALOS
(CENTRAL)
SINNOH

TYPE: NORMAL

With nerves of steel, nothing can perturb it. It is more agile and active than it appears.

It constantly gnaws on logs and rocks to whittle down its front teeth. It nests alongside water.

HOW TO SAY IT: BEE-doof
IMPERIAL HEIGHT: 1'08"
IMPERIAL WEIGHT: 44.1 lbs.
METRIC HEIGHT: 0.5 m
METRIC WEIGHT: 20.0 kg

POSSIBLE MOVES: Tackle, Growl, Defense Curl, Rollout, Headbutt, Hyper Fang, Yawn, Crunch, Take Down, Super Fang, Swords Dance, Amnesia, Superpower, Curse

BIDOOF   BIBAREL

TYPE: ROCK-WATER

BINACLE
Two-Handed Pokémon

After two Binacle find a suitably sized rock, they adhere themselves to it and live together. They cooperate to gather food during high tide.

If the two don't work well together, both their offense and defense fall apart. Without good teamwork, they won't survive.

HOW TO SAY IT: BY-nuh-kull **METRIC HEIGHT:** 0.5 m
IMPERIAL HEIGHT: 1'08" **METRIC WEIGHT:** 31.0 kg
IMPERIAL WEIGHT: 68.3 lbs.

POSSIBLE MOVES: Ancient Power, Cross Chop, Fury Cutter, Fury Swipes, Hone Claws, Mud-Slap, Razor Shell, Rock Polish, Scratch, Shell Smash, Slash, Water Gun, Withdraw

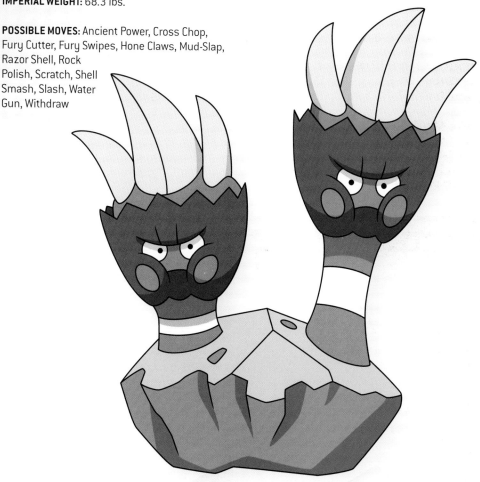

BINACLE

BARBARACLE

BISHARP

Sword Blade Pokémon

REGIONS:
ALOLA
GALAR
KALOS
(MOUNTAIN)
UNOVA

TYPE: DARK-STEEL

It's accompanied by a large retinue of Pawniard. Bisharp keeps a keen eye on its minions, ensuring none of them even think of double-crossing it.

Violent conflicts erupt between Bisharp and Fraxure over places where sharpening stones can be found.

HOW TO SAY IT: BIH-sharp
IMPERIAL HEIGHT: 5'03"
IMPERIAL WEIGHT: 154.3 lbs.
METRIC HEIGHT: 1.6 m
METRIC WEIGHT: 70.0 kg

POSSIBLE MOVES: Assurance, Fury Cutter, Guillotine, Iron Defense, Iron Head, Laser Focus, Leer, Metal Burst, Metal Claw, Metal Sound, Night Slash, Scary Face, Scratch, Slash, Swords Dance, Torment

PAWNIARD

BISHARP

BLACEPHALON

Fireworks Pokémon

TYPE: FIRE-GHOST

It slithers toward people. Then, without warning, it triggers the explosion of its own head. It's apparently one kind of Ultra Beast.

A UB that appeared from an Ultra Wormhole, it causes explosions, then takes advantage of opponents' surprise to rob them of their vitality.

HOW TO SAY IT: blass-SEF-uh-lawn
IMPERIAL HEIGHT: 5'11"
IMPERIAL WEIGHT: 28.7 lbs.
METRIC HEIGHT: 1.8 m
METRIC WEIGHT: 13.0 kg

POSSIBLE MOVES: Ember, Astonish, Magic Coat, Stored Power, Flame Burst, Night Shade, Light Screen, Calm Mind, Fire Blast, Shadow Ball, Trick, Mind Blown

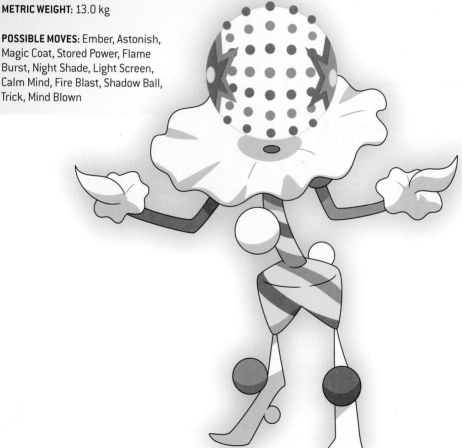

DOES NOT EVOLVE

BLASTOISE

Shellfish Pokémon

TYPE: WATER

It crushes its foe under its heavy body to cause fainting. In a pinch, it will withdraw inside its shell.

The rocket cannons on its shell fire jets of water capable of punching holes through thick steel.

HOW TO SAY IT: BLAS-toyce
IMPERIAL HEIGHT: 5'03"
IMPERIAL WEIGHT: 188.5 lbs.
METRIC HEIGHT: 1.6 m
METRIC WEIGHT: 85.5 kg

POSSIBLE MOVES: Flash Cannon, Tackle, Tail Whip, Water Gun, Withdraw, Bubble, Bite, Rapid Spin, Protect, Water Pulse, Aqua Tail, Skull Bash, Iron Defense, Rain Dance, Hydro Pump

MEGA BLASTOISE
Shellfish Pokémon

TYPE: WATER

IMPERIAL HEIGHT: 5'03"
IMPERIAL WEIGHT: 222.9 lbs.
METRIC HEIGHT: 1.6 m
METRIC WEIGHT: 101.1 kg

SQUIRTLE   WARTORTLE   BLASTOISE   MEGA BLASTOISE

Alternate Form:
GIGANTAMAX BLASTOISE

It's not very good at precision shooting. When attacking, it just fires its thirty-one cannons over and over and over.

Water fired from this Pokémon's central main cannon has enough power to blast a hole into a mountain.

IMPERIAL HEIGHT: 82'00"+
IMPERIAL WEIGHT: ????.? lbs.
METRIC HEIGHT: 25.0+ m
METRIC WEIGHT: ???.? kg

BLAZIKEN
Blaze Pokémon

TYPE: FIRE-FIGHTING

In battle, Blaziken blows out intense flames from its wrists and attacks foes courageously. The stronger the foe, the more intensely this Pokémon's wrists burn.

Blaziken has incredibly strong legs—it can easily clear a thirty-story building in one leap. This Pokémon's blazing punches leave its foes scorched and blackened.

HOW TO SAY IT: BLAZE-uh-ken
IMPERIAL HEIGHT: 6'03"
IMPERIAL WEIGHT: 114.6 lbs.
METRIC HEIGHT: 1.9 m
METRIC WEIGHT: 52.0 kg

POSSIBLE MOVES: Blaze Kick, Double Kick, Flare Blitz, Fire Punch, High Jump Kick, Scratch, Growl, Ember, Sand Attack, Peck, Flame Charge, Quick Attack, Bulk Up, Focus Energy, Slash, Brave Bird, Sky Uppercut

MEGA BLAZIKEN
Blaze Pokémon

TYPE: FIRE-FIGHTING

IMPERIAL HEIGHT: 6'03"
IMPERIAL WEIGHT: 114.6 lbs.
METRIC HEIGHT: 1.9 m
METRIC WEIGHT: 52.0 kg

TORCHIC → COMBUSKEN → BLAZIKEN → MEGA BLAZIKEN

BLIPBUG
Larva Pokémon

TYPE: BUG

A constant collector of information, this Pokémon is very smart. Very strong is what it isn't.

Often found in gardens, this Pokémon has hairs on its body that it uses to assess its surroundings.

HOW TO SAY IT: BLIP-bug
IMPERIAL HEIGHT: 1'04"
IMPERIAL WEIGHT: 17.6 lbs.
METRIC HEIGHT: 0.4 m
METRIC WEIGHT: 8.0 kg

POSSIBLE MOVE: Struggle Bug

BLIPBUG ⇨ **DOTTLER** ⇨ **ORBEETLE**

TYPE: NORMAL

BLISSEY
Happiness Pokémon

Whenever a Blissey finds a weakened Pokémon, it will share its egg and offer its care until the other Pokémon is all better.

Blissey lays mysterious eggs that are filled with happiness. It's said that anyone who eats a Blissey egg will start acting kindly to all others.

HOW TO SAY IT: BLISS-sey
IMPERIAL HEIGHT: 4'11"
IMPERIAL WEIGHT: 103.2 lbs.
METRIC HEIGHT: 1.5 m
METRIC WEIGHT: 46.8 kg

POSSIBLE MOVES: Defense Curl, Pound, Growl, Tail Whip, Refresh, Double Slap, Soft-Boiled, Bestow, Minimize, Take Down, Sing, Fling, Heal Pulse, Egg Bomb, Light Screen, Healing Wish, Double-Edge

HAPPINY ⇨ **CHANSEY** ⇨ **BLISSEY**

BLITZLE

Electrified Pokémon

TYPE: ELECTRIC

When thunderclouds cover the sky, it will appear. It can catch lightning with its mane and store the electricity.

Its mane shines when it discharges electricity. It uses the frequency and rhythm of these flashes to communicate.

HOW TO SAY IT: BLIT-zul
METRIC HEIGHT: 0.8 m
IMPERIAL HEIGHT: 2'07"
METRIC WEIGHT: 29.8 kg
IMPERIAL WEIGHT: 65.7 lbs.

POSSIBLE MOVES: Quick Attack, Tail Whip, Charge, Shock Wave, Thunder Wave, Flame Charge, Pursuit, Spark, Stomp, Discharge, Agility, Wild Charge, Thrash

BLITZLE   ZEBSTRIKA

BOLDORE

Ore Pokémon

TYPE: ROCK

If you see its orange crystals start to glow, be wary. It's about to fire off bursts of energy.

It relies on sound in order to monitor what's in its vicinity. When angered, it will attack without ever changing the direction it's facing.

HOW TO SAY IT: BOHL-dohr
IMPERIAL HEIGHT: 2'11"
IMPERIAL WEIGHT: 224.9 lbs.
METRIC HEIGHT: 0.9 m
METRIC WEIGHT: 102.0 kg

POSSIBLE MOVES: Explosion, Harden, Headbutt, Iron Defense, Mud-Slap, Power Gem, Rock Blast, Rock Slide, Sand Attack, Sandstorm, Smack Down, Stealth Rock, Stone Edge, Tackle

ROGGENROLA   BOLDORE   GIGALITH

BOLTUND

Dog Pokémon

TYPE: ELECTRIC

This Pokémon generates electricity and channels it into its legs to keep them going strong. Boltund can run nonstop for three full days.

It sends electricity through its legs to boost their strength. Running at top speed, it easily breaks 50 mph.

HOW TO SAY IT: BOHL-tund
IMPERIAL HEIGHT: 3'03"
IMPERIAL WEIGHT: 75.0 lbs.
METRIC HEIGHT: 1.0 m
METRIC WEIGHT: 34.0 kg

POSSIBLE MOVES: Bite, Charge, Charm, Crunch, Electric Terrain, Electrify, Nuzzle, Play Rough, Roar, Spark, Tackle, Tail Whip, Wild Charge

YAMPER → BOLTUND

REGION: ALOLA GALAR KALOS (MOUNTAIN) SINNOH

BONSLY

Bonsai Pokémon

TYPE: ROCK

It expels both sweat and tears from its eyes. The sweat is a little salty, while the tears have a slight bitterness.

This Pokémon lives in dry, rocky areas. As its green spheres dry out, their dull luster increases.

HOW TO SAY IT: BON-slye   **METRIC HEIGHT:** 0.8 m
IMPERIAL HEIGHT: 1'08"   **METRIC WEIGHT:** 46.8 kg
IMPERIAL WEIGHT: 33.1 lbs.

POSSIBLE MOVES: Block, Copycat, Counter, Double-Edge, Fake Tears, Flail, Low Kick, Mimic, Rock Slide, Rock Throw, Rock Tomb, Sucker Punch, Tearful Look

BONSLY   SUDOWOODO

BOUFFALANT

Bash Buffalo Pokémon

TYPE: NORMAL

These Pokémon can crush a car with no more than a headbutt. Bouffalant with more hair on their heads hold higher positions within the herd.

These Pokémon live in herds of about twenty individuals. Bouffalant that betray the herd will lose the hair on their heads for some reason.

HOW TO SAY IT: BOO-fuh-lahnt
IMPERIAL HEIGHT: 5'03"
IMPERIAL WEIGHT: 208.6 lbs.
METRIC HEIGHT: 1.6 m
METRIC WEIGHT: 94.6 kg

POSSIBLE MOVES: Pursuit, Leer, Rage, Fury Attack, Horn Attack, Scary Face, Revenge, Head Charge, Focus Energy, Megahorn, Reversal, Thrash, Swords Dance, Giga Impact

DOES NOT EVOLVE

BOUNSWEET

Fruit Pokémon

REGIONS: ALOLA GALAR

TYPE: GRASS

Its body gives off a sweet, fruity scent that is extremely appetizing to bird Pokémon.

When under attack, it secretes a sweet and delicious sweat. The scent only calls more enemies to it.

HOW TO SAY IT: BOWN-sweet
IMPERIAL HEIGHT: 1'00"
IMPERIAL WEIGHT: 7.1 lbs.
METRIC HEIGHT: 0.3 m
METRIC WEIGHT: 3.2 kg

POSSIBLE MOVES: Aromatherapy, Aromatic Mist, Flail, Magical Leaf, Play Nice, Rapid Spin, Razor Leaf, Splash, Sweet Scent, Teeter Dance

BOUNSWEET   STEENEE   TSAREENA

BRAIXEN

Fox Pokémon

TYPE: FIRE

It has a twig stuck in its tail. With friction from its tail fur, it sets the twig on fire and launches into battle.

When the twig is plucked from its tail, friction sets the twig alight. The flame is used to send signals to its allies.

HOW TO SAY IT: BRAKE-sen **METRIC HEIGHT:** 1.0 m
IMPERIAL HEIGHT: 3'03" **METRIC WEIGHT:** 14.5 kg
IMPERIAL WEIGHT: 32.0 lbs.

POSSIBLE MOVES: Scratch, Tail Whip, Ember, Howl, Flame Charge, Psybeam, Fire Spin, Lucky Chant, Light Screen, Psyshock, Flamethrower, Will-O-Wisp, Psychic, Sunny Day, Magic Room, Fire Blast

FENNEKIN ➤ **BRAIXEN** ➤ **DELPHOX**

BRAVIARY

Valiant Pokémon

TYPE: NORMAL-FLYING

Known for its bravery and pride, this majestic Pokémon is often seen as a motif for various kinds of emblems.

Because this Pokémon is hotheaded and belligerent, it's Corviknight that's taken the role of transportation in Galar.

HOW TO SAY IT: BRAY-vee-air-ee
IMPERIAL HEIGHT: 4'11"
IMPERIAL WEIGHT: 90.4 lbs.
METRIC HEIGHT: 1.5 m
METRIC WEIGHT: 41.0 kg

POSSIBLE MOVES: Aerial Ace, Air Slash, Brave Bird, Crush Claw, Defog, Hone Claws, Leer, Peck, Scary Face, Sky Attack, Slash, Superpower, Tailwind, Thrash, Whirlwind, Wing Attack

RUFFLET ➤ **BRAVIARY**

BRELOOM

Mushroom Pokémon

REGION: HOENN

TYPE: GRASS-FIGHTING

Breloom closes in on its foe with light and sprightly footwork, then throws punches with its stretchy arms. This Pokémon's fighting technique puts boxers to shame.

The seeds ringing Breloom's tail are made of hardened toxic spores. It is horrible to eat the seeds. Just taking a bite of this Pokémon's seed will cause your stomach to rumble.

HOW TO SAY IT: brell-LOOM
IMPERIAL HEIGHT: 3'11"
IMPERIAL WEIGHT: 86.4 lbs.

METRIC HEIGHT: 1.2 m
METRIC WEIGHT: 39.2 kg

POSSIBLE MOVES: Absorb, Tackle, Stun Spore, Leech Seed, Mega Drain, Headbutt, Mach Punch, Feint, Counter, Force Palm, Sky Uppercut, Mind Reader, Seed Bomb, Dynamic Punch

SHROOMISH   BRELOOM

BRIONNE

Pop Star Pokémon

REGION: ALOLA

TYPE: WATER

It gets excited when it sees a dance it doesn't know. This hard worker practices diligently until it can learn that dance.

It attacks by smacking its enemies with the exploding water balloons that it creates.

HOW TO SAY IT: bree-AHN
IMPERIAL HEIGHT: 2'00"
IMPERIAL WEIGHT: 38.6 lbs.

METRIC HEIGHT: 0.6 m
METRIC WEIGHT: 17.5 kg

POSSIBLE MOVES: Pound, Water Gun, Growl, Disarming Voice, Baby-Doll Eyes, Aqua Jet, Icy Wind, Encore, Bubble Beam, Sing, Double Slap, Hyper Voice, Moonblast, Captivate, Hydro Pump, Misty Terrain

POPPLIO   BRIONNE   PRIMARINA

TYPE: STEEL-PSYCHIC

BRONZONG
Bronze Bell Pokémon

Some believe it to be a deity that summons rain clouds. When angered, it lets out a warning cry that rings out like the tolling of a bell.

Many scientists suspect that this Pokémon originated outside the Galar region, based on the patterns on its body.

HOW TO SAY IT: brawn-ZONG
IMPERIAL HEIGHT: 4'03"
IMPERIAL WEIGHT: 412.3 lbs.
METRIC HEIGHT: 1.3 m
METRIC WEIGHT: 187.0 kg

POSSIBLE MOVES: Block, Confuse Ray, Confusion, Extrasensory, Future Sight, Gyro Ball, Heavy Slam, Hypnosis, Imprison, Iron Defense, Metal Sound, Payback, Rain Dance, Safeguard, Sunny Day, Tackle, Weather Ball

BRONZOR   BRONZONG

BRONZOR
Bronze Pokémon

TYPE: STEEL-PSYCHIC

It appears in ancient ruins. The pattern on its body doesn't come from any culture in the Galar region, so it remains shrouded in mystery.

Polishing Bronzor to a shine makes its surface reflect the truth, according to common lore. Be that as it may, Bronzor hates being polished.

HOW TO SAY IT: BRAWN-zor   **METRIC HEIGHT:** 0.5 m
IMPERIAL HEIGHT: 1'08"   **METRIC WEIGHT:** 60.5 kg
IMPERIAL WEIGHT: 133.4 lbs.

POSSIBLE MOVES: Confuse Ray, Confusion, Extrasensory, Future Sight, Gyro Ball, Heavy Slam, Hypnosis, Imprison, Iron Defense, Metal Sound, Payback, Safeguard, Tackle

BRONZOR   BRONZONG

BRUXISH
Gnash Teeth Pokémon

REGION: ALOLA

TYPE: WATER-PSYCHIC

It burrows beneath the sand, radiating psychic power from the protuberance on its head. It waits for prey as it surveys the area.

Its skin is thick enough to fend off Mareanie's spikes. With its robust teeth, Bruxish crunches up the spikes and eats them.

HOW TO SAY IT: BRUCK-sish
IMPERIAL HEIGHT: 2'11"
IMPERIAL WEIGHT: 41.9 lbs.
METRIC HEIGHT: 0.9 m
METRIC WEIGHT: 19.0 kg

DOES NOT EVOLVE

POSSIBLE MOVES: Water Gun, Astonish, Confusion, Bite, Aqua Jet, Disable, Psywave, Crunch, Aqua Tail, Screech, Psychic Fangs, Synchronoise

BUDEW
Bud Pokémon

REGIONS: GALAR KALOS (CENTRAL) SINNOH

TYPE: GRASS-POISON

The pollen it releases contains poison. If this Pokémon is raised on clean water, the poison's toxicity is increased.

This Pokémon is highly sensitive to temperature changes. When its bud starts to open, that means spring is right around the corner.

HOW TO SAY IT: buh-DOO
IMPERIAL HEIGHT: 0'08"
IMPERIAL WEIGHT: 2.6 lbs.
METRIC HEIGHT: 0.2 m
METRIC WEIGHT: 1.2 kg

POSSIBLE MOVES: Absorb, Growth, Water Sport, Stun Spore, Mega Drain, Worry Seed

BUDEW　　ROSELIA　　ROSERADE

BUIZEL

Sea Weasel Pokémon

TYPE: WATER

It swims by rotating its two tails like a screw. When it dives, its flotation sac collapses.

It inflates the flotation sac around its neck and pokes its head out of the water to see what is going on.

HOW TO SAY IT: BWEE-zul   **METRIC HEIGHT:** 0.7 m
IMPERIAL HEIGHT: 2'04"   **METRIC WEIGHT:** 29.5 kg
IMPERIAL WEIGHT: 65.0 lbs.

POSSIBLE MOVES: Sonic Boom, Growl, Water Sport, Quick Attack, Water Gun, Pursuit, Swift, Aqua Jet, Double Hit, Whirlpool, Razor Wind, Aqua Tail, Agility, Hydro Pump

BUIZEL   **FLOATZEL**

BULBASAUR

Seed Pokémon

TYPE: GRASS-POISON

There is a plant seed on its back right from the day this Pokémon is born. The seed slowly grows larger.

While it is young, it uses the nutrients that are stored in the seed on its back in order to grow.

HOW TO SAY IT: BUL-ba-sore   **METRIC HEIGHT:** 0.7 m
IMPERIAL HEIGHT: 2'04"   **METRIC WEIGHT:** 6.9 kg
IMPERIAL WEIGHT: 15.2 lbs.

POSSIBLE MOVES: Tackle, Growl, Leech Seed, Vine Whip, Poison Powder, Sleep Powder, Take Down, Razor Leaf, Sweet Scent, Growth, Double Edge, Worry Seed, Synthesis, Seed Bomb

BULBASAUR   **IVYSAUR**   **VENUSAUR**   **MEGA VENUSAUR**

BUNEARY

Rabbit Pokémon

TYPE: NORMAL

If both of Buneary's ears are rolled up, something is wrong with its body or mind. It's a sure sign the Pokémon is in need of care.

Buneary can attack by rolling up their ears and then striking with the force created by unrolling them. This attack becomes stronger with training.

HOW TO SAY IT: buh-NEAR-ee
IMPERIAL HEIGHT: 1'04"
IMPERIAL WEIGHT: 12.1 lbs.
METRIC HEIGHT: 0.4 m
METRIC WEIGHT: 5.5 kg

POSSIBLE MOVES: Splash, Pound, Defense Curl, Foresight, Endure, Frustration, Quick Attack, Jump Kick, Baton Pass, Agility, Dizzy Punch, After You, Charm, Entrainment, Bounce, Healing Wish, Baby-Doll Eyes

BUNEARY → **LOPUNNY** → **MEGA LOPUNNY**

BUNNELBY

Digging Pokémon

TYPE: NORMAL

It excels at digging holes. Using its ears, it can dig a nest 33 feet deep in one night.

It's very sensitive to danger. The sound of Corviknight's flapping will have Bunnelby digging a hole to hide underground in moments.

HOW TO SAY IT: BUN-ell-bee
IMPERIAL HEIGHT: 1'04"
IMPERIAL WEIGHT: 11.0 lbs.
METRIC HEIGHT: 0.4 m
METRIC WEIGHT: 5.0 kg

POSSIBLE MOVES: Bounce, Bulldoze, Dig, Double Kick, Earthquake, Flail, Laser Focus, Leer, Mud Shot, Mud-Slap, Quick Attack, Super Fang, Swords Dance, Tackle, Take Down

BUNNELBY → **DIGGERSBY**

BURMY

Bagworm Pokémon

TYPE: BUG

To shelter itself from cold, wintry winds, it covers itself with a cloak made of twigs and leaves.

If its cloak is broken in battle, it quickly remakes the cloak with materials nearby.

HOW TO SAY IT: BURR-mee
IMPERIAL HEIGHT: 0'08"
IMPERIAL WEIGHT: 7.5 lbs.
METRIC HEIGHT: 0.2 m
METRIC WEIGHT: 3.4 kg

POSSIBLE MOVES: Protect, Tackle, Bug Bite, Hidden Power

PLANT CLOAK

SANDY CLOAK

TRASH CLOAK

WORMADAM

BURMY

MOTHIM

67

BUTTERFREE

Butterfly Pokémon

REGIONS:
ALOLA
GALAR
KALOS
(CENTRAL)
KANTO

TYPE: BUG-FLYING

In battle, it flaps its wings at great speed to release highly toxic dust into the air.

It collects honey every day. It rubs honey onto the hairs on its legs to carry it back to its nest.

HOW TO SAY IT: BUT-er-free
IMPERIAL HEIGHT: 3'07"
IMPERIAL WEIGHT: 70.5 lbs.
METRIC HEIGHT: 1.1 m
METRIC WEIGHT: 32.0 kg

POSSIBLE MOVES: Air Slash, Bug Bite, Bug Buzz, Confusion, Gust, Harden, Poison Powder, Psybeam, Quiver Dance, Rage Powder, Safeguard, Sleep Powder, String Shot, Stun Spore, Supersonic, Tackle, Tailwind, Whirlwind

CATERPIE   **METAPOD**   **BUTTERFREE**

Alternate Form:
GIGANTAMAX BUTTERFREE

Crystallized Gigantamax energy makes up this Pokémon's blindingly bright and highly toxic scales.

Once it has opponents trapped in a tornado that could blow away a 10-ton truck, it finishes them off with its poisonous scales.

IMPERIAL HEIGHT: 55'09"+
IMPERIAL WEIGHT: ????.? lbs.
METRIC HEIGHT: 17.0+ m
METRIC WEIGHT: ???.? kg

REGION: ALOLA

BUZZWOLE
Swollen Pokémon

TYPE: BUG-FIGHTING

Although it's alien to this world and a danger here, it's apparently a common organism in the world where it normally lives.

Buzzwole goes around showing off its abnormally swollen muscles. It is one kind of Ultra Beast.

HOW TO SAY IT: BUZZ-wole
IMPERIAL HEIGHT: 7'10"
IMPERIAL WEIGHT: 735.5 lbs.
METRIC HEIGHT: 2.4 m
METRIC WEIGHT: 333.6 kg

POSSIBLE MOVES: Fell Stinger, Thunder Punch, Ice Punch, Reversal, Harden, Power-Up Punch, Focus Energy, Comet Punch, Bulk Up, Vital Throw, Endure, Leech Life, Taunt, Mega Punch, Counter, Hammer Arm, Lunge, Dynamic Punch, Superpower, Focus Punch

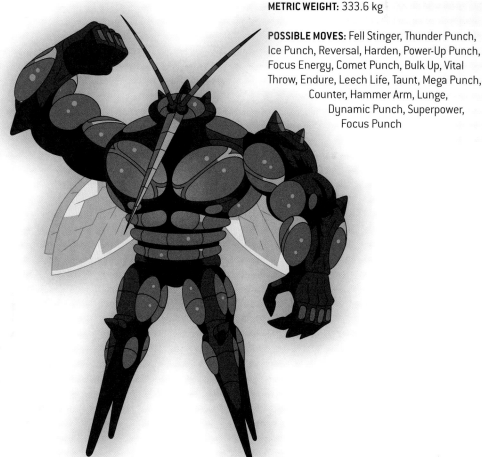

DOES NOT EVOLVE

CACNEA
Cactus Pokémon

TYPE: GRASS

Cacnea lives in arid locations such as deserts. It releases a strong aroma from its flower to attract prey. When prey comes near, this Pokémon shoots sharp thorns from its body to bring the victim down.

The more arid and harsh the environment, the more pretty and fragrant a flower Cacnea grows. This Pokémon battles by wildly swinging its thorny arms.

HOW TO SAY IT: CACK-nee-uh
IMPERIAL HEIGHT: 1'04"
IMPERIAL WEIGHT: 113.1 lbs.
METRIC HEIGHT: 0.4 m
METRIC WEIGHT: 51.3 kg

POSSIBLE MOVES: Poison Sting, Leer, Absorb, Growth, Leech Seed, Sand Attack, Pin Missile, Ingrain, Feint Attack, Spikes, Sucker Punch, Payback, Needle Arm, Cotton Spore, Sandstorm, Destiny Bond, Energy Ball

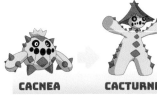

CACNEA   CACTURNE

CACTURNE
Scarecrow Pokémon

TYPE: GRASS-DARK

During the daytime, Cacturne remains unmoving so that it does not lose any moisture to the harsh desert sun. This Pokémon becomes active at night when the temperature drops.

If a traveler is going through a desert in the thick of night, Cacturne will follow in a ragtag group. The Pokémon are biding their time, waiting for the traveler to tire and become incapable of moving.

HOW TO SAY IT: CACK-turn
IMPERIAL HEIGHT: 4'03"
IMPERIAL WEIGHT: 170.6 lbs.
METRIC HEIGHT: 1.3 m
METRIC WEIGHT: 77.4 kg

POSSIBLE MOVES: Spiky Shield, Destiny Bond, Revenge, Poison Sting, Leer, Absorb, Growth, Leech Seed, Sand Attack, Needle Arm, Feint Attack, Ingrain, Payback, Spikes, Sucker Punch, Pin Missile, Energy Ball, Cotton Spore, Sandstorm

CACNEA   CACTURNE

CAMERUPT

Eruption Pokémon

TYPE: FIRE-GROUND

Camerupt has a volcano inside its body. Magma of 18,000 degrees Fahrenheit courses through its body. Occasionally, the humps on this Pokémon's back erupt, spewing the superheated magma.

The humps on Camerupt's back are formed by a transformation of its bones. They sometimes blast out molten magma. This Pokémon apparently erupts often when it is enraged.

HOW TO SAY IT: CAM-err-rupt
IMPERIAL HEIGHT: 6'03"
IMPERIAL WEIGHT: 485.0 lbs.
METRIC HEIGHT: 1.9 m
METRIC WEIGHT: 220.0 kg

POSSIBLE MOVES: Rock Slide, Fissure, Eruption, Growl, Tackle, Ember, Focus Energy, Magnitude, Flame Burst, Amnesia, Lava Plume, Earth Power, Curse, Take Down, Yawn, Earthquake

MEGA CAMERUPT

Eruption Pokémon

TYPE: FIRE-GROUND

IMPERIAL HEIGHT: 8'02"
IMPERIAL WEIGHT: 706.6 lbs.
METRIC HEIGHT: 2.5 m
METRIC WEIGHT: 320.5 kg

NUMEL CAMERUPT MEGA CAMERUPT

CARBINK
Jewel Pokémon

TYPE: ROCK-FAIRY

Some say that deep beneath the surface of the world, a pack of Carbink live with their queen in a kingdom of jewels.

To keep the jewels on their bodies free of tarnish, packs of Carbink use their soft manes to polish one another's jewels.

HOW TO SAY IT: CAR-bink
IMPERIAL HEIGHT: 1'00"
IMPERIAL WEIGHT: 12.6 lbs.
METRIC HEIGHT: 0.3 m
METRIC WEIGHT: 5.7 kg

POSSIBLE MOVES: Tackle, Harden, Rock Throw, Sharpen, Smack Down, Reflect, Stealth Rock, Guard Split, Ancient Power, Flail, Skill Swap, Power Gem, Stone Edge, Moonblast, Light Screen, Safeguard

DOES NOT EVOLVE

CARKOL
Coal Pokémon

TYPE: ROCK-FIRE

It forms coal inside its body. Coal dropped by this Pokémon once helped fuel the lives of people in the Galar region.

By rapidly rolling its legs, it can travel at over 18 mph. The temperature of the flames it breathes exceeds 1,800 degrees Fahrenheit.

HOW TO SAY IT: KAR-kohl
IMPERIAL HEIGHT: 3'07"
IMPERIAL WEIGHT: 172.0 lbs.
METRIC HEIGHT: 1.1 m
METRIC WEIGHT: 78.0 kg

POSSIBLE MOVES: Ancient Power, Burn Up, Flame Charge, Heat Crash, Incinerate, Rapid Spin, Rock Blast, Rock Polish, Smack Down, Smokescreen, Stealth Rock, Tackle

ROLYCOLY

CARKOL

COALOSSAL

CARNIVINE

Bug Catcher Pokémon

REGIONS:
KALOS
(MOUNTAIN)
SINNOH

TYPE: GRASS

It attracts prey with its sweet-smelling saliva, then chomps down. It takes a whole day to eat prey.

It binds itself to trees in marshes. It attracts prey with its sweet-smelling drool and gulps them down.

HOW TO SAY IT: CAR-neh-vine
IMPERIAL HEIGHT: 4'07"
IMPERIAL WEIGHT: 59.5 lbs.
METRIC HEIGHT: 1.4 m
METRIC WEIGHT: 27.0 kg

POSSIBLE MOVES: Bind, Growth, Bite, Vine Whip, Sweet Scent, Ingrain, Feint Attack, Leaf Tornado, Stockpile, Spit Up, Swallow, Crunch, Wring Out, Power Whip

DOES NOT EVOLVE

CARRACOSTA

Prototurtle Pokémon

REGIONS:
ALOLA
UNOVA

TYPE: WATER-ROCK

Its jaws are terrifyingly powerful. It could eat Omastar and Omanyte whole and not be bothered in the slightest by their shells.

Carracosta eats every last bit of the prey it catches, even the shells and bones, to further strengthen its sturdy shell.

HOW TO SAY IT: care-a-KOSS-tah
IMPERIAL HEIGHT: 3'11"
IMPERIAL WEIGHT: 178.6 lbs.
METRIC HEIGHT: 1.2 m
METRIC WEIGHT: 81.0 kg

POSSIBLE MOVES: Bide, Withdraw, Water Gun, Rollout, Bite, Protect, Aqua Jet, Ancient Power, Crunch, Wide Guard, Brine, Smack Down, Curse, Shell Smash, Aqua Tail, Rock Slide, Rain Dance, Hydro Pump

TIRTOUGA   **CARRACOSTA**

CARVANHA
Savage Pokémon

TYPE: WATER-DARK

It won't attack while it's alone—not even if it spots prey. Instead, it waits for other Carvanha to join it, and then the Pokémon attack as a group.

These Pokémon have sharp fangs and powerful jaws. Sailors avoid Carvanha dens at all costs.

HOW TO SAY IT: car-VAH-na
IMPERIAL HEIGHT: 2'07"
IMPERIAL WEIGHT: 45.9 lbs.
METRIC HEIGHT: 0.8 m
METRIC WEIGHT: 20.8 kg

POSSIBLE MOVES: Leer, Bite, Rage, Focus Energy, Aqua Jet, Assurance, Screech, Swagger, Ice Fang, Scary Face, Poison Fang, Crunch, Agility, Take Down

CARVANHA   SHARPEDO   MEGA SHARPEDO

CASCOON
Cocoon Pokémon

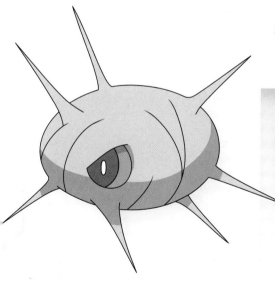

TYPE: BUG

Cascoon makes its protective cocoon by wrapping its body entirely with a fine silk from its mouth. Once the silk goes around its body, it hardens. This Pokémon prepares for its evolution inside the cocoon.

If it is attacked, Cascoon remains motionless however badly it may be hurt. It does so because if it were to move, its body would be weak upon evolution. This Pokémon will also not forget the pain it endured.

HOW TO SAY IT: CAS-koon
IMPERIAL HEIGHT: 2'04"
IMPERIAL WEIGHT: 25.4 lbs.
METRIC HEIGHT: 0.7 m
METRIC WEIGHT: 11.5 kg

WURMPLE   CASCOON   DUSTOX

POSSIBLE MOVE: Harden

CASTFORM
Weather Pokémon

REGULAR FORM

SNOWY FORM

RAINY FORM

SUNNY FORM

REGIONS:
ALOLA
HOENN

TYPE: NORMAL

Although its form changes with the weather, that is apparently the result of a chemical reaction and not the result of its own free will.

Its form changes depending on the weather. The rougher conditions get, the rougher Castform's disposition!

HOW TO SAY IT: CAST-form
IMPERIAL HEIGHT: 1'00"
IMPERIAL WEIGHT: 1.8 lbs.
METRIC HEIGHT: 0.3 m
METRIC WEIGHT: 0.8 kg

POSSIBLE MOVES: Tackle, Water Gun, Ember, Powder Snow, Headbutt, Rain Dance, Sunny Day, Hail, Weather Ball, Hydro Pump, Fire Blast, Blizzard, Hurricane

DOES NOT EVOLVE

CATERPIE
Worm Pokémon

REGIONS:
ALOLA
GALAR
KALOS
(CENTRAL)
KANTO

TYPE: BUG

For protection, it releases a horrible stench from the antenna on its head to drive away enemies.

Its short feet are tipped with suction pads that enable it to tirelessly climb slopes and walls.

HOW TO SAY IT: CAT-ur-pee
IMPERIAL HEIGHT: 1'00"
IMPERIAL WEIGHT: 6.4 lbs.
METRIC HEIGHT: 0.3 m
METRIC WEIGHT: 2.9 kg

POSSIBLE MOVES: Bug Bite, String Shot, Tackle

CATERPIE METAPOD BUTTERFREE

MYTHICAL POKÉMON

CELEBI
Time Travel Pokémon

TYPE: PSYCHIC-GRASS

This Pokémon came from the future by crossing over time. It is thought that so long as Celebi appears, a bright and shining future awaits us.

HOW TO SAY IT: SEL-ih-bee
IMPERIAL HEIGHT: 2'00"
IMPERIAL WEIGHT: 11.0 lbs.
METRIC HEIGHT: 0.6 m
METRIC WEIGHT: 5.0 kg

POSSIBLE MOVES: Leech Seed, Confusion, Recover, Heal Bell, Safeguard, Magical Leaf, Ancient Power, Baton Pass, Natural Gift, Heal Block, Future Sight, Healing Wish, Leaf Storm, Perish Song

DOES NOT EVOLVE

CELESTEELA
Launch Pokémon

ULTRA BEAST

TYPE: STEEL-FLYING

One of the dangerous UBs, high energy readings can be detected coming from both of its huge arms.

Although it's alien to this world and a danger here, it's apparently a common organism in the world where it normally lives.

HOW TO SAY IT: sell-uh-STEEL-uh
IMPERIAL HEIGHT: 30'02"
IMPERIAL WEIGHT: 2,204.4 lbs.
METRIC HEIGHT: 9.2 m
METRIC WEIGHT: 999.9 kg

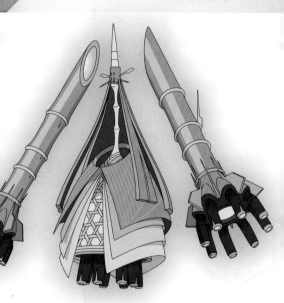

POSSIBLE MOVES: Wide Guard, Air Slash, Ingrain, Absorb, Harden, Tackle, Smack Down, Mega Drain, Leech Seed, Metal Sound, Iron Head, Giga Drain, Flash Cannon, Autotomize, Seed Bomb, Skull Bash, Iron Defense, Heavy Slam, Double-Edge

DOES NOT EVOLVE

CENTISKORCH
Radiator Pokémon

TYPE: FIRE-BUG

When it heats up, its body temperature reaches about 1,500 degrees Fahrenheit. It lashes its body like a whip and launches itself at enemies.

While its burning body is already dangerous on its own, this excessively hostile Pokémon also has large and very sharp fangs.

HOW TO SAY IT: SEN-tih-scorch
IMPERIAL HEIGHT: 9'10"
IMPERIAL WEIGHT: 264.6 lbs.
METRIC HEIGHT: 3.0 m
METRIC WEIGHT: 120.0 kg

POSSIBLE MOVES: Bite, Bug Bite, Burn Up, Coil, Crunch, Ember, Fire Lash, Fire Spin, Flame Wheel, Inferno, Lunge, Slam, Smokescreen, Wrap

SIZZLIPEDE   CENTISKORCH

Alternate Form:
GIGANTAMAX CENTISKORCH

Gigantamax energy has evoked a rise in its body temperature, now reaching over 1,800 degrees Fahrenheit. Its heat waves incinerate its enemies.

The heat that comes off a Gigantamax Centiskorch may destabilize air currents. Sometimes it can even cause storms.

IMPERIAL HEIGHT: 246'01"+
IMPERIAL WEIGHT: ????.? lbs.
METRIC HEIGHT: 75.0+ mm
METRIC WEIGHT: ???.? kg

CHANDELURE
Luring Pokémon

TYPE: GHOST-FIRE

This Pokémon haunts dilapidated mansions. It sways its arms to hypnotize opponents with the ominous dancing of its flames.

In homes illuminated by Chandelure instead of lights, funerals were a constant occurrence—or so it's said.

HOW TO SAY IT: shan-duh-LOOR
IMPERIAL HEIGHT: 3'03"
IMPERIAL WEIGHT: 75.6 lbs.
METRIC HEIGHT: 1.0 m
METRIC WEIGHT: 34.3 kg

POSSIBLE MOVES: Astonish, Confuse Ray, Curse, Ember, Fire Spin, Hex, Imprison, Inferno, Memento, Minimize, Night Shade, Overheat, Pain Split, Shadow Ball, Smog, Will-O-Wisp

LITWICK   LAMPENT   CHANDELURE

CHANSEY
Egg Pokémon

TYPE: NORMAL

The egg Chansey carries is not only delicious but also packed with nutrition. It's used as a high-class cooking ingredient.

This species was once very slow. To protect their eggs from other creatures, these Pokémon became able to flee quickly.

HOW TO SAY IT: CHAN-see
IMPERIAL HEIGHT: 3'07"
IMPERIAL WEIGHT: 76.3 lbs.
METRIC HEIGHT: 1.1 m
METRIC WEIGHT: 34.6 kg

POSSIBLE MOVES: Double-Edge, Defense Curl, Pound, Growl, Tail Whip, Refresh, Double Slap, Soft-Boiled, Bestow, Minimize, Take Down, Sing, Fling, Heal Pulse, Egg Bomb, Light Screen, Healing Wish

HAPPINY   CHANSEY   BLISSEY

CHARIZARD

Flame Pokémon

TYPE: FIRE-FLYING

It spits fire that is hot enough to melt boulders. It may cause forest fires by blowing flames.

Its wings can carry this Pokémon close to an altitude of 4,600 feet. It blows out fire at very high temperatures.

HOW TO SAY IT: CHAR-iz-ard
IMPERIAL HEIGHT: 5'07"
IMPERIAL WEIGHT: 199.5 lbs.
METRIC HEIGHT: 1.7 m
METRIC WEIGHT: 90.5 kg

POSSIBLE MOVES: Air Slash, Dragon Breath, Dragon Claw, Ember, Fire Fang, Fire Spin, Flamethrower, Flare Blitz, Growl, Heat Wave, Inferno, Scary Face, Scratch, Slash, Smokescreen

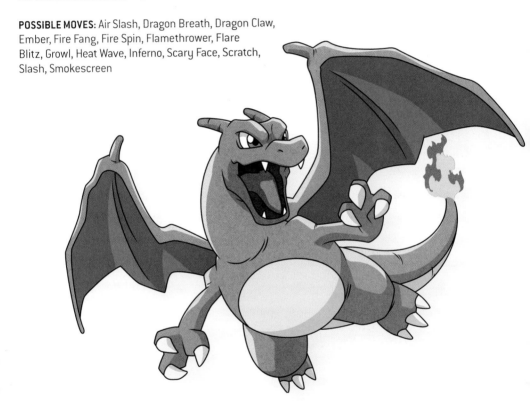

MEGA
CHARIZARD X

MEGA
CHARIZARD Y

CHARMANDER

CHARMELEON

CHARIZARD

MEGA CHARIZARD X
Flame Pokémon

TYPE: FIRE-DRAGON

IMPERIAL HEIGHT: 5'07"
IMPERIAL WEIGHT: 243.6 lbs.

METRIC HEIGHT: 1.7 m
METRIC WEIGHT: 110.5 kg

MEGA CHARIZARD Y
Flame Pokémon

TYPE: FIRE-FLYING

IMPERIAL HEIGHT: 5'07"
IMPERIAL WEIGHT: 221.6 lbs.

METRIC HEIGHT: 1.7 m
METRIC WEIGHT: 100.5 kg

Alternate Form:
GIGANTAMAX CHARIZARD

This colossal, flame-winged figure of a Charizard was brought about by Gigantamax energy.

The flame inside its body burns hotter than 3,600 degrees Fahrenheit. When Charizard roars, that temperature climbs even higher.

IMPERIAL HEIGHT: 91'10"+
IMPERIAL WEIGHT: ????.? lbs.
METRIC HEIGHT: 28.0+ m
METRIC WEIGHT: ???.? kg

CHARJABUG

Battery Pokémon

REGION:
ALOLA
GALAR

TYPE: BUG-ELECTRIC

While its durable shell protects it from attacks, Charjabug strikes at enemies with jolts of electricity discharged from the tips of its jaws.

Its digestive processes convert the leaves it eats into electricity. An electric sac in its belly stores the electricity for later use.

HOW TO SAY IT: CHAR-juh-bug   **METRIC HEIGHT:** 0.5 m
IMPERIAL HEIGHT: 1'08"   **METRIC WEIGHT:** 10.5 kg
IMPERIAL WEIGHT: 23.1 lbs.

POSSIBLE MOVES: Bite, Bug Bite, Charge, Crunch, Dig, Discharge, Iron Defense, Mud-Slap, Spark, Sticky Web, String Shot, Vise Grip, X-Scissor

GRUBBIN   **CHARJABUG**   **VIKAVOLT**

CHARMANDER

Lizard Pokémon

REGIONS:
GALAR
KALOS
(CENTRAL)
KANTO

TYPE: FIRE

It has a preference for hot things. When it rains, steam is said to spout from the tip of its tail.

From the time it is born, a flame burns at the tip of its tail. Its life would end if the flame were to go out.

HOW TO SAY IT: CHAR-man-der   **METRIC HEIGHT:** 0.6 m
IMPERIAL HEIGHT: 2'00"   **METRIC WEIGHT:** 8.5 kg
IMPERIAL WEIGHT: 18.7 lbs.

POSSIBLE MOVES: Dragon Breath, Ember, Fire Fang, Fire Spin, Flamethrower, Flare Blitz, Growl, Inferno, Scary Face, Scratch, Slash, Smokescreen

MEGA CHARIZARD X

CHARMANDER   **CHARMELEON**   **CHARIZARD**

MEGA CHARIZARD Y

REGIONS:
GALAR
KALOS
(CENTRAL)
KANTO

CHARMELEON
Flame Pokémon

TYPE: FIRE

It has a barbaric nature. In battle, it whips its fiery tail around and slashes away with sharp claws.

If it becomes agitated during battle, it spouts intense flames, incinerating its surroundings.

HOW TO SAY IT: char-MEE-lee-un
IMPERIAL HEIGHT: 3'07"
IMPERIAL WEIGHT: 41.9 lbs.
METRIC HEIGHT: 1.1 m
METRIC WEIGHT: 19.0 kg

POSSIBLE MOVES: Dragon Breath, Ember, Fire Fang, Fire Spin, Flamethrower, Flare Blitz, Growl, Inferno, Scary Face, Scratch, Slash, Smokescreen

MEGA CHARIZARD X

MEGA CHARIZARD Y

CHARMANDER → CHARMELEON → CHARIZARD

REGIONS:
KALOS
(COASTAL)
SINNOH

CHATOT
Music Note Pokémon

TYPE: NORMAL-FLYING

It mimics the cries of other Pokémon to trick them into thinking it's one of them. This way they won't attack it.

It can learn and speak human words. If they gather, they all learn the same saying.

HOW TO SAY IT: CHAT-tot
IMPERIAL HEIGHT: 1'08"
IMPERIAL WEIGHT: 4.2 lbs.
METRIC HEIGHT: 0.5 m
METRIC WEIGHT: 1.9 kg

POSSIBLE MOVES: Hyper Voice, Chatter, Confide, Taunt, Peck, Growl, Mirror Move, Sing, Fury Attack, Round, Mimic, Echoed Voice, Roost, Uproar, Synchronoise, Feather Dance

DOES NOT EVOLVE

83

CHERRIM

Blossom Pokémon

TYPE: GRASS

As a bud, it barely moves. It sits still, placidly waiting for sunlight to appear.

Its folded petals are pretty tough. Bird Pokémon can peck at them all they want, and Cherrim won't be bothered at all.

HOW TO SAY IT: chuh-RIM
IMPERIAL HEIGHT: 1'08"
IMPERIAL WEIGHT: 20.5 lbs.
METRIC HEIGHT: 0.5 m
METRIC WEIGHT: 9.3 kg

POSSIBLE MOVES: Flower Shield, Growth, Helping Hand, Leafage, Leech Seed, Magical Leaf, Morning Sun, Petal Blizzard, Petal Dance, Solar Beam, Sunny Day, Tackle, Take Down, Worry Seed

CHERUBI   CHERRIM

TYPE: GRASS

It nimbly dashes about to avoid getting pecked by bird Pokémon that would love to make off with its small, nutrient-rich storage ball.

The deeper a Cherubi's red, the more nutrients it has stockpiled in its body. And the sweeter and tastier its small ball!

HOW TO SAY IT: chuh-ROO-bee
IMPERIAL HEIGHT: 1'04"
IMPERIAL WEIGHT: 7.3 lbs.
METRIC HEIGHT: 0.4 m
METRIC WEIGHT: 3.3 kg

POSSIBLE MOVES: Growth, Helping Hand, Leafage, Leech Seed, Magical Leaf, Morning Sun, Petal Blizzard, Solar Beam, Tackle, Take Down, Worry Seed

CHERUBI

Cherry Pokémon

CHERUBI   CHERRIM

CHESNAUGHT

Spiny Armor Pokémon

TYPE: GRASS-FIGHTING

Its Tackle is forceful enough to flip a 50-ton tank. It shields its allies from danger with its own body.

When it takes a defensive posture with its fists guarding its face, it could withstand a bomb blast.

HOW TO SAY IT: CHESS-nawt
IMPERIAL HEIGHT: 5'03"
IMPERIAL WEIGHT: 198.4 lbs.
METRIC HEIGHT: 1.6 m
METRIC WEIGHT: 90.0 kg

POSSIBLE MOVES: Feint, Hammer Arm, Belly Drum, Tackle, Growl, Vine Whip, Rollout, Bite, Leech Seed, Pin Missile, Needle Arm, Take Down, Seed Bomb, Spiky Shield, Mud Shot, Bulk Up, Body Slam, Pain Split, Wood Hammer, Giga Impact

CHESPIN   QUILLADIN   CHESNAUGHT

CHESPIN

Spiny Nut Pokémon

TYPE: GRASS

The quills on its head are usually soft. When it flexes them, the points become so hard and sharp that they can pierce rock.

Such a thick shell of wood covers its head and back that even a direct hit from a truck wouldn't faze it.

HOW TO SAY IT: CHESS-pin
IMPERIAL HEIGHT: 1'04"
IMPERIAL WEIGHT: 19.8 lbs.
METRIC HEIGHT: 0.4 m
METRIC WEIGHT: 9.0 kg

POSSIBLE MOVES: Growl, Vine Whip, Rollout, Bite, Leech Seed, Pin Missile, Take Down, Seed Bomb, Mud Shot, Bulk Up, Body Slam, Pain Split, Wood Hammer

CHESPIN   QUILLADIN   CHESNAUGHT

CHEWTLE
Snapping Pokémon

REGION: GALAR

TYPE: WATER

Apparently the itch of its teething impels it to snap its jaws at anything in front of it.

It starts off battles by attacking with its rock-hard horn, but as soon as the opponent flinches, this Pokémon bites down and never lets go.

HOW TO SAY IT: CHOO-tull
IMPERIAL HEIGHT: 1'00"
IMPERIAL WEIGHT: 18.7 lbs.
METRIC HEIGHT: 0.3 m
METRIC WEIGHT: 8.5 kg

POSSIBLE MOVES: Bite, Body Slam, Counter, Headbutt, Jaw Lock, Liquidation, Protect, Tackle, Water Gun

CHEWTLE **DREDNAW**

TYPE: GRASS

In battle, Chikorita waves its leaf around to keep the foe at bay. However, a sweet fragrance also wafts from the leaf, becalming the battling Pokémon and creating a cozy, friendly atmosphere all around.

HOW TO SAY IT: CHICK-oh-REE-ta
IMPERIAL HEIGHT: 2'11"
IMPERIAL WEIGHT: 14.1 lbs.
METRIC HEIGHT: 0.9 m
METRIC WEIGHT: 6.4 kg

POSSIBLE MOVES: Tackle, Growl, Razor Leaf, Poison Powder, Synthesis, Reflect, Magical Leaf, Natural Gift, Sweet Scent, Light Screen, Body Slam, Safeguard, Aromatherapy, Solar Beam

CHIKORITA
Leaf Pokémon

CHIKORITA ➡ **BAYLEEF** ➡ **MEGANIUM**

REGION: SINNOH

CHIMCHAR
Chimp Pokémon

TYPE: FIRE

Its fiery rear end is fueled by gas made in its belly. Even rain can't extinguish the fire.

The gas made in its belly burns from its rear end. The fire burns weakly when it feels sick.

HOW TO SAY IT: CHIM-char
IMPERIAL HEIGHT: 1'08"
IMPERIAL WEIGHT: 13.7 lbs.
METRIC HEIGHT: 0.5 m
METRIC WEIGHT: 6.2 kg

POSSIBLE MOVES: Scratch, Leer, Ember, Taunt, Fury Swipes, Flame Wheel, Nasty Plot, Torment, Facade, Fire Spin, Acrobatics, Slack Off, Flamethrower

CHIMCHAR ➡ **MONFERNO** ➡ **INFERNAPE**

CHIMECHO

Wind Chime Pokémon

TYPE: PSYCHIC

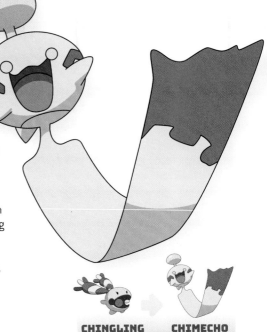

Chimecho makes its cries echo inside its hollow body. When this Pokémon becomes enraged, its cries result in ultrasonic waves that have the power to knock foes flying.

In high winds, Chimecho cries as it hangs from a tree branch or the eaves of a building using a suction cup on its head. This Pokémon plucks berries with its long tail and eats them.

HOW TO SAY IT: chime-ECK-ko
IMPERIAL HEIGHT: 2'00"
IMPERIAL WEIGHT: 2.2 lbs.
METRIC HEIGHT: 0.6 m
METRIC WEIGHT: 1.0 kg

POSSIBLE MOVES: Healing Wish, Synchronoise, Wrap, Growl, Astonish, Confusion, Uproar, Take Down, Yawn, Psywave, Double-Edge, Heal Bell, Safeguard, Extrasensory, Heal Pulse

CHINGLING → CHIMECHO

CHINCHOU

Angler Pokémon

TYPE: WATER-ELECTRIC

Its antennae, which evolved from a fin, have both positive and negative charges flowing through them.

On the dark ocean floor, its only means of communication is its constantly flashing lights.

HOW TO SAY IT: CHIN-chow
IMPERIAL HEIGHT: 1'08"
IMPERIAL WEIGHT: 26.5 lbs.
METRIC HEIGHT: 0.5 m
METRIC WEIGHT: 12.0 kg

POSSIBLE MOVES: Aqua Ring, Bubble Beam, Charge, Confuse Ray, Discharge, Electro Ball, Flail, Hydro Pump, Spark, Supersonic, Take Down, Thunder Wave, Water Gun

CHINCHOU → LANTURN

CHINGLING

Bell Pokémon

TYPE: PSYCHIC

Each time it hops, it makes a ringing sound. It deafens foes by emitting high-frequency cries.

There is an orb inside its mouth. When it hops, the orb bounces all over and makes a ringing sound.

HOW TO SAY IT: CHING-ling
IMPERIAL HEIGHT: 0'08"
IMPERIAL WEIGHT: 1.3 lbs.
METRIC HEIGHT: 0.2 m
METRIC WEIGHT: 0.6 kg

POSSIBLE MOVES: Wrap, Growl, Astonish, Confusion, Yawn, Last Resort, Entrainment, Uproar

CHINGLING   CHIMECHO

CINCCINO

Scarf Pokémon

TYPE: NORMAL

Its body secretes oil that this Pokémon spreads over its nest as a coating to protect it from dust. Cinccino won't tolerate even a speck of the stuff.

A special oil that seeps through their fur helps them avoid attacks. The oil fetches a high price at market.

HOW TO SAY IT: chin-CHEE-noh
IMPERIAL HEIGHT: 1'08"
IMPERIAL WEIGHT: 16.5 lbs.
METRIC HEIGHT: 0.5 m
METRIC WEIGHT: 7.5 kg

POSSIBLE MOVES: After You, Baby-Doll Eyes, Bullet Seed, Charm, Echoed Voice, Encore, Helping Hand, Hyper Voice, Last Resort, Pound, Rock Blast, Sing, Slam, Swift, Tail Slap, Tickle

MINCCINO   CINCCINO

CINDERACE

Striker Pokémon

TYPE: FIRE

It juggles a pebble with its feet, turning it into a burning soccer ball. Its shots strike opponents hard and leave them scorched.

It's skilled at both offense and defense, and it gets pumped up when cheered on. But if it starts showboating, it could put itself in a tough spot.

HOW TO SAY IT: SIN-deh-race
IMPERIAL HEIGHT: 4'07"
IMPERIAL WEIGHT: 72.8 lbs.
METRIC HEIGHT: 1.4 m
METRIC WEIGHT: 33.0 kg

POSSIBLE MOVES: Agility, Bounce, Counter, Court Change, Double Kick, Double-Edge, Ember, Feint, Flame Charge, Growl, Headbutt, Pyro Ball, Quick Attack, Tackle

SCORBUNNY ➡ **RABOOT** ➡ **CINDERACE**

Alternate Form:
GIGANTAMAX CINDERACE

Infused with Cinderace's fighting spirit, the gigantic Pyro Ball never misses its targets and completely roasts opponents.

Gigantamax energy can sometimes cause the diameter of this Pokémon's fireball to exceed 300 feet.

IMPERIAL HEIGHT: 88'07"+
IMPERIAL WEIGHT: ????.? lbs.
METRIC HEIGHT: 27.0+ m
METRIC WEIGHT: ???.? kg

CLAMPERL
Bivalve Pokémon

TYPE: WATER

Despite its appearance, it's carnivorous. It clamps down on its prey with both sides of its shell and doesn't let go until they stop moving.

Clamperl's pearls are exceedingly precious. They can be more than ten times as costly as Shellder's pearls.

HOW TO SAY IT: CLAM-perl
IMPERIAL HEIGHT: 1'04"
IMPERIAL WEIGHT: 115.7 lbs.
METRIC HEIGHT: 0.4 m
METRIC WEIGHT: 52.5 kg

POSSIBLE MOVES: Clamp, Water Gun, Whirlpool, Iron Defense, Shell Smash

CLAMPERL

HUNTAIL

GOREBYSS

CLAUNCHER
Water Gun Pokémon

TYPE: WATER

Claruncher's claws can fall off during battle, but they'll regenerate. The meat inside the claws is popular as a delicacy in Galar.

By detonating gas that accumulates in its right claw, this Pokémon launches water like a bullet. This is how Clauncher defeats its enemies.

HOW TO SAY IT: CLAWN-chur
IMPERIAL HEIGHT: 1'08"
IMPERIAL WEIGHT: 18.3 lbs.
METRIC HEIGHT: 0.5 m
METRIC WEIGHT: 8.3 kg

POSSIBLE MOVES: Splash, Water Gun, Water Sport, Vice Grip, Bubble, Flail, Bubble Beam, Swords Dance, Crabhammer, Water Pulse, Smack Down, Aqua Jet, Muddy Water

CLAUNCHER   CLAWITZER

CLAWITZER

Howitzer Pokémon

TYPE: WATER

After using the feelers on its oversized claw to detect the location of prey, Clawitzer launches a cannonball of water at its target.

Clawitzer's right arm is a cannon that launches projectiles made of seawater. Shots from a Clawitzer's cannon arm can sink a tanker.

HOW TO SAY IT: CLOW-wit-zur
IMPERIAL HEIGHT: 4'03"
IMPERIAL WEIGHT: 77.8 lbs.
METRIC HEIGHT: 1.3 m
METRIC WEIGHT: 35.3 kg

POSSIBLE MOVES: Heal Pulse, Dark Pulse, Dragon Pulse, Aura Sphere, Splash, Water Gun, Water Sport, Vice Grip, Bubble, Flail, Bubble Beam, Swords Dance, Crabhammer, Water Pulse, Smack Down, Aqua Jet, Muddy Water

CLAUNCHER → CLAWITZER

CLAYDOL

Clay Doll Pokémon

TYPE: GROUND-PSYCHIC

This mysterious Pokémon started life as an ancient clay figurine made over 20,000 years ago.

It appears to have been born from clay dolls made by ancient people. It uses telekinesis to float and move.

HOW TO SAY IT: CLAY-doll
IMPERIAL HEIGHT: 4'11"
IMPERIAL WEIGHT: 238.1 lbs.
METRIC HEIGHT: 1.5 m
METRIC WEIGHT: 108.0 kg

POSSIBLE MOVES: Ancient Power, Confusion, Cosmic Power, Earth Power, Explosion, Extrasensory, Guard Split, Harden, Hyper Beam, Imprison, Mud-Slap, Power Split, Power Trick, Psybeam, Rapid Spin, Rock Tomb, Sandstorm, Self-Destruct, Teleport

BALTOY → CLAYDOL

CLEFABLE

Fairy Pokémon

TYPE: FAIRY

A timid fairy Pokémon that is rarely seen, it will run and hide the moment it senses people.

Their ears are sensitive enough to hear a pin drop from over a mile away, so they're usually found in quiet places.

HOW TO SAY IT: kleh-FAY-bull
IMPERIAL HEIGHT: 4'03"
IMPERIAL WEIGHT: 88.2 lbs.
METRIC HEIGHT: 1.3 m
METRIC WEIGHT: 40.0 kg

POSSIBLE MOVES: After You, Charm, Copycat, Cosmic Power, Disarming Voice, Encore, Follow Me, Gravity, Healing Wish, Life Dew, Meteor Mash, Metronome, Minimize, Moonblast, Moonlight, Pound, Sing, Splash, Stored Power, Sweet Kiss

CLEFFA ⇒ CLEFAIRY ⇒ CLEFABLE

REGIONS:
ALOLA
GALAR
KANTO

CLEFAIRY

Fairy Pokémon

TYPE: FAIRY

It is said that happiness will come to those who see a gathering of Clefairy dancing under a full moon.

Its adorable behavior and cry make it highly popular. However, this cute Pokémon is rarely found.

HOW TO SAY IT: kleh-FAIR-ee   **METRIC HEIGHT:** 0.6 m
IMPERIAL HEIGHT: 2'00"   **METRIC WEIGHT:** 7.5 kg
IMPERIAL WEIGHT: 16.5 lbs.

POSSIBLE MOVES: After You, Charm, Copycat, Cosmic Power, Defense Curl, Disarming Voice, Encore, Follow Me, Gravity, Growl, Healing Wish, Life Dew, Meteor Mash, Metronome, Minimize, Moonblast, Moonlight, Pound, Sing, Splash, Stored Power, Sweet Kiss

CLEFFA ⇒ CLEFAIRY ⇒ CLEFABLE

CLEFFA
Star Shape Pokémon

TYPE: FAIRY

According to local rumors, Cleffa are often seen in places where shooting stars have fallen.

Because of its unusual, starlike silhouette, people believe that it came here on a meteor.

HOW TO SAY IT: CLEFF-uh
IMPERIAL HEIGHT: 1'00" **METRIC HEIGHT:** 0.3 m
IMPERIAL WEIGHT: 6.6 lbs. **METRIC WEIGHT:** 3.0 kg

POSSIBLE MOVES: Charm, Copycat, Disarming Voice, Encore, Pound, Sing, Splash, Sweet Kiss

CLEFFA   CLEFAIRY   CLEFABLE

CLOBBOPUS
Tantrum Pokémon

TYPE: NORMAL

It's very curious, but its means of investigating things is to try to punch them with its tentacles. The search for food is what brings it onto land.

Its tentacles tear off easily, but it isn't alarmed when that happens—it knows they'll grow back. It's about as smart as a three-year-old.

HOW TO SAY IT: KLAH-buh-puss
IMPERIAL HEIGHT: 2'00"
IMPERIAL WEIGHT: 8.8 lbs.
METRIC HEIGHT: 0.6 m
METRIC WEIGHT: 4.0 kg

POSSIBLE MOVES: Bind, Brick Break, Bulk Up, Detect, Feint, Leer, Reversal, Rock Smash, Submission, Superpower, Taunt

CLOBBOPUS   GRAPPLOCT

REGIONS:
ALOLA
GALAR
KALOS
(COASTAL)
KANTO

CLOYSTER

Bivalve Pokémon

TYPE: WATER-ICE

Its shell is extremely hard. It cannot be shattered, even with a bomb. The shell opens only when it is attacking.

Once it slams its shell shut, it is impossible to open, even by those with superior strength.

HOW TO SAY IT: CLOY-stur
IMPERIAL HEIGHT: 4'11"
IMPERIAL WEIGHT: 292.1 lbs.
METRIC HEIGHT: 1.5 m
METRIC WEIGHT: 132.5 kg

POSSIBLE MOVES: Aurora Beam, Hydro Pump, Ice Beam, Ice Shard, Icicle Crash, Icicle Spear, Iron Defense, Leer, Protect, Razor Shell, Shell Smash, Spikes, Supersonic, Tackle, Toxic Spikes, Water Gun, Whirlpool, Withdraw

SHELLDER   CLOYSTER

COALOSSAL

Coal Pokémon

TYPE: FIRE

It's usually peaceful, but the vandalism of mines enrages it. Offenders will be incinerated with flames that reach 2,700 degrees Fahrenheit.

While it's engaged in battle, its mountain of coal will burn bright red, sending off sparks that scorch the surrounding area.

HOW TO SAY IT: koh-LAHS-ull
IMPERIAL HEIGHT: 9'02"
IMPERIAL WEIGHT: 684.5 lbs.
METRIC HEIGHT: 2.8 m
METRIC WEIGHT: 310.5 kg

POSSIBLE MOVES: Ancient Power, Burn Up, Flame Charge, Heat Crash, Incinerate, Rapid Spin, Rock Blast, Rock Polish, Smack Down, Smokescreen, Stealth Rock, Tackle, Tar Shot

ROLYCOLY   **CARKOL**   **COALOSSAL**

Alternate Form:
GIGANTAMAX COALOSSAL

Its body is a colossal stove. With Gigantamax energy stoking the fire, this Pokémon's flame burns hotter than 3,600 degrees Fahrenheit.

When Galar was hit by a harsh cold wave, this Pokémon served as a giant heating stove and saved many lives.

IMPERIAL HEIGHT: 137'10"+
IMPERIAL WEIGHT: ????.? lbs.
METRIC HEIGHT: 42.0+m
METRIC WEIGHT: ???.? kg

LEGENDARY POKÉMON

COBALION
Iron Will Pokémon

TYPE: STEEL-FIGHTING

It has a body and heart of steel. Its glare is sufficient to make even an unruly Pokémon obey it.

It has a body and heart of steel. It worked with its allies to punish people when they hurt Pokémon.

HOW TO SAY IT: koh-BAY-lee-un **METRIC HEIGHT:** 2.1 m
IMPERIAL HEIGHT: 6'11" **METRIC WEIGHT:** 250.0 kg
IMPERIAL WEIGHT: 551.2 lbs.

POSSIBLE MOVES: Quick Attack, Leer, Double Kick, Metal Claw, Take Down, Helping Hand, Retaliate, Iron Head, Sacred Sword, Swords Dance, Quick Guard, Work Up, Metal Burst, Close Combat

DOES NOT EVOLVE

COFAGRIGUS
Coffin Pokémon

TYPE: GHOST

This Pokémon has a body of sparkling gold. People say it no longer remembers that it was once human.

There are many depictions of Cofagrigus decorating ancient tombs. They're symbols of the wealth that kings of bygone eras had.

HOW TO SAY IT: kof-uh-GREE-guss
IMPERIAL HEIGHT: 5'07"
IMPERIAL WEIGHT: 168.7 lbs.
METRIC HEIGHT: 1.7 m
METRIC WEIGHT: 76.5 kg

POSSIBLE MOVES: Astonish, Crafty Shield, Curse, Dark Pulse, Destiny Bond, Disable, Grudge, Guard Split, Haze, Hex, Mean Look, Night Shade, Power Split, Protect, Scary Face, Shadow Ball, Shadow Claw, Will-O-Wisp

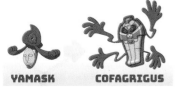

YAMASK COFAGRIGUS

COMBEE
Tiny Bee Pokémon

REGIONS:
KALOS (CENTRAL)
SINNOH

TYPE: BUG-FLYING

The members of the trio spend all their time together. Each one has a slightly different taste in nectar.

It ceaselessly gathers nectar from sunrise to sundown, all for the sake of Vespiquen and the swarm.

HOW TO SAY IT: COMB-bee
IMPERIAL HEIGHT: 1'00"
IMPERIAL WEIGHT: 12.1 lbs.
METRIC HEIGHT: 0.3 m
METRIC WEIGHT: 5.5 kg

POSSIBLE MOVES: Sweet Scent, Gust, Bug Bite, Bug Buzz

COMBEE   **VESPIQUEN**

COMBUSKEN
Young Fowl Pokémon

REGION:
HOENN

TYPE: FIRE-FIGHTING

Combusken toughens up its legs and thighs by running through fields and mountains. This Pokémon's legs possess both speed and power, enabling it to dole out ten kicks in one second.

Combusken battles with the intensely hot flames it spews from its beak and with outstandingly destructive kicks. This Pokémon's cry is very loud and distracting.

HOW TO SAY IT: com-BUS-ken
IMPERIAL HEIGHT: 2'11"
IMPERIAL WEIGHT: 43.0 lbs.
METRIC HEIGHT: 0.9 m
METRIC WEIGHT: 19.5 kg

POSSIBLE MOVES: Scratch, Growl, Focus Energy, Ember, Double Kick, Peck, Sand Attack, Bulk Up, Quick Attack, Slash, Mirror Move, Sky Uppercut, Flare Blitz, Flame Charge

TORCHIC   **COMBUSKEN**   **BLAZIKEN**   **MEGA BLAZIKEN**

COMFEY
Posy Picker Pokémon

TYPE: FAIRY

Comfey picks flowers with its vine and decorates itself with them. For some reason, flowers won't wither once they're attached to a Comfey.

These Pokémon smell very nice. All Comfey wear different flowers, so each of these Pokémon has its own individual scent.

HOW TO SAY IT: KUM-fay
IMPERIAL HEIGHT: 0'04"
IMPERIAL WEIGHT: 0.7 lbs.
METRIC HEIGHT: 0.1 m
METRIC WEIGHT: 0.3 kg

POSSIBLE MOVES: Helping Hand, Vine Whip, Flower Shield, Leech Seed, Draining Kiss, Magical Leaf, Growth, Wrap, Sweet Kiss, Natural Gift, Petal Blizzard, Synthesis, Sweet Scent, Grass Knot, Floral Healing, Petal Dance, Aromatherapy, Grassy Terrain, Play Rough

DOES NOT EVOLVE

CONKELDURR
Muscular Pokémon

TYPE: FIGHTING

Concrete mixed by Conkeldurr is much more durable than normal concrete, even when the compositions of the two materials are the same.

When going all out, this Pokémon throws aside its concrete pillars and leaps at opponents to pummel them with its fists.

HOW TO SAY IT: kon-KELL-dur
IMPERIAL HEIGHT: 4'07"
IMPERIAL WEIGHT: 191.8 lbs.
METRIC HEIGHT: 1.4 m
METRIC WEIGHT: 87.0 kg

POSSIBLE MOVES: Bulk Up, Dynamic Punch, Focus Energy, Focus Punch, Hammer Arm, Leer, Low Kick, Pound, Rock Slide, Rock Throw, Scary Face, Slam, Stone Edge, Superpower

TIMBURR

GURDURR

CONKELDURR

COPPERAJAH

Copperderm Pokémon

TYPE: STEEL

They came over from another region long ago and worked together with humans. Their green skin is resistant to water.

These Pokémon live in herds. Their trunks have incredible grip strength, strong enough to crush giant rocks into powder.

HOW TO SAY IT: KAH-peh-RAH-zhah
IMPERIAL HEIGHT: 9'10"
IMPERIAL WEIGHT: 1,433.0 lbs.
METRIC HEIGHT: 3.0 m
METRIC WEIGHT: 650.0 kg

POSSIBLE MOVES: Bulldoze, Dig, Growl, Heavy Slam, High Horsepower, Iron Defense, Iron Head, Play Rough, Rock Smash, Rollout, Stomp, Strength, Superpower, Tackle

CUFANT

COPPERAJAH

Alternate Form:
GIGANTAMAX COPPERAJAH

So much power is packed within its trunk that if it were to unleash that power, the resulting blast could level mountains and change the landscape.

After this Pokémon has Gigantamaxed, its massive nose can utterly demolish large structures with a single smashing blow.

IMPERIAL HEIGHT: 75'06"+
IMPERIAL WEIGHT: ????.? lbs.
METRIC HEIGHT: 23.0+ m
METRIC WEIGHT: ???.? kg

CORPHISH
Ruffian Pokémon

TYPE: WATER

No matter how dirty the water in the river, it will adapt and thrive. It has a strong will to survive.

It was originally a Pokémon from afar that escaped to the wild. It can adapt to the dirtiest river.

HOW TO SAY IT: COR-fish
IMPERIAL HEIGHT: 2'00"
IMPERIAL WEIGHT: 25.4 lbs.
METRIC HEIGHT: 0.6 m
METRIC WEIGHT: 11.5 kg

POSSIBLE MOVES:
Bubble Beam, Crabhammer, Crunch, Double Hit, Endeavor, Guillotine, Harden, Knock Off, Leer, Night Slash, Protect, Razor Shell, Swords Dance, Taunt, Water Gun

CORPHISH   CRAWDAUNT

CORSOLA

Coral Pokémon

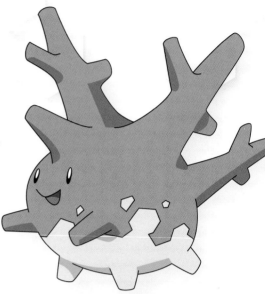

TYPE: WATER-ROCK

It will regrow any branches that break off its head. People keep particularly beautiful Corsola branches as charms to promote safe childbirth.

These Pokémon live in warm seas. In prehistoric times, many lived in the oceans around the Galar region as well.

HOW TO SAY IT: COR-soh-la
IMPERIAL HEIGHT: 2'00"
IMPERIAL WEIGHT: 11.0 lbs.
METRIC HEIGHT: 0.6 m
METRIC WEIGHT: 5.0 kg

POSSIBLE MOVES: Ancient Power, Aqua Ring, Bubble Beam, Earth Power, Endure, Flail, Harden, Life Dew, Mirror Coat, Power Gem, Recover, Tackle, Water Gun

DOES NOT EVOLVE

GALARIAN CORSOLA

Coral Pokémon

TYPE: GHOST

Watch your step when wandering areas oceans once covered. What looks like a stone could be this Pokémon, and it will curse you if you kick it.

Sudden climate change wiped out this ancient kind of Corsola. This Pokémon absorbs others' life force through its branches.

HOW TO SAY IT: COR-soh-la
IMPERIAL HEIGHT: 2'00"
IMPERIAL WEIGHT: 1.1 lbs.
METRIC HEIGHT: 0.6 m
METRIC WEIGHT: 0.5 kg

POSSIBLE MOVES: Ancient Power, Astonish, Curse, Disable, Grudge, Harden, Hex, Mirror Coat, Night Shade, Power Gem, Spite, Strength Sap, Tackle

GALARIAN CORSOLA → CURSOLA

REGION: GALAR

CORVIKNIGHT
Raven Pokémon

TYPE: FLYING-STEEL

This Pokémon reigns supreme in the skies of the Galar region. The black luster of its steel body could drive terror into the heart of any foe.

With their great intellect and flying skills, these Pokémon very successfully act as the Galar region's airborne taxi service.

HOW TO SAY IT: KOR-vih-nyte
IMPERIAL HEIGHT: 7'3"
IMPERIAL WEIGHT: 165.3 lbs.
METRIC HEIGHT: 2.2 m
METRIC WEIGHT: 75.0 kg

POSSIBLE MOVES: Brave Bird, Drill Peck, Fury Attack, Hone Claws, Iron Defense, Leer, Metal Sound, Peck, Pluck, Power Trip, Scary Face, Steel Wing, Swagger, Taunt

ROOKIDEE → **CORVISQUIRE** → **CORVIKNIGHT**

Alternate Form:
GIGANTAMAX CORVIKNIGHT

Imbued with Gigantamax energy, its wings can whip up winds more forceful than any a hurricane could muster. The gusts blow everything away.

The eight feathers on its back are called blade birds, and they can launch off its body to attack foes independently.

IMPERIAL HEIGHT: 45'11"+
IMPERIAL WEIGHT: ????.? lbs.
METRIC HEIGHT: 14.0+ m
METRIC WEIGHT: ???.? kg

CORVISQUIRE

Raven Pokémon

TYPE: FLYING

Smart enough to use tools in battle, these Pokémon have been seen picking up rocks and flinging them or using ropes to wrap up enemies.

The lessons of many harsh battles have taught it how to accurately judge an opponent's strength.

HOW TO SAY IT: KOR-vih-skwyre
IMPERIAL HEIGHT: 2'07"
IMPERIAL WEIGHT: 35.3 lbs.
METRIC HEIGHT: 0.8 m
METRIC WEIGHT: 16.0 kg

POSSIBLE MOVES: Brave Bird, Drill Peck, Fury Attack, Hone Claws, Leer, Peck, Pluck, Power Trip, Scary Face, Swagger, Taunt

ROOKIDEE → CORVISQUIRE → CORVIKNIGHT

COSMOEM

Protostar Pokémon

LEGENDARY POKÉMON

TYPE: PSYCHIC

The king who ruled Alola in times of antiquity called it the "cocoon of the stars" and built an altar to worship it.

As it absorbs light, Cosmoem continues to grow. Its golden shell is surprisingly solid.

HOW TO SAY IT: KOZ-mo-em
IMPERIAL HEIGHT: 0'04"
IMPERIAL WEIGHT: 2,204.4 lbs.
METRIC HEIGHT: 0.1 m
METRIC WEIGHT: 999.9 kg

POSSIBLE MOVES: Cosmic Power, Teleport

COSMOG → COSMOEM

SOLGALEO

LUNALA

TYPE: PSYCHIC

Even though its helpless, gaseous body can be blown away by the slightest breeze, it doesn't seem to care.

Whether or not it's a Pokémon from this world is a mystery. When it's in a jam, it warps away to a safe place to hide.

HOW TO SAY IT: KOZ-mog
IMPERIAL HEIGHT: 0'08"
IMPERIAL WEIGHT: 0.2 lbs.
METRIC HEIGHT: 0.2 m
METRIC WEIGHT: 0.1 kg

POSSIBLE MOVES: Splash, Teleport

COSMOG

COSMOEM

SOLGALEO

LUNALA

COTTONEE

Cotton Puff Pokémon

TYPE: GRASS-FAIRY

It shoots cotton from its body to protect itself. If it gets caught up in hurricane-strength winds, it can get sent to the other side of the Earth.

Weaving together the cotton of both Cottonee and Eldegoss produces exquisite cloth that's highly prized by many luxury brands.

HOW TO SAY IT: KAHT-ton-ee
IMPERIAL HEIGHT: 1'00"
IMPERIAL WEIGHT: 1.3 lbs.
METRIC HEIGHT: 0.3 m
METRIC WEIGHT: 0.6 kg

POSSIBLE MOVES: Absorb, Charm, Cotton Guard, Cotton Spore, Endeavor, Energy Ball, Fairy Wind, Giga Drain, Growth, Helping Hand, Leech Seed, Mega Drain, Poison Powder, Razor Leaf, Solar Beam, Stun Spore, Sunny Day

COTTONEE   WHIMSICOTT

CRABOMINABLE

Woolly Crab Pokémon

TYPE: FIGHTING-ICE

It stores coldness in its pincers and pummels its foes. It can even smash thick walls of ice to bits!

Before it stops to think, it just starts pummeling. There are records of it turning back avalanches with a flurry of punches.

HOW TO SAY IT: crab-BAH-min-uh-bull
IMPERIAL HEIGHT: 5'07"
IMPERIAL WEIGHT: 396.8 lbs.
METRIC HEIGHT: 1.7 m
METRIC WEIGHT: 180.0 kg

POSSIBLE MOVES: Ice Punch, Bubble, Rock Smash, Leer, Pursuit, Bubble Beam, Power-Up Punch, Dizzy Punch, Avalanche, Reversal, Ice Hammer, Iron Defense, Dynamic Punch, Close Combat

CRABRAWLER   CRABOMINABLE

CRABRAWLER
Boxing Pokémon

TYPE: FIGHTING

Its hard pincers are well suited to both offense and defense. Fights between two Crabrawler are like boxing matches.

Crabrawler has been known to mistake Exeggutor for a coconut tree and climb it. The enraged Exeggutor shakes it off and stomps it.

HOW TO SAY IT: crab-BRAW-ler
IMPERIAL HEIGHT: 2'00"
IMPERIAL WEIGHT: 15.4 lbs.
METRIC HEIGHT: 0.6 m
METRIC WEIGHT: 7.0 kg

POSSIBLE MOVES: Bubble, Rock Smash, Leer, Pursuit, Bubble Beam, Power-Up Punch, Dizzy Punch, Payback, Reversal, Crabhammer, Iron Defense, Dynamic Punch, Close Combat

CRABRAWLER   **CRABOMINABLE**

CRADILY
Barnacle Pokémon

TYPE: ROCK-GRASS

Normally, it lived on shallow sea shoals. When the tide went out, this Pokémon came up on land to search for prey.

This carnivorous Pokémon lived in primordial seas. It catches prey in its eight tentacles and dissolves them with digestive fluid as it eats.

HOW TO SAY IT: cray-DILLY
IMPERIAL HEIGHT: 4'11"
IMPERIAL WEIGHT: 133.2 lbs.
METRIC HEIGHT: 1.5 m
METRIC WEIGHT: 60.4 kg

POSSIBLE MOVES: Wring Out, Astonish, Constrict, Acid, Ingrain, Confuse Ray, Ancient Power, Brine, Giga Drain, Gastro Acid, Amnesia, Energy Ball, Stockpile, Spit Up, Swallow

LILEEP   **CRADILY**

CRAMORANT

Gulp Pokémon

REGION: GALAR

TYPE: FLYING-WATER

It's so strong that it can knock out some opponents in a single hit, but it also may forget what it's battling midfight.

This hungry Pokémon swallows Arrokuda whole. Occasionally, it makes a mistake and tries to swallow a Pokémon other than its preferred prey.

HOW TO SAY IT: KRAM-uh-rent
IMPERIAL HEIGHT: 2'07"
IMPERIAL WEIGHT: 39.7 lbs.
METRIC HEIGHT: 0.8 m
METRIC WEIGHT: 18.0 kg

POSSIBLE MOVES: Amnesia, Belch, Dive, Drill Peck, Fury Attack, Hydro Pump, Peck, Pluck, Spit Up, Stockpile, Swallow, Thrash, Water Gun

DOES NOT EVOLVE

CRANIDOS

Head Butt Pokémon

REGIONS: ALOLA SINNOH

TYPE: ROCK

A primeval Pokémon, it possesses a hard and sturdy skull, lacking any intelligence within.

Its hard skull is its distinguishing feature. It snapped trees by headbutting them, and then it fed on their ripe berries.

HOW TO SAY IT: CRANE-ee-dose
IMPERIAL HEIGHT: 2'11"
IMPERIAL WEIGHT: 69.4 lbs.
METRIC HEIGHT: 0.9 m
METRIC WEIGHT: 31.5 kg

POSSIBLE MOVES: Headbutt, Leer, Focus Energy, Pursuit, Take Down, Scary Face, Assurance, Chip Away, Ancient Power, Zen Headbutt, Screech, Head Smash

CRANIDOS   RAMPARDOS

REGIONS:
ALOLA
GALAR
HOENN
KALOS
(CENTRAL)

CRAWDAUNT
Rogue Pokémon

TYPE: WATER-DARK

A rough customer that wildly flails its giant claws. It is said to be extremely hard to raise.

A brutish Pokémon that loves to battle. It will crash itself into any foe that approaches its nest.

HOW TO SAY IT: CRAW-daunt
IMPERIAL HEIGHT: 3'07"
IMPERIAL WEIGHT: 72.3 lbs.
METRIC HEIGHT: 1.1 m
METRIC WEIGHT: 32.8 kg

POSSIBLE MOVES: Bubble Beam, Crabhammer, Crunch, Double Hit, Endeavor, Guillotine, Harden, Knock Off, Leer, Night Slash, Protect, Razor Shell, Swift, Swords Dance, Taunt, Water Gun

CORPHISH → **CRAWDAUNT**

LEGENDARY POKÉMON

REGION:
SINNOH

CRESSELIA
Lunar Pokémon

TYPE: PSYCHIC

Shiny particles are released from its wings like a veil. It is said to represent the crescent moon.

Those who sleep holding Cresselia's feather are assured of joyful dreams. It is said to represent the crescent moon.

HOW TO SAY IT: creh-SELL-ee-ah
IMPERIAL HEIGHT: 4'11"
IMPERIAL WEIGHT: 188.7 lbs.
METRIC HEIGHT: 1.5 m
METRIC WEIGHT: 85.6 kg

POSSIBLE MOVES: Lunar Dance, Psycho Shift, Psycho Cut, Moonlight, Confusion, Double Team, Safeguard, Mist, Aurora Beam, Future Sight, Slash, Psychic, Moonblast

DOES NOT EVOLVE

CROAGUNK

Toxic Mouth Pokémon

CROAGUNK → TOXICROAK

TYPE: POISON-FIGHTING

It makes frightening noises with its poison-filled cheek sacs. When opponents flinch, Croagunk hits them with a poison jab.

Once diluted, its poison becomes medicinal. This Pokémon came into popularity after a pharmaceutical company chose it as a mascot.

HOW TO SAY IT: CROW-gunk
IMPERIAL HEIGHT: 2'04"
IMPERIAL WEIGHT: 50.7 lbs.
METRIC HEIGHT: 0.7 m
METRIC WEIGHT: 23.0 kg

POSSIBLE MOVES: Astonish, Belch, Flatter, Mud-Slap, Nasty Plot, Poison Jab, Poison Sting, Revenge, Sludge Bomb, Sucker Punch, Swagger, Taunt, Toxic, Venoshock

---

CROBAT

Bat Pokémon

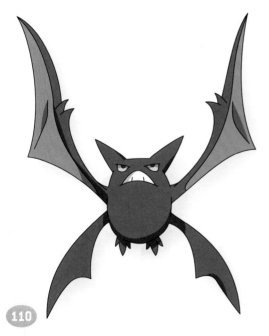

TYPE: POISON-FLYING

Its fangs are so sharp, if it bites you in the dark and sucks your blood, you won't notice any pain or realize you've been bitten.

It feeds on the blood of living people and Pokémon. If it can't drink any blood for even a short while, it becomes weak and unable to fly.

HOW TO SAY IT: CROW-bat
IMPERIAL HEIGHT: 5'11"
IMPERIAL WEIGHT: 165.3 lbs.
METRIC HEIGHT: 1.8 m
METRIC WEIGHT: 75.0 kg

POSSIBLE MOVES: Cross Poison, Screech, Absorb, Supersonic, Astonish, Bite, Wing Attack, Confuse Ray, Air Cutter, Swift, Poison Fang, Mean Look, Leech Life, Haze, Venoshock, Air Slash, Quick Guard

ZUBAT → GOLBAT → CROBAT

CROCONAW
Big Jaw Pokémon

TYPE: WATER

Once Croconaw has clamped its jaws on its foe, it will absolutely not let go. Because the tips of its fangs are forked back like barbed fishhooks, they become impossible to remove when they have sunk in.

HOW TO SAY IT: CROCK-oh-naw
IMPERIAL HEIGHT: 3'07"
IMPERIAL WEIGHT: 55.1 lbs.
METRIC HEIGHT: 1.1 m
METRIC WEIGHT: 25.0 kg

POSSIBLE MOVES: Scratch, Leer, Water Gun, Rage, Bite, Scary Face, Ice Fang, Flail, Crunch, Chip Away, Slash, Screech, Thrash, Aqua Tail, Superpower, Hydro Pump

TOTODILE ➡ **CROCONAW** ➡ **FERALIGATR**

TYPE: BUG-ROCK

This highly territorial Pokémon prefers dry climates. It won't come out of its boulder on rainy days.

Its thick claws are its greatest weapons. They're mighty enough to crack Rhyperior's carapace.

HOW TO SAY IT: KRUS-tul
IMPERIAL HEIGHT: 4'07"
IMPERIAL WEIGHT: 440.9 lbs.
METRIC HEIGHT: 1.4 m
METRIC WEIGHT: 200.0 kg

POSSIBLE MOVES: Bug Bite, Flail, Fury Cutter, Rock Blast, Rock Polish, Rock Slide, Rock Wrecker, Sand Attack, Shell Smash, Slash, Smack Down, Stealth Rock, Withdraw, X-Scissor

CRUSTLE
Stone Home Pokémon

DWEBBLE ➡ **CRUSTLE**

CRYOGONAL
Crystallizing Pokémon

TYPE: ICE

They are born in snow clouds. They use chains made of ice crystals to capture prey.

They are composed of ice crystals. They capture prey with chains of ice, freezing the prey at −148 degrees Fahrenheit.

HOW TO SAY IT: kry-AH-guh-nul
IMPERIAL HEIGHT: 3'07"
IMPERIAL WEIGHT: 326.3 lbs.
METRIC HEIGHT: 1.1 m
METRIC WEIGHT: 148.0 kg

POSSIBLE MOVES: Bind, Ice Shard, Sharpen, Rapid Spin, Icy Wind, Mist, Haze, Aurora Beam, Acid Armor, Ancient Power, Ice Beam, Light Screen, Reflect, Slash, Confuse Ray, Recover, Freeze-Dry, Solar Beam, Night Slash, Sheer Cold

DOES NOT EVOLVE

CUBCHOO
Chill Pokémon

TYPE: ICE

When this Pokémon is in good health, its snot becomes thicker and stickier. It will smear its snot on anyone it doesn't like.

It sniffles before performing a move, using its frosty snot to provide an icy element to any move that needs it.

HOW TO SAY IT: cub-CHOO
IMPERIAL HEIGHT: 1'08"
IMPERIAL WEIGHT: 18.7 lbs.
METRIC HEIGHT: 0.5 m
METRIC WEIGHT: 8.5 kg

POSSIBLE MOVES: Blizzard, Brine, Charm, Endure, Flail, Frost Breath, Fury Swipes, Growl, Hail, Icy Wind, Play Nice, Powder Snow, Rest, Sheer Cold, Slash, Thrash

CUBCHOO   BEARTIC

CUBONE

MAROWAK

ALOLAN MAROWAK

CUBONE
Lonely Pokémon

TYPE: GROUND

When the memory of its departed mother brings it to tears, its cries echo mournfully within the skull it wears on its head.

This Pokémon wears the skull of its deceased mother. Sometimes Cubone's dreams make it cry, but each tear Cubone sheds makes it stronger.

HOW TO SAY IT: CUE-bone
IMPERIAL HEIGHT: 1'04"
IMPERIAL WEIGHT: 14.3 lbs.
METRIC HEIGHT: 0.4 m
METRIC WEIGHT: 6.5 kg

POSSIBLE MOVES: Growl, Tail Whip, Bone Club, Headbutt, Leer, Focus Energy, Bonemerang, Rage, False Swipe, Thrash, Fling, Stomping Tantrum, Endeavor, Double-Edge, Retaliate, Bone Rush

TYPE: STEEL

It digs up the ground with its trunk. It's also very strong, being able to carry loads of over five tons without any problem at all.

If a job requires serious strength, this Pokémon will excel at it. Its copper body tarnishes in the rain, turning a vibrant green color.

HOW TO SAY IT: KYOO-funt
IMPERIAL HEIGHT: 3'11"
IMPERIAL WEIGHT: 220.5 lbs.
METRIC HEIGHT: 1.2 m
METRIC WEIGHT: 100.0 kg

POSSIBLE MOVES: Bulldoze, Dig, Growl, High Horsepower, Iron Defense, Iron Head, Play Rough, Rock Smash, Rollout, Stomp, Strength, Superpower, Tackle

CUFANT
Copperderm Pokémon

CUFANT   **COPPERAJAH**

CURSOLA

Coral Pokémon

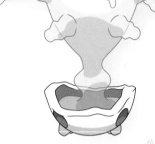

TYPE: GHOST

Its shell is overflowing with its heightened otherworldly energy. The ectoplasm serves as protection for this Pokémon's core spirit.

Be cautious of the ectoplasmic body surrounding its soul. You'll become stiff as stone if you touch it.

HOW TO SAY IT: KURR-suh-luh
IMPERIAL HEIGHT: 3'03"
IMPERIAL WEIGHT: 0.9 lbs.
METRIC HEIGHT: 1.0 m
METRIC WEIGHT: 0.4 kg

POSSIBLE MOVES: Ancient Power, Astonish, Curse, Disable, Grudge, Harden, Hex, Mirror Coat, Night Shade, Perish Song, Power Gem, Spite, Strength Sap, Tackle

GALARIAN CORSOLA → CURSOLA

CUTIEFLY

Bee Fly Pokémon

REGIONS: ALOLA GALAR

TYPE: BUG-FAIRY

Nectar and pollen are its favorite fare. You can find Cutiefly hovering around Gossifleur, trying to get some of Gossifleur's pollen.

An opponent's aura can tell Cutiefly what that opponent's next move will be. Then Cutiefly can glide around the attack and strike back.

HOW TO SAY IT: KYOO-tee-fly
IMPERIAL HEIGHT: 0'04"
IMPERIAL WEIGHT: 0.4 lbs.
METRIC HEIGHT: 0.1 m
METRIC WEIGHT: 0.2 kg

POSSIBLE MOVES: Absorb, Aromatherapy, Bug Buzz, Dazzling Gleam, Draining Kiss, Fairy Wind, Quiver Dance, Struggle Bug, Stun Spore, Sweet Scent, Switcheroo

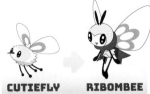

CUTIEFLY → RIBOMBEE

REGION: JOHTO

CYNDAQUIL
Fire Mouse Pokémon

TYPE: FIRE

Cyndaquil protects itself by flaring up the flames on its back. The flames are vigorous if the Pokémon is angry. However, if it is tired, the flames splutter fitfully with incomplete combustion.

HOW TO SAY IT: SIN-da-kwill
IMPERIAL HEIGHT: 1'08"
IMPERIAL WEIGHT: 17.4 lbs.
METRIC HEIGHT: 0.5 m
METRIC WEIGHT: 7.9 kg

POSSIBLE MOVES: Tackle, Leer, Smokescreen, Ember, Quick Attack, Flame Wheel, Defense Curl, Flame Charge, Swift, Lava Plume, Flamethrower, Inferno, Rollout, Double-Edge, Burn Up, Eruption

CYNDAQUIL ➡ **QUILAVA** ➡ **TYPHLOSION**

MYTHICAL POKÉMON

REGION: SINNOH

DARKRAI
Pitch-Black Pokémon

TYPE: DARK

It chases people and Pokémon from its territory by causing them to experience deep, nightmarish slumbers.

It can lull people to sleep and make them dream. It is active during nights of the new moon.

HOW TO SAY IT: DARK-rye
IMPERIAL HEIGHT: 4'11"
IMPERIAL WEIGHT: 111.3 lbs.
METRIC HEIGHT: 1.5 m
METRIC WEIGHT: 50.5 kg

POSSIBLE MOVES: Ominous Wind, Disable, Quick Attack, Hypnosis, Feint Attack, Nightmare, Double Team, Haze, Dark Void, Nasty Plot, Dream Eater, Dark Pulse

DOES NOT EVOLVE

DARMANITAN

Blazing Pokémon

TYPE: FIRE

The thick arms of this hot-blooded Pokémon can deliver punches capable of obliterating a dump truck.

This Pokémon's power level rises along with the temperature of its fire, which can reach 2,500 degrees Fahrenheit.

HOW TO SAY IT: dar-MAN-ih-tan **METRIC HEIGHT:** 1.3 m
IMPERIAL HEIGHT: 4'03" **METRIC WEIGHT:** 92.9 kg
IMPERIAL WEIGHT: 204.8 lbs.

POSSIBLE MOVES: Belly Drum, Bite, Ember, Fire Fang, Fire Punch, Flare Blitz, Hammer Arm, Headbutt, Incinerate, Superpower, Tackle, Taunt, Thrash, Uproar, Work Up

DARUMAKA   DARMANITAN

GALARIAN DARMANITAN

Zen Charm Pokémon

TYPE: ICE

On days when blizzards blow through, it comes down to where people live. It stashes food in the snowball on its head, taking it home for later.

Though it has a gentle disposition, it's also very strong. It will quickly freeze the snowball on its head before going for a headbutt.

HOW TO SAY IT: dar-MAN-ih-tan **METRIC HEIGHT:** 1.7 m
IMPERIAL HEIGHT: 5'07" **METRIC WEIGHT:** 120.0 kg
IMPERIAL WEIGHT: 264.6 lbs.

POSSIBLE MOVES: Avalanche, Belly Drum, Bite, Blizzard, Headbutt, Ice Fang, Ice Punch, Icicle Crash, Powder Snow, Superpower, Tackle, Taunt, Thrash, Uproar, Work Up

GALARIAN   GALARIAN
DARUMAKA   DARMANITAN

DARTRIX

Blade Quill Pokémon

TYPE: GRASS-FLYING

This narcissistic Pokémon is a clean freak. If you don't groom it diligently, it will stop listening to you.

Supremely sensitive to the presence of others, it can detect opponents standing behind it, flinging its sharp feathers to take them out.

HOW TO SAY IT: DAR-trix
IMPERIAL HEIGHT: 2'04"
IMPERIAL WEIGHT: 35.3 lbs.
METRIC HEIGHT: 0.7 m
METRIC WEIGHT: 16.0 kg

POSSIBLE MOVES: Tackle, Leafage, Growl, Peck, Astonish, Razor Leaf, Ominous Wind, Foresight, Pluck, Synthesis, Fury Attack, Sucker Punch, Leaf Blade, Feather Dance, Brave Bird, Nasty Plot

ROWLET **DARTRIX** **DECIDUEYE**

DARUMAKA

Zen Charm Pokémon

TYPE: FIRE

It derives its power from fire burning inside its body. If the fire dwindles, this Pokémon will immediately fall asleep.

This popular symbol of good fortune will never fall over in its sleep, no matter how it's pushed or pulled.

HOW TO SAY IT: dah-roo-MAH-kuh
IMPERIAL HEIGHT: 2'00"
IMPERIAL WEIGHT: 82.7 lbs.
METRIC HEIGHT: 0.6 m
METRIC WEIGHT: 37.5 kg

POSSIBLE MOVES: Belly Drum, Bite, Ember, Fire Fang, Fire Punch, Flare Blitz, Headbutt, Incinerate, Superpower, Tackle, Taunt, Thrash, Uproar, Work Up

DARUMAKA → DARMANITAN

GALARIAN DARUMAKA

Zen Charm Pokémon

TYPE: ICE

It lived in snowy areas for so long that its fire sac cooled off and atrophied. It now has an organ that generates cold instead.

The colder they get, the more energetic they are. They freeze their breath to make snowballs, using them as ammo for playful snowball fights.

HOW TO SAY IT: dah-roo-MAH-kuh
IMPERIAL HEIGHT: 2'04"
IMPERIAL WEIGHT: 88.2 lbs.
METRIC HEIGHT: 0.7 m
METRIC WEIGHT: 40.0 kg

POSSIBLE MOVES: Avalanche, Belly Drum, Bite, Blizzard, Headbutt, Ice Fang, Ice Punch, Powder Snow, Superpower, Tackle, Taunt, Thrash, Uproar, Work Up

GALARIAN DARUMAKA → GALARIAN DARMANITAN

TYPE: GRASS-GHOST

REGION: ALOLA

DECIDUEYE
Arrow Quill Pokémon

It nocks its arrow quills and shoots them at opponents. When it simply can't afford to miss, it tugs the vine on its head to improve its focus.

Decidueye can nock and fire an arrow at an enemy in a tenth of a second, so its battles are decided in the blink of an eye.

HOW TO SAY IT: deh-SIH-joo-eye
IMPERIAL HEIGHT: 5'03"
IMPERIAL WEIGHT: 80.7 lbs.

METRIC HEIGHT: 1.6 m
METRIC WEIGHT: 36.6 kg

POSSIBLE MOVES: Spirit Shackle, Phantom Force, Leaf Storm, U-turn, Shadow Sneak, Tackle, Leafage, Growl, Peck, Astonish, Razor Leaf, Ominous Wind, Foresight, Pluck, Synthesis, Fury Attack, Sucker Punch, Leaf Blade, Feather Dance, Brave Bird, Nasty Plot

ROWLET

DARTRIX

DECIDUEYE

DEDENNE

Antenna Pokémon

REGIONS:
ALOLA
KALOS
(COASTAL)

TYPE: ELECTRIC-FAIRY

A Dedenne's whiskers pick up electrical waves other Dedenne send out. These Pokémon share locations of food or electricity with one another.

Since Dedenne can't generate much electricity on its own, it steals electricity from outlets or other electric Pokémon.

HOW TO SAY IT: deh-DEN-nay
IMPERIAL HEIGHT: 0'08"
IMPERIAL WEIGHT: 4.9 lbs.
METRIC HEIGHT: 0.2 m
METRIC WEIGHT: 2.2 kg

POSSIBLE MOVES: Tackle, Tail Whip, Thunder Shock, Charge, Charm, Parabolic Charge, Nuzzle, Thunder Wave, Volt Switch, Rest, Snore, Charge Beam, Entrainment, Play Rough, Thunder, Discharge

DOES NOT EVOLVE

DEERLING

Season Pokémon

REGION:
UNOVA

TYPE: NORMAL-GRASS

Their coloring changes according to the seasons and can be slightly affected by the temperature and humidity as well.

The turning of the seasons changes the color and scent of this Pokémon's fur. People use it to mark the seasons.

HOW TO SAY IT: DEER-ling
IMPERIAL HEIGHT: 2'00"
IMPERIAL WEIGHT: 43.0 lbs.
METRIC HEIGHT: 0.6 m
METRIC WEIGHT: 19.5 kg

POSSIBLE MOVES: Tackle, Camouflage, Growl, Sand Attack, Double Kick, Leech Seed, Feint Attack, Take Down, Jump Kick, Aromatherapy, Energy Ball, Charm, Nature Power, Double-Edge, Solar Beam

DEERLING → SAWSBUCK

SPRING FORM

SUMMER FORM

AUTUMN FORM

WINTER FORM

TYPE: DARK-DRAGON

When it encounters something, its first urge is usually to bite it. If it likes what it tastes, it will commit the associated scent to memory.

Because it can't see, this Pokémon is constantly biting at everything it touches, trying to keep track of its surroundings.

HOW TO SAY IT: DY-noh
METRIC HEIGHT: 0.8 m
IMPERIAL HEIGHT: 2'07"
METRIC WEIGHT: 17.3 kg
IMPERIAL WEIGHT: 38.1 lbs.

POSSIBLE MOVES: Assurance, Bite, Body Slam, Crunch, Dragon Breath, Dragon Pulse, Dragon Rush, Focus Energy, Headbutt, Hyper Voice, Nasty Plot, Outrage, Roar, Scary Face, Slam, Tackle, Work Up

DEINO **ZWEILOUS** **HYDREIGON**

DEINO
Irate Pokémon

DELCATTY
Prim Pokémon

TYPE: NORMAL

Delcatty prefers to live an unfettered existence in which it can do as it pleases at its own pace. Because this Pokémon eats and sleeps whenever it decides, its daily routines are completely random.

Delcatty sleeps anywhere it wants without keeping a permanent nest. If other Pokémon approach it as it sleeps, this Pokémon will never fight—it will just move away somewhere else.

HOW TO SAY IT: dell-CAT-tee
METRIC HEIGHT: 1.1 m
IMPERIAL HEIGHT: 3'07"
METRIC WEIGHT: 32.6 kg
IMPERIAL WEIGHT: 71.9 lbs.

POSSIBLE MOVES: Fake Out, Attract, Sing, Double Slap

SKITTY **DELCATTY**

DELIBIRD

Delivery Pokémon

REGIONS:
ALOLA
GALAR
JOHTO
KALOS
(MOUNTAIN)

TYPE: ICE-FLYING

It carries food all day long. There are tales about lost people who were saved by the food it had.

It has a generous habit of sharing its food with people and Pokémon, so it's always scrounging around for more food.

HOW TO SAY IT: DELL-ee-bird
IMPERIAL HEIGHT: 2'11"
IMPERIAL WEIGHT: 35.3 lbs.
METRIC HEIGHT: 0.9 m
METRIC WEIGHT: 16.0 kg

POSSIBLE MOVES: Present, Drill Peck

DOES NOT EVOLVE

DELPHOX

Fox Pokémon

REGION:
KALOS
(CENTRAL)

TYPE: FIRE-PSYCHIC

It gazes into the flame at the tip of its branch to achieve a focused state, which allows it to see into the future.

Using psychic power, it generates a fiery vortex of 5,400 degrees Fahrenheit, incinerating foes swept into this whirl of flame.

HOW TO SAY IT: DELL-fox
IMPERIAL HEIGHT: 4'11"
IMPERIAL WEIGHT: 86.0 lbs.
METRIC HEIGHT: 1.5 m
METRIC WEIGHT: 39.0 kg

POSSIBLE MOVES: Future Sight, Role Play, Switcheroo, Shadow Ball, Scratch, Tail Whip, Ember, Howl, Flame Charge, Psybeam, Fire Spin, Lucky Chant, Light Screen, Psyshock, Mystical Fire, Flamethrower, Will-O-Wisp, Psychic, Sunny Day, Magic Room, Fire Blast

FENNEKIN → BRAIXEN → DELPHOX

DEOXYS
DNA Pokémon

ATTACK FORME

DEFENSE FORME

SPEED FORME

TYPE: PSYCHIC

The DNA of a space virus underwent a sudden mutation upon exposure to a laser beam and resulted in Deoxys. The crystalline organ on this Pokémon's chest appears to be its brain.

Deoxys emerged from a virus that came from space. It is highly intelligent and wields psychokinetic powers. This Pokémon shoots lasers from the crystalline organ on its chest.

HOW TO SAY IT: dee-OCKS-iss
IMPERIAL HEIGHT: 5'07"
IMPERIAL WEIGHT: 134.0 lbs.
METRIC HEIGHT: 1.7 m
METRIC WEIGHT: 60.8 kg

POSSIBLE MOVES: Leer, Wrap, Night Shade, Teleport, Knock Off, Pursuit, Psychic, Snatch, Psycho Shift, Zen Headbutt, Cosmic Power, Recover, Psycho Boost, Hyper Beam

NORMAL FORME

DOES NOT EVOLVE

DEWGONG
Sea Lion Pokémon

REGIONS:
**ALOLA
KANTO**

TYPE: WATER-ICE

Its entire body is a snowy white. Unharmed by even intense cold, it swims powerfully in icy waters.

HOW TO SAY IT: DOO-gong
IMPERIAL HEIGHT: 5'07"
IMPERIAL WEIGHT: 264.6 lbs.
METRIC HEIGHT: 1.7 m
METRIC WEIGHT: 120.0 kg

POSSIBLE MOVES: Headbutt, Growl, Signal Beam, Icy Wind, Encore, Ice Shard, Rest, Aqua Ring, Aurora Beam, Aqua Jet, Brine, Sheer Cold, Take Down, Dive, Aqua Tail, Ice Beam, Safeguard, Hail

SEEL   DEWGONG

DEWOTT
Discipline Pokémon

REGION:
UNOVA

TYPE: WATER

Strict training is how it learns its flowing double-scalchop technique.

As a result of strict training, each Dewott learns different forms for using the scalchops.

HOW TO SAY IT: DOO-wot
IMPERIAL HEIGHT: 2'07"
IMPERIAL WEIGHT: 54.0 lbs.
METRIC HEIGHT: 0.8 m
METRIC WEIGHT: 24.5 kg

POSSIBLE MOVES: Tackle, Tail Whip, Water Gun, Water Sport, Focus Energy, Razor Shell, Fury Cutter, Water Pulse, Revenge, Aqua Jet, Encore, Aqua Tail, Retaliate, Swords Dance, Hydro Pump

OSHAWOTT   DEWOTT   SAMUROTT

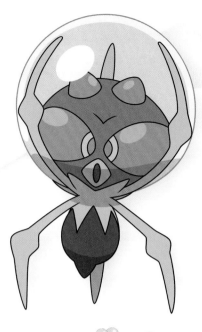

DEWPIDER
Water Bubble Pokémon

TYPE: WATER-BUG

It forms a water bubble at the rear of its body and then covers its head with it. Meeting another Dewpider means comparing water-bubble sizes.

Dewpider normally lives underwater. When it comes onto land in search of food, it takes water with it in the form of a bubble on its head.

HOW TO SAY IT: DOO-pih-der
IMPERIAL HEIGHT: 1'00"
IMPERIAL WEIGHT: 8.8 lbs.
METRIC HEIGHT: 0.3 m
METRIC WEIGHT: 4.0 kg

POSSIBLE MOVES: Aqua Ring, Bite, Bubble Beam, Bug Bite, Crunch, Entrainment, Headbutt, Infestation, Leech Life, Liquidation, Lunge, Mirror Coat, Soak, Water Gun

DEWPIDER   **ARAQUANID**

DHELMISE
Sea Creeper Pokémon

TYPE: GHOST-GRASS

After a piece of seaweed merged with debris from a sunken ship, it was reborn as this ghost Pokémon.

After lowering its anchor, it waits for its prey. It catches large Wailord and drains their life force.

HOW TO SAY IT: dell-MIZE
IMPERIAL HEIGHT: 12'10"
IMPERIAL WEIGHT: 463.0 lbs.
METRIC HEIGHT: 3.9 m
METRIC WEIGHT: 210.0 kg

POSSIBLE MOVES: Absorb, Anchor Shot, Astonish, Energy Ball, Giga Drain, Growth, Gyro Ball, Heavy Slam, Mega Drain, Metal Sound, Phantom Force, Power Whip, Rapid Spin, Shadow Ball, Slam, Switcheroo, Whirlpool, Wrap

DOES NOT EVOLVE

DIALGA

Temporal Pokémon

LEGENDARY POKÉMON

TYPE: STEEL-DRAGON

A Pokémon spoken of in legend. It is said that time began moving when Dialga was born.

It has the power to control time. It appears in Sinnoh-region myths as an ancient deity.

HOW TO SAY IT: dee-AWL-gah
IMPERIAL HEIGHT: 17'09"
IMPERIAL WEIGHT: 1,505.8 lbs.
METRIC HEIGHT: 5.4 m
METRIC WEIGHT: 683.0 kg

POSSIBLE MOVES: Dragon Breath, Scary Face, Metal Claw, Ancient Power, Slash, Power Gem, Metal Burst, Dragon Claw, Earth Power, Aura Sphere, Iron Tail, Roar of Time, Flash Cannon

DOES NOT EVOLVE

DIANCIE

Jewel Pokémon

TYPE: ROCK-FAIRY

A sudden transformation of Carbink, its pink, glimmering body is said to be the loveliest sight in the whole world.

It can instantly create many diamonds by compressing the carbon in the air between its hands.

HOW TO SAY IT: die-AHN-see
IMPERIAL HEIGHT: 2'04"
IMPERIAL WEIGHT: 19.4 lbs.
METRIC HEIGHT: 0.7 m
METRIC WEIGHT: 8.8 kg

POSSIBLE MOVES: Tackle, Harden, Rock Throw, Sharpen, Smack Down, Reflect, Stealth Rock, Guard Split, Ancient Power, Flail, Skill Swap, Trick Room, Power Gem, Stone Edge, Moonblast, Diamond Storm, Light Screen, Safeguard

MEGA DIANCIE

Jewel Pokémon

TYPE: ROCK-FAIRY

IMPERIAL HEIGHT: 3'07"
IMPERIAL WEIGHT: 61.3 lbs.
METRIC HEIGHT: 1.1 m
METRIC WEIGHT: 27.8 kg

DIANCIE   **MEGA DIANCIE**

DIGGERSBY
Digging Pokémon

TYPE: NORMAL-GROUND

With power equal to an excavator, it can dig through dense bedrock. It's a huge help during tunnel construction.

The fur on its belly retains heat exceptionally well. People used to make heavy winter clothing from fur shed by this Pokémon.

HOW TO SAY IT: DIH-gurz-bee
IMPERIAL HEIGHT: 3'03"
IMPERIAL WEIGHT: 93.5 lbs.

METRIC HEIGHT: 1.0 m
METRIC WEIGHT: 42.4 kg

POSSIBLE MOVES: Bounce, Bulldoze, Dig, Double Kick, Earthquake, Flail, Hammer Arm, Laser Focus, Leer, Mud Shot, Mud-Slap, Quick Attack, Super Fang, Swords Dance, Tackle, Take Down

BUNNELBY   DIGGERSBY

DIGLETT
Mole Pokémon

TYPE: GROUND

If a Diglett digs through a field, it leaves the soil perfectly tilled and ideal for planting crops.

It burrows through the ground at a shallow depth. It leaves raised earth in its wake, making it easy to spot.

HOW TO SAY IT: DIG-let
IMPERIAL HEIGHT: 0'08"
IMPERIAL WEIGHT: 1.8 lbs.
METRIC HEIGHT: 0.2 m
METRIC WEIGHT: 0.8 kg

POSSIBLE MOVES: Astonish, Bulldoze, Dig, Earth Power, Earthquake, Fissure, Growl, Mud-Slap, Sand Attack, Sandstorm, Scratch, Slash, Sucker Punch

DIGLETT   **DUGTRIO**

ALOLAN DIGLETT
Mole Pokémon

TYPE: GROUND-STEEL

The metal-rich geology of this Pokémon's habitat caused it to develop steel whiskers on its head.

Its three hairs change shape depending on Diglett's mood. They're a useful communication tool among these Pokémon.

HOW TO SAY IT: uh-LO-luhn DIG-let
IMPERIAL HEIGHT: 0'08"
IMPERIAL WEIGHT: 2.2 lbs.
METRIC HEIGHT: 0.2 m
METRIC WEIGHT: 1.0 kg

POSSIBLE MOVES: Astonish, Bulldoze, Dig, Earth Power, Earthquake, Fissure, Growl, Iron Head, Metal Claw, Mud-Slap, Sand Attack, Sandstorm, Sucker Punch

ALOLAN DIGLETT   ALOLAN DUGTRIO

DITTO
Transform Pokémon

REGIONS:
ALOLA
GALAR
KALOS
(MOUNTAIN)
KANTO

TYPE: NORMAL

It can reconstitute its entire cellular structure to change into what it sees, but it returns to normal when it relaxes.

When it encounters another Ditto, it will move faster than normal to duplicate that opponent exactly.

HOW TO SAY IT: DIT-toe
IMPERIAL HEIGHT: 1'00"
IMPERIAL WEIGHT: 8.8 lbs.
METRIC HEIGHT: 0.3 m
METRIC WEIGHT: 4.0 kg

POSSIBLE MOVE: Transform

DOES NOT EVOLVE

DODRIO
Triple Bird Pokémon

REGIONS:
KALOS
(CENTRAL)
KANTO

TYPE: NORMAL-FLYING

One of Doduo's two heads splits to form a unique species. It runs close to 40 mph in prairies.

HOW TO SAY IT: doe-DREE-oh
IMPERIAL HEIGHT: 5'11"
IMPERIAL WEIGHT: 187.8 lbs.
METRIC HEIGHT: 1.8 m
METRIC WEIGHT: 85.2 kg

POSSIBLE MOVES: Tri Attack, Peck, Growl, Quick Attack, Rage, Fury Attack, Pursuit, Pluck, Double Hit, Agility, Uproar, Acupressure, Swords Dance, Jump Kick, Drill Peck, Endeavor, Thrash

DODUO → DODRIO

DODUO
Twin Bird Pokémon

TYPE: NORMAL-FLYING

Its short wings make flying difficult. Instead, this Pokémon runs at high speed on developed legs.

HOW TO SAY IT: doe-DOO-oh
IMPERIAL HEIGHT: 4'07"
IMPERIAL WEIGHT: 86.4 lbs.
METRIC HEIGHT: 1.4 m
METRIC WEIGHT: 39.2 kg

POSSIBLE MOVES: Peck, Growl, Quick Attack, Rage, Fury Attack, Pursuit, Pluck, Double Hit, Agility, Uproar, Acupressure, Swords Dance, Jump Kick, Drill Peck, Endeavor, Thrash

DODUO DODRIO

TYPE: GROUND

Donphan's favorite attack is curling its body into a ball, then charging at its foe while rolling at high speed. Once it starts rolling, this Pokémon can't stop very easily.

If Donphan were to tackle with its hard body, even a house could be destroyed. Using its massive strength, the Pokémon helps clear rock and mud slides that block mountain trails.

REGION: JOHTO

DONPHAN
Armor Pokémon

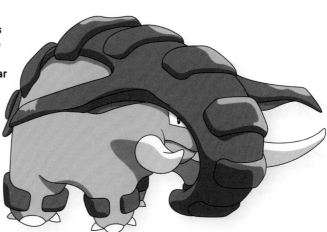

HOW TO SAY IT: DON-fan
IMPERIAL HEIGHT: 3'07"
IMPERIAL WEIGHT: 264.6 lbs.
METRIC HEIGHT: 1.1 m
METRIC WEIGHT: 120.0 kg

POSSIBLE MOVES: Fury Attack, Fire Fang, Thunder Fang, Horn Attack, Bulldoze, Growl, Defense Curl, Rapid Spin, Rollout, Assurance, Knock Off, Slam, Magnitude, Scary Face, Earthquake, Giga Impact

PHANPY DONPHAN

DOTTLER

Radome Pokémon

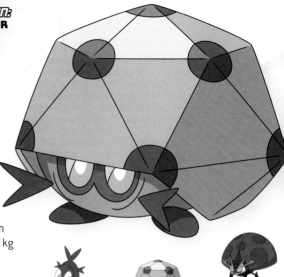

TYPE: BUG

It barely moves, but it's still alive. Hiding in its shell without food or water seems to have awakened its psychic powers.

As it grows inside its shell, it uses its psychic abilities to monitor the outside world and prepare for evolution.

HOW TO SAY IT: DOT-ler
IMPERIAL HEIGHT: 1'04"
IMPERIAL WEIGHT: 43.0 lbs.
METRIC HEIGHT: 0.4 m
METRIC WEIGHT: 19.5 kg

POSSIBLE MOVES: Confusion, Light Screen, Reflect, Struggle Bug

BLIPBUG　　DOTTLER　　ORBEETLE

DOUBLADE

Sword Pokémon

TYPE: STEEL-GHOST

Honedge evolves into twins. The two blades rub together to emit a metallic sound that unnerves opponents.

The two swords employ a strategy of rapidly alternating between offense and defense to bring down their prey.

HOW TO SAY IT: DUH-blade
IMPERIAL HEIGHT: 2'07"
IMPERIAL WEIGHT: 9.9 lbs.
METRIC HEIGHT: 0.8 m
METRIC WEIGHT: 4.5 kg

POSSIBLE MOVES: Aerial Ace, Autotomize, Fury Cutter, Iron Defense, Iron Head, Metal Sound, Night Slash, Power Trick, Retaliate, Sacred Sword, Shadow Sneak, Slash, Swords Dance, Tackle

HONEDGE　　DOUBLADE　　AEGISLASH

DRACOVISH
Fossil Pokémon

TYPE: WATER-DRAGON

Powerful legs and jaws made it the apex predator of its time. Its own overhunting of its prey was what drove it to extinction.

Its mighty legs are capable of running at speeds exceeding 40 mph, but this Pokémon can't breathe unless it's underwater.

HOW TO SAY IT: DRAK-oh-vish
IMPERIAL HEIGHT: 7'07"
IMPERIAL WEIGHT: 474.0 lbs.
METRIC HEIGHT: 2.3 m
METRIC WEIGHT: 215.0 kg

POSSIBLE MOVES: Ancient Power, Bite, Brutal Swing, Crunch, Dragon Breath, Dragon Pulse, Dragon Rush, Fishious Rend, Protect, Stomp, Super Fang, Tackle, Water Gun

DOES NOT EVOLVE

REGION: GALAR

DRACOZOLT
Fossil Pokémon

TYPE: ELECTRIC-DRAGON

In ancient times, it was unbeatable thanks to its powerful lower body, but it went extinct anyway after it depleted all its plant-based food sources.

The powerful muscles in its tail generate its electricity. Compared to its lower body, its upper half is entirely too small.

HOW TO SAY IT: DRAK-oh-zohlt
IMPERIAL HEIGHT: 5'11"
IMPERIAL WEIGHT: 418.9 lbs.
METRIC HEIGHT: 1.8 m
METRIC WEIGHT: 190.0 kg

POSSIBLE MOVES: Aerial Ace, Ancient Power, Bolt Beak, Charge, Discharge, Dragon Pulse, Dragon Rush, Dragon Tail, Pluck, Slam, Stomp, Tackle, Thunder Shock

DOES NOT EVOLVE

DRAGALGE
Mock Kelp Pokémon

TYPE: POISON-DRAGON

Dragalge uses a poisonous liquid capable of corroding metal to send tankers that enter its territory to the bottom of the sea.

Dragalge generates dragon energy by sticking the plume on its head out above the ocean's surface and bathing it in sunlight.

HOW TO SAY IT: druh-GAL-jee **METRIC HEIGHT:** 1.8 m
IMPERIAL HEIGHT: 5'11" **METRIC WEIGHT:** 81.5 kg
IMPERIAL WEIGHT: 179.7 lbs.

POSSIBLE MOVES: Dragon Tail, Twister, Tackle, Smokescreen, Water Gun, Feint Attack, Tail Whip, Bubble, Acid, Camouflage, Poison Tail, Water Pulse, Double Team, Toxic, Aqua Tail, Sludge Bomb, Hydro Pump, Dragon Pulse

SKRELP   DRAGALGE

DRAGAPULT
Stealth Pokémon

TYPE: DRAGON-GHOST

When it isn't battling, it keeps Dreepy in the holes on its horns. Once a fight starts, it launches the Dreepy like supersonic missiles.

Apparently the Dreepy inside Dragapult's horns eagerly look forward to being launched out at Mach speeds.

HOW TO SAY IT: DRAG-uh-pult
IMPERIAL HEIGHT: 9'10"
IMPERIAL WEIGHT: 110.2 lbs.
METRIC HEIGHT: 3.0 m
METRIC WEIGHT: 50.0 kg

POSSIBLE MOVES: Agility, Assurance, Astonish, Bite, Double Hit, Double-Edge, Dragon Breath, Dragon Dance, Dragon Darts, Dragon Rush, Hex, Infestation, Last Resort, Lock-On, Phantom Force, Quick Attack, Sucker Punch, Take Down, U-turn

DREEPY   DRAKLOAK   DRAGAPULT

DRAGONAIR
Dragon Pokémon

TYPE: DRAGON

According to a witness, its body was surrounded by a strange aura that gave it a mystical look.

HOW TO SAY IT: DRAG-gon-AIR
IMPERIAL HEIGHT: 13'01"
IMPERIAL WEIGHT: 36.4 lbs.
METRIC HEIGHT: 4.0 m
METRIC WEIGHT: 16.5 kg

POSSIBLE MOVES: Wrap, Leer, Thunder Wave, Twister, Dragon Rage, Slam, Agility, Dragon Tail, Aqua Tail, Dragon Rush, Safeguard, Dragon Dance, Outrage, Hyper Beam

DRATINI   DRAGONAIR   DRAGONITE

DRAGONITE
Dragon Pokémon

TYPE: DRAGON-FLYING

It is said that this Pokémon lives somewhere in the sea and that it flies. However, these are only rumors.

HOW TO SAY IT: DRAG-gon-ite
IMPERIAL HEIGHT: 7'03"
IMPERIAL WEIGHT: 463.0 lbs.
METRIC HEIGHT: 2.2 m
METRIC WEIGHT: 210.0 kg

POSSIBLE MOVES: Wing Attack, Hurricane, Fire Punch, Thunder Punch, Roost, Wrap, Leer, Thunder Wave, Twister, Dragon Rage, Slam, Agility, Dragon Tail, Aqua Tail, Dragon Rush, Safeguard, Dragon Dance, Outrage, Hyper Beam, Hurricane

DRATINI   DRAGONAIR   DRAGONITE

DRAKLOAK

Caretaker Pokémon

TYPE: DRAGON-GHOST

It's capable of flying faster than 120 mph. It battles alongside Dreepy and dotes on them until they successfully evolve.

Without a Dreepy to place on its head and care for, it gets so uneasy it'll try to substitute any Pokémon it finds for the missing Dreepy.

HOW TO SAY IT: DRAK-klohk
IMPERIAL HEIGHT: 4'4"
IMPERIAL WEIGHT: 24.3 lbs.
METRIC HEIGHT: 1.8 m
METRIC WEIGHT: 11.0 kg

POSSIBLE MOVES: Agility, Assurance, Astonish, Bite, Double Hit, Double-Edge, Dragon Dance, Dragon Pulse, Dragon Rush, Hex, Infestation, Last Resort, Lock-On, Phantom Force, Quick Attack, Take Down, U-turn

DREEPY   **DRAKLOAK**   **DRAGAPULT**

DRAMPA

Placid Pokémon

TYPE: NORMAL-DRAGON

The mountains it calls home are nearly two miles in height. On rare occasions, it descends to play with the children living in the towns below.

Drampa is a kind and friendly Pokémon—until it's angered. When that happens, it stirs up a gale and flattens everything around.

HOW TO SAY IT: DRAM-puh
IMPERIAL HEIGHT: 9'10"
IMPERIAL WEIGHT: 407.9 lbs.
METRIC HEIGHT: 3.0 m
METRIC WEIGHT: 185.0 kg

POSSIBLE MOVES: Dragon Breath, Dragon Pulse, Echoed Voice, Extrasensory, Fly, Glare, Hyper Voice, Light Screen, Outrage, Play Nice, Protect, Safeguard, Twister

DOES NOT EVOLVE

TYPE: POISON-DARK

Its poison is potent, but it rarely sees use. This Pokémon prefers to use physical force instead, going on rampages with its car-crushing strength.

It's so vicious that it's called the Sand Demon. Yet when confronted by Hippowdon, Drapion keeps a low profile and will never pick a fight.

HOW TO SAY IT: DRAP-ee-on
IMPERIAL HEIGHT: 4'03"
IMPERIAL WEIGHT: 135.6 lbs.
METRIC HEIGHT: 1.3 m
METRIC WEIGHT: 61.5 kg

POSSIBLE MOVES: Acupressure, Bite, Bug Bite, Cross Poison, Crunch, Fell Stinger, Fire Fang, Hone Claws, Ice Fang, Knock Off, Leer, Night Slash, Pin Missile, Poison Fang, Poison Sting, Scary Face, Thunder Fang, Toxic, Toxic Spikes, Venoshock, X-Scissor

DRAPION
Ogre Scorpion Pokémon

SKORUPI   DRAPION

DRATINI
Dragon Pokémon

TYPE: DRAGON

Long thought to be a myth, this Pokémon's existence was only recently confirmed by a fisherman who caught one.

HOW TO SAY IT: dra-TEE-nee
IMPERIAL HEIGHT: 5'11"
IMPERIAL WEIGHT: 7.3 lbs.
METRIC HEIGHT: 1.8 m
METRIC WEIGHT: 3.3 kg

POSSIBLE MOVES: Wrap, Leer, Thunder Wave, Twister, Dragon Rage, Slam, Agility, Dragon Tail, Aqua Tail, Dragon Rush, Safeguard, Dragon Dance, Outrage, Hyper Beam

DRATINI   DRAGONAIR   DRAGONITE

DREDNAW
Bite Pokémon

REGION: GALAR

TYPE: WATER-ROCK

With jaws that can shear through steel rods, this highly aggressive Pokémon chomps down on its unfortunate prey.

This Pokémon rapidly extends its retractable neck to sink its sharp fangs into distant enemies and take them down.

HOW TO SAY IT: DRED-naw
IMPERIAL HEIGHT: 3'03"
IMPERIAL WEIGHT: 254.6 lbs.
METRIC HEIGHT: 1.0 m
METRIC WEIGHT: 115.5 kg

POSSIBLE MOVES: Bite, Body Slam, Counter, Crunch, Head Smash, Headbutt, Jaw Lock, Liquidation, Protect, Razor Shell, Rock Polish, Rock Tomb, Tackle, Water Gun

CHEWTLE   **DREDNAW**

Alternate Form:
GIGANTAMAX DREDNAW

It responded to Gigantamax energy by becoming bipedal. First it comes crashing down on foes, and then it finishes them off with its massive jaws.

In the Galar region, there's a tale about this Pokémon chewing up a mountain and using the rubble to stop a flood.

IMPERIAL HEIGHT: 78'09"+
IMPERIAL WEIGHT: ????.? lbs.
METRIC HEIGHT: 24.0+ m
METRIC WEIGHT: ???.? kg

DREEPY
Lingering Pokémon

TYPE: DRAGON-GHOST

After being reborn as a ghost Pokémon, Dreepy wanders the areas it used to inhabit back when it was alive in prehistoric seas.

If this weak Pokémon is by itself, a mere child could defeat it. But if Dreepy has friends to help it train, it can evolve and become much stronger.

HOW TO SAY IT: DREE-pee
IMPERIAL HEIGHT: 1'08"
IMPERIAL WEIGHT: 4.4 lbs.
METRIC HEIGHT: 0.5 m
METRIC WEIGHT: 2.0 kg

POSSIBLE MOVES: Astonish, Bite, Infestation, Quick Attack

DREEPY   **DRAKLOAK**   **DRAGAPULT**

REGIONS:
ALOLA
GALAR
KALOS
(COASTAL)
SINNOH

DRIFBLIM
Blimp Pokémon

TYPE: GHOST-FLYING

Some say this Pokémon is a collection of souls burdened with regrets, silently drifting through the dusk.

It grabs people and Pokémon and carries them off somewhere. Where do they go? Nobody knows.

HOW TO SAY IT: DRIFF-blim
IMPERIAL HEIGHT: 3'11"
IMPERIAL WEIGHT: 33.1 lbs.
METRIC HEIGHT: 1.2 m
METRIC WEIGHT: 15.0 kg

POSSIBLE MOVES: Astonish, Baton Pass, Destiny Bond, Explosion, Focus Energy, Gust, Hex, Minimize, Payback, Phantom Force, Self-Destruct, Shadow Ball, Spit Up, Stockpile, Strength Sap, Swallow, Tailwind

DRIFLOON   **DRIFBLIM**

DRIFLOON

Balloon Pokémon

REGIONS:
ALOLA
GALAR
KALOS
(COASTAL)
SINNOH

TYPE: GHOST-FLYING

Perhaps seeking company, it approaches children. However, it often quickly runs away again when the children play too roughly with it.

The gathering of many souls gave rise to this Pokémon. During humid seasons, they seem to appear in abundance.

HOW TO SAY IT: DRIFF-loon
IMPERIAL HEIGHT: 1'04"
IMPERIAL WEIGHT: 2.6 lbs.
METRIC HEIGHT: 0.4 m
METRIC WEIGHT: 1.2 kg

POSSIBLE MOVES: Astonish, Baton Pass, Destiny Bond, Explosion, Focus Energy, Gust, Hex, Minimize, Payback, Self-Destruct, Shadow Ball, Spit Up, Stockpile, Swallow, Tailwind

DRIFLOON   DRIFBLIM

DRILBUR

Mole Pokémon

TYPE: GROUND

It brings its claws together and whirls around at high speed before rushing toward its prey.

It's a digger, using its claws to burrow through the ground. It causes damage to vegetable crops, so many farmers have little love for it.

HOW TO SAY IT: DRIL-bur
IMPERIAL HEIGHT: 1'00"
IMPERIAL WEIGHT: 18.7 lbs.
METRIC HEIGHT: 0.3 m
METRIC WEIGHT: 8.5 kg

POSSIBLE MOVES: Crush Claw, Dig, Drill Run, Earthquake, Fissure, Fury Swipes, Hone Claws, Metal Claw, Mud-Slap, Rapid Spin, Rock Slide, Sandstorm, Scratch, Swords Dance

DRILBUR   EXCADRILL

DRIZZILE
Water Lizard Pokémon

TYPE: WATER

A clever combatant, this Pokémon battles using water balloons created with moisture secreted from its palms.

Highly intelligent but also very lazy, it keeps enemies out of its territory by laying traps everywhere.

HOW TO SAY IT: DRIZ-zyle
IMPERIAL HEIGHT: 2'04"
IMPERIAL WEIGHT: 25.4 lbs.
METRIC HEIGHT: 0.7 m
METRIC WEIGHT: 11.5 kg

POSSIBLE MOVES: Bind, Growl, Liquidation, Pound, Rain Dance, Soak, Sucker Punch, Tearful Look, U-turn, Water Gun, Water Pulse

SOBBLE   DRIZZILE   INTELEON

DROWZEE
Hypnosis Pokémon

TYPE: PSYCHIC

If you sleep by it all the time, it will sometimes show you dreams it had eaten in the past.

HOW TO SAY IT: DROW-zee
IMPERIAL HEIGHT: 3'03"
IMPERIAL WEIGHT: 71.4 lbs.
METRIC HEIGHT: 1.0 m
METRIC WEIGHT: 32.4 kg

POSSIBLE MOVES: Pound, Hypnosis, Disable, Confusion, Headbutt, Poison Gas, Meditate, Psybeam, Wake-Up Slap, Psych Up, Synchronoise, Zen Headbutt, Swagger, Psychic, Nasty Plot, Psyshock, Future Sight

DROWZEE   HYPNO

DRUDDIGON

Cave Pokémon

TYPE: DRAGON

Druddigon lives in caves, but it never skips sunbathing—it won't be able to move if its body gets too cold.

Druddigon are vicious and cunning. They take up residence in nests dug out by other Pokémon, treating the stolen nests as their own lairs.

HOW TO SAY IT: DRUD-dih-guhn
IMPERIAL HEIGHT: 5'03"
IMPERIAL WEIGHT: 306.4 lbs.
METRIC HEIGHT: 1.6 m
METRIC WEIGHT: 139.0 kg

POSSIBLE MOVES: Leer, Scratch, Hone Claws, Bite, Scary Face, Dragon Rage, Slash, Crunch, Dragon Claw, Chip Away, Revenge, Night Slash, Dragon Tail, Rock Climb, Superpower, Outrage

DOES NOT EVOLVE

DUBWOOL

Sheep Pokémon

TYPE: GROUND

Weave a carpet from its springy wool, and you end up with something closer to a trampoline. You'll start to bounce the moment you set foot on it.

Its majestic horns are meant only to impress the opposite gender. They never see use in battle.

HOW TO SAY IT: DUB-wool
IMPERIAL HEIGHT: 4'03"
IMPERIAL WEIGHT: 94.8 lbs.
METRIC HEIGHT: 1.3 m
METRIC WEIGHT: 43.0 kg

POSSIBLE MOVES: Copycat, Cotton Guard, Defense Curl, Double Kick, Double-Edge, Growl, Guard Split, Guard Swap, Headbutt, Last Resort, Reversal, Tackle, Take Down

WOOLOO   DUBWOOL

DUCKLETT

Water Bird Pokémon

TYPE: WATER-FLYING

When attacked, it uses its feathers to splash water, escaping under cover of the spray.

They are better at swimming than flying, and they happily eat their favorite food, peat moss, as they dive underwater.

HOW TO SAY IT: DUK-lit
IMPERIAL HEIGHT: 1'08"
IMPERIAL WEIGHT: 12.1 lbs.
METRIC HEIGHT: 0.5 m
METRIC WEIGHT: 5.5 kg

POSSIBLE MOVES: Water Gun, Water Sport, Defog, Wing Attack, Water Pulse, Aerial Ace, Bubble Beam, Feather Dance, Aqua Ring, Air Slash, Roost, Rain Dance, Tailwind, Brave Bird, Hurricane

DUCKLETT   SWANNA

DUGTRIO

Mole Pokémon

TYPE: GROUND

A team of Diglett triplets. It triggers huge earthquakes by burrowing sixty miles underground.

These Diglett triplets dig over sixty miles below sea level. No one knows what it's like underground.

HOW TO SAY IT: DUG-TREE-oh
IMPERIAL HEIGHT: 2'04"
IMPERIAL WEIGHT: 73.4 lbs.
METRIC HEIGHT: 0.7 m
METRIC WEIGHT: 33.3 kg

POSSIBLE MOVES: Rototiller, Night Slash, Tri Attack, Scratch, Sand Attack, Growl, Astonish, Mud-Slap, Magnitude, Bulldoze, Sucker Punch, Sand Tomb, Mud Bomb, Earth Power, Dig, Slash, Earthquake, Fissure

DIGLETT

DUGTRIO

ALOLAN DUGTRIO

Mole Pokémon

TYPE: GROUND-STEEL

Their beautiful, metallic whiskers create a sort of protective helmet on their heads, and they also function as highly precise sensors.

The three of them get along very well. Through their formidable teamwork, they defeat powerful opponents.

HOW TO SAY IT: uh-LO-luhn DUG-TREE-oh
IMPERIAL HEIGHT: 2'04"
IMPERIAL WEIGHT: 146.8 lbs.
METRIC HEIGHT: 0.7 m
METRIC WEIGHT: 66.6 kg

POSSIBLE MOVES: Sand Tomb, Rototiller, Night Slash, Tri Attack, Sand Attack, Metal Claw, Growl, Astonish, Mud-Slap, Magnitude, Bulldoze, Sucker Punch, Mud Bomb, Earth Power, Dig, Iron Head, Earthquake, Fissure

ALOLAN DIGLETT   ALOLAN DUGTRIO

TYPE: NORMAL

DUNSPARCE
Land Snake Pokémon

This Pokémon's tiny wings have some scientists saying that Dunsparce used to fly through the sky in ancient times.

The nests Dunsparce live in are mazes of tunnels. They never get lost in their own nests—they can tell where they are by the scent of the dirt.

HOW TO SAY IT: DUN-sparce
IMPERIAL HEIGHT: 4'11"
IMPERIAL WEIGHT: 30.9 lbs.
METRIC HEIGHT: 1.5 m
METRIC WEIGHT: 14.0 kg

POSSIBLE MOVES: Rage, Defense Curl, Rollout, Spite, Pursuit, Screech, Mud-Slap, Yawn, Ancient Power, Body Slam, Drill Run, Roost, Take Down, Coil, Dig, Glare, Double-Edge, Endeavor, Air Slash, Dragon Rush, Endure, Flail

DOES NOT EVOLVE

DUOSION
Mitosis Pokémon

TYPE: PSYCHIC

Its psychic power can supposedly cover a range of more than half a mile—but only if its two brains can agree with each other.

Its brain has split into two, and the two halves rarely think alike. Its actions are utterly unpredictable.

HOW TO SAY IT: doo-OH-zhun
IMPERIAL HEIGHT: 2'00"
IMPERIAL WEIGHT: 17.6 lbs.
METRIC HEIGHT: 0.6 m
METRIC WEIGHT: 8.0 kg

POSSIBLE MOVES: Ally Switch, Charm, Confusion, Endeavor, Future Sight, Light Screen, Pain Split, Protect, Psybeam, Psychic, Psyshock, Recover, Reflect, Skill Swap, Wonder Room

SOLOSIS **DUOSION** **REUNICLUS**

145

DURALUDON

Alloy Pokémon

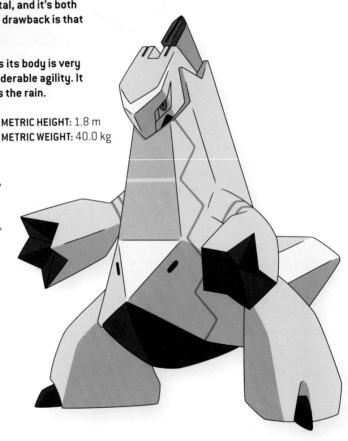

REGION: GALAR

TYPE: STEEL-DRAGON

Its body resembles polished metal, and it's both lightweight and strong. The only drawback is that it rusts easily.

The special metal that composes its body is very light, so this Pokémon has considerable agility. It lives in caves because it dislikes the rain.

HOW TO SAY IT: duh-RAL-uh-dahn
IMPERIAL HEIGHT: 5'11"
IMPERIAL WEIGHT: 88.2 lbs.
METRIC HEIGHT: 1.8 m
METRIC WEIGHT: 40.0 kg

POSSIBLE MOVES: Breaking Swipe, Dragon Claw, Dragon Tail, Flash Cannon, Hone Claws, Hyper Beam, Iron Defense, Laser Focus, Leer, Metal Burst, Metal Claw, Metal Sound, Rock Smash

DOES NOT EVOLVE

Alternate Form:
GIGANTAMAX DURALUDON

It's grown to resemble a skyscraper. Parts of its towering body glow due to a profusion of energy.

The hardness of its cells is exceptional, even among Steel types. It also has a body structure that's resistant to earthquakes.

IMPERIAL HEIGHT: 141'01"+
IMPERIAL WEIGHT: ????.? lbs.
METRIC HEIGHT: 43.0+ m
METRIC WEIGHT: ???.? kg

TYPE: BUG-STEEL

DURANT
Iron Ant Pokémon

They lay their eggs deep inside their nests. When attacked by Heatmor, they retaliate using their massive mandibles.

With their large mandibles, these Pokémon can crunch their way through rock. They work together to protect their eggs from Sandaconda.

HOW TO SAY IT: dur-ANT
IMPERIAL HEIGHT: 1'00"
IMPERIAL WEIGHT: 72.8 lbs.
METRIC HEIGHT: 0.3 m
METRIC WEIGHT: 33.0 kg

POSSIBLE MOVES: Guillotine, Iron Defense, Metal Sound, Vice Grip, Sand Attack, Fury Cutter, Bite, Agility, Metal Claw, Bug Bite, Crunch, Iron Head, Dig, Entrainment, X-Scissor

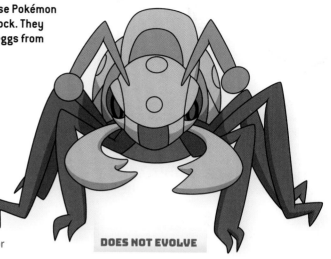

DOES NOT EVOLVE

TYPE: GHOST

DUSCLOPS
Beckon Pokémon

Its body is entirely hollow. When it opens its mouth, it sucks everything in as if it were a black hole.

It seeks drifting will-o'-the-wisps and sucks them into its empty body. What happens inside is a mystery.

HOW TO SAY IT: DUS-klops
IMPERIAL HEIGHT: 5'03"
IMPERIAL WEIGHT: 67.5 lbs.
METRIC HEIGHT: 1.6 m
METRIC WEIGHT: 30.6 kg

POSSIBLE MOVES: Astonish, Bind, Confuse Ray, Curse, Disable, Fire Punch, Future Sight, Gravity, Hex, Ice Punch, Leer, Mean Look, Night Shade, Payback, Shadow Ball, Shadow Punch, Shadow Sneak, Thunder Punch, Will-O-Wisp

DUSKULL   **DUSCLOPS**   **DUSKNOIR**

DUSKNOIR

Gripper Pokémon

REGIONS:
GALAR
HOENN

TYPE: GHOST

At the bidding of transmissions from the spirit world, it steals people and Pokémon away. No one knows whether it has a will of its own.

With the mouth on its belly, Dusknoir swallows its target whole. The soul is the only thing eaten—Dusknoir disgorges the body before departing.

HOW TO SAY IT: DUSK-nwar **METRIC HEIGHT:** 2.2 m
IMPERIAL HEIGHT: 7'03" **METRIC WEIGHT:** 106.6 kg
IMPERIAL WEIGHT: 235.0 lbs.

POSSIBLE MOVES: Astonish, Bind, Confuse Ray, Curse, Destiny Bond, Disable, Fire Punch, Future Sight, Gravity, Hex, Ice Punch, Leer, Mean Look, Night Shade, Payback, Shadow Ball, Shadow Punch, Shadow Sneak, Thunder Punch, Will-O-Wisp

DUSKULL   **DUSCLOPS**   **DUSKNOIR**

DUSKULL

Requiem Pokémon

REGIONS:
GALAR
HOENN

TYPE: GHOST

If it finds bad children who won't listen to their parents, it will spirit them away—or so it's said.

Making itself invisible, it silently sneaks up to prey. It has the ability to slip through thick walls.

HOW TO SAY IT: DUS-kull
IMPERIAL HEIGHT: 2'07"
IMPERIAL WEIGHT: 33.1 lbs.
METRIC HEIGHT: 0.8 m
METRIC WEIGHT: 15.0 kg

POSSIBLE MOVES: Astonish, Confuse Ray, Curse, Disable, Future Sight, Hex, Leer, Mean Look, Night Shade, Payback, Shadow Ball, Shadow Sneak, Will-O-Wisp

DUSKULL   **DUSCLOPS**   **DUSKNOIR**

TYPE: BUG-POISON

DUSTOX
Poison Moth Pokémon

Dustox is instinctively drawn to light. Swarms of this Pokémon are attracted by the bright lights of cities, where they wreak havoc by stripping the leaves off roadside trees for food.

When Dustox flaps its wings, a fine dust is scattered all over. This dust is actually a powerful poison that will even make a pro wrestler sick. This Pokémon searches for food using its antennae-like radar.

HOW TO SAY IT: DUS-tocks
IMPERIAL HEIGHT: 3'11"
IMPERIAL WEIGHT: 69.7 lbs.
METRIC HEIGHT: 1.2 m
METRIC WEIGHT: 31.6 kg

POSSIBLE MOVES: Gust, Confusion, Poison Power, Moonlight, Venoshock, Psybeam, Silver Wind, Light Screen, Whirlwind, Toxic, Bug Buzz, Protect, Quiver Dance

WURMPLE   **CASCOON**   **DUSTOX**

DWEBBLE
Rock Inn Pokémon

TYPE: BUG-ROCK

When it finds a stone appealing, it creates a hole inside it and uses it as its home. This Pokémon is the natural enemy of Roggenrola and Rolycoly.

It first tries to find a rock to live in, but if there are no suitable rocks to be found, Dwebble may move in to the ports of a Hippowdon.

HOW TO SAY IT: DWEHB-bul   **METRIC HEIGHT:** 0.3 m
IMPERIAL HEIGHT: 1'00"   **METRIC WEIGHT:** 14.5 kg
IMPERIAL WEIGHT: 32.0 lbs.

POSSIBLE MOVES: Bug Bite, Flail, Fury Cutter, Rock Blast, Rock Polish, Rock Slide, Rock Wrecker, Sand Attack, Shell Smash, Slash, Smack Down, Stealth Rock, Withdraw, X-Scissor

DWEBBLE   **CRUSTLE**

EELEKTRIK
EleFish Pokémon

REGION: UNOVA

TYPE: ELECTRIC

It wraps itself around its prey and paralyzes it with electricity from the round spots on its sides. Then it chomps.

These Pokémon have a big appetite. When they spot their prey, they attack it and paralyze it with electricity.

HOW TO SAY IT: ee-LEK-trik
IMPERIAL HEIGHT: 3'11"
IMPERIAL WEIGHT: 48.5 lbs.
METRIC HEIGHT: 1.2 m
METRIC WEIGHT: 22.0 kg

POSSIBLE MOVES: Headbutt, Thunder Wave, Spark, Charge Beam, Bind, Acid, Discharge, Crunch, Thunderbolt, Acid Spray, Coil, Wild Charge, Gastro Acid, Zap Cannon, Thrash

TYNAMO   EELEKTRIK   EELEKTROSS

EELEKTROSS
EleFish Pokémon

REGION: UNOVA

TYPE: ELECTRIC

With their sucker mouths, they suck in prey. Then they use their fangs to shock the prey with electricity.

They crawl out of the ocean using their arms. They will attack prey on shore and immediately drag it into the ocean.

HOW TO SAY IT: ee-LEK-trahs
IMPERIAL HEIGHT: 6'11"
IMPERIAL WEIGHT: 177.5 lbs.
METRIC HEIGHT: 2.1 m
METRIC WEIGHT: 80.5 kg

POSSIBLE MOVES: Crunch, Thrash, Zap Cannon, Gastro Acid, Coil, Ion Deluge, Crush Claw, Headbutt, Acid

TYNAMO   EELEKTRIK   EELEKTROSS

REGIONS:
ALOLA
GALAR
KALOS
(COASTAL)
KANTO

EEVEE
Evolution Pokémon

TYPE: NORMAL

It has the ability to alter the composition of its body to suit its surrounding environment.

Thanks to its unstable genetic makeup, this special Pokémon conceals many different possible evolutions.

HOW TO SAY IT: EE-vee
IMPERIAL HEIGHT: 1'00"
IMPERIAL WEIGHT: 14.3 lbs.
METRIC HEIGHT: 0.3 m
METRIC WEIGHT: 6.5 kg

POSSIBLE MOVES: Baby-Doll Eyes, Baton Pass, Bite, Charm, Copycat, Covet, Double-Edge, Growl, Helping Hand, Last Resort, Quick Attack, Sand Attack, Swift, Tackle, Tail Whip, Take Down

JOLTEON · FLAREON · GLACEON · VAPOREON · EEVEE · ESPEON · UMBREON · LEAFEON · SYLVEON

Alternate Form:
GIGANTAMAX EEVEE

Gigantamax energy upped the fluffiness of the fur around Eevee's neck. The fur will envelop a foe, capturing its body and captivating its mind.

Having gotten even friendlier and more innocent, Eevee tries to play with anyone around, only to end up crushing them with its immense body.

IMPERIAL HEIGHT: 59'01"+
IMPERIAL WEIGHT: ????.? lbs.
METRIC HEIGHT: 180+ m
METRIC WEIGHT: ???.? kg

EISCUE

Penguin Pokémon

TYPE: ICE

It drifted in on the flow of ocean waters from a frigid place. It keeps its head iced constantly to make sure it stays nice and cold.

This Pokémon keeps its heat-sensitive head cool with ice. It fishes for its food, dangling its single hair into the sea to lure in prey.

HOW TO SAY IT: ICE-kyoo
IMPERIAL HEIGHT: 4'07"
IMPERIAL WEIGHT: 196.2 lbs.
METRIC HEIGHT: 1.4 m
METRIC WEIGHT: 89.0 kg

POSSIBLE MOVES: Amnesia, Aurora Veil, Blizzard, Freeze-Dry, Hail, Headbutt, Icy Wind, Mist, Powder Snow, Surf, Tackle, Weather Ball

DOES NOT EVOLVE

EKANS

Snake Pokémon

REGIONS:
ALOLA
KALOS
(MOUNTAIN)
KANTO

TYPE: POISON

The older it gets, the longer it grows. At night, it wraps its long body around tree branches to rest.

HOW TO SAY IT: ECK-kins
IMPERIAL HEIGHT: 6'07"
IMPERIAL WEIGHT: 15.2 lbs.
METRIC HEIGHT: 2.0 m
METRIC WEIGHT: 6.9 kg

POSSIBLE MOVES: Wrap, Leer, Poison Sting, Bite, Glare, Screech, Acid, Stockpile, Swallow, Spit Up, Acid Spray, Mud Bomb, Gastro Acid, Belch, Haze, Coil, Gunk Shot

EKANS → ARBOK

ELDEGOSS
Cotton Bloom Pokémon

TYPE: GRASS

The seeds attached to its cotton fluff are full of nutrients. It spreads them on the wind so that plants and other Pokémon can benefit from them.

The cotton on the head of this Pokémon can be spun into a glossy, gorgeous yarn—a Galar regional specialty.

HOW TO SAY IT: EL-duh-gahs
IMPERIAL HEIGHT: 1'08"
IMPERIAL WEIGHT: 5.5 lbs.
METRIC HEIGHT: 0.5 m
METRIC WEIGHT: 2.5 kg

POSSIBLE MOVES: Aromatherapy, Cotton Guard, Cotton Spore, Hyper Voice, Leaf Storm, Leaf Tornado, Leafage, Rapid Spin, Razor Leaf, Round, Sing, Sweet Scent, Synthesis

GOSSIFLEUR → ELDEGOSS

ELECTABUZZ
Electric Pokémon

TYPE: ELECTRIC

If a major power outage occurs, it is certain that this Pokémon has eaten electricity at a power plant.

HOW TO SAY IT: eh-LECK-ta-buzz
IMPERIAL HEIGHT: 3'07"
IMPERIAL WEIGHT: 66.1 lbs.
METRIC HEIGHT: 1.1 m
METRIC WEIGHT: 30.0 kg

POSSIBLE MOVES: Quick Attack, Leer, Thunder Shock, Low Kick, Swift, Shock Wave, Thunder Wave, Electro Ball, Light Screen, Thunder Punch, Discharge, Screech, Thunderbolt, Thunder

ELEKID → ELECTABUZZ → ELECTIVIRE

153

ELECTIVIRE

Thunderbolt Pokémon

TYPE: ELECTRIC

It grips its tail, which spews electricity, and then beats down opponents with the power of its electrified fist.

A single Electivire can provide enough electricity for all the buildings in a big city for a year.

HOW TO SAY IT: el-LECT-uh-vire
IMPERIAL HEIGHT: 5'11"
IMPERIAL WEIGHT: 305.6 lbs.
METRIC HEIGHT: 1.8 m
METRIC WEIGHT: 138.6 kg

POSSIBLE MOVES: Electric Terrain, Ion Deluge, Fire Punch, Quick Attack, Leer, Thunder Shock, Low Kick, Swift, Shock Wave, Thunder Wave, Electro Ball, Light Screen, Thunder Punch, Discharge, Screech, Thunderbolt, Thunder, Giga Impact

ELEKID   ELECTABUZZ   ELECTIVIRE

TYPE: ELECTRIC

It stores static electricity in its fur for discharging. It gives off sparks if a storm approaches.

It stores electricity in its fur. It gives off sparks from all over its body in seasons when the air is dry.

REGIONS:
ALOLA
GALAR
HOENN
KALOS
(COASTAL)

ELECTRIKE

Lightning Pokémon

HOW TO SAY IT: eh-LEK-trike
IMPERIAL HEIGHT: 2'00"
IMPERIAL WEIGHT: 33.5 lbs.
METRIC HEIGHT: 0.6 m
METRIC WEIGHT: 15.2 kg

POSSIBLE MOVES: Bite, Charge, Discharge, Howl, Leer, Quick Attack, Roar, Shock Wave, Tackle, Thunder, Thunder Fang, Thunder Wave, Wild Charge

ELECTRIKE   MANECTRIC   MEGA MANECTRIC

ELECTRODE
Ball Pokémon

TYPE: ELECTRIC

Stores electrical energy inside its body. Even the slightest shock could trigger a huge explosion.

HOW TO SAY IT: ee-LECK-trode
IMPERIAL HEIGHT: 3'11"
IMPERIAL WEIGHT: 146.8 lbs.
METRIC HEIGHT: 1.2 m
METRIC WEIGHT: 66.6 kg

POSSIBLE MOVES: Magnetic Flux, Charge, Tackle, Sonic Boom, Spark, Eerie Impulse, Rollout, Screech, Charge Beam, Light Screen, Electro Ball, Self-Destruct, Swift, Magnet Rise, Gyro Ball, Explosion, Mirror Coat, Discharge

VOLTORB   ELECTRODE

ELEKID
Electric Pokémon

TYPE: ELECTRIC

When it hears the crash of thunder, Elekid's mood improves. It can be useful to record that sound and play it when Elekid's feeling down.

When its horns shine a bluish white, that's the sign it's fully charged. You'll get a shocking jolt if you touch it!

HOW TO SAY IT: EL-eh-kid   **METRIC HEIGHT:** 0.6 m
IMPERIAL HEIGHT: 2'00"   **METRIC WEIGHT:** 23.5 kg
IMPERIAL WEIGHT: 51.8 lbs.

POSSIBLE MOVES: Quick Attack, Leer, Thunder Shock, Low Kick, Swift, Shock Wave, Thunder Wave, Electro Ball, Light Screen, Thunder Punch, Discharge, Screech, Thunderbolt, Thunder

ELEKID   ELECTABUZZ   ELECTIVIRE   **155**

ELGYEM

Cerebral Pokémon

TYPE: PSYCHIC

If this Pokémon stands near a TV, strange scenery will appear on the screen. That scenery is said to be from its home.

This Pokémon was discovered about fifty years ago. Its highly developed brain enables it to exert its psychic powers.

HOW TO SAY IT: ELL-jee-ehm
IMPERIAL HEIGHT: 1'08"
IMPERIAL WEIGHT: 19.8 lbs.
METRIC HEIGHT: 0.5 m
METRIC WEIGHT: 9.0 kg

POSSIBLE MOVES: Calm Mind, Confusion, Growl, Guard Split, Headbutt, Imprison, Power Split, Psybeam, Psychic, Recover, Teleport, Wonder Room, Zen Headbutt

ELGYEM   BEHEEYEM

EMBOAR

Mega Fire Pig Pokémon

REGION: UNOVA

TYPE: FIRE-FIGHTING

It can throw a fire punch by setting its fists on fire with its fiery chin. It cares deeply about its friends.

It has mastered fast and powerful fighting moves. It grows a beard of fire.

HOW TO SAY IT: EHM-bohr
IMPERIAL HEIGHT: 5'03"
IMPERIAL WEIGHT: 330.7 lbs.
METRIC HEIGHT: 1.6 m
METRIC WEIGHT: 150.0 kg

POSSIBLE MOVES: Hammer Arm, Tackle, Tail Whip, Ember, Odor Sleuth, Defense Curl, Flame Charge, Arm Thrust, Smog, Rollout, Take Down, Heat Crash, Assurance, Flamethrower, Head Smash, Roar, Flare Blitz

TEPIG   PIGNITE   EMBOAR

EMOLGA
Sky Squirrel Pokémon

TYPE: ELECTRIC-FLYING

As Emolga flutters through the air, it crackles with electricity. This Pokémon is cute, but it can cause a lot of trouble.

This Pokémon absolutely loves sweet berries. Sometimes it stuffs its cheeks full of so much food that it can't fly properly.

HOW TO SAY IT: ee-MAHL-guh
IMPERIAL HEIGHT: 1'04"
IMPERIAL WEIGHT: 11.0 lbs.
METRIC HEIGHT: 0.4 m
METRIC WEIGHT: 5.0 kg

POSSIBLE MOVES: Thunder Shock, Quick Attack, Tail Whip, Charge, Spark, Nuzzle, Pursuit, Double Team, Shock Wave, Electro Ball, Acrobatics, Light Screen, Encore, Volt Switch, Agility, Discharge

DOES NOT EVOLVE

REGION:
SINNOH

EMPOLEON
Emperor Pokémon

TYPE: WATER-STEEL

It swims as fast as a jet boat. The edges of its wings are sharp and can slice apart drifting ice.

The three horns that extend from its beak attest to its power. The leader has the biggest horns.

HOW TO SAY IT: em-POH-lee-on
IMPERIAL HEIGHT: 5'07"
IMPERIAL WEIGHT: 186.3 lbs.
METRIC HEIGHT: 1.7 m
METRIC WEIGHT: 84.5 kg

POSSIBLE MOVES: Tackle, Growl, Bubble, Swords Dance, Peck, Metal Claw, Bubble Beam, Swagger, Fury Attack, Brine, Aqua Jet, Whirlpool, Mist, Drill Peck, Hydro Pump

PIPLUP   **PRINPLUP**   **EMPOLEON**

ENTEI
Volcano Pokémon

REGION: JOHTO

LEGENDARY POKÉMON

TYPE: FIRE

Entei embodies the passion of magma. This Pokémon is thought to have been born in the eruption of a volcano. It sends up massive bursts of fire that utterly consume all that they touch.

HOW TO SAY IT: EN-tay
IMPERIAL HEIGHT: 6'11"
IMPERIAL WEIGHT: 436.5 lbs.
METRIC HEIGHT: 2.1 m
METRIC WEIGHT: 198.0 kg

POSSIBLE MOVES: Sacred Fire, Eruption, Extrasensory, Lava Plume, Bite, Leer, Ember, Roar, Fire Spin, Stomp, Flamethrower, Swagger, Fire Fang, Fire Blast, Calm Mind

DOES NOT EVOLVE

ESCAVALIER
Cavalry Pokémon

REGIONS: GALAR KALOS (MOUNTAIN) UNOVA

TYPE: BUG-STEEL

They use shells they've stolen from Shelmet to arm and protect themselves. They're very popular Pokémon in the Galar region.

It charges its enemies, lances at the ready. An image of one of its duels is captured in a famous painting of Escavalier clashing with Sirfetch'd.

HOW TO SAY IT: ess-KAV-a-LEER
IMPERIAL HEIGHT: 3'03"
IMPERIAL WEIGHT: 72.8 lbs.
METRIC HEIGHT: 1.0 m
METRIC WEIGHT: 33.0 kg

POSSIBLE MOVES: Acid Spray, Bug Buzz, Double-Edge, Endure, False Swipe, Fell Stinger, Flail, Fury Cutter, Giga Impact, Headbutt, Iron Defense, Iron Head, Leer, Metal Burst, Peck, Quick Guard, Reversal, Scary Face, Swords Dance, Take Down, X-Scissor

KARRABLAST ➡ **ESCAVALIER**

REGIONS:
ALOLA
GALAR
JOHTO
KALOS
(COASTAL)

ESPEON
Sun Pokémon

TYPE: PSYCHIC

By reading air currents, it can predict things such as the weather or its foe's next move.

It unleashes psychic power from the orb on its forehead. When its power is exhausted, the orb grows dull and dark.

HOW TO SAY IT: ESS-pee-on
IMPERIAL HEIGHT: 2'11"
IMPERIAL WEIGHT: 58.4 lbs.
METRIC HEIGHT: 0.9 m
METRIC WEIGHT: 26.5 kg

POSSIBLE MOVES: Baby-Doll Eyes, Baton Pass, Bite, Charm, Confusion, Copycat, Covet, Double-Edge, Future Sight, Growl, Helping Hand, Last Resort, Morning Sun, Power Swap, Psybeam, Psych Up, Psychic, Quick Attack, Sand Attack, Swift, Tackle, Tail Whip, Take Down

EEVEE → ESPEON

ESPURR
Restraint Pokémon

TYPE: PSYCHIC

Though Espurr's expression never changes, behind that blank stare is an intense struggle to contain its devastating psychic power.

There's enough psychic power in Espurr to send a wrestler flying, but because this power can't be controlled, Espurr finds it troublesome.

HOW TO SAY IT: ESS-purr
IMPERIAL HEIGHT: 1'00"
IMPERIAL WEIGHT: 7.7 lbs.
METRIC HEIGHT: 0.3 m
METRIC WEIGHT: 3.5 kg

POSSIBLE MOVES: Confusion, Covet, Disarming Voice, Fake Out, Leer, Light Screen, Psybeam, Psyshock, Reflect, Scratch

ESPURR → MEOWSTIC

ETERNATUS

Gigantic Pokémon

TYPE: POISON-DRAGON

The core on its chest absorbs energy emanating from the lands of the Galar region. This energy is what allows Eternatus to stay active.

It was inside a meteorite that fell 20,000 years ago. There seems to be a connection between this Pokémon and the Dynamax phenomenon.

HOW TO SAY IT: ee-TURR-nuh-tuss
IMPERIAL HEIGHT: 65'07"
IMPERIAL WEIGHT: 2094.4 lbs.
METRIC HEIGHT: 20.0 m
METRIC WEIGHT: 950.0 kg

POSSIBLE MOVES: Agility, Confuse Ray, Cosmic Power, Cross Poison, Dragon Dance, Dragon Pulse, Dragon Tail, Dynamax Cannon, Eternabeam, Flamethrower, Hyper Beam, Poison Tail, Recover, Toxic, Venoshock

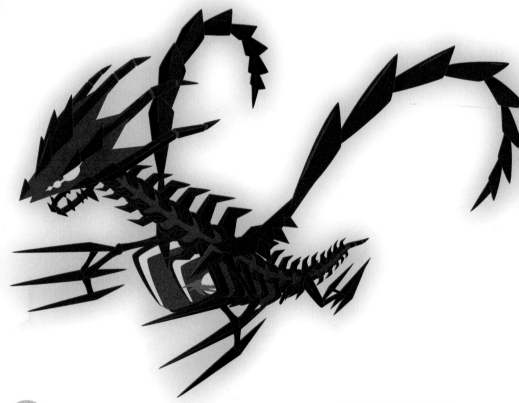

160

DOES NOT EVOLVE

EXCADRILL
Subterrene Pokémon

TYPE: GROUND-STEEL

It's not uncommon for tunnels that appear to have formed naturally to actually be a result of Excadrill's rampant digging.

Known as the Drill King, this Pokémon can tunnel through the terrain at speeds of over 90 mph.

HOW TO SAY IT: EKS-kuh-dril
IMPERIAL HEIGHT: 2'04"
IMPERIAL WEIGHT: 89.1 lbs.
METRIC HEIGHT: 0.7 m
METRIC WEIGHT: 40.4 kg

POSSIBLE MOVES: Crush Claw, Dig, Drill Run, Earthquake, Fissure, Fury Swipes, Hone Claws, Horn Drill, Metal Claw, Mud-Slap, Rapid Spin, Rock Slide, Sandstorm, Scratch, Swords Dance

DRILBUR   EXCADRILL

EXEGGCUTE
Egg Pokémon

TYPE: GRASS-PSYCHIC

Though it may look like it's just a bunch of eggs, it's a proper Pokémon. Exeggcute communicates with others of its kind via telepathy, apparently.

These Pokémon get nervous when they're not in a group of six. The minute even one member of the group goes missing, Exeggcute become cowardly.

HOW TO SAY IT: ECKS-egg-cute
IMPERIAL HEIGHT: 1'04"
IMPERIAL WEIGHT: 5.5 lbs.
METRIC HEIGHT: 0.4 m
METRIC WEIGHT: 2.5 kg

POSSIBLE MOVES: Barrage, Uproar, Hypnosis, Reflect, Leech Seed, Bullet Seed, Stun Spore, Poison Powder, Sleep Powder, Confusion, Worry Seed, Natural Gift, Solar Beam, Extrasensory, Bestow

EXEGGUTOR

EXEGGCUTE

ALOLAN
EXEGGUTOR

161

EXEGGUTOR

Coconut Pokémon

REGIONS: KALOS (COASTAL) KANTO

TYPE: GRASS-PSYCHIC

Each of Exeggutor's three heads is thinking different thoughts. The three don't seem to be very interested in one another.

When they work together, Exeggutor's three heads can put out powerful psychic energy. Cloudy days make this Pokémon sluggish.

HOW TO SAY IT: ecks-EGG-u-tore
IMPERIAL HEIGHT: 6'07"
IMPERIAL WEIGHT: 264.6 lbs.
METRIC HEIGHT: 2.0 m
METRIC WEIGHT: 120.0 kg

POSSIBLE MOVES: Seed Bomb, Barrage, Hypnosis, Confusion, Stomp, Psyshock, Egg Bomb, Wood Hammer, Leaf Storm

EXEGGCUTE ➡ EXEGGUTOR

ALOLAN EXEGGUTOR

Coconut Pokémon

REGION: ALOLA

TYPE: GRASS-DRAGON

Blazing sunlight has brought out the true form and powers of this Pokémon.

This Pokémon's psychic powers aren't as strong as they once were. The head on this Exeggutor's tail scans surrounding areas with weak telepathy.

HOW TO SAY IT: ecks-EGG-u-tore
IMPERIAL HEIGHT: 35'09"
IMPERIAL WEIGHT: 916.2 lbs.
METRIC HEIGHT: 10.9 m
METRIC WEIGHT: 415.6 kg

POSSIBLE MOVES: Dragon Hammer, Seed Bomb, Barrage, Hypnosis, Confusion, Psyshock, Egg Bomb, Wood Hammer, Leaf Storm

EXEGGCUTE ➡ ALOLAN EXEGGUTOR

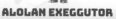

TYPE: NORMAL

In the past, people would use the loud voices of these Pokémon as a means of communication between distant cities.

This Pokémon can do more than just shout. To communicate with others of its kind, it'll emit all sorts of sounds from the holes in its body.

HOW TO SAY IT: ecks-PLOWD
IMPERIAL HEIGHT: 4'11"
IMPERIAL WEIGHT: 185.2 lbs.
METRIC HEIGHT: 1.5 m
METRIC WEIGHT: 84.0 kg

POSSIBLE MOVES: Crunch, Bite, Boomburst, Ice Fang, Fire Fang, Thunder Fang, Pound, Echoed Voice, Astonish, Howl, Screech, Supersonic, Stomp, Uproar, Roar, Rest, Sleep Talk, Hyper Voice, Synchronoise, Hyper Beam

REGIONS:
HOENN
KALOS
(CENTRAL)

EXPLOUD
Loud Noise Pokémon

WHISMUR → LOUDRED → EXPLOUD

REGION:
GALAR

FALINKS
Formation Pokémon

TYPE: FIGHTING

Five of them are troopers, and one is the brass. The brass's orders are absolute.

The six of them work together as one Pokémon. Teamwork is also their battle strategy, and they constantly change their formation as they fight.

HOW TO SAY IT: FAY-links
IMPERIAL HEIGHT: 9'10"
IMPERIAL WEIGHT: 136.7 lbs.
METRIC HEIGHT: 3.0 m
METRIC WEIGHT: 62.0 kg

POSSIBLE MOVES: Bulk Up, Close Combat, Counter, Endure, First Impression, Focus Energy, Headbutt, Iron Defense, Megahorn, No Retreat, Protect, Reversal, Rock Smash, Tackle

DOES NOT EVOLVE

FARFETCH'D
Wild Duck Pokémon

TYPE: NORMAL-FLYING

The stalk this Pokémon carries in its wings serves as a sword to cut down opponents. In a dire situation, the stalk can also serve as food.

They use a plant stalk as a weapon, but not all of them use it in the same way. Several distinct styles of stalk fighting have been observed.

HOW TO SAY IT: FAR-fetched
IMPERIAL HEIGHT: 2'07"
IMPERIAL WEIGHT: 33.1 lbs.
METRIC HEIGHT: 0.8 m
METRIC WEIGHT: 15.0 kg

POSSIBLE MOVES: Aerial Ace, Agility, Air Cutter, Air Slash, Brave Bird, Cut, False Swipe, Fury Cutter, Knock Off, Leaf Blade, Leer, Peck, Sand Attack, Slash, Swords Dance

DOES NOT EVOLVE

GALARIAN FARFETCH'D
Wild Duck Pokémon

TYPE: FIGHTING

The Farfetch'd of the Galar region are brave warriors, and they wield thick, tough leeks in battle.

The stalks of leeks are thicker and longer in the Galar region. Farfetch'd that adapted to these stalks took on a unique form.

HOW TO SAY IT: FAR-fetched
IMPERIAL HEIGHT: 2'07"
IMPERIAL WEIGHT: 92.6 lbs.
METRIC HEIGHT: 0.8 m
METRIC WEIGHT: 42.0 kg

POSSIBLE MOVES: Brave Bird, Brick Break, Brutal Swing, Defog, Detect, Final Gambit, Fury Cutter, Knock Off, Leaf Blade, Leer, Peck, Rock Smash, Sand Attack, Slam, Swords Dance

GALARIAN
FARFETCH'D ➡ SIRFETCH'D

FEAROW
Beak Pokémon

TYPE: NORMAL-FLYING

A Pokémon that dates back many years. If it senses danger, it flies high and away, instantly.

HOW TO SAY IT: FEER-oh
IMPERIAL HEIGHT: 3'11"
IMPERIAL WEIGHT: 83.8 lbs.
METRIC HEIGHT: 1.2 m
METRIC WEIGHT: 38.0 kg

POSSIBLE MOVES: Drill Run, Pluck, Peck, Growl, Leer, Pursuit, Fury Attack, Aerial Ace, Mirror Move, Assurance, Agility, Focus Energy, Roost, Drill Peck

SPEAROW   FEAROW

FEEBAS
Fish Pokémon

TYPE: WATER

Although unattractive and unpopular, this Pokémon's marvelous vitality has made it a subject of research.

It is a shabby and ugly Pokémon. However, it is very hardy and can survive on little water.

HOW TO SAY IT: FEE-bass
IMPERIAL HEIGHT: 2'00"
IMPERIAL WEIGHT: 16.3 lbs.
METRIC HEIGHT: 0.6 m
METRIC WEIGHT: 7.4 kg

POSSIBLE MOVES: Flail, Splash, Tackle

FEEBAS   MILOTIC

FENNEKIN
Fox Pokémon

TYPE: FIRE

Eating a twig fills it with energy, and its roomy ears give vent to air hotter than 390 degrees Fahrenheit.

As it walks, it munches on a twig in place of a snack. It intimidates opponents by puffing hot air out of its ears.

HOW TO SAY IT: FEN-ik-in
IMPERIAL HEIGHT: 1'04"
IMPERIAL WEIGHT: 20.7 lbs.
METRIC HEIGHT: 0.4 m
METRIC WEIGHT: 9.4 kg

POSSIBLE MOVES: Scratch, Tail Whip, Ember, Howl, Flame Charge, Psybeam, Fire Spin, Lucky Chant, Light Screen, Psyshock, Flamethrower, Will-O-Wisp, Psychic, Sunny Day, Magic Room, Fire Blast

FENNEKIN **BRAIXEN** **DELPHOX**

FERALIGATR
Big Jaw Pokémon

TYPE: WATER

Feraligatr intimidates its foes by opening its huge mouth. In battle, it will kick the ground hard with its thick and powerful hind legs to charge at the foe at an incredible speed.

HOW TO SAY IT: fer-AL-ee-gay-tur
IMPERIAL HEIGHT: 7'07"
IMPERIAL WEIGHT: 195.8 lbs.
METRIC HEIGHT: 2.3 m
METRIC WEIGHT: 88.8 kg

POSSIBLE MOVES: Scratch, Leer, Water Gun, Rage, Bite, Scary Face, Ice Fang, Flail, Agility, Crunch, Chip Away, Slash, Screech, Thrash, Aqua Tail, Superpower, Hydro Pump

TOTODILE **CROCONAW** **FERALIGATR**

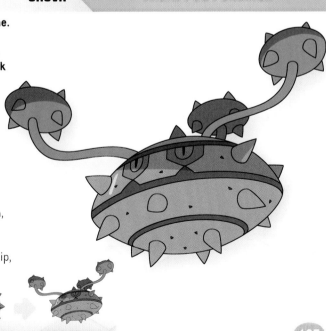

FERROSEED
Thorn Seed Pokémon

TYPE: GRASS-STEEL

It defends itself by launching spikes, but its aim isn't very good at first. Only after a lot of practice will it improve.

Mossy caves are their preferred dwellings. Enzymes contained in mosses help Ferroseed's spikes grow big and strong.

HOW TO SAY IT: fer-AH-seed
IMPERIAL HEIGHT: 2'00"
IMPERIAL WEIGHT: 41.4 lbs.
METRIC HEIGHT: 0.6 m
METRIC WEIGHT: 18.8 kg

POSSIBLE MOVES: Curse, Explosion, Flash Cannon, Gyro Ball, Harden, Ingrain, Iron Defense, Iron Head, Metal Claw, Pin Missile, Self-Destruct, Tackle

FERROSEED → FERROTHORN

TYPE: GRASS-STEEL

FERROTHORN
Thorn Pod Pokémon

This Pokémon scrapes its spikes across rocks, and then uses the tips of its feelers to absorb the nutrients it finds within the stone.

Its spikes are harder than steel. This Pokémon crawls across rock walls by stabbing the spikes on its feelers into the stone.

HOW TO SAY IT: fer-AH-thorn
IMPERIAL HEIGHT: 3'03"
IMPERIAL WEIGHT: 242.5 lbs.
METRIC HEIGHT: 1.0 m
METRIC WEIGHT: 110.0 kg

POSSIBLE MOVES: Curse, Explosion, Flash Cannon, Gyro Ball, Harden, Ingrain, Iron Defense, Iron Head, Metal Claw, Pin Missile, Power Whip, Self-Destruct, Tackle

FERROSEED → FERROTHORN

FINNEON
Wing Fish Pokémon

REGIONS:
ALOLA
SINNOH

TYPE: WATER

When night falls, their pink patterns begin to shine. They're popular with divers, so there are resorts that feed them to keep them close.

It lures in prey with its shining tail fins. It stays near the surface during the day and moves to the depths when night falls.

HOW TO SAY IT: FINN-ee-on
IMPERIAL HEIGHT: 1'04"
IMPERIAL WEIGHT: 15.4 lbs.
METRIC HEIGHT: 0.4 m
METRIC WEIGHT: 7.0 kg

POSSIBLE MOVES: Pound, Water Gun, Attract, Rain Dance, Gust, Water Pulse, Captivate, Safeguard, Aqua Ring, Whirlpool, U-turn, Bounce, Silver Wind, Soak

FINNEON   LUMINEON

FLAAFFY
Wool Pokémon

REGIONS:
ALOLA
JOHTO
KALOS
(COASTAL)

TYPE: ELECTRIC

In the places on its body where fleece doesn't grow, its skin is rubbery and doesn't conduct electricity. Those spots are safe to touch.

It stores electricity in its fluffy fleece. If it stores up too much, it will start to go bald in those patches.

HOW TO SAY IT: FLAH-fee
IMPERIAL HEIGHT: 2'07"
IMPERIAL WEIGHT: 29.3 lbs.
METRIC HEIGHT: 0.8 m
METRIC WEIGHT: 13.3 kg

POSSIBLE MOVES: Tackle, Growl, Thunder Wave, Thunder Shock, Cotton Spore, Charge, Take Down, Electro Ball, Confuse Ray, Power Gem, Discharge, Cotton Guard, Signal Beam, Light Screen, Thunder

MAREEP   FLAAFFY   AMPHAROS   MEGA AMPHAROS

FLABÉBÉ
Single Bloom Pokémon

TYPE: FAIRY

It's not safe without the power of a flower, but it will keep traveling around until it finds one with the color and shape it wants.

Flabébé wears a crown made from pollen it's collected from its flower. The crown has hidden healing properties.

HOW TO SAY IT: flah-BAY-BAY
IMPERIAL HEIGHT: 0'04"
IMPERIAL WEIGHT: 0.2 lbs.
METRIC HEIGHT: 0.1 m
METRIC WEIGHT: 0.1 kg

POSSIBLE MOVES: Tackle, Vine Whip, Fairy Wind, Lucky Chant, Razor Leaf, Wish, Magical Leaf, Grassy Terrain, Petal Blizzard, Aromatherapy, Misty Terrain, Moonblast, Petal Dance, Solar Beam

FLABÉBÉ   FLOETTE   FLORGES

FLAPPLE

Apple Wing Pokémon

TYPE: GRASS-DRAGON

It ate a sour apple, and that induced its evolution. In its cheeks, it stores an acid capable of causing chemical burns.

It flies on wings of apple skin and spits a powerful acid. It can also change its shape into that of an apple.

HOW TO SAY IT: FLAP-puhl
IMPERIAL WEIGHT: 2.2 lbs.
IMPERIAL HEIGHT: 1'00"
METRIC HEIGHT: 0.3 m
METRIC WEIGHT: 1.0 kg

POSSIBLE MOVES: Acid Spray, Acrobatics, Astonish, Dragon Breath, Dragon Dance, Dragon Pulse, Dragon Rush, Fly, Grav Apple, Growth, Iron Defense, Leech Seed, Protect, Recycle, Twister, Wing Attack, Withdraw

APPLIN   FLAPPLE

Alternate Form:
GIGANTAMAX FLAPPLE

Under the influence of Gigantamax energy, it produces much more sweet nectar, and its shape has changed to resemble a giant apple.

If it stretches its neck, the strong aroma of its nectar pours out. The scent is so sickeningly sweet that one whiff makes other Pokémon faint.

IMPERIAL HEIGHT: 78'09"+
IMPERIAL WEIGHT: ????.? lbs.
METRIC HEIGHT: 24.0+ m
METRIC WEIGHT: ???.? kg

REGIONS:
ALOLA
GALAR
KALOS
(COASTAL)
KANTO

FLAREON
Flame Pokémon

TYPE: FIRE

Once it has stored up enough heat, this Pokémon's body temperature can reach up to 1,700 degrees Fahrenheit.

It stores some of the air it inhales in its internal flame pouch, which heats it to over 3,000 degrees Fahrenheit.

HOW TO SAY IT: FLAIR-ee-on
IMPERIAL HEIGHT: 2'11"
IMPERIAL WEIGHT: 55.1 lbs.
METRIC HEIGHT: 0.9 m
METRIC WEIGHT: 25.0 kg

POSSIBLE MOVES: Baby-Doll Eyes, Baton Pass, Bite, Charm, Copycat, Covet, Double-Edge, Ember, Fire Fang, Fire Spin, Flare Blitz, Growl, Helping Hand, Last Resort, Lava Plume, Quick Attack, Sand Attack, Scary Face, Smog, Swift, Tackle, Tail Whip, Take Down

EEVEE → FLAREON

FLETCHINDER
Ember Pokémon

TYPE: FIRE-FLYING

Fletchinder launches embers into the den of its prey. When the prey comes leaping out, Fletchinder's sharp talons finish it off.

Fletchinder are exceedingly territorial and aggressive. These Pokémon fight among themselves over feeding grounds.

HOW TO SAY IT: FLETCH-in-der
IMPERIAL HEIGHT: 2'04"
IMPERIAL WEIGHT: 35.3 lbs.
METRIC HEIGHT: 0.7 m
METRIC WEIGHT: 16.0 kg

POSSIBLE MOVES: Ember, Tackle, Growl, Quick Attack, Peck, Agility, Flail, Roost, Razor Wind, Natural Gift, Flame Charge, Acrobatics, Me First, Tailwind, Steel Wing

FLETCHLING → FLETCHINDER → TALONFLAME

FLETCHLING

Tiny Robin Pokémon

TYPE: NORMAL-FLYING

Its melodious cries are actually warnings. Fletchling will mercilessly peck at anything that enters its territory.

When this Pokémon gets excited, its body temperature increases sharply. If you touch a Fletchling with bare hands, you might get burned.

HOW TO SAY IT: FLETCH-ling
IMPERIAL HEIGHT: 1'00"
IMPERIAL WEIGHT: 3.7 lbs.
METRIC HEIGHT: 0.3 m
METRIC WEIGHT: 1.7 kg

POSSIBLE MOVES: Tackle, Growl, Quick Attack, Peck, Agility, Flail, Roost, Razor Wind, Natural Gift, Flame Charge, Acrobatics, Me First, Tailwind, Steel Wing

FLETCHLING   FLETCHINDER   TALONFLAME

FLOATZEL

Sea Weasel Pokémon

TYPE: WATER

It floats using its well-developed flotation sac. It assists in the rescues of drowning people.

Its flotation sac developed as a result of pursuing aquatic prey. It can double as a rubber raft.

HOW TO SAY IT: FLOAT-zul
IMPERIAL HEIGHT: 3'07"
IMPERIAL WEIGHT: 73.9 lbs.
METRIC HEIGHT: 1.1 m
METRIC WEIGHT: 33.5 kg

POSSIBLE MOVES: Ice Fang, Crunch, Sonic Boom, Growl, Water Sport, Quick Attack, Water Gun, Pursuit, Swift, Aqua Jet, Double Hit, Whirlpool, Razor Wind, Aqua Tail, Agility, Hydro Pump

BUIZEL   FLOATZEL

FLOETTE

Single Bloom Pokémon

TYPE: FAIRY

It raises flowers and uses them as weapons. The more gorgeous the blossom, the more power it contains.

It gives its own power to flowers, pouring its heart into caring for them. Floette never forgives anyone who messes up a flower bed.

HOW TO SAY IT: floh-ET
IMPERIAL HEIGHT: 0'08"
IMPERIAL WEIGHT: 2.0 lbs.
METRIC HEIGHT: 0.2 m
METRIC WEIGHT: 0.9 kg

POSSIBLE MOVES: Tackle, Vine Whip, Fairy Wind, Lucky Chant, Razor Leaf, Wish, Magical Leaf, Grassy Terrain, Petal Blizzard, Aromatherapy, Misty Terrain, Moonblast, Petal Dance, Solar Beam

FLABÉBÉ　　**FLOETTE**　　**FLORGES**

FLORGES

Garden Pokémon

TYPE: FAIRY

It controls the flowers it grows. The petal blizzards that Florges triggers are overwhelming in their beauty and power.

Its life can span several hundred years. It's said to devote its entire life to protecting gardens.

HOW TO SAY IT: FLORE-jess
IMPERIAL HEIGHT: 3'07"
IMPERIAL WEIGHT: 22.0 lbs.
METRIC HEIGHT: 1.1 m
METRIC WEIGHT: 10.0 kg

POSSIBLE MOVES: Disarming Voice, Lucky Chant, Wish, Magical Leaf, Flower Shield, Grass Knot, Grassy Terrain, Petal Blizzard, Misty Terrain

FLABÉBÉ　　**FLOETTE**　　**FLORGES**

FLYGON
Mystic Pokémon

REGIONS:
ALOLA
GALAR
HOENN
KALOS
(MOUNTAIN)

TYPE: GROUND-DRAGON

This Pokémon hides in the heart of sandstorms it creates and seldom appears where people can see it.

It is nicknamed the Desert Spirit because the flapping of its wings sounds like a woman singing.

HOW TO SAY IT: FLY-gon
IMPERIAL HEIGHT: 6'07"
IMPERIAL WEIGHT: 180.8 lbs.
METRIC HEIGHT: 2.0 m
METRIC WEIGHT: 82.0 kg

POSSIBLE MOVES: Astonish, Bite, Boomburst, Bug Buzz, Bulldoze, Crunch, Dig, Dragon Breath, Dragon Claw, Dragon Dance, Dragon Rush, Dragon Tail, Earth Power, Earthquake, Feint, Fissure, Laser Focus, Mud-Slap, Sand Attack, Sand Tomb, Sandstorm, Screech, Superpower, Supersonic, Uproar

TRAPINCH　　**VIBRAVA**　　**FLYGON**

FOMANTIS
Sickle Grass Pokémon

TYPE: GRASS

When bathed in sunlight, this Pokémon emits a pleasantly sweet scent, which causes bug Pokémon to gather around it.

During the day, Fomantis basks in sunlight and sleeps peacefully. It wakes and moves around at night.

HOW TO SAY IT: fo-MAN-tis
IMPERIAL HEIGHT: 1'00"
IMPERIAL WEIGHT: 3.3 lbs.
METRIC HEIGHT: 0.3 m
METRIC WEIGHT: 1.5 kg

POSSIBLE MOVES: Fury Cutter, Leafage, Razor Leaf, Growth, Ingrain, Leaf Blade, Synthesis, Slash, Sweet Scent, Solar Beam, Sunny Day

FOMANTIS　　**LURANTIS**

FOONGUS
Mushroom Pokémon

TYPE: GRASS-POISON

No one knows what the Poké Ball-like pattern on Foongus means or why Foongus has it.

The spores released from this Pokémon's hands are highly poisonous, but when thoroughly dried, the spores can be used as stomach medicine.

HOW TO SAY IT: FOON-gus **METRIC HEIGHT:** 0.2 m
IMPERIAL HEIGHT: 0'08" **METRIC WEIGHT:** 1.0 kg
IMPERIAL WEIGHT: 2.2 lbs.

POSSIBLE MOVES: Absorb, Growth, Astonish, Bide, Mega Drain, Ingrain, Feint Attack, Sweet Scent, Giga Drain, Toxic, Synthesis, Clear Smog, Solar Beam, Rage Powder, Spore

FOONGUS   **AMOONGUSS**

FORRETRESS
Bagworm Pokémon

TYPE: BUG-STEEL

When something approaches it, it fires off fragments of its steel shell in attack. This is not a conscious action but a conditioned reflex.

In the moment that it gulps down its prey, the inside of its shell is exposed, but to this day, no one has ever seen that sight.

HOW TO SAY IT: FOR-it-tress **METRIC HEIGHT:** 1.2 m
IMPERIAL HEIGHT: 3'11" **METRIC WEIGHT:** 125.8 kg
IMPERIAL WEIGHT: 277.3 lbs.

POSSIBLE MOVES: Toxic Spikes, Tackle, Protect, Self-Destruct, Bug Bite, Take Down, Rapid Spin, Bide, Natural Gift, Spikes, Mirror Shot, Autotomize, Payback, Explosion, Iron Defense, Gyro Ball, Double-Edge, Magnet Rise, Zap Cannon, Heavy Slam

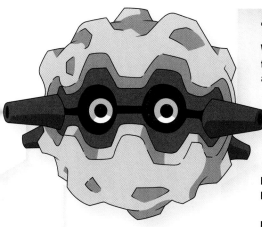

PINECO   **FORRETRESS**

175

FRAXURE

Axe Jaw Pokémon

TYPE: DRAGON

After battle, this Pokémon carefully sharpens its tusks on river rocks. It needs to take care of its tusks—if one breaks, it will never grow back.

Its skin is as hard as a suit of armor. Fraxure's favorite strategy is to tackle its opponents, stabbing them with its tusks at the same time.

HOW TO SAY IT: FRAK-shur   **METRIC HEIGHT:** 1.0 m
IMPERIAL HEIGHT: 3'03"   **METRIC WEIGHT:** 36.0 kg
IMPERIAL WEIGHT: 79.4 lbs.

POSSIBLE MOVES: Assurance, Bite, Crunch, Dragon Claw, Dragon Dance, Dragon Pulse, Dual Chop, False Swipe, Giga Impact, Guillotine, Laser Focus, Leer, Outrage, Scary Face, Scratch, Slash, Swords Dance, Taunt

AXEW   FRAXURE   HAXORUS

FRILLISH

Floating Pokémon

TYPE: WATER-GHOST

It envelops its prey in its veil-like arms and draws it down to the deeps, five miles below the ocean's surface.

Legend has it that the residents of a sunken ancient city changed into these Pokémon.

HOW TO SAY IT: FRIL-lish   **METRIC HEIGHT:** 1.2 m
IMPERIAL HEIGHT: 3'11"   **METRIC WEIGHT:** 33.0 kg
IMPERIAL WEIGHT: 72.8 lbs.

POSSIBLE MOVES: Absorb, Brine, Destiny Bond, Hex, Hydro Pump, Night Shade, Poison Sting, Rain Dance, Recover, Shadow Ball, Water Gun, Water Pulse, Water Spout, Whirlpool

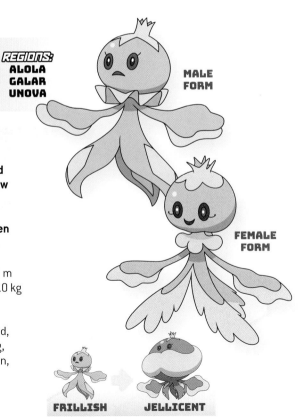

MALE FORM

FEMALE FORM

FRILLISH   JELLICENT

FROAKIE

Bubble Frog Pokémon

TYPE: WATER

It secretes flexible bubbles from its chest and back. The bubbles reduce the damage it would otherwise take when attacked.

It protects its skin by covering its body in delicate bubbles. Beneath its happy-go-lucky air, it keeps a watchful eye on its surroundings.

HOW TO SAY IT: FRO-kee **METRIC HEIGHT:** 0.3 m
IMPERIAL HEIGHT: 1'00" **METRIC WEIGHT:** 7.0 kg
IMPERIAL WEIGHT: 15.4 lbs.

POSSIBLE MOVES: Pound, Growl, Bubble, Quick Attack, Lick, Water Pulse, Smokescreen, Round, Fling, Smack Down, Substitute, Bounce, Double Team, Hydro Pump

FROAKIE   **FROGADIER**   **GRENINJA**

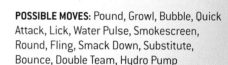

FROGADIER

Bubble Frog Pokémon

TYPE: WATER

It can throw bubble-covered pebbles with precise control, hitting empty cans up to a hundred feet away.

Its swiftness is unparalleled. It can scale a tower of more than 2,000 feet in a minute's time.

HOW TO SAY IT: FROG-uh-deer **METRIC HEIGHT:** 0.6 m
IMPERIAL HEIGHT: 2'00" **METRIC WEIGHT:** 10.9 kg
IMPERIAL WEIGHT: 24.0 lbs.

POSSIBLE MOVES: Pound, Growl, Bubble, Quick Attack, Lick, Water Pulse, Smokescreen, Round, Fling, Smack Down, Substitute, Bounce, Double Team, Hydro Pump

FROAKIE   **FROGADIER**   **GRENINJA**

FROSLASS

Snow Land Pokémon

REGIONS: ALOLA GALAR SINNOH

TYPE: ICE-GHOST

After a woman met her end on a snowy mountain, her regrets lingered on. From them, this Pokémon was born. Its favorite food is frozen souls.

It spits out cold air of nearly −60 degrees Fahrenheit to freeze its quarry. It brings frozen prey back to its lair and neatly lines them up.

HOW TO SAY IT: FROS-lass
IMPERIAL HEIGHT: 4'03"
IMPERIAL WEIGHT: 58.6 lbs.
METRIC HEIGHT: 1.3 m
METRIC WEIGHT: 26.6 kg

POSSIBLE MOVES: Astonish, Aurora Veil, Bite, Blizzard, Confuse Ray, Crunch, Destiny Bond, Double Team, Draining Kiss, Frost Breath, Hail, Headbutt, Hex, Ice Fang, Ice Shard, Icy Wind, Leer, Powder Snow, Protect, Shadow Ball, Will-O-Wisp

SNORUNT **FROSLASS**

FROSMOTH

Frost Moth Pokémon

REGION: GALAR

TYPE: ICE-BUG

Icy scales fall from its wings like snow as it flies over fields and mountains. The temperature of its wings is less than −290 degrees Fahrenheit.

It shows no mercy to any who desecrate fields and mountains. It will fly around on its icy wings, causing a blizzard to chase offenders away.

HOW TO SAY IT: FRAHS-mahth
IMPERIAL HEIGHT: 4'03"
IMPERIAL WEIGHT: 92.6 lbs.
METRIC HEIGHT: 1.3 m
METRIC WEIGHT: 42.0 kg

POSSIBLE MOVES: Attract, Aurora Beam, Aurora Veil, Blizzard, Bug Buzz, Defog, Feather Dance, Hail, Helping Hand, Icy Wind, Infestation, Mist, Powder Snow, Quiver Dance, Struggle Bug, Stun Spore, Tailwind, Wide Guard

SNOM **FROSMOTH**

FURFROU

Poodle Pokémon

TYPE: NORMAL

There was an era when aristocrats would compete to see who could trim their Furfrou's fur into the most exquisite style.

Left alone, its fur will grow longer and longer, but it will only allow someone it trusts to cut it.

HOW TO SAY IT: FUR-froo
IMPERIAL HEIGHT: 3'11"
IMPERIAL WEIGHT: 61.7 lbs.
METRIC HEIGHT: 1.2 m
METRIC WEIGHT: 28.0 kg

POSSIBLE MOVES: Tackle, Growl, Sand Attack, Baby-Doll Eyes, Headbutt, Tail Whip, Bite, Odor Sleuth, Retaliate, Take Down, Charm, Sucker Punch, Cotton Guard

DOES NOT EVOLVE

FURRET

Long Body Pokémon

TYPE: NORMAL

Furret has a very slim build. When under attack, it can slickly squirm through narrow spaces and get away. In spite of its short limbs, this Pokémon is very nimble and fleet.

HOW TO SAY IT: FUR-ret
IMPERIAL HEIGHT: 5'11"
IMPERIAL WEIGHT: 71.6 lbs.
METRIC HEIGHT: 1.8 m
METRIC WEIGHT: 32.5 kg

POSSIBLE MOVES: Agility, Coil, Scratch, Foresight, Defense Curl, Quick Attack, Fury Swipes, Helping Hand, Follow Me, Slam, Rest, Sucker Punch, Amnesia, Baton Pass, Me First, Hyper Voice

SENTRET   FURRET

GABITE
Cave Pokémon

TYPE: DRAGON-GROUND

It loves shiny things. When it finds a Sableye trying to catch a Carbink, Gabite becomes furiously angry and attacks the Sableye.

It sheds its skin and gradually grows larger. Its scales can be ground into a powder and used as raw materials for traditional medicine.

HOW TO SAY IT: gab-BITE
IMPERIAL HEIGHT: 4'07"
IMPERIAL WEIGHT: 123.5 lbs.
METRIC HEIGHT: 1.4 m
METRIC WEIGHT: 56.0 kg

POSSIBLE MOVES: Dual Chop, Tackle, Sand Attack, Dragon Rage, Sandstorm, Take Down, Sand Tomb, Slash, Dragon Claw, Dig, Dragon Rush

GIBLE → GABITE → GARCHOMP → MEGA GARCHOMP

GALLADE
Blade Pokémon

TYPE: PSYCHIC-FIGHTING

True to its honorable-warrior image, it uses the blades on its elbows only in defense of something or someone.

Sharply attuned to others' wishes for help, this Pokémon seeks out those in need and aids them in battle.

HOW TO SAY IT: guh-LADE
IMPERIAL HEIGHT: 5'03"
IMPERIAL WEIGHT: 114.6 lbs.
METRIC HEIGHT: 1.6 m
METRIC WEIGHT: 52.0 kg

POSSIBLE MOVES: Aerial Ace, Calm Mind, Charm, Close Combat, Confusion, Disarming Voice, Double Team, Draining Kiss, Dream Eater, False Swipe, Feint, Fury Cutter, Future Sight, Growl, Heal Pulse, Helping Hand, Hypnosis, Imprison, Leer, Life Dew, Night Slash, Protect, Psybeam, Psychic, Psycho Cut, Quick Guard, Slash, Swords Dance, Teleport, Wide Guard

MEGA GALLADE
Blade Pokémon

TYPE: PSYCHIC-FIGHTING

IMPERIAL HEIGHT: 5'03"
IMPERIAL WEIGHT: 124.3 lbs.
METRIC HEIGHT: 1.6 m
METRIC WEIGHT: 56.4 kg

RALTS → KIRLIA → GALLADE → MEGA GALLADE

GALVANTULA

EleSpider Pokémon

TYPE: BUG-ELECTRIC

It launches electrified fur from its abdomen as its means of attack. Opponents hit by the fur could be in for three full days and nights of paralysis.

It lays traps of electrified threads near the nests of bird Pokémon, aiming to snare chicks that are not yet good at flying.

HOW TO SAY IT: gal-VAN-choo-luh
IMPERIAL HEIGHT: 2'07"
IMPERIAL WEIGHT: 31.5 lbs.
METRIC HEIGHT: 0.8 m
METRIC WEIGHT: 14.3 kg

POSSIBLE MOVES: Absorb, Agility, Bug Bite, Bug Buzz, Discharge, Electro Ball, Electroweb, Fury Cutter, Gastro Acid, Screech, Slash, Sticky Web, String Shot, Sucker Punch, Thunder Wave

JOLTIK → GALVANTULA

TYPE: POISON

This Pokémon eats trash, which turns into poison inside its body. The main component of the poison depends on what sort of trash was eaten.

The toxic liquid it launches from its right arm is so virulent that it can kill a weakened creature instantly.

HOW TO SAY IT: gar-BOH-dur
IMPERIAL HEIGHT: 6'03"
IMPERIAL WEIGHT: 236.6 lbs.
METRIC HEIGHT: 1.9 m
METRIC WEIGHT: 107.3 kg

POSSIBLE MOVES: Acid Spray, Amnesia, Belch, Body Slam, Clear Smog, Explosion, Gunk Shot, Metal Claw, Pain Split, Poison Gas, Pound, Recycle, Sludge, Sludge Bomb, Stockpile, Swallow, Take Down, Toxic, Toxic Spikes

REGIONS:
ALOLA
GALAR
KALOS
(MOUNTAIN)
UNOVA

GARBODOR
Trash Heap Pokémon

TRUBBISH   **GARBODOR**

Alternate Form:
GIGANTAMAX GARBODOR

Due to Gigantamax energy, this Pokémon's toxic gas has become much thicker, congealing into masses shaped like discarded toys.

It sprays toxic gas from its mouth and fingers. If the gas engulfs you, the toxins will seep in all the way down to your bones.

IMPERIAL HEIGHT: 68'11"+
IMPERIAL WEIGHT: ????.? lbs.
METRIC HEIGHT: 21.0+ m
METRIC WEIGHT: ???.? kg

GARCHOMP

Mach Pokémon

TYPE: DRAGON-GROUND

It flies at the speed of sound while searching for prey, and it has midair battles with Salamence as the two compete for food.

Its fine scales don't just reduce wind resistance—their sharp edges also cause injury to any opponent who attacks it.

HOW TO SAY IT: GAR-chomp
IMPERIAL HEIGHT: 6'03"
IMPERIAL WEIGHT: 209.4 lbs.
METRIC HEIGHT: 1.9 m
METRIC WEIGHT: 95.0 kg

POSSIBLE MOVES: Crunch, Dual Chop, Fire Fang, Tackle, Sand Attack, Dragon Rage, Sandstorm, Take Down, Sand Tomb, Slash, Dragon Claw, Dig, Dragon Rush

MEGA GARCHOMP

Mach Pokémon

TYPE: DRAGON-GROUND

IMPERIAL HEIGHT: 6'03"
IMPERIAL WEIGHT: 209.4 lbs.
METRIC HEIGHT: 1.9 m
METRIC WEIGHT: 95.0 kg

GIBLE

GABITE

GARCHOMP

MEGA GARCHOMP

TYPE: PSYCHIC-FAIRY

It has the power to predict the future. Its power peaks when it is protecting its Trainer.

To protect its Trainer, it will expend all its psychic power to create a small black hole.

HOW TO SAY IT: GAR-dee-VWAR
IMPERIAL HEIGHT: 5'03"
IMPERIAL WEIGHT: 106.7 lbs.
METRIC HEIGHT: 1.6 m
METRIC WEIGHT: 48.4 kg

POSSIBLE MOVES: Calm Mind, Charm, Confusion, Dazzling Gleam, Disarming Voice, Double Team, Draining Kiss, Dream Eater, Future Sight, Growl, Heal Pulse, Healing Wish, Hypnosis, Life Dew, Misty Terrain, Moonblast, Psybeam, Psychic, Teleport, Wish

GARDEVOIR
Embrace Pokémon

MEGA GARDEVOIR
Embrace Pokémon

TYPE: PSYCHIC-FAIRY

IMPERIAL HEIGHT: 5'03"
IMPERIAL WEIGHT: 106.7 lbs.
METRIC HEIGHT: 1.6 m
METRIC WEIGHT: 48.4 kg

RALTS ➡ **KIRLIA** ➡ **GARDEVOIR** ➡ **MEGA GARDEVOIR**

GASTLY
Gas Pokémon

REGIONS:
ALOLA
GALAR
KALOS
(MOUNTAIN)
KANTO

TYPE: GHOST-POISON

Born from gases, anyone would faint if engulfed by its gaseous body, which contains poison.

With its gas-like body, it can sneak into any place it desires. However, it can be blown away by wind.

HOW TO SAY IT: GAST-lee
IMPERIAL HEIGHT: 4'03"
IMPERIAL WEIGHT: 0.2 lbs.
METRIC HEIGHT: 1.3 m
METRIC WEIGHT: 0.1 kg

POSSIBLE MOVES: Confuse Ray, Curse, Dark Pulse, Destiny Bond, Dream Eater, Hex, Hypnosis, Lick, Mean Look, Night Shade, Payback, Shadow Ball, Spite, Sucker Punch

GASTLY   **HAUNTER**   **GENGAR**   **MEGA GENGAR**

GASTRODON (EAST SEA)
Sea Slug Pokémon

TYPE: WATER-GROUND

It secretes a purple fluid to deter enemies. This fluid isn't poisonous—instead, it's super sticky, and once it sticks, it's very hard to unstick.

Its body is covered in a sticky slime. It's very susceptible to dehydration, so it can't spend too much time on land.

HOW TO SAY IT: GAS-stroh-don
IMPERIAL HEIGHT: 2'11"
IMPERIAL WEIGHT: 65.9 lbs.
METRIC HEIGHT: 0.9 m
METRIC WEIGHT: 29.9 kg

POSSIBLE MOVES: Ancient Power, Body Slam, Earth Power, Harden, Memento, Muddy Water, Mud-Slap, Rain Dance, Recover, Water Gun, Water Pulse

SHELLOS   **GASTRODON**
(EAST SEA)   **(EAST SEA)**

GASTRODON (WEST SEA)
Sea Slug Pokémon

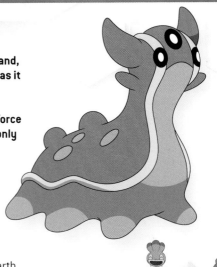

TYPE: WATER-GROUND

Its search for food sometimes leads it onto land, where it leaves behind a sticky trail of slime as it passes through.

The softness of its body helps disperse the force of impacts, so although its body is uncommonly squishy, it's also surprisingly resilient.

HOW TO SAY IT: GAS-stroh-don
IMPERIAL HEIGHT: 2'11"
IMPERIAL WEIGHT: 65.9 lbs.
METRIC HEIGHT: 0.9 m
METRIC WEIGHT: 29.9 kg

POSSIBLE MOVES: Ancient Power, Body Slam, Earth Power, Harden, Memento, Muddy Water, Mud-Slap, Rain Dance, Recover, Water Gun, Water Pulse

SHELLOS
(WEST SEA)

GASTRODON
(WEST SEA)

MYTHICAL POKÉMON

GENESECT
Paleozoic Pokémon

TYPE: BUG-STEEL

This ancient bug Pokémon was altered by Team Plasma. They upgraded the cannon on its back.

This Pokémon existed 300 million years ago. Team Plasma altered it and attached a cannon to its back.

HOW TO SAY IT: JEN-uh-sekt
IMPERIAL HEIGHT: 4'11"
IMPERIAL WEIGHT: 181.9 lbs.
METRIC HEIGHT: 1.5 m
METRIC WEIGHT: 82.5 kg

POSSIBLE MOVES: Fell Stinger, Techno Blast, Quick Attack, Magnet Rise, Metal Claw, Screech, Fury Cutter, Lock-On, Flame Charge, Magnet Bomb, Slash, Metal Sound, Signal Beam, Tri Attack, X-Scissor, Bug Buzz, Simple Beam, Zap Cannon, Hyper Beam, Self-Destruct

DOES NOT EVOLVE

GENGAR
Shadow Pokémon

REGIONS:
ALOLA
GALAR
KALOS
(MOUNTAIN)
KANTO

TYPE: GHOST-POISON

On the night of a full moon, if shadows move on their own and laugh, it must be Gengar's doing.

It is said to emerge from darkness to steal the lives of those who become lost in mountains.

HOW TO SAY IT: GHEN-gar
IMPERIAL HEIGHT: 4'11"
IMPERIAL WEIGHT: 89.3 lbs.
METRIC HEIGHT: 1.5 m
METRIC WEIGHT: 40.5 kg

POSSIBLE MOVES: Confuse Ray, Curse, Dark Pulse, Destiny Bond, Dream Eater, Hex, Hypnosis, Lick, Mean Look, Night Shade, Payback, Perish Song, Reflect Type, Shadow Ball, Shadow Punch, Spite, Sucker Punch

GASTLY   HAUNTER   GENGAR   MEGA GENGAR

MEGA GENGAR
Shadow Pokémon

TYPE: GHOST-POISON

IMPERIAL HEIGHT: 4'07"
IMPERIAL WEIGHT: 89.3 lbs.
METRIC HEIGHT: 1.4 m
METRIC WEIGHT: 40.5 kg

Alternate Form:
GIGANTAMAX GENGAR

Rumor has it that its gigantic mouth leads not into its body, filled with cursed energy, but instead directly to the afterlife.

It lays traps, hoping to steal the lives of those it catches. If you stand in front of its mouth, you'll hear your loved ones' voices calling out to you.

IMPERIAL HEIGHT: 65'07"+
IMPERIAL WEIGHT: ????.? lbs.
METRIC HEIGHT: 20.0 m+
METRIC WEIGHT: ???.? kg

GEODUDE
Rock Pokémon

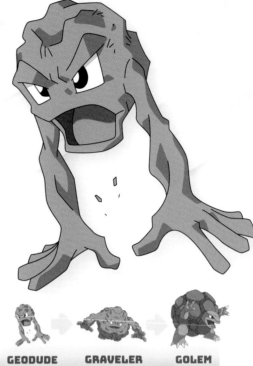

TYPE: ROCK-GROUND

Commonly found near mountain trails and the like. If you step on one by accident, it gets angry.

HOW TO SAY IT: JEE-oh-dude
IMPERIAL HEIGHT: 1'04"
IMPERIAL WEIGHT: 44.1 lbs.
METRIC HEIGHT: 0.4 m
METRIC WEIGHT: 20.0 kg

POSSIBLE MOVES: Tackle, Defense Curl, Mud Sport, Rock Polish, Rollout, Magnitude, Rock Throw, Rock Blast, Smack Down, Self-Destruct, Bulldoze, Stealth Rock, Earthquake, Explosion, Double-Edge, Stone Edge

GEODUDE   GRAVELER   GOLEM

ALOLAN GEODUDE
Rock Pokémon

TYPE: ROCK-ELECTRIC

Its stone head is imbued with electricity and magnetism. If you carelessly step on one, you'll be in for a painful shock.

HOW TO SAY IT: JEE-oh-dude
IMPERIAL HEIGHT: 1'04"
IMPERIAL WEIGHT: 44.8 lbs.
METRIC HEIGHT: 0.4 m
METRIC WEIGHT: 20.3 kg

POSSIBLE MOVES: Tackle, Defense Curl, Charge, Rock Polish, Rollout, Spark, Rock Throw, Smack Down, Thunder Punch, Self-Destruct, Stealth Rock, Rock Blast, Discharge, Explosion, Double-Edge, Stone Edge

ALOLAN GEODUDE   ALOLAN GRAVELER   ALOLAN GOLEM

TYPE: DRAGON-GROUND

GIBLE
Land Shark Pokémon

It reacts to anything that moves—flies right at it and bites it. Sometimes it injures itself, but it doesn't care too much.

Its original home is an area much hotter than Alola. If you're planning to live with one, your heating bill will soar.

HOW TO SAY IT: GIB-bull
IMPERIAL HEIGHT: 2'04"
IMPERIAL WEIGHT: 45.2 lbs.
METRIC HEIGHT: 0.7 m
METRIC WEIGHT: 20.5 kg

POSSIBLE MOVES: Tackle, Sand Attack, Dragon Rage, Sandstorm, Take Down, Sand Tomb, Slash, Dragon Claw, Dig, Dragon Rush

GIBLE ➡ **GABITE** ➡ **GARCHOMP** ➡ **MEGA GARCHOMP**

TYPE: ROCK

REGIONS:
ALOLA
GALAR
KALOS
(COASTAL)
UNOVA

GIGALITH
Compressed Pokémon

This hardy Pokémon can often be found on construction sites and in mines, working alongside people and Copperajah.

Although its energy blasts can blow away a dump truck, they have a limitation— they can only be fired when the sun is out.

HOW TO SAY IT: GIH-gah-lith
IMPERIAL HEIGHT: 5'07"
IMPERIAL WEIGHT: 573.2 lbs.
METRIC HEIGHT: 1.7 m
METRIC WEIGHT: 260.0 kg

POSSIBLE MOVES: Explosion, Harden, Headbutt, Iron Defense, Mud-Slap, Power Gem, Rock Blast, Rock Slide, Sand Attack, Sandstorm, Smack Down, Stealth Rock, Stone Edge, Tackle

ROGGENROLA ➡ **BOLDORE** ➡ **GIGALITH**

GIRAFARIG

Long Neck Pokémon

TYPE: NORMAL-PSYCHIC

Girafarig's rear head also has a brain, but it is small. The rear head attacks in response to smells and sounds. Approaching this Pokémon from behind can cause the rear head to suddenly lash out and bite.

HOW TO SAY IT: jir-RAF-uh-rig
IMPERIAL HEIGHT: 4'11"
IMPERIAL WEIGHT: 91.5 lbs.
METRIC HEIGHT: 1.5 m
METRIC WEIGHT: 41.5 kg

POSSIBLE MOVES: Power Swap, Guard Swap, Astonish, Tackle, Growl, Confusion, Odor Sleuth, Stomp, Agility, Psybeam, Baton Pass, Assurance, Double Hit, Psychic, Zen Headbutt, Crunch, Nasty Plot

DOES NOT EVOLVE

GIRATINA ALTERED FORME

Renegade Pokémon

TYPE: GHOST-DRAGON

This Pokémon is said to live in a world on the reverse side of ours, where common knowledge is distorted and strange.

It was banished for its violence. It silently gazed upon the old world from the Distortion World.

HOW TO SAY IT: geer-ah-TEE-na
IMPERIAL HEIGHT: 14'09"
IMPERIAL WEIGHT: 1,653.5 lbs.
METRIC HEIGHT: 4.5 m
METRIC WEIGHT: 750.0 kg

POSSIBLE MOVES: Dragon Breath, Scary Face, Ominous Wind, Ancient Power, Slash, Shadow Sneak, Destiny Bond, Dragon Claw, Earth Power, Aura Sphere, Shadow Claw, Shadow Force, Hex

GIRATINA ORIGIN FORME

Renegade Pokémon

TYPE: GHOST-DRAGON

IMPERIAL HEIGHT: 22'08"
IMPERIAL WEIGHT: 1,443.0 lbs.
METRIC HEIGHT: 6.9 m
METRIC WEIGHT: 650.0 kg

DOES NOT EVOLVE

GLACEON
Fresh Snow Pokémon

REGIONS:
ALOLA
GALAR
KALOS
(COASTAL)
SINNOH

TYPE: ICE

Any who become captivated by the beauty of the snowfall that Glaceon creates will be frozen before they know it.

The coldness emanating from Glaceon causes powdery snow to form, making it quite a popular Pokémon at ski resorts.

HOW TO SAY IT: GLAY-cee-on
IMPERIAL HEIGHT: 2'07"
IMPERIAL WEIGHT: 57.1 lbs.
METRIC HEIGHT: 0.8 m
METRIC WEIGHT: 25.9 kg

POSSIBLE MOVES: Baby-Doll Eyes, Baton Pass, Bite, Blizzard, Charm, Copycat, Covet, Double-Edge, Freeze-Dry, Growl, Hail, Helping Hand, Ice Fang, Ice Shard, Icy Wind, Last Resort, Mirror Coat, Quick Attack, Sand Attack, Swift, Tackle, Tail Whip, Take Down

EEVEE ➡ GLACEON

194

GLALIE
Face Pokémon

TYPE: ICE

It has a body of ice that won't melt, even with fire. It can instantly freeze moisture in the atmosphere.

It can instantly freeze moisture in the atmosphere. It uses this power to freeze its foes.

HOW TO SAY IT: GLAY-lee
IMPERIAL HEIGHT: 4'11"
IMPERIAL WEIGHT: 565.5 lbs.
METRIC HEIGHT: 1.5 m
METRIC WEIGHT: 256.5 kg

POSSIBLE MOVES: Astonish, Bite, Blizzard, Crunch, Double Team, Freeze-Dry, Frost Breath, Hail, Headbutt, Ice Fang, Ice Shard, Icy Wind, Leer, Powder Snow, Protect, Sheer Cold

MEGA GLALIE
Face Pokémon

TYPE: ICE

IMPERIAL HEIGHT: 6'11"
IMPERIAL WEIGHT: 772.1 lbs.
METRIC HEIGHT: 2.1 m
METRIC WEIGHT: 350.2 kg

SNORUNT　　**GLALIE**　　**MEGA GLALIE**

GLAMEOW

Catty Pokémon

TYPE: NORMAL

It claws if displeased and purrs when affectionate. Its fickleness is very popular among some.

When it's happy, Glameow demonstrates beautiful movements of its tail, like a dancing ribbon.

HOW TO SAY IT: GLAM-meow
IMPERIAL HEIGHT: 1'08"
IMPERIAL WEIGHT: 8.6 lbs.
METRIC HEIGHT: 0.5 m
METRIC WEIGHT: 3.9 kg

POSSIBLE MOVES: Fake Out, Scratch, Growl, Hypnosis, Feint Attack, Fury Swipes, Charm, Assist, Captivate, Slash, Sucker Punch, Attract, Hone Claws, Play Rough

GLAMEOW   PURUGLY

GLIGAR

Fly Scorpion Pokémon

TYPE: GROUND-FLYING

Gligar glides through the air without a sound as if it were sliding. This Pokémon hangs on to the face of its foe using its clawed hind legs
and the large pincers on its forelegs, then injects the prey with its poison barb.

HOW TO SAY IT: GLY-gar
IMPERIAL HEIGHT: 3'07"
IMPERIAL WEIGHT: 142.9 lbs.
METRIC HEIGHT: 1.1 m
METRIC WEIGHT: 64.8 kg

POSSIBLE MOVES: Poison Sting, Sand Attack, Harden, Knock Off, Quick Attack, Fury Cutter, Feint Attack, Acrobatics, Slash, U-turn, Screech, X-Scissor, Sky Uppercut, Swords Dance, Guillotine

GLIGAR   GLISCOR

GLISCOR
Fang Scorpion Pokémon

TYPE: GROUND-FLYING

It observes prey while hanging inverted from branches. When the chance presents itself, it swoops!

Its flight is soundless. It uses its lengthy tail to carry off its prey . . . Then its elongated fangs do the rest.

HOW TO SAY IT: GLY-score
IMPERIAL HEIGHT: 6'07"
IMPERIAL WEIGHT: 93.7 lbs.
METRIC HEIGHT: 2.0 m
METRIC WEIGHT: 42.5 kg

POSSIBLE MOVES: Guillotine, Thunder Fang, Ice Fang, Fire Fang, Poison Jab, Sand Attack, Harden, Knock Off, Quick Attack, Fury Cutter, Feint Attack, Acrobatics, Night Slash, U-turn, Screech, X-Scissor, Sky Uppercut, Swords Dance

GLIGAR   GLISCOR

TYPE: GRASS-POISON

Its pistils exude an incredibly foul odor. The horrid stench can cause fainting at a distance of 1.25 miles.

What appears to be drool is actually sweet honey. It is very sticky and clings stubbornly if touched.

HOW TO SAY IT: GLOOM
IMPERIAL HEIGHT: 2'07"
IMPERIAL WEIGHT: 19.0 lbs.
METRIC HEIGHT: 0.8 m
METRIC WEIGHT: 8.6 kg

POSSIBLE MOVES: Absorb, Acid, Giga Drain, Grassy Terrain, Growth, Mega Drain, Moonblast, Moonlight, Petal Dance, Poison Powder, Sleep Powder, Stun Spore, Sweet Scent, Toxic

GLOOM
Weed Pokémon

VILEPLUME

BELLOSSOM

ODDISH   GLOOM

GOGOAT

Mount Pokémon

TYPE: GRASS

It can tell how its Trainer is feeling by subtle shifts in the grip on its horns. This empathic sense lets them run as if one being.

They inhabit mountainous regions. The leader of the herd is decided by a battle of clashing horns.

HOW TO SAY IT: GO-goat
IMPERIAL HEIGHT: 5'07"
IMPERIAL WEIGHT: 200.6 lbs.
METRIC HEIGHT: 1.7 m
METRIC WEIGHT: 91.0 kg

POSSIBLE MOVES: Aerial Ace, Earthquake, Tackle, Growth, Vine Whip, Tail Whip, Leech Seed, Razor Leaf, Synthesis, Take Down, Bulldoze, Seed Bomb, Bulk Up, Double-Edge, Horn Leaf, Leaf Blade, Milk Drink

SKIDDO   GOGOAT

GOLBAT

Bat Pokémon

TYPE: POISON-FLYING

It attacks in a stealthy manner, without warning. Its sharp fangs are used to bite and to suck blood.

HOW TO SAY IT: GOHL-bat
IMPERIAL HEIGHT: 5'03"
IMPERIAL WEIGHT: 121.3 lbs.
METRIC HEIGHT: 1.6 m
METRIC WEIGHT: 55.0 kg

POSSIBLE MOVES: Screech, Absorb, Supersonic, Astonish, Bite, Wing Attack, Confuse Ray, Air Cutter, Swift, Poison Fang, Mean Look, Leech Life, Haze, Venoshock, Air Slash, Quick Guard

ZUBAT   GOLBAT   CROBAT

TYPE: WATER

Its dorsal, pectoral, and tail fins wave elegantly in water. That is why it is known as the Water Dancer.

Its dorsal and pectoral fins are strongly developed like muscles. It can swim at a speed of five knots.

HOW TO SAY IT: GOL-deen
IMPERIAL HEIGHT: 2'00"
IMPERIAL WEIGHT: 33.1 lbs.
METRIC HEIGHT: 0.6 m
METRIC WEIGHT: 15.0 kg

POSSIBLE MOVES: Agility, Aqua Ring, Flail, Horn Attack, Horn Drill, Megahorn, Peck, Soak, Supersonic, Tail Whip, Water Pulse, Waterfall

REGIONS:
ALOLA
GALAR
KALOS
(CENTRAL)
KANTO

GOLDEEN
Goldfish Pokémon

GOLDEEN → SEAKING

TYPE: WATER

This Pokémon lives in gently flowing rivers. It paddles through the water with its long limbs, putting its graceful swimming skills on display.

Old tales tell of Golduck punishing those that defiled its river. The guilty were dragged into the water and taken away.

HOW TO SAY IT: GOL-duck
IMPERIAL HEIGHT: 5'07"
IMPERIAL WEIGHT: 168.9 lbs.
METRIC HEIGHT: 1.7 m
METRIC WEIGHT: 76.6 kg

POSSIBLE MOVES: Me First, Aqua Jet, Water Sport, Scratch, Tail Whip, Water Gun, Confusion, Fury Swipes, Water Pulse, Disable, Screech, Zen Headbutt, Aqua Tail, Soak, Psych Up, Amnesia, Hydro Pump, Wonder Room

REGIONS:
ALOLA
KALOS
(CENTRAL)
KANTO

GOLDUCK
Duck Pokémon

PSYDUCK → GOLDUCK

GOLEM

Megaton Pokémon

TYPE: ROCK-GROUND

Once it sheds its skin, its body turns tender and whitish. Its hide hardens when it's exposed to air.

HOW TO SAY IT: GO-lum
IMPERIAL HEIGHT: 4'07"
IMPERIAL WEIGHT: 661.4 lbs.
METRIC HEIGHT: 1.4 m
METRIC WEIGHT: 300.0 kg

POSSIBLE MOVES: Heavy Slam, Tackle, Defense Curl, Mud Sport, Rock Polish, Steamroller, Magnitude, Rock Throw, Rock Blast, Smack Down, Self-Destruct, Bulldoze, Stealth Rock, Earthquake, Explosion, Double-Edge, Stone Edge

GEODUDE   GRAVELER   GOLEM

ALOLAN GOLEM

Megaton Pokémon

REGION:
ALOLA

TYPE: ROCK-ELECTRIC

It uses magnetism to accelerate and fire off rocks tinged with electricity. Even if it doesn't score a direct hit, the jolt of electricity will do the job.

HOW TO SAY IT: GO-lum
IMPERIAL HEIGHT: 5'07"
IMPERIAL WEIGHT: 696.7 lbs.
METRIC HEIGHT: 1.7 m
METRIC WEIGHT: 316.0 kg

POSSIBLE MOVES: Heavy Slam, Tackle, Defense Curl, Charge, Rock Polish, Steamroller, Spark, Rock Throw, Smack Down, Thunder Punch, Self-Destruct, Stealth Rock, Rock Blast, Discharge, Explosion, Double-Edge, Stone Edge

ALOLAN
GEODUDE

ALOLAN
GRAVELER

ALOLAN
GOLEM

REGIONS:
ALOLA
GALAR
KALOS
(COASTAL)
UNOVA

GOLETT

Automaton Pokémon

TYPE: GROUND-GHOST

They were sculpted from clay in ancient times. No one knows why, but some of them are driven to continually line up boulders.

This Pokémon was created from clay. It received orders from its master many thousands of years ago, and it still follows those orders to this day.

HOW TO SAY IT: GO-let
IMPERIAL HEIGHT: 3'03"
IMPERIAL WEIGHT: 202.8 lbs.
METRIC HEIGHT: 1.0 m
METRIC WEIGHT: 92.0 kg

POSSIBLE MOVES: Astonish, Curse, Defense Curl, Dynamic Punch, Earthquake, Hammer Arm, Heavy Slam, Iron Defense, Mega Punch, Mud-Slap, Night Shade, Phantom Force, Pound, Shadow Ball, Shadow Punch, Stomping Tantrum

GOLETT → GOLURK

GOLISOPOD

Hard Scale Pokémon

TYPE: BUG-WATER

It will do anything to win, taking advantage of every opening and finishing opponents off with the small claws on its front legs.

They live in sunken ships or in holes in the seabed. When Golisopod and Grapploct battle, the loser becomes the winner's meal.

HOW TO SAY IT: go-LIE-suh-pod
IMPERIAL HEIGHT: 6'07"
IMPERIAL WEIGHT: 238.1 lbs.
METRIC HEIGHT: 2.0 m
METRIC WEIGHT: 108.0 kg

POSSIBLE MOVES: Bug Bite, Defense Curl, First Impression, Fury Cutter, Iron Defense, Liquidation, Mud Shot, Pin Missile, Razor Shell, Rock Smash, Sand Attack, Slash, Spite, Struggle Bug, Sucker Punch, Swords Dance

WIMPOD → GOLISOPOD

201

GOLURK
Automaton Pokémon

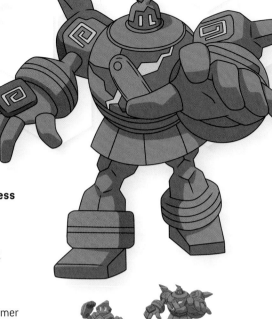

REGIONS:
ALOLA
GALAR
KALOS
(COASTAL)
UNOVA

TYPE: GROUND-GHOST

Artillery platforms built into the walls of ancient castles served as perches from which Golurk could fire energy beams.

There's a theory that inside Golurk is a perpetual motion machine that produces limitless energy, but this belief hasn't been proven.

HOW TO SAY IT: GO-lurk
IMPERIAL HEIGHT: 9'02"
IMPERIAL WEIGHT: 727.5 lbs.
METRIC HEIGHT: 2.8 m
METRIC WEIGHT: 330.0 kg

POSSIBLE MOVES: Astonish, Curse, Defense Curl, Dynamic Punch, Earthquake, Focus Punch, Hammer Arm, Heavy Slam, High Horsepower, Iron Defense, Mega Punch, Mud-Slap, Night Shade, Phantom Force, Pound, Shadow Ball, Shadow Punch, Stomping Tantrum

GOLETT   GOLURK

GOODRA
Dragon Pokémon

REGIONS:
ALOLA
GALAR
KALOS
(MOUNTAIN)

TYPE: DRAGON

Sometimes it misunderstands instructions and appears dazed or bewildered. Many Trainers don't mind, finding this behavior to be adorable.

Its form of offense is forcefully stretching out its horns. The strikes land one hundred times harder than any blow from a heavyweight boxer.

HOW TO SAY IT: GOO-druh
IMPERIAL HEIGHT: 6'07"
IMPERIAL WEIGHT: 331.8 lbs.
METRIC HEIGHT: 2.0 m
METRIC WEIGHT: 150.5 kg

POSSIBLE MOVES: Absorb, Acid Spray, Aqua Tail, Body Slam, Curse, Dragon Breath, Dragon Pulse, Feint, Flail, Muddy Water, Poison Tail, Power Whip, Protect, Rain Dance, Tackle, Tearful Look, Water Gun, Water Pulse

GOOMY   SLIGGOO   GOODRA

GOOMY

Soft Tissue Pokémon

TYPE: DRAGON

Because most of its body is water, it will dry up if the weather becomes too arid. It's considered the weakest dragon Pokémon.

Their horns are powerful sensors. As soon as Goomy pick up any sign of enemies, they go into hiding. This is how they've survived.

HOW TO SAY IT: GOO-mee
IMPERIAL HEIGHT: 1'00"
IMPERIAL WEIGHT: 6.2 lbs.
METRIC HEIGHT: 0.3 m
METRIC WEIGHT: 2.8 kg

POSSIBLE MOVES: Absorb, Body Slam, Curse, Dragon Breath, Dragon Pulse, Flail, Muddy Water, Protect, Rain Dance, Tackle, Water Gun, Water Pulse

GOOMY   SLIGGOO   GOODRA

GOREBYSS

South Sea Pokémon

TYPE: WATER

The color of its body changes with the water temperature. The coloration of Gorebyss in Alola is almost blindingly vivid.

It sucks bodily fluids out of its prey. The leftover meat sinks to the seafloor, where it becomes food for other Pokémon.

HOW TO SAY IT: GORE-a-biss
IMPERIAL HEIGHT: 5'11"
IMPERIAL WEIGHT: 49.8 lbs.
METRIC HEIGHT: 1.8 m
METRIC WEIGHT: 22.6 kg

POSSIBLE MOVES: Whirlpool, Confusion, Water Sport, Agility, Draining Kiss, Water Pulse, Amnesia, Aqua Ring, Captivate, Dive, Baton Pass, Psychic, Aqua Tail, Coil, Hydro Pump

CLAMPERL   GOREBYSS

GOSSIFLEUR

Flowering Pokémon

TYPE: GRASS

It anchors itself in the ground with its single leg, then basks in the sun. After absorbing enough sunlight, its petals spread as it blooms brilliantly.

It whirls around in the wind while singing a joyous song. This delightful display has charmed many into raising this Pokémon.

HOW TO SAY IT: GAH-sih-fluhr
IMPERIAL HEIGHT: 1'04"
IMPERIAL WEIGHT: 4.9 lbs.
METRIC HEIGHT: 0.4 m
METRIC WEIGHT: 2.2 kg

POSSIBLE MOVES:
Aromatherapy, Hyper Voice, Leaf Storm, Leaf Tornado, Leafage, Rapid Spin, Razor Leaf, Round, Sing, Sweet Scent, Synthesis

GOSSIFLEUR

ELDEGOSS

GOTHITA

Fixation Pokémon

TYPE: PSYCHIC

Though they're still only babies, there's psychic power stored in their ribbonlike feelers, and sometimes they use that power to fight.

Even when nobody seems to be around, Gothita can still be heard making a muted cry. Many believe it's speaking to something only it can see.

HOW TO SAY IT: GAH-THEE-tah
IMPERIAL HEIGHT: 1'04"
IMPERIAL WEIGHT: 12.8 lbs.
METRIC HEIGHT: 0.4 m
METRIC WEIGHT: 5.8 kg

POSSIBLE MOVES: Charm, Confusion, Fake Tears, Flatter, Future Sight, Hypnosis, Magic Room, Play Nice, Pound, Psybeam, Psych Up, Psychic, Psyshock, Tickle

GOTHITA ➡ **GOTHORITA** ➡ **GOTHITELLE**

GOTHITELLE

Astral Body Pokémon

TYPE: PSYCHIC

It has tremendous psychic power, but it dislikes conflict. It's also able to predict the future based on the movement of the stars.

A criminal who was shown his fate by a Gothitelle went missing that same day and was never seen again.

HOW TO SAY IT: GAH-thih-tell
IMPERIAL HEIGHT: 4'11"
IMPERIAL WEIGHT: 97.0 lbs.
METRIC HEIGHT: 1.5 m
METRIC WEIGHT: 44.0 kg

POSSIBLE MOVES: Charm, Confusion, Fake Tears, Flatter, Future Sight, Hypnosis, Magic Room, Play Nice, Pound, Psybeam, Psych Up, Psychic, Psyshock, Tickle

GOTHITA ➡ **GOTHORITA** ➡ **GOTHITELLE**

GOTHORITA

Manipulate Pokémon

TYPE: PSYCHIC

It's said that when stars shine in the night sky, this Pokémon will spirit away sleeping children. Some call it the Witch of Punishment.

On nights when the stars shine, this Pokémon's psychic power is at its strongest. It's unknown just what link Gothorita has to the greater universe.

HOW TO SAY IT: GAH-thoh-REE-tah
IMPERIAL HEIGHT: 2'04"
IMPERIAL WEIGHT: 39.7 lbs.
METRIC HEIGHT: 0.7 m
METRIC WEIGHT: 18.0 kg

POSSIBLE MOVES: Charm, Confusion, Fake Tears, Flatter, Future Sight, Hypnosis, Magic Room, Play Nice, Pound, Psybeam, Psych Up, Psychic, Psyshock, Tickle

GOTHITA   GOTHORITA   GOTHITELLE

GOURGEIST

Pumpkin Pokémon

TYPE: GHOST-GRASS

Eerie cries emanate from its body in the dead of night. The sounds are said to be the wails of spirits who are suffering in the afterlife.

In the darkness of a new-moon night, Gourgeist will come knocking. Whoever answers the door will be swept off to the afterlife.

HOW TO SAY IT: GORE-guyst
IMPERIAL HEIGHT: 2'11"
IMPERIAL WEIGHT: 27.6 lbs.
METRIC HEIGHT: 0.9 m
METRIC WEIGHT: 12.5 kg

POSSIBLE MOVES: Astonish, Bullet Seed, Confuse Ray, Explosion, Leech Seed, Moonblast, Pain Split, Phantom Force, Razor Leaf, Scary Face, Seed Bomb, Shadow Ball, Shadow Sneak, Trick, Trick-or-Treat, Worry Seed

PUMPKABOO   GOURGEIST

GRANBULL

Fairy Pokémon

TYPE: FAIRY

While it has powerful jaws, it doesn't care for disputes, so it rarely has a chance to display their might.

Although it's popular with young people, Granbull is timid and sensitive, so it's totally incompetent as a watchdog.

HOW TO SAY IT: GRAN-bull
IMPERIAL HEIGHT: 4'07"
IMPERIAL WEIGHT: 107.4 lbs.
METRIC HEIGHT: 1.4 m
METRIC WEIGHT: 48.7 kg

POSSIBLE MOVES: Outrage, Ice Fang, Fire Fang, Thunder Fang, Tackle, Scary Face, Tail Whip, Charm, Bite, Lick, Headbutt, Roar, Rage, Play Rough, Payback, Crunch

SNUBBULL   **GRANBULL**

GRAPPLOCT

Jujitsu Pokémon

TYPE: FIGHTING

A body made up of nothing but muscle makes the grappling moves this Pokémon performs with its tentacles tremendously powerful.

Searching for an opponent to test its skills against, it emerges onto land. Once the battle is over, it returns to the sea.

HOW TO SAY IT: GRAP-lahct
IMPERIAL HEIGHT: 5'03"
IMPERIAL WEIGHT: 86.0 lbs.
METRIC HEIGHT: 1.6 m
METRIC WEIGHT: 39.0 kg

POSSIBLE MOVES: Bind, Brick Break, Bulk Up, Detect, Feint, Leer, Octazooka, Octolock, Reversal, Rock Smash, Submission, Superpower, Taunt, Topsy-Turvy

CLOBBOPUS   **GRAPPLOCT**

GRAVELER

Rock Pokémon

TYPE: ROCK-GROUND

Often seen rolling down mountain trails. Obstacles are just things to roll straight over, not avoid.

HOW TO SAY IT: GRAV-el-ler
IMPERIAL HEIGHT: 3'03"
IMPERIAL WEIGHT: 231.5 lbs.
METRIC HEIGHT: 1.0 m
METRIC WEIGHT: 105.0 kg

POSSIBLE MOVES: Tackle, Defense Curl, Mud Sport, Rock Polish, Rollout, Magnitude, Rock Throw, Rock Blast, Smack Down, Self-Destruct, Bulldoze, Stealth Rock, Earthquake, Explosion, Double-Edge, Stone Edge

GEODUDE   GRAVELER   GOLEM

ALOLAN GRAVELER

Rock Pokémon

TYPE: ROCK-ELECTRIC

When it comes rolling down a mountain path, anything in its way gets zapped by electricity and sent flying.

HOW TO SAY IT: GRAV-el-ler
IMPERIAL HEIGHT: 3'03"
IMPERIAL WEIGHT: 242.5 lbs.
METRIC HEIGHT: 1.0 m
METRIC WEIGHT: 110.0 kg

POSSIBLE MOVES: Tackle, Defense Curl, Charge, Rock Polish, Rollout, Spark, Rock Throw, Smack Down, Thunder Punch, Self-Destruct, Stealth Rock, Rock Blast, Discharge, Explosion, Double-Edge, Stone Edge

ALOLAN   ALOLAN   ALOLAN
GEODUDE   GRAVELER   GOLEM

GREEDENT
Greedy Pokémon

TYPE: NORMAL

It stashes berries in its tail—so many berries that they fall out constantly. But this Pokémon is a bit slow-witted, so it doesn't notice the loss.

Common throughout the Galar region, this Pokémon has strong teeth and can chew through the toughest of berry shells.

HOW TO SAY IT: GREE-dent
IMPERIAL HEIGHT: 2'00"
IMPERIAL WEIGHT: 13.2 lbs.
METRIC HEIGHT: 0.6 m
METRIC WEIGHT: 6.0 kg

POSSIBLE MOVES: Belch, Bite, Body Slam, Bullet Seed, Counter, Covet, Rest, Spit Up, Stockpile, Stuff Cheeks, Super Fang, Swallow, Tackle, Tail Whip

SKWOVET   GREEDENT

TYPE: WATER-DARK

It creates throwing stars out of compressed water. When it spins them and throws them at high speed, these stars can split metal in two.

It appears and vanishes with a ninja's grace. It toys with its enemies using swift movements, while slicing them with throwing stars of sharpest water.

GRENINJA
Ninja Pokémon

HOW TO SAY IT: greh-NIN-jah
IMPERIAL HEIGHT: 4'11"
IMPERIAL WEIGHT: 88.2 lbs.
METRIC HEIGHT: 1.5 m
METRIC WEIGHT: 40.0 kg

POSSIBLE MOVES: Night Slash, Role Play, Mat Block, Pound, Growl, Bubble, Quick Attack, Lick, Water Pulse, Smokescreen, Shadow Sneak, Spikes, Feint Attack, Water Shuriken, Substitute, Extrasensory, Double Team, Haze, Hydro Pump

FROAKIE   FROGADIER   GRENINJA

GRIMER

Sludge Pokémon

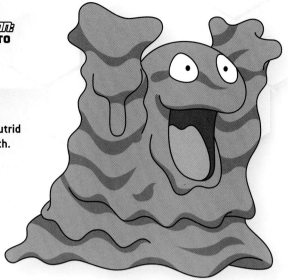

TYPE: POISON

Made of congealed sludge. It smells too putrid to touch. Even weeds won't grow in its path.

HOW TO SAY IT: GRY-mur
IMPERIAL HEIGHT: 2'11"
IMPERIAL WEIGHT: 66.1 lbs.
METRIC HEIGHT: 0.9 m
METRIC WEIGHT: 30.0 kg

POSSIBLE MOVES: Poison Gas, Pound, Harden, Bite, Disable, Acid Spray, Poison Fang, Minimize, Fling, Knock Off, Crunch, Screech, Gunk Shot, Acid Armor, Belch, Memento

GRIMER   MUK

ALOLAN GRIMER

Sludge Pokémon

REGION: ALOLA

TYPE: POISON-DARK

It has a passion for trash above all else, speedily digesting it and creating brilliant crystals of sparkling poison.

HOW TO SAY IT: GRY-mur
IMPERIAL HEIGHT: 2'04"
IMPERIAL WEIGHT: 92.6 lbs.
METRIC HEIGHT: 0.7 m
METRIC WEIGHT: 42.0 kg

POSSIBLE MOVES: Pound, Poison Gas, Harden, Bite, Disable, Acid Spray, Poison Fang, Minimize, Fling, Knock Off, Crunch, Screech, Gunk Shot, Acid Armor, Belch, Memento

ALOLAN GRIMER   ALOLAN MUK

GRIMMSNARL
Bulk Up Pokémon

TYPE: DARK-FAIRY

With the hair wrapped around its body helping to enhance its muscles, this Pokémon can overwhelm even Machamp.

Its hairs work like muscle fibers. When its hairs unfurl, they latch on to opponents, ensnaring them as tentacles would.

HOW TO SAY IT: GRIM-snarl
IMPERIAL HEIGHT: 4'11"
IMPERIAL WEIGHT: 134.5 lbs.
METRIC HEIGHT: 1.5 m
METRIC WEIGHT: 61.0 kg

POSSIBLE MOVES: Assurance, Bite, Bulk Up, Confide, Dark Pulse, Fake Out, Fake Tears, False Surrender, Flatter, Foul Play, Hammer Arm, Nasty Plot, Play Rough, Power-Up Punch, Spirit Break, Sucker Punch, Swagger, Torment

IMPIDIMP MORGREM

GRIMMSNARL

Alternate Form:
GIGANTAMAX GRIMMSNARL

By transforming its leg hair, this Pokémon delivers power-packed drill kicks that can bore huge holes in Galar's terrain.

Gigantamax energy has caused more hair to sprout all over its body. With the added strength, it can jump over the world's tallest building.

IMPERIAL HEIGHT: 105'00"+
IMPERIAL WEIGHT: ????.? lbs.
METRIC HEIGHT: 32.0+ m
METRIC WEIGHT: ???.? kg

GROOKEY

Chimp Pokémon

TYPE: GRASS

When it uses its special stick to strike up a beat, the sound waves produced carry revitalizing energy to the plants and flowers in the area.

It attacks with rapid beats of its stick. As it strikes with amazing speed, it gets more and more pumped.

HOW TO SAY IT: GROO-kee **METRIC HEIGHT:** 0.3 m
IMPERIAL HEIGHT: 1'00" **METRIC WEIGHT:** 5.0 kg
IMPERIAL WEIGHT: 11.0 lbs.

POSSIBLE MOVES: Branch Poke, Endeavor, Growl, Knock Off, Razor Leaf, Scratch, Screech, Slam, Taunt, Uproar, Wood Hammer

GROOKEY　　THWACKEY　　RILLABOOM

GROTLE

Grove Pokémon

TYPE: GRASS

It lives along water in forests. In the daytime, it leaves the forest to sunbathe its treed shell.

It knows where pure water wells up. It carries fellow Pokémon there on its back.

HOW TO SAY IT: GRAH-tul
IMPERIAL HEIGHT: 3'07"
IMPERIAL WEIGHT: 213.8 lbs.
METRIC HEIGHT: 1.1 m
METRIC WEIGHT: 97.0 kg

POSSIBLE MOVES: Tackle, Withdraw, Absorb, Razor Leaf, Curse, Bite, Mega Drain, Leech Seed, Synthesis, Crunch, Giga Drain, Leaf Storm

TURTWIG　　GROTLE　　TORTERRA

REGION: HOENN

GROUDON
Continent Pokémon

TYPE: GROUND

Groudon is said to be the personification of the land itself. Legends tell of its many clashes against Kyogre, as each sought to gain the power of nature.

Through Primal Reversion and with nature's full power, it will take back its true form. It can cause magma to erupt and expand the landmass of the world.

HOW TO SAY IT: GRAU-DON
IMPERIAL HEIGHT: 11'06"
IMPERIAL WEIGHT: 2,094.4 lbs.
METRIC HEIGHT: 3.5 m
METRIC WEIGHT: 950.0 kg

POSSIBLE MOVES: Ancient Power, Mud Shot, Scary Face, Earth Power, Lava Plume, Rest, Earthquake, Precipice Blades, Bulk Up, Solar Beam, Fissure, Fire Blast, Hammer Arm, Eruption

PRIMAL GROUDON
Continent Pokémon

TYPE: GROUND-FIRE

IMPERIAL HEIGHT: 16'05"
IMPERIAL WEIGHT: 2,204.0 lbs.
METRIC HEIGHT: 5.0 m
METRIC WEIGHT: 999.7 kg

GROUDON → PRIMAL GROUDON

213

GROVYLE

Wood Gecko Pokémon

TYPE: GRASS

The leaves growing out of Grovyle's body are convenient for camouflaging it from enemies in the forest. This Pokémon is a master at climbing trees in jungles.

This Pokémon adeptly flies from branch to branch in trees. In a forest, no Pokémon can ever hope to catch a fleeing Grovyle however fast they may be.

HOW TO SAY IT: GROW-vile **METRIC HEIGHT:** 0.9 m
IMPERIAL HEIGHT: 2'11" **METRIC WEIGHT:** 21.6 kg
IMPERIAL WEIGHT: 47.6 lbs.

POSSIBLE MOVES: Fury Cutter, Pound, Leer, Absorb, Quick Attack, Mega Drain, Pursuit, Leaf Blade, Agility, Slam, Detect, X-Scissor, False Swipe, Quick Guard, Leaf Storm, Screech

TREECKO   **GROVYLE**   **SCEPTILE**   **MEGA SCEPTILE**

GROWLITHE

Puppy Pokémon

REGIONS: ALOLA GALAR KANTO

TYPE: FIRE

It has a brave and trustworthy nature. It fearlessly stands up to bigger and stronger foes.

Extremely loyal, it will fearlessly bark at any opponent to protect its own Trainer from harm.

HOW TO SAY IT: GROWL-lith **METRIC HEIGHT:** 0.7 m
IMPERIAL HEIGHT: 2'04" **METRIC WEIGHT:** 19.0 kg
IMPERIAL WEIGHT: 41.9 lbs.

POSSIBLE MOVES: Agility, Bite, Crunch, Ember, Fire Fang, Flame Wheel, Flamethrower, Flare Blitz, Helping Hand, Howl, Leer, Play Rough, Retaliate, Reversal, Roar, Take Down

GROWLITHE   **ARCANINE**

TYPE: BUG

Its natural enemies, like Rookidee, may flee rather than risk getting caught in its large mandibles that can snap thick tree branches.

It uses its big jaws to dig nests into the forest floor, and it loves to feed on sweet tree sap.

HOW TO SAY IT: GRUB-bin
IMPERIAL HEIGHT: 1'04"
IMPERIAL WEIGHT: 9.7 lbs.
METRIC HEIGHT: 0.4 m
METRIC WEIGHT: 4.4 kg

POSSIBLE MOVES: Bite, Bug Bite, Crunch, Dig, Mud-Slap, Spark, Sticky Web, String Shot, Vise Grip, X-Scissor

REGIONS:
ALOLA
GALAR

GRUBBIN
Larva Pokémon

GRUBBIN   **CHARJABUG**   **VIKAVOLT**

REGIONS:
HOENN
KALOS
(COASTAL)

GRUMPIG
Manipulate Pokémon

TYPE: PSYCHIC

Grumpig uses the black pearls on its body to amplify its psychic power waves for gaining total control over its foe. When this Pokémon uses its special power, its snorting breath grows labored.

Grumpig uses the black pearls on its body to wield its fantastic powers. When it is doing so, it dances bizarrely. This Pokémon's black pearls are valuable as works of art.

HOW TO SAY IT: GRUM-pig   **METRIC HEIGHT:** 0.9 m
IMPERIAL HEIGHT: 2'11"   **METRIC WEIGHT:** 71.5 kg
IMPERIAL WEIGHT: 157.6 lbs.

POSSIBLE MOVES: Teeter Dance, Belch, Splash, Psywave, Odor Sleuth, Psybeam, Psych Up, Confuse Ray, Magic Coat, Zen Headbutt, Rest, Snore, Power Gem, Psyshock, Payback, Psychic, Bounce

SPOINK   **GRUMPIG**

GULPIN
Stomach Pokémon

TYPE: POISON

Virtually all of Gulpin's body is its stomach. As a result, it can swallow something its own size. This Pokémon's stomach contains a special fluid that digests anything.

Most of Gulpin's body is made up of its stomach—its heart and brain are very small in comparison. This Pokémon's stomach contains special enzymes that dissolve anything.

HOW TO SAY IT: GULL-pin   **METRIC HEIGHT:** 0.4 m
IMPERIAL HEIGHT: 1'04"   **METRIC WEIGHT:** 10.3 kg
IMPERIAL WEIGHT: 22.7 lbs.

POSSIBLE MOVES: Pound, Yawn, Poison Gas, Sludge, Amnesia, Encore, Toxic, Acid Spray, Stockpile, Spit Up, Swallow, Belch, Sludge Bomb, Gastro Acid, Wring Out, Gunk Shot

GULPIN   SWALOT

GUMSHOOS
Stakeout Pokémon

TYPE: NORMAL

Although it wasn't originally found in Alola, this Pokémon was brought over a long time ago when there was a huge Rattata outbreak.

Patient by nature, this Pokémon loses control of itself and pounces when it spots its favorite meal—Rattata!

HOW TO SAY IT: GUM-shooss
IMPERIAL HEIGHT: 2'04"
IMPERIAL WEIGHT: 31.3 lbs.
METRIC HEIGHT: 0.7 m
METRIC WEIGHT: 14.2 kg

POSSIBLE MOVES: Tackle, Leer, Pursuit, Sand Attack, Odor Sleuth, Bide, Bite, Mud-Slap, Super Fang, Take Down, Scary Face, Crunch, Hyper Fang, Yawn, Thrash, Rest

YUNGOOS   GUMSHOOS

TYPE: FIGHTING

GURDURR
Muscular Pokémon

It shows off its muscles to Machoke and other Gurdurr. If it fails to measure up to the other Pokémon, it lies low for a little while.

Gurdurr excels at demolition—construction is not its forte. In any case, there's skill in the way this Pokémon wields its metal beam.

HOW TO SAY IT: GUR-dur   **METRIC HEIGHT:** 1.2 m
IMPERIAL HEIGHT: 3'11"   **METRIC WEIGHT:** 40.0 kg
IMPERIAL WEIGHT: 88.2 lbs.

POSSIBLE MOVES: Bulk Up, Dynamic Punch, Focus Energy, Focus Punch, Hammer Arm, Leer, Low Kick, Pound, Rock Slide, Rock Throw, Scary Face, Slam, Stone Edge, Superpower

TIMBURR　**GURDURR**　**CONKELDURR**

ULTRA BEAST

GUZZLORD
Junkivore Pokémon

TYPE: DARK-DRAGON

Although it's alien to this world and a danger here, it's apparently a common organism in the world where it normally lives.

An unknown life-form called a UB. It may be constantly hungry—it is certainly always devouring something.

HOW TO SAY IT: GUZZ-lord   **METRIC HEIGHT:** 5.5 m
IMPERIAL HEIGHT: 18'01"   **METRIC WEIGHT:** 888.0 kg
IMPERIAL WEIGHT: 1,957.7 lbs.

POSSIBLE MOVES: Belch, Wide Guard, Swallow, Stockpile, Dragon Rage, Bite, Stomp, Brutal Swing, Steamroller, Dragon Tail, Iron Tail, Stomping Tantrum, Crunch, Hammer Arm, Thrash, Gastro Acid, Heavy Slam, Wring Out, Dragon Rush

DOES NOT EVOLVE

GYARADOS

Atrocious Pokémon

REGIONS:
ALOLA
GALAR
KALOS
(CENTRAL)
KANTO

TYPE: WATER-FLYING

It has an extremely aggressive nature. The Hyper Beam it shoots from its mouth totally incinerates all targets.

Once it begins to rampage, a Gyarados will burn everything down, even in a harsh storm.

HOW TO SAY IT: GARE-uh-dos
IMPERIAL HEIGHT: 21'04"
IMPERIAL WEIGHT: 518.1 lbs.
METRIC HEIGHT: 6.5 m
METRIC WEIGHT: 235.0 kg

POSSIBLE MOVES: Aqua Tail, Bite, Brine, Crunch, Dragon Dance, Flail, Hurricane, Hydro Pump, Hyper Beam, Ice Fang, Leer, Rain Dance, Scary Face, Splash, Tackle, Thrash, Twister, Waterfall, Whirlpool

MEGA GYARADOS

Atrocious Pokémon

TYPE: WATER-DARK

IMPERIAL HEIGHT: 21'04"
IMPERIAL WEIGHT: 672.4 lbs.
METRIC HEIGHT: 6.5 m
METRIC WEIGHT: 305.0 kg

MAGIKARP → **GYARADOS** → **MEGA GYARADOS**

HAKAMO-O
Scaly Pokémon

TYPE: DRAGON-FIGHTING

The scaleless, scarred parts of its body are signs of its strength. It shows them off to defeated opponents.

Before attacking its enemies, it clashes its scales together and roars. Its sharp claws shred the opposition.

HOW TO SAY IT: HAH-kah-MOH-oh
IMPERIAL HEIGHT: 3'11"
IMPERIAL WEIGHT: 103.6 lbs.
METRIC HEIGHT: 1.2 m
METRIC WEIGHT: 47.0 kg

POSSIBLE MOVES: Autotomize, Close Combat, Dragon Claw, Dragon Dance, Dragon Tail, Headbutt, Iron Defense, Leer, Noble Roar, Outrage, Protect, Scary Face, Screech, Tackle, Work Up

JANGMO-O ➡ HAKAMO-O ➡ KOMMO-O

HAPPINY
Playhouse Pokémon

TYPE: NORMAL

Mimicking Chansey, Happiny will place an egg-shaped stone in its belly pouch. Happiny will treasure this stone.

Happiny's willing to lend its precious round stone to those it's friendly with, but if the stone isn't returned, Happiny will cry and throw a tantrum.

HOW TO SAY IT: hap-PEE-nee
IMPERIAL HEIGHT: 2'00"
IMPERIAL WEIGHT: 53.8 lbs.
METRIC HEIGHT: 0.6 m
METRIC WEIGHT: 24.4 kg

POSSIBLE MOVES: Pound, Charm, Copycat, Refresh, Sweet Kiss

HAPPINY ➡ CHANSEY ➡ BLISSEY

HARIYAMA

Arm Thrust Pokémon

REGIONS:
ALOLA
HOENN
KALOS
(COASTAL)

TYPE: FIGHTING

Although they enjoy comparing their strength, they're also kind. They value etiquette, praising opponents they battle.

Hariyama that are big and fat aren't necessarily strong. There are some small ones that move nimbly and use moves skillfully.

HOW TO SAY IT: HAR-ee-YAH-mah
IMPERIAL HEIGHT: 7'07"
IMPERIAL WEIGHT: 559.5 lbs.
METRIC HEIGHT: 2.3 m
METRIC WEIGHT: 253.8 kg

POSSIBLE MOVES: Brine, Tackle, Focus Energy, Sand Attack, Arm Thrust, Fake Out, Force Palm, Whirlwind, Knock Off, Vital Throw, Belly Drum, Smelling Salts, Seismic Toss, Wake-Up Slap, Endure, Close Combat, Reversal, Heavy Slam

MAKUHITA   HARIYAMA

HATENNA

Calm Pokémon

REGION:
GALAR

TYPE: PSYCHIC

Via the protrusion on its head, it senses other creatures' emotions. If you don't have a calm disposition, it will never warm up to you.

If this Pokémon senses a strong emotion, it will run away as fast as it can. It prefers areas without people.

HOW TO SAY IT: hat-EN-nuh
IMPERIAL HEIGHT: 1'04"
IMPERIAL WEIGHT: 7.5 lbs.
METRIC HEIGHT: 0.4 m
METRIC WEIGHT: 3.4 kg

POSSIBLE MOVES: Aromatherapy, Calm Mind, Confusion, Dazzling Gleam, Disarming Voice, Heal Pulse, Healing Wish, Life Dew, Play Nice, Psybeam, Psychic

HATENNA   HATTREM   HATTERENE

HATTERENE
Silent Pokémon

TYPE: PSYCHIC-FAIRY

It emits psychic power strong enough to cause headaches as a deterrent to the approach of others.

If you're too loud around it, you risk being torn apart by the claws on its tentacle. This Pokémon is also known as the Forest Witch.

HOW TO SAY IT: HAT-eh-reen
IMPERIAL HEIGHT: 6'11"
IMPERIAL WEIGHT: 11.2 lbs.
METRIC HEIGHT: 2.1 m
METRIC WEIGHT: 5.1 kg

POSSIBLE MOVES: Aromatherapy, Brutal Swing, Calm Mind, Confusion, Dazzling Gleam, Disarming Voice, Heal Pulse, Healing Wish, Life Dew, Magic Powder, Play Nice, Psybeam, Psychic, Psycho Cut

HATENNA   HATTREM   HATTERENE

Alternate Form:
GIGANTAMAX HATTERENE

This Pokémon can read the emotions of creatures over thirty miles away. The minute it senses hostility, it goes on the attack.

Beams like lightning shoot down from its tentacles. It's known to some as the Raging Goddess.

IMPERIAL HEIGHT: 85'04"+
IMPERIAL WEIGHT: ????.? lbs.
METRIC HEIGHT: 26.0+ m
METRIC WEIGHT: ???.? kg

HATTREM

Serene Pokémon

TYPE: PSYCHIC

No matter who you are, if you bring strong emotions near this Pokémon, it will silence you violently.

Using the braids on its head, it pummels foes to get them to quiet down. One blow from those braids would knock out a professional boxer.

HOW TO SAY IT: HAT-trum **METRIC HEIGHT:** 0.6 m
IMPERIAL HEIGHT: 2'00" **METRIC WEIGHT:** 4.8 kg
IMPERIAL WEIGHT: 10.6 lbs.

POSSIBLE MOVES: Aromatherapy, Brutal Swing, Calm Mind, Confusion, Dazzling Gleam, Disarming Voice, Heal Pulse, Healing Wish, Life Dew, Play Nice, Psybeam, Psychic

HATENNA   HATTREM   HATTERENE

HAUNTER

Gas Pokémon

TYPE: GHOST-POISON

Its tongue is made of gas. If licked, its victim starts shaking constantly until death eventually comes.

If you get the feeling of being watched in darkness when nobody is around, Haunter is there.

HOW TO SAY IT: HAUNT-ur **METRIC HEIGHT:** 1.6 m
IMPERIAL HEIGHT: 5'03" **METRIC WEIGHT:** 0.1 kg
IMPERIAL WEIGHT: 0.2 lbs.

POSSIBLE MOVES: Confuse Ray, Curse, Dark Pulse, Destiny Bond, Dream Eater, Hex, Hypnosis, Lick, Mean Look, Night Shade, Payback, Shadow Ball, Shadow Punch, Spite, Sucker Punch

GASTLY   HAUNTER   GENGAR   MEGA GENGAR

TYPE: FIGHTING-FLYING

It drives its opponents to exhaustion with its agile maneuvers, then ends the fight with a flashy finishing move.

It always strikes a pose before going for its finishing move. Sometimes opponents take advantage of that time to counterattack.

HOW TO SAY IT: haw-LOO-cha
IMPERIAL HEIGHT: 2'07"
IMPERIAL WEIGHT: 47.4 lbs.
METRIC HEIGHT: 0.8 m
METRIC WEIGHT: 21.5 kg

POSSIBLE MOVES: Aerial Ace, Bounce, Detect, Encore, Endeavor, Feather Dance, Flying Press, High Jump Kick, Hone Claws, Roost, Sky Attack, Submission, Swords Dance, Tackle, Taunt, Wing Attack

REGIONS:
ALOLA
GALAR
KALOS
(COASTAL)

HAWLUCHA
Wrestling Pokémon

DOES NOT EVOLVE

REGIONS:
GALAR
KALOS
(CENTRAL)
UNOVA

HAXORUS
Axe Jaw Pokémon

TYPE: DRAGON

Its resilient tusks are its pride and joy. It licks up dirt to take in the minerals it needs to keep its tusks in top condition.

While usually kindhearted, it can be terrifying if angered. Tusks that can slice through steel beams are how Haxorus deals with its adversaries.

HOW TO SAY IT: HAK-soar-us
IMPERIAL HEIGHT: 5'11"
IMPERIAL WEIGHT: 232.6 lbs.
METRIC HEIGHT: 1.8 m
METRIC WEIGHT: 105.5 kg

POSSIBLE MOVES: Assurance, Bite, Crunch, Dragon Claw, Dragon Dance, Dragon Pulse, Dual Chop, False Swipe, Giga Impact, Guillotine, Laser Focus, Leer, Outrage, Scary Face, Scratch, Slash, Swords Dance, Taunt

AXEW → FRAXURE → HAXORUS

HEATMOR

Anteater Pokémon

TYPE: FIRE

There's a hole in its tail that allows it to draw in the air it needs to keep its fire burning. If the hole gets blocked, this Pokémon will fall ill.

A flame serves as its tongue, melting through the hard shell of Durant so that Heatmor can devour their insides.

HOW TO SAY IT: HEET-mohr
IMPERIAL HEIGHT: 4'07"
IMPERIAL WEIGHT: 127.9 lbs.
METRIC HEIGHT: 1.4 m
METRIC WEIGHT: 58.0 kg

POSSIBLE MOVES: Amnesia, Bind, Bug Bite, Fire Lash, Fire Spin, Flare Blitz, Fury Swipes, Hone Claws, Incinerate, Inferno, Lick, Slash, Spit Up, Stockpile, Swallow, Tackle

DOES NOT EVOLVE

HEATRAN

Lava Dome Pokémon

REGION:
SINNOH

LEGENDARY POKÉMON

TYPE: FIRE-STEEL

It dwells in volcanic caves. It digs in with its cross-shaped feet to crawl on ceilings and walls.

Boiling blood, like magma, circulates through its body. It makes its dwelling place in volcanic caves.

HOW TO SAY IT: HEET-tran
IMPERIAL HEIGHT: 5'07"
IMPERIAL WEIGHT: 948.0 lbs.
METRIC HEIGHT: 1.7 m
METRIC WEIGHT: 430.0 kg

POSSIBLE MOVES: Ancient Power, Leer, Fire Fang, Metal Sound, Crunch, Scary Face, Lava Plume, Fire Spin, Iron Head, Earth Power, Heat Wave, Stone Edge, Magma Storm

DOES NOT EVOLVE

TYPE: ELECTRIC-NORMAL

A now-vanished desert culture treasured these Pokémon. Appropriately, when Heliolisk came to the Galar region, treasure came with them.

One Heliolisk basking in the sun with its frill outspread is all it would take to produce enough electricity to power a city.

HOW TO SAY IT: HEE-lee-oh-lisk
IMPERIAL HEIGHT: 3'03"
IMPERIAL WEIGHT: 46.3 lbs.
METRIC HEIGHT: 1.0 m
METRIC WEIGHT: 21.0 kg

POSSIBLE MOVES: Bulldoze, Charge, Discharge, Eerie Impulse, Electrify, Mud-Slap, Parabolic Charge, Pound, Quick Attack, Tail Whip, Thunder, Thunder Shock, Thunder Wave, Thunderbolt, Volt Switch

REGIONS:
GALAR
KALOS
(COASTAL)

HELIOLISK
Generator Pokémon

HELIOPTILE   HELIOLISK

REGIONS:
GALAR
KALOS
(COASTAL)

HELIOPTILE
Generator Pokémon

TYPE: ELECTRIC-NORMAL

When spread, the frills on its head act like solar panels, generating the power behind this Pokémon's electric moves.

The sun powers this Pokémon's electricity generation. Interruption of that process stresses Helioptile to the point of weakness.

HOW TO SAY IT: hee-lee-AHP-tile
IMPERIAL HEIGHT: 1'08"
IMPERIAL WEIGHT: 13.2 lbs.
METRIC HEIGHT: 0.5 m
METRIC WEIGHT: 6.0 kg

POSSIBLE MOVES: Bulldoze, Charge, Electrify, Mud-Slap, Parabolic Charge, Pound, Quick Attack, Tail Whip, Thunder, Thunder Shock, Thunder Wave, Thunderbolt, Volt Switch

HELIOPTILE   HELIOLISK

HERACROSS
Single Horn Pokémon

TYPE: BUG-FIGHTING

Heracross loves sweet sap and will go looking through forests for it. The Pokémon uses its two antennae to pick up scents as it searches.

This Pokémon takes pride in its strength, which allows it to lift things one hundred times heavier than itself with no trouble at all.

HOW TO SAY IT: HAIR-uh-cross
IMPERIAL HEIGHT: 4'11"
IMPERIAL WEIGHT: 119.0 lbs.
METRIC HEIGHT: 1.5 m
METRIC WEIGHT: 54.0 kg

POSSIBLE MOVES: Arm Thrust, Bullet Seed, Night Slash, Tackle, Leer, Horn Attack, Endure, Fury Attack, Aerial Ace, Chip Away, Counter, Brick Break, Take Down, Pin Missile, Close Combat, Feint, Reversal, Megahorn

MEGA HERACROSS
Single Horn Pokémon

TYPE: BUG-FIGHTING

IMPERIAL HEIGHT: 5'07"
IMPERIAL WEIGHT: 137.8 lbs.
METRIC HEIGHT: 1.7 m
METRIC WEIGHT: 62.5 kg

HERACROSS   MEGA HERACROSS

TYPE: NORMAL

Herdier is a very smart and friendly Pokémon. So much so that there's a theory that Herdier was the first Pokémon to partner with people.

The black fur that covers this Pokémon's body is dense and springy. Even sharp fangs bounce right off.

HERDIER
Loyal Dog Pokémon

HOW TO SAY IT: HERD-ee-er
IMPERIAL HEIGHT: 2'11"
IMPERIAL WEIGHT: 32.4 lbs.
METRIC HEIGHT: 0.9 m
METRIC WEIGHT: 14.7 kg

POSSIBLE MOVES: Leer, Tackle, Odor Sleuth, Bite, Helping Hand, Take Down, Work Up, Crunch, Roar, Retaliate, Reversal, Last Resort, Giga Impact, Play Rough

LILLIPUP   **HERDIER**   **STOUTLAND**

HIPPOPOTAS
Hippo Pokémon

TYPE: GROUND

It moves through the sands with its mouth open, swallowing sand along with its prey. It gets rid of the sand by spouting it from its nose.

This Pokémon is active during the day and passes the cold desert nights burrowed snugly into the sand.

HOW TO SAY IT: HIP-poh-puh-TOSS
IMPERIAL HEIGHT: 2'07"
IMPERIAL WEIGHT: 109.1 lbs.
METRIC HEIGHT: 0.8 m
METRIC WEIGHT: 49.5 kg

POSSIBLE MOVES: Bite, Crunch, Dig, Double-Edge, Earthquake, Fissure, Rest, Roar, Sand Attack, Sand Tomb, Sandstorm, Slack Off, Tackle, Take Down, Yawn

HIPPOPOTAS   **HIPPOWDON**

HIPPOWDON

Heavyweight Pokémon

REGIONS:
GALAR
KALOS
(COASTAL)
SINNOH

TYPE: GROUND

Stones can get stuck in the ports on their bodies. Dwebble help dislodge such stones, so Hippowdon look after these Pokémon.

When roused to violence by its rage, it spews out the quantities of sand it has swallowed and whips up a sandstorm.

HOW TO SAY IT: hip-POW-don
IMPERIAL HEIGHT: 6'07"
IMPERIAL WEIGHT: 661.4 lbs.
METRIC HEIGHT: 2.0 m
METRIC WEIGHT: 300.0 kg

POSSIBLE MOVES: Bite, Crunch, Dig, Double-Edge, Earthquake, Fire Fang, Fissure, Ice Fang, Rest, Roar, Sand Attack, Sand Tomb, Sandstorm, Slack Off, Tackle, Take Down, Thunder Fang, Yawn

HIPPOPOTAS   **HIPPOWDON**

HITMONCHAN

Punching Pokémon

REGIONS:
GALAR
KANTO

TYPE: FIGHTING

Its punches slice the air. They are launched at such high speed, even a slight graze could cause a burn.

Its punches slice the air. However, it seems to need a short break after fighting for three minutes.

HOW TO SAY IT: HIT-mon-CHAN
IMPERIAL HEIGHT: 4'07"
IMPERIAL WEIGHT: 110.7 lbs.
METRIC HEIGHT: 1.4 m
METRIC WEIGHT: 50.2 kg

POSSIBLE MOVES: Agility, Bullet Punch, Close Combat, Counter, Detect, Drain Punch, Fake Out, Feint, Fire Punch, Focus Energy, Focus Punch, Helping Hand, Ice Punch, Mach Punch, Mega Punch, Power-Up Punch, Quick Guard, Revenge, Tackle, Thunder Punch, Vacuum Wave

TYROGUE   **HITMONCHAN**

TYPE: FIGHTING

This amazing Pokémon has an awesome sense of balance. It can kick in succession from any position.

The legs freely contract and stretch. The stretchy legs allow it to hit a distant foe with a rising kick.

HOW TO SAY IT: HIT-mon-LEE
IMPERIAL HEIGHT: 4'11"
IMPERIAL WEIGHT: 109.8 lbs.
METRIC HEIGHT: 1.5m
METRIC WEIGHT: 49.8 kg

POSSIBLE MOVES: Blaze Kick, Brick Break, Close Combat, Double Kick, Endure, Fake Out, Feint, Focus Energy, Helping Hand, High Jump Kick, Low Kick, Low Sweep, Mega Kick, Mind Reader, Revenge, Reversal, Tackle, Wide Guard

REGIONS: GALAR KANTO

HITMONLEE
Kicking Pokémon

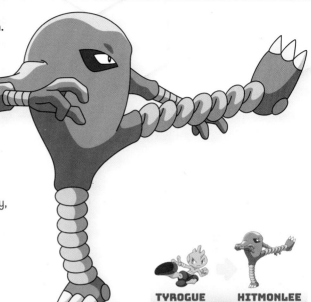

TYROGUE   HITMONLEE

REGIONS: GALAR JOHTO

HITMONTOP
Handstand Pokémon

TYPE: FIGHTING

It launches kicks while spinning. If it spins at high speed, it may bore its way into the ground.

After doing a handstand to throw off the opponent's timing, it presents its fancy kick moves.

HOW TO SAY IT: HIT-mon-TOP
IMPERIAL HEIGHT: 4'07"
IMPERIAL WEIGHT: 105.8 lbs.
METRIC HEIGHT: 1.4 m
METRIC WEIGHT: 48.0 kg

POSSIBLE MOVES: Agility, Close Combat, Counter, Detect, Dig, Endeavor, Fake Out, Feint, Focus Energy, Gyro Ball, Helping Hand, Quick Attack, Quick Guard, Rapid Spin, Revenge, Sucker Punch, Tackle, Triple Kick, Wide Guard

TYROGUE   HITMONTOP

TYPE: FIRE-FLYING

Ho-Oh's feathers glow in seven colors depending on the angle at which they are struck by light. These feathers are said to bring happiness to the bearers. This Pokémon is said to live at the foot of a rainbow.

HOW TO SAY IT: HOE-OH
IMPERIAL HEIGHT: 12'06"
IMPERIAL WEIGHT: 438.7 lbs.

METRIC HEIGHT: 3.8 m
METRIC WEIGHT: 199.0 kg

POSSIBLE MOVES: Whirlwind, Weather Ball, Gust, Brave Bird, Extrasensory, Sunny Day, Fire Blast, Sacred Fire, Punishment, Ancient Power, Safeguard, Recover, Future Sight, Natural Gift, Calm Mind, Sky Attack

DOES NOT EVOLVE

TYPE: DARK-FLYING

It will absolutely not forgive failure from or betrayal by its goons. It has no choice in this if it wants to maintain the order of the flock.

Its goons take care of most of the fighting for it. The only time it dirties its own hands is in delivering a final blow to finish off an opponent.

HOW TO SAY IT: HONCH-krow
IMPERIAL HEIGHT: 2'11"
IMPERIAL WEIGHT: 60.2 lbs.

METRIC HEIGHT: 0.9 m
METRIC WEIGHT: 27.3 kg

POSSIBLE MOVES: Night Slash, Sucker Punch, Astonish, Pursuit, Haze, Wing Attack, Swagger, Nasty Plot, Foul Play, Quash, Dark Pulse

REGIONS:
ALOLA
KALOS (MOUNTAIN)
SINNOH

HONCHKROW
Big Boss Pokémon

MURKROW → HONCHKROW

REGIONS:
GALAR
KALOS (CENTRAL)

HONEDGE
Sword Pokémon

TYPE: STEEL-GHOST

Honedge's soul once belonged to a person who was killed a long time ago by the sword that makes up Honedge's body.

The blue eye on the sword's handguard is the true body of Honedge. With its old cloth, it drains people's lives away.

HOW TO SAY IT: HONE-ej
IMPERIAL HEIGHT: 2'07"
IMPERIAL WEIGHT: 4.4 lbs.

METRIC HEIGHT: 0.8 m
METRIC WEIGHT: 2.0 kg

POSSIBLE MOVES: Aerial Ace, Autotomize, Fury Cutter, Iron Defense, Iron Head, Metal Sound, Night Slash, Power Trick, Retaliate, Sacred Sword, Shadow Sneak, Slash, Swords Dance, Tackle

HONEDGE   DOUBLADE   AEGISLASH

HOOPA CONFINED

Mischief Pokémon

MYTHICAL POKÉMON

TYPE: PSYCHIC-GHOST

In its true form, it possesses a huge amount of power. Legends of its avarice tell how it once carried off an entire castle to gain the treasure hidden within.

It is said to be able to seize anything it desires with its six rings and six huge arms. With its power sealed, it is transformed into a much smaller form.

HOW TO SAY IT: HOO-puh
IMPERIAL HEIGHT: 1'08"
IMPERIAL WEIGHT: 19.8 lbs.
METRIC HEIGHT: 0.5 m
METRIC WEIGHT: 9.0 kg

POSSIBLE MOVES: Trick, Destiny Bond, Ally Switch, Confusion, Astonish, Magic Coat, Light Screen, Psybeam, Skill Swap, Power Split, Guard Split, Phantom Force, Zen Headbutt, Wonder Room, Trick Room, Shadow Ball, Nasty Plot, Psychic, Hyperspace Hole

HOOPA UNBOUND

Djinn Pokémon

TYPE: PSYCHIC-DARK

IMPERIAL HEIGHT: 21'04"
IMPERIAL WEIGHT: 1,080.3 lbs.
METRIC HEIGHT: 6.5 m
METRIC WEIGHT: 490.0 kg

DOES NOT EVOLVE

HOOTHOOT
Owl Pokémon

TYPE: NORMAL-FLYING

It always stands on one foot. It changes feet so fast, the movement can rarely be seen.

It begins to hoot at the same time every day. Some Trainers use them in place of clocks.

HOW TO SAY IT: HOOT-HOOT
IMPERIAL HEIGHT: 2'04"
IMPERIAL WEIGHT: 46.7 lbs.
METRIC HEIGHT: 0.7 m
METRIC WEIGHT: 21.2 kg

POSSIBLE MOVES: Air Slash, Confusion, Dream Eater, Echoed Voice, Extrasensory, Growl, Hypnosis, Moonblast, Peck, Psycho Shift, Reflect, Roost, Tackle, Take Down, Uproar

HOOTHOOT   NOCTOWL

HOPPIP
Cottonweed Pokémon

TYPE: GRASS-FLYING

This Pokémon drifts and floats with the wind. If it senses the approach of strong winds, Hoppip links its leaves with other Hoppip to prepare against being blown away.

HOW TO SAY IT: HOP-pip
IMPERIAL HEIGHT: 1'04"
IMPERIAL WEIGHT: 1.1 lbs.
METRIC HEIGHT: 0.4 m
METRIC WEIGHT: 0.5 kg

POSSIBLE MOVES:
Splash, Absorb, Synthesis, Tail Whip, Tackle, Fairy Wind, Poison Powder, Stun Spore, Sleep Powder, Bullet Seed, Leech Seed, Mega Drain, Acrobatics, Rage Powder, Cotton Spore, U-turn, Worry Seed, Giga Drain, Bounce, Memento

HOPPIP   SKIPLOOM   JUMPLUFF

HORSEA
Dragon Pokémon

TYPE: WATER

Horsea makes its home in oceans with gentle currents. If this Pokémon is under attack, it spits out pitch-black ink and escapes.

They swim with dance-like motions and cause whirlpools to form. Horsea compete to see which of them can generate the biggest whirlpool.

HOW TO SAY IT: HOR-see
IMPERIAL HEIGHT: 1'04"
IMPERIAL WEIGHT: 17.6 lbs.
METRIC HEIGHT: 0.4 m
METRIC WEIGHT: 8.0 kg

POSSIBLE MOVES: Water Gun, Smokescreen, Leer, Bubble, Focus Energy, Bubble Beam, Agility, Twister, Brine, Hydro Pump, Dragon Dance, Dragon Pulse

HORSEA   SEADRA   KINGDRA

HOUNDOOM
Dark Pokémon

TYPE: DARK-FIRE

They spew flames mixed with poison to finish off their opponents. They divvy up their prey evenly among the members of their pack.

Identifiable by its eerie howls, people a long time ago thought it was the grim reaper and feared it.

HOW TO SAY IT: HOWN-doom
IMPERIAL HEIGHT: 4' 07"
IMPERIAL WEIGHT: 77.2 lbs.
METRIC HEIGHT: 1.4 m
METRIC WEIGHT: 35.0 kg

POSSIBLE MOVES: Inferno, Nasty Plot, Thunder Fang, Leer, Ember, Howl, Smog, Roar, Bite, Odor Sleuth, Beat Up, Fire Fang, Feint Attack, Embargo, Foul Play, Flamethrower, Crunch

MEGA HOUNDOOM
Dark Pokémon

TYPE: DARK-FIRE

IMPERIAL HEIGHT: 6'03"
IMPERIAL WEIGHT: 109.1 lbs.
METRIC HEIGHT: 1.9 m
METRIC WEIGHT: 49.5 kg

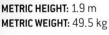
HOUNDOUR   HOUNDOOM   MEGA HOUNDOOM

HOUNDOUR
Dark Pokémon

TYPE: DARK-FIRE

It cooperates with others skillfully. When it becomes your partner, it's very loyal to you as its Trainer and will obey your orders.

They make repeated eerie howls before dawn to call attention to their pack.

HOW TO SAY IT: HOWN-dowr
IMPERIAL HEIGHT: 2' 00"
IMPERIAL WEIGHT: 23.8 lbs.
METRIC HEIGHT: 0.6 m
METRIC WEIGHT: 10.8 kg

POSSIBLE MOVES: Leer, Ember, Howl, Smog, Roar, Bite, Odor Sleuth, Beat Up, Fire Fang, Feint Attack, Embargo, Foul Play, Flamethrower, Crunch, Nasty Plot, Inferno

HOUNDOUR ➡️ **HOUNDOOM** ➡️ **MEGA HOUNDOOM**

HUNTAIL
Deep Sea Pokémon

TYPE: WATER

It's not the strongest swimmer. It wags its tail to lure in its prey and then gulps them down as soon as they get close.

Deep seas are their habitat. According to tradition, when Huntail wash up onshore, something unfortunate will happen.

HOW TO SAY IT: HUN-tail
IMPERIAL HEIGHT: 5'07"
IMPERIAL WEIGHT: 59.5 lbs.
METRIC HEIGHT: 1.7 m
METRIC WEIGHT: 27.0 kg

POSSIBLE MOVES: Whirlpool, Bite, Screech, Scary Face, Feint Attack, Water Pulse, Ice Fang, Brine, Sucker Punch, Dive, Baton Pass, Crunch, Aqua Tail, Coil, Hydro Pump

CLAMPERL ➡️ **HUNTAIL**

HYDREIGON

Brutal Pokémon

TYPE: DARK-DRAGON

There are a slew of stories about villages that were destroyed by Hydreigon. It bites anything that moves.

The three heads take turns sinking their teeth into the opponent. Their attacks won't slow until their target goes down.

HOW TO SAY IT: hy-DRY-gahn
IMPERIAL HEIGHT: 5'11"
IMPERIAL WEIGHT: 352.7 lbs.
METRIC HEIGHT: 1.8 m
METRIC WEIGHT: 160.0 kg

POSSIBLE MOVES: Assurance, Bite, Body Slam, Crunch, Double Hit, Dragon Breath, Dragon Pulse, Dragon Rush, Focus Energy, Headbutt, Hyper Beam, Hyper Voice, Nasty Plot, Outrage, Roar, Scary Face, Slam, Tackle, Tri Attack, Work Up

DEINO   ZWEILOUS   HYDREIGON

HYPNO

Hypnosis Pokémon

REGIONS:
ALOLA
KANTO

TYPE: PSYCHIC

Avoid eye contact if you come across one. It will try to put you to sleep by using its pendulum.

HOW TO SAY IT: HIP-no
IMPERIAL HEIGHT: 5'03"
IMPERIAL WEIGHT: 166.7 lbs.
METRIC HEIGHT: 1.6 m
METRIC WEIGHT: 75.6 kg

POSSIBLE MOVES: Future Sight, Nasty Plot, Nightmare, Switcheroo, Pound, Hypnosis, Disable, Confusion, Headbutt, Poison Gas, Meditate, Psybeam, Wake-Up Slap, Psych Up, Synchronoise, Zen Headbutt, Swagger, Psychic, Psyshock

DROWZEE   HYPNO

IGGLYBUFF
Balloon Pokémon

TYPE: NORMAL-FAIRY

Igglybuff loves to sing. Its marshmallow-like body gives off a faint sweet smell.

Taking advantage of the softness of its body, Igglybuff moves as if bouncing. Its body turns a deep pink when its temperature rises.

HOW TO SAY IT: IG-lee-buff
IMPERIAL HEIGHT: 1'00"
IMPERIAL WEIGHT: 2.2 lbs.
METRIC HEIGHT: 0.3 m
METRIC WEIGHT: 1.0 kg

POSSIBLE MOVES: Sing, Charm, Defense Curl, Pound, Sweet Kiss, Copycat

IGGLYBUFF   **JIGGLYPUFF**   **WIGGLYTUFF**

ILLUMISE
Firefly Pokémon

TYPE: BUG

Illumise attracts a swarm of Volbeat using a sweet fragrance. Once the Volbeat have gathered, this Pokémon leads the lit-up swarm in drawing geometric designs on the canvas of the night sky.

Illumise leads a flight of illuminated Volbeat to draw signs in the night sky. This Pokémon is said to earn greater respect from its peers by composing more complex designs in the sky.

HOW TO SAY IT: EE-loom-MEE-zay
IMPERIAL HEIGHT: 2'00"
IMPERIAL WEIGHT: 39.0 lbs.
METRIC HEIGHT: 0.6 m
METRIC WEIGHT: 17.7 kg

POSSIBLE MOVES: Play Nice, Tackle, Sweet Scent, Charm, Quick Attack, Struggle Bug, Moonlight, Wish, Encore, Flatter, Zen Headbutt, Helping Hand, Bug Buzz, Play Rough, Covet, Infestation

DOES NOT EVOLVE

IMPIDIMP

Wily Pokémon

REGION: GALAR

TYPE: DARK-FAIRY

Through its nose, it sucks in the emanations produced by people and Pokémon when they feel annoyed. It thrives off this negative energy.

It sneaks into people's homes, stealing things and feasting on the negative energy of the frustrated occupants.

HOW TO SAY IT: IMP-ih-dimp **METRIC HEIGHT:** 0.4 m
IMPERIAL HEIGHT: 1'04" **METRIC WEIGHT:** 5.5 kg
IMPERIAL WEIGHT: 12.1 lbs.

POSSIBLE MOVES: Assurance, Bite, Confide, Dark Pulse, Fake Out, Fake Tears, Flatter, Foul Play, Nasty Plot, Play Rough, Sucker Punch, Swagger, Torment

IMPIDIMP **MORGREM** **GRIMMSNARL**

INCINEROAR

Heel Pokémon

REGION: ALOLA

TYPE: FIRE-DARK

Although it's rough mannered and egotistical, it finds beating down unworthy opponents boring. It gets motivated for stronger opponents.

When its fighting spirit is set alight, the flames around its waist become especially intense.

HOW TO SAY IT: in-SIN-uh-roar **METRIC HEIGHT:** 1.8 m
IMPERIAL HEIGHT: 5'11" **METRIC WEIGHT:** 83.0 kg
IMPERIAL WEIGHT: 183.0 lbs.

POSSIBLE MOVES: Darkest Lariat, Bulk Up, Throat Chop, Scratch, Ember, Growl, Lick, Leer, Fire Fang, Double Kick, Roar, Bite, Swagger, Fury Swipes, Thrash, Flamethrower, Scary Face, Flare Blitz, Outrage, Cross Chop

LITTEN **TORRACAT** **INCINEROAR**

TYPE: PSYCHIC-NORMAL

INDEEDEE
Emotion Pokémon

These intelligent Pokémon touch horns with each other to share information between them.

They diligently serve people and Pokémon so they can gather feelings of gratitude. The females are particularly good at babysitting.

HOW TO SAY IT: in-DEE-dee
IMPERIAL HEIGHT: 2'11"
IMPERIAL WEIGHT: 61.7 lbs.
METRIC HEIGHT: 0.9 m
METRIC WEIGHT: 28.0 kg

POSSIBLE MOVES: Aromatherapy, Baton Pass, Calm Mind, Disarming Voice, Follow Me, Guard Split, Healing Wish, Helping Hand, Play Nice, Psybeam, Psychic, Psychic Terrain, Stored Power

FEMALE FORM

MALE FORM

INFERNAPE
Flame Pokémon

TYPE: FIRE-FIGHTING

Its crown of fire is indicative of its fiery nature. It is beaten by none in terms of quickness.

It tosses its enemies around with agility. It uses all its limbs to fight in its own unique style.

HOW TO SAY IT: in-FUR-nape
IMPERIAL HEIGHT: 3'11"
IMPERIAL WEIGHT: 121.3 lbs.
METRIC HEIGHT: 1.2 m
METRIC WEIGHT: 55.0 kg

POSSIBLE MOVES: Scratch, Leer, Ember, Taunt, Mach Punch, Fury Swipes, Flame Wheel, Feint, Punishment, Close Combat, Fire Spin, Acrobatics, Calm Mind, Flare Blitz

CHIMCHAR   **MONFERNO**   **INFERNAPE**

INKAY
Revolving Pokémon

TYPE: DARK-PSYCHIC

It spins while making its luminescent spots flash. These spots allow it to communicate with others by using different patterns of light.

By exposing foes to the blinking of its luminescent spots, Inkay demoralizes them, and then it seizes the chance to flee.

HOW TO SAY IT: IN-kay
IMPERIAL HEIGHT: 1'04"
IMPERIAL WEIGHT: 7.7 lbs.
METRIC HEIGHT: 0.4 m
METRIC WEIGHT: 3.5 kg

POSSIBLE MOVES: Foul Play, Hypnosis, Night Slash, Payback, Peck, Pluck, Psybeam, Psycho Cut, Slash, Superpower, Swagger, Switcheroo, Tackle, Topsy-Turvy, Wrap

INKAY   **MALAMAR**

INTELEON
Secret Agent Pokémon

TYPE: WATER

It has many hidden capabilities, such as fingertips that can shoot water and a membrane on its back that it can use to glide through the air.

Its nictitating membranes let it pick out foes' weak points so it can precisely blast them with water that shoots from its fingertips at Mach 3.

HOW TO SAY IT: in-TELL-ee-un
IMPERIAL HEIGHT: 6'03"
IMPERIAL WEIGHT: 99.6 lbs.
METRIC HEIGHT: 1.9 m
METRIC WEIGHT: 45.2 kg

POSSIBLE MOVES: Acrobatics, Bind, Growl, Hydro Pump, Liquidation, Pound, Rain Dance, Snipe Shot, Soak, Sucker Punch, Tearful Look, U-turn, Water Gun, Water Pulse

SOBBLE   **DRIZZILE**   **INTELEON**

Alternate Form:
GIGANTAMAX INTELEON

Gigantamax Inteleon's Water Gun move fires at Mach 7. As the Pokémon takes aim, it uses the crest on its head to gauge wind and temperature.

It has excellent sniping skills. Shooting a berry rolling along over nine miles away is a piece of cake for this Pokémon.

IMPERIAL HEIGHT: 131'03"+
IMPERIAL WEIGHT: ????.? lbs.
METRIC HEIGHT: 40.0+ m
METRIC WEIGHT: ???.? kg

IVYSAUR
Seed Pokémon

REGIONS:
KALOS
(CENTRAL)
KANTO

TYPE: GRASS-POISON

When the bulb on its back grows large, it appears to lose the ability to stand on its hind legs.

Exposure to sunlight adds to its strength. Sunlight also makes the bud on its back grow larger.

HOW TO SAY IT: EYE-vee-sore
IMPERIAL HEIGHT: 3'03"
IMPERIAL WEIGHT: 28.7 lbs.

METRIC HEIGHT: 1.0 m
METRIC WEIGHT: 13.0 kg

POSSIBLE MOVES: Tackle, Growl, Leech Seed, Vine Whip, Poison Powder, Sleep Powder, Take Down, Razor Leaf, Sweet Scent, Growth, Double Edge, Worry Seed, Synthesis, Solar Beam

BULBASAUR

IVYSAUR

VENUSAUR

MEGA VENUSAUR

JANGMO-O
Scaly Pokémon

REGIONS:
ALOLA
GALAR

TYPE: DRAGON

They learn to fight by smashing their head scales together. The dueling strengthens both their skills and their spirits.

Jangmo-o strikes its scales to communicate with others of its kind. Its scales are actually fur that's become as hard as metal.

HOW TO SAY IT: JANG-MOH-oh
IMPERIAL HEIGHT: 2'00"
IMPERIAL WEIGHT: 65.5 lbs.

METRIC HEIGHT: 0.6 m
METRIC WEIGHT: 29.7 kg

POSSIBLE MOVES: Dragon Claw, Dragon Dance, Dragon Tail, Headbutt, Iron Defense, Leer, Noble Roar, Outrage, Protect, Scary Face, Screech, Tackle, Work Up

JANGMO-O

HAKAMO-O

KOMMO-O

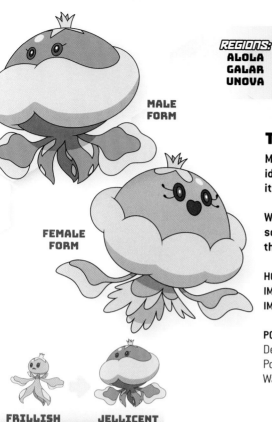

MALE FORM

FEMALE FORM

FRILLISH → JELLICENT

JELLICENT
Floating Pokémon

TYPE: WATER-GHOST

Most of this Pokémon's body composition is identical to sea water. It makes sunken ships its lair.

Whenever a full moon hangs in the night sky, schools of Jellicent gather near the surface of the sea, waiting for their prey to appear.

HOW TO SAY IT: JEL-ih-sent **METRIC HEIGHT:** 2.2 m
IMPERIAL HEIGHT: 7'03"   **METRIC WEIGHT:** 135.0 kg
IMPERIAL WEIGHT: 297.6 lbs.

POSSIBLE MOVES: Absorb, Acid Armor, Brine, Destiny Bond, Hex, Hydro Pump, Night Shade, Poison Sting, Rain Dance, Recover, Shadow Ball, Water Gun, Water Pulse, Water Spout, Whirlpool

IGGLYBUFF → JIGGLYPUFF → WIGGLYTUFF

REGIONS:
ALOLA
GALAR
KALOS
(MOUNTAIN)
KANTO

JIGGLYPUFF
Balloon Pokémon

TYPE: NORMAL-FAIRY

Jigglypuff has top-notch lung capacity, even by comparison to other Pokémon. It won't stop singing its lullabies until its foes fall asleep.

By freely changing the wavelength of its voice, Jigglypuff sings a mysterious melody sure to make any listener sleepy.

HOW TO SAY IT: JIG-lee-puff **METRIC HEIGHT:** 0.5 m
IMPERIAL HEIGHT: 1'08"   **METRIC WEIGHT:** 5.5 kg
IMPERIAL WEIGHT: 12.1 lbs.

POSSIBLE MOVES: Sing, Defense Curl, Pound, Play Nice, Disarming Voice, Disable, Double Slap, Rollout, Round, Stockpile, Swallow, Spit Up, Wake-Up Slap, Rest, Body Slam, Gyro Ball, Mimic, Hyper Voice, Double-Edge

TYPE: STEEL-PSYCHIC

A legend states that Jirachi will make true any wish that is written on notes attached to its head when it awakens. If this Pokémon senses danger, it will fight without awakening.

Jirachi will awaken from its sleep of a thousand years if you sing to it in a voice of purity. It is said to make true any wish that people desire.

HOW TO SAY IT: jir-AH-chi
IMPERIAL HEIGHT: 1'00"
IMPERIAL WEIGHT: 2.4 lbs.
METRIC HEIGHT: 0.3 m
METRIC WEIGHT: 1.1 kg

POSSIBLE MOVES: Wish, Confusion, Rest, Swift, Helping Hand, Psychic, Refresh, Lucky Chant, Zen Headbutt, Double-Edge, Gravity, Healing Wish, Future Sight, Cosmic Power, Last Resort, Doom Desire

DOES NOT EVOLVE

REGIONS:
ALOLA
GALAR
KALOS
(COASTAL)
KANTO

JOLTEON
Lightning Pokémon

TYPE: ELECTRIC

If it is angered or startled, the fur all over its body bristles like sharp needles that pierce foes.

It accumulates negative ions in the atmosphere to blast out 10,000-volt lightning bolts.

HOW TO SAY IT: JOL-tee-on
IMPERIAL HEIGHT: 2'07"
METRIC HEIGHT: 0.8 m
METRIC WEIGHT: 24.5 kg
IMPERIAL WEIGHT: 54.0 lbs.

POSSIBLE MOVES: Agility, Baby-Doll Eyes, Baton Pass, Bite, Charm, Copycat, Covet, Discharge, Double Kick, Double-Edge, Growl, Helping Hand, Last Resort, Pin Missile, Quick Attack, Sand Attack, Swift, Tackle, Tail Whip, Take Down, Thunder, Thunder Fang, Thunder Shock, Thunder Wave

EEVEE → JOLTEON

JOLTIK
Attaching Pokémon

TYPE: BUG-ELECTRIC

Joltik can be found clinging to other Pokémon. It's soaking up static electricity because it can't produce a charge on its own.

Joltik latch on to other Pokémon and suck out static electricity. They're often found sticking to Yamper's hindquarters.

HOW TO SAY IT: JOHL-tik
IMPERIAL HEIGHT: 0'04"
IMPERIAL WEIGHT: 1.3 lbs.
METRIC HEIGHT: 0.1 m
METRIC WEIGHT: 0.6 kg

POSSIBLE MOVES: Absorb, Agility, Bug Bite, Bug Buzz, Discharge, Electro Ball, Electroweb, Fury Cutter, Gastro Acid, Screech, Slash, String Shot, Sucker Punch, Thunder Wave

JOLTIK → GALVANTULA

JUMPLUFF
Cottonweed Pokémon

REGIONS:
JOHTO
KALOS
(CENTRAL)

TYPE: GRASS-FLYING

Jumpluff rides warm southern winds to cross the sea and fly to foreign lands. The Pokémon descends to the ground when it encounters cold air while it is floating.

HOW TO SAY IT: JUM-pluff
IMPERIAL HEIGHT: 2'07"
IMPERIAL WEIGHT: 6.6 lbs.
METRIC HEIGHT: 0.8 m
METRIC WEIGHT: 3.0 kg

POSSIBLE MOVES: Splash, Absorb, Synthesis, Tail Whip, Tackle, Fairy Wind, Poison Powder, Stun Spore, Sleep Powder, Bullet Seed, Leech Seed, Mega Drain, Acrobatics, Rage Powder, Cotton Spore, U-turn, Worry Seed, Giga Drain, Bounce, Memento

HOPPIP   SKIPLOOM   JUMPLUFF

JYNX
Human Shape Pokémon

REGIONS:
ALOLA
KALOS
(MOUNTAIN)
KANTO

TYPE: ICE-PSYCHIC

Appears to move to a rhythm of its own, as if it were dancing. It wiggles its hips as it walks.

HOW TO SAY IT: JINX
IMPERIAL HEIGHT: 4'07"
IMPERIAL WEIGHT: 89.5 lbs.
METRIC HEIGHT: 1.4 m
METRIC WEIGHT: 40.6 kg

POSSIBLE MOVES: Draining Kiss, Perish Song, Pound, Lick, Lovely Kiss, Powder Snow, Double Slap, Ice Punch, Heart Stamp, Mean Look, Fake Tears, Wake-Up Slap, Avalanche, Body Slam, Wring Out, Blizzard

SMOOCHUM   JYNX

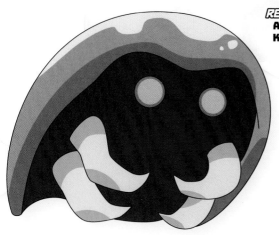

KABUTO
Shellfish Pokémon

TYPE: ROCK-WATER

This species is almost entirely extinct. Kabuto molt every three days, making their shells harder and harder.

While some say this species has gone extinct, Kabuto sightings are apparently fairly common in some places.

HOW TO SAY IT: ka-BOO-toe
IMPERIAL HEIGHT: 1'08"
IMPERIAL WEIGHT: 25.4 lbs.
METRIC HEIGHT: 0.5 m
METRIC WEIGHT: 11.5 kg

POSSIBLE MOVES: Scratch, Harden, Absorb, Leer, Mud Shot, Sand Attack, Endure, Aqua Jet, Mega Drain, Metal Sound, Ancient Power, Wring Out

KABUTO   KABUTOPS

KABUTOPS
Shellfish Pokémon

TYPE: ROCK-WATER

Kabutops slices its prey apart and sucks out the fluids. The discarded body parts become food for other Pokémon.

The cause behind the extinction of this species is unknown. Kabutops were aggressive Pokémon that inhabited warm seas.

HOW TO SAY IT: KA-boo-tops
IMPERIAL HEIGHT: 4'03"
IMPERIAL WEIGHT: 89.3 lbs.
METRIC HEIGHT: 1.3 m
METRIC WEIGHT: 40.5 kg

POSSIBLE MOVES: Feint, Scratch, Harden, Absorb, Leer, Mud Shot, Sand Attack, Endure, Aqua Jet, Mega Drain, Slash, Metal Sound, Ancient Power, Wring Out, Night Slash

KABUTO   KABUTOPS

KADABRA
Psi Pokémon

TYPE: PSYCHIC

Using its psychic power, Kadabra levitates as it sleeps. It uses its springy tail as a pillow.

This Pokémon's telekinesis is immensely powerful. To prepare for evolution, Kadabra stores up psychic energy in the star on its forehead.

HOW TO SAY IT: kuh-DAB-ra
IMPERIAL HEIGHT: 4'03"
IMPERIAL WEIGHT: 124.6 lbs.
METRIC HEIGHT: 1.3 m
METRIC WEIGHT: 56.5 kg

POSSIBLE MOVES: Kinesis, Teleport, Confusion, Disable, Psybeam, Miracle Eye, Reflect, Psycho Cut, Recover, Telekinesis, Ally Switch, Psychic, Role Play, Future Sight, Trick

ABRA　　**KADABRA**　　**ALAKAZAM**　　**MEGA ALAKAZAM**

KAKUNA
Cocoon Pokémon

TYPE: BUG-POISON

Able to move only slightly. When endangered, it may stick out its stinger and poison its enemy.

HOW TO SAY IT: kah-KOO-na
IMPERIAL HEIGHT: 2'00"
IMPERIAL WEIGHT: 22.0 lbs.
METRIC HEIGHT: 0.6 m
METRIC WEIGHT: 10.0 kg

POSSIBLE MOVE: Harden

WEEDLE　　**KAKUNA**　　**BEEDRILL**　　**MEGA BEEDRILL**

KANGASKHAN
Parent Pokémon

TYPE: NORMAL

Although it's carrying its baby in a pouch on its belly, Kangaskhan is swift on its feet. It intimidates its opponents with quick jabs.

There are records of a lost human child being raised by a childless Kangaskhan.

HOW TO SAY IT: KANG-gas-con
IMPERIAL HEIGHT: 7'03"
IMPERIAL WEIGHT: 176.4 lbs.
METRIC HEIGHT: 2.2 m
METRIC WEIGHT: 80.0 kg

POSSIBLE MOVES: Comet Punch, Leer, Fake Out, Tail Whip, Bite, Double Hit, Rage, Mega Punch, Chip Away, Dizzy Punch, Crunch, Endure, Outrage, Sucker Punch, Reversal

MEGA KANGASKHAN
Parent Pokémon

TYPE: NORMAL

IMPERIAL HEIGHT: 7'03"
IMPERIAL WEIGHT: 220.5 lbs.
METRIC HEIGHT: 2.2 m
METRIC WEIGHT: 100.0 kg

KANGASKHAN → **MEGA KANGASKHAN**

KARRABLAST

Clamping Pokémon

TYPE: BUG

Its strange physiology reacts to electrical energy in interesting ways. The presence of a Shelmet will cause this Pokémon to evolve.

It spits a liquid from its mouth to melt through Shelmet's shell. Karrablast doesn't eat the shell—it eats only the contents.

HOW TO SAY IT: KAIR-ruh-blast
IMPERIAL HEIGHT: 1'08"
IMPERIAL WEIGHT: 13.0 lbs.
METRIC HEIGHT: 0.5 m
METRIC WEIGHT: 5.9 kg

POSSIBLE MOVES: Acid Spray, Bug Buzz, Double-Edge, Endure, False Swipe, Flail, Fury Cutter, Headbutt, Leer, Peck, Scary Face, Swords Dance, Take Down, X-Scissor

KARRABLAST   ESCAVALIER

KARTANA

Drawn Sword Pokémon

REGION:
ALOLA

ULTRA BEAST

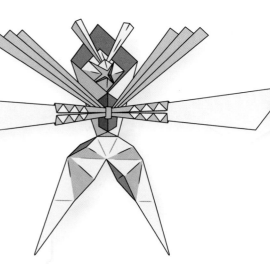

TYPE: GRASS-STEEL

This Ultra Beast's body, which is as thin as paper, is like a sharpened sword.

Although it's alien to this world and a danger here, it's apparently a common organism in the world where it normally lives.

HOW TO SAY IT: kar-TAH-nuh
IMPERIAL HEIGHT: 1'00"
IMPERIAL WEIGHT: 0.2 lbs.
METRIC HEIGHT: 0.3 m
METRIC WEIGHT: 0.1 kg

POSSIBLE MOVES: Sacred Sword, Defog, Vacuum Wave, Air Cutter, Fury Cutter, Cut, False Swipe, Razor Leaf, Synthesis, Aerial Ace, Laser Focus, Night Slash, Swords Dance, Leaf Blade, X-Scissor, Detect, Air Slash, Psycho Cut, Guillotine

DOES NOT EVOLVE

KECLEON
Color Swap Pokémon

TYPE: NORMAL

It changes its hue to blend into its surroundings. If no one takes notice of it for too long, it will pout and never reveal itself.

Its color changes for concealment and also when its mood or health changes. The darker the color, the healthier it is.

HOW TO SAY IT: KEH-clee-on
IMPERIAL HEIGHT: 3'03"
IMPERIAL WEIGHT: 48.5 lbs.
METRIC HEIGHT: 1.0 m
METRIC WEIGHT: 22.0 kg

POSSIBLE MOVES: Synchronoise, Ancient Power, Thief, Tail Whip, Astonish, Lick, Scratch, Bind, Feint Attack, Fury Swipes, Feint, Psybeam, Shadow Sneak, Slash, Screech, Substitute, Sucker Punch, Shadow Claw

DOES NOT EVOLVE

MYTHICAL POKÉMON

KELDEO
Colt Pokémon

ORDINARY FORM

RESOLUTE FORM

TYPE: WATER-FIGHTING

It crosses the world, running over the surfaces of oceans and rivers. It appears at scenic waterfronts.

When it is resolute, its body fills with power and it becomes swifter. Its jumps are then too fast to follow.

HOW TO SAY IT: KELL-dee-oh
IMPERIAL HEIGHT: 4'07"
IMPERIAL WEIGHT: 106.9 lbs.
METRIC HEIGHT: 1.4 m
METRIC WEIGHT: 48.5 kg

POSSIBLE MOVES: Aqua Jet, Leer, Double Kick, Bubble Beam, Take Down, Helping Hand, Retaliate, Aqua Tail, Sacred Sword, Swords Dance, Quick Guard, Work Up, Hydro Pump, Close Combat

DOES NOT EVOLVE

KINGDRA
Dragon Pokémon

TYPE: WATER-DRAGON

With the arrival of a storm at sea, this Pokémon will show itself on the surface. When a Kingdra and a Dragonite meet, a fierce battle ensues.

Scales shed by this Pokémon have such a splendorous gleam to them that they've been given to royalty as gifts.

HOW TO SAY IT: KING-dra
IMPERIAL HEIGHT: 5'11"
IMPERIAL WEIGHT: 335.1 lbs.
METRIC HEIGHT: 1.8 m
METRIC WEIGHT: 152.0 kg

POSSIBLE MOVES: Dragon Pulse, Yawn, Water Gun, Smokescreen, Leer, Bubble, Focus Energy, Bubble Beam, Agility, Twister, Brine, Hydro Pump, Dragon Dance

 HORSEA

 SEADRA

 KINGDRA

KINGLER

Pincer Pokémon

TYPE: WATER

Its large and hard pincer has 10,000-horsepower strength. However, being so big, it is unwieldy to move.

Its oversized claw is very powerful, but when it's not in battle, the claw just gets in the way.

HOW TO SAY IT: KING-lur
METRIC HEIGHT: 1.3 m
IMPERIAL HEIGHT: 4'03"
METRIC WEIGHT: 60.0 kg
IMPERIAL WEIGHT: 132.3 lbs.

POSSIBLE MOVES: Bubble Beam, Crabhammer, Flail, Guillotine, Hammer Arm, Harden, Leer, Metal Claw, Mud Shot, Protect, Razor Shell, Slam, Stomp, Swords Dance, Water Gun, Wide Guard

KRABBY   **KINGLER**

Alternate Form:
GIGANTAMAX KINGLER

The flow of Gigantamax energy has spurred this Pokémon's left pincer to grow to an enormous size. That claw can pulverize anything.

The bubbles it spews out are strongly alkaline. Any opponents hit by them will have their bodies quickly melted away.

IMPERIAL HEIGHT: 62'04"+
IMPERIAL WEIGHT: ?????.? lbs.
METRIC HEIGHT: 19.0+ m
METRIC WEIGHT: ???.? kg

KIRLIA

Emotion Pokémon

TYPE: PSYCHIC-FAIRY

If its Trainer becomes happy, it overflows with energy, dancing joyously while spinning about.

It has a psychic power that enables it to distort the space around it and see into the future.

HOW TO SAY IT: KERL-lee-ah
IMPERIAL HEIGHT: 2'07"
IMPERIAL WEIGHT: 44.5 lbs.

METRIC HEIGHT: 0.8 m
METRIC WEIGHT: 20.2 kg

POSSIBLE MOVES: Calm Mind, Charm, Confusion, Disarming Voice, Double Team, Draining Kiss, Dream Eater, Future Sight, Growl, Heal Pulse, Hypnosis, Life Dew, Psybeam, Psychic, Teleport

RALTS   KIRLIA

GARDEVOIR   MEGA GARDEVOIR

GALLADE   MEGA GALLADE

KLANG

Gear Pokémon

TYPE: STEEL

When Klang goes all out, the minigear links up perfectly with the outer part of the big gear, and this Pokémon's rotation speed increases sharply.

Many companies in the Galar region choose Klang as their logo. This Pokémon is considered the symbol of industrial technology.

HOW TO SAY IT: KLANG
IMPERIAL HEIGHT: 2'00"
IMPERIAL WEIGHT: 112.4 lbs.

METRIC HEIGHT: 0.6 m
METRIC WEIGHT: 51.0 kg

POSSIBLE MOVES: Autotomize, Bind, Charge, Charge Beam, Discharge, Gear Grind, Hyper Beam, Lock-On, Metal Sound, Screech, Shift Gear, Thunder Shock, Vise Grip, Zap Cannon

KLINK   KLANG   KLINKLANG

TYPE: STEEL-FAIRY

This Pokémon is constantly collecting keys. Entrust a Klefki with important keys, and the Pokémon will protect them no matter what.

Klefki sucks in metal ions with the horn topping its head. It seems this Pokémon loves keys so much that its head needed to look like one, too.

HOW TO SAY IT: KLEF-key
IMPERIAL HEIGHT: 0'08"
IMPERIAL WEIGHT: 6.6 lbs.
METRIC HEIGHT: 0.2 m
METRIC WEIGHT: 3.0 kg

POSSIBLE MOVES: Fairy Lock, Tackle, Fairy Wind, Astonish, Metal Sound, Spikes, Draining Kiss, Crafty Shield, Foul Play, Torment, Mirror Shot, Imprison, Recycle, Play Rough, Magic Room, Heal Block

REGIONS:
ALOLA
KALOS
(MOUNTAIN)

KLEFKI
Key Ring Pokémon

DOES NOT EVOLVE

TYPE: STEEL

The two minigears that compose this Pokémon are closer than twins. They mesh well only with each other.

It's suspected that Klink were the inspiration behind ancient people's invention of the first gears.

HOW TO SAY IT: KLEENK
IMPERIAL HEIGHT: 1'00"
IMPERIAL WEIGHT: 46.3 lbs.
METRIC HEIGHT: 0.3 m
METRIC WEIGHT: 21.0 kg

POSSIBLE MOVES: Autotomize, Bind, Charge, Charge Beam, Discharge, Gear Grind, Hyper Beam, Lock-On, Metal Sound, Screech, Shift Gear, Thunder Shock, Vise Grip, Zap Cannon

REGIONS:
GALAR
UNOVA

KLINK
Gear Pokémon

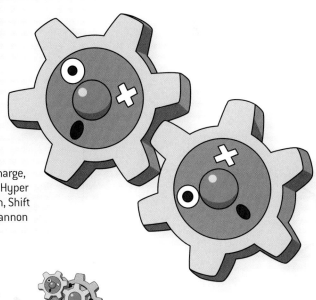

KLINK → KLANG → KLINKLANG

KLINKLANG

Gear Pokémon

TYPE: STEEL

From its spikes, it launches powerful blasts of electricity. Its red core contains an enormous amount of energy.

The three gears that compose this Pokémon spin at high speed. Its new spiked gear isn't a living creature.

HOW TO SAY IT: KLEENK-klang
IMPERIAL HEIGHT: 2'00"
IMPERIAL WEIGHT: 178.6 lbs.
METRIC HEIGHT: 0.6 m
METRIC WEIGHT: 81.0 kg

POSSIBLE MOVES: Autotomize, Bind, Charge, Charge Beam, Discharge, Electric Terrain, Gear Grind, Gear Up, Hyper Beam, Lock-On, Magnetic Flux, Metal Sound, Screech, Shift Gear, Thunder Shock, Vise Grip, Zap Cannon

KLINK   KLANG   KLINKLANG

KOFFING

Poison Gas Pokémon

TYPE: POISON

Its body is full of poisonous gas. It floats into garbage dumps, seeking out the fumes of raw, rotting trash.

It adores polluted air. Some claim that Koffing used to be more plentiful in the Galar region than they are now.

HOW TO SAY IT: KOFF-ing
IMPERIAL HEIGHT: 2'00"
IMPERIAL WEIGHT: 2.2 lbs.
METRIC HEIGHT: 0.6 m
METRIC WEIGHT: 1.0 kg

POSSIBLE MOVES: Assurance, Belch, Clear Smog, Destiny Bond, Explosion, Haze, Memento, Poison Gas, Self-Destruct, Sludge, Sludge Bomb, Smog, Smokescreen, Tackle, Toxic

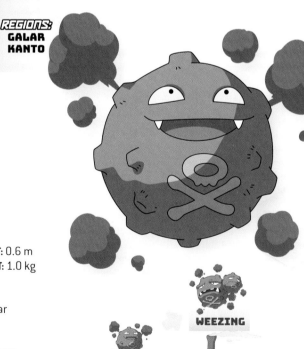

WEEZING

KOFFING

GALARIAN WEEZING

KOMALA
Drowsing Pokémon

TYPE: NORMAL

It stays asleep from the moment it's born. When it falls into a deep sleep, it stops moving altogether.

It remains asleep from birth to death as a result of the sedative properties of the leaves that form its diet.

HOW TO SAY IT: koh-MAH-luh **METRIC HEIGHT:** 0.4 m
IMPERIAL HEIGHT: 1'04" **METRIC WEIGHT:** 19.9 kg
IMPERIAL WEIGHT: 43.9 lbs.

POSSIBLE MOVES: Defense Curl, Rollout, Stockpile, Spit Up, Swallow, Rapid Spin, Yawn, Slam, Flail, Sucker Punch, Psych Up, Wood Hammer, Thrash

DOES NOT EVOLVE

KOMMO-O
Scaly Pokémon

TYPE: DRAGON-FIGHTING

It clatters its tail scales to unnerve opponents. This Pokémon will battle only those who stand steadfast in the face of this display.

Certain ruins have paintings of ancient warriors wearing armor made of Kommo-o scales.

HOW TO SAY IT: koh-MOH-oh **METRIC HEIGHT:** 1.6 m
IMPERIAL HEIGHT: 5'03" **METRIC WEIGHT:** 78.2 kg
IMPERIAL WEIGHT: 172.4 lbs.

POSSIBLE MOVES: Autotomize, Belly Drum, Boomburst, Clanging Scales, Clangorous Soul, Close Combat, Dragon Claw, Dragon Dance, Dragon Tail, Headbutt, Iron Defense, Leer, Noble Roar, Outrage, Protect, Scary Face, Screech, Tackle, Work Up

JANGMO-O   HAKAMO-O   KOMMO-O

KRABBY

River Crab Pokémon

TYPE: WATER

It can be found near the sea. The large pincers grow back if they are torn out of their sockets.

If it senses danger approaching, it cloaks itself with bubbles from its mouth so it will look bigger.

HOW TO SAY IT: KRAB-ee
IMPERIAL HEIGHT: 1'04"
IMPERIAL WEIGHT: 14.3 lbs.
METRIC HEIGHT: 0.4 m
METRIC WEIGHT: 6.5 kg

POSSIBLE MOVES: Bubble Beam, Crabhammer, Flail, Guillotine, Harden, Leer, Metal Claw, Mud Shot, Protect, Razor Shell, Slam, Stomp, Swords Dance, Water Gun

KRABBY   KINGLER

KRICKETOT

Cricket Pokémon

TYPE: BUG

It chats with others using the sounds of its colliding antennae. These sounds are fall hallmarks.

When its antennae hit each other, it sounds like the music of a xylophone.

HOW TO SAY IT: KRICK-eh-tot
IMPERIAL HEIGHT: 1'00"
IMPERIAL WEIGHT: 4.9 lbs.
METRIC HEIGHT: 0.3 m
METRIC WEIGHT: 2.2 kg

POSSIBLE MOVES: Growl, Bide, Struggle Bug, Bug Bite

KRICKETOT   KRICKETUNE

TYPE: BUG

It crosses its knifelike arms in front of its chest when it cries. It can compose melodies ad lib.

It signals its emotions with its melodies. Scientists are studying these melodic patterns.

REGION: SINNOH

KRICKETUNE
Cricket Pokémon

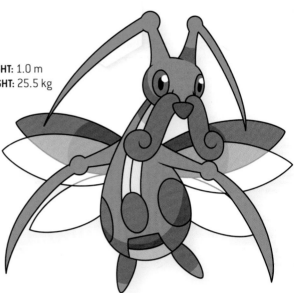

HOW TO SAY IT: KRICK-eh-toon
IMPERIAL HEIGHT: 3'03"
IMPERIAL WEIGHT: 56.2 lbs.
METRIC HEIGHT: 1.0 m
METRIC WEIGHT: 25.5 kg

POSSIBLE MOVES: Growl, Bide, Fury Cutter, Absorb, Sing, Focus Energy, Slash, X-Scissor, Screech, Fell Stinger, Taunt, Night Slash, Sticky Web, Bug Buzz, Perish Song

KRICKETOT ➤ **KRICKETUNE**

REGIONS: ALOLA KALOS (COASTAL) UNOVA

KROKOROK
Desert Croc Pokémon

TYPE: GROUND-DARK

Krokorok has specialized eyes that enable it to see in the dark. This ability lets Krokorok hunt in the dead of night without getting lost.

Although this Pokémon has specialized eyes that allow it to see in the dark, Krokorok won't move much at night—the desert gets cold after sunset.

HOW TO SAY IT: KRAHK-oh-rahk
IMPERIAL HEIGHT: 3'03"
IMPERIAL WEIGHT: 73.6 lbs.
METRIC HEIGHT: 1.0 m
METRIC WEIGHT: 33.4 kg

POSSIBLE MOVES: Leer, Rage, Bite, Sand Attack, Torment, Sand Tomb, Assurance, Mud-Slap, Embargo, Swagger, Crunch, Dig, Scary Face, Foul Play, Sandstorm, Earthquake, Thrash

SANDILE ➤ **KROKOROK** ➤ **KROOKODILE**

KROOKODILE

Intimidation Pokémon

TYPE: GROUND-DARK

This Pokémon is known as the Bully of the Sands. Krookodile's mighty jaws can bite through heavy plates of iron with almost no effort at all.

While terribly aggressive, Krookodile also has the patience to stay hidden under sand for days, lying in wait for prey.

HOW TO SAY IT: KROOK-oh-dyle
IMPERIAL HEIGHT: 4'11"
IMPERIAL WEIGHT: 212.3 lbs.
METRIC HEIGHT: 1.5 m
METRIC WEIGHT: 96.3 kg

POSSIBLE MOVES: Power Trip, Leer, Rage, Bite, Sand Attack, Torment, Sand Tomb, Assurance, Mud-Slap, Embargo, Swagger, Crunch, Dig, Scary Face, Foul Play, Sandstorm, Earthquake, Outrage

SANDILE   KROKOROK   KROOKODILE

LEGENDARY POKÉMON

KYOGRE
Sea Basin Pokémon

TYPE: WATER

Through Primal Reversion and with nature's full power, it will take back its true form. It can summon storms that cause the sea levels to rise.

Kyogre is said to be the personification of the sea itself. Legends tell of its many clashes against Groudon, as each sought to gain the power of nature.

HOW TO SAY IT: kai-OH-gurr
IMPERIAL HEIGHT: 14'09"
IMPERIAL WEIGHT: 776.0 lbs.
METRIC HEIGHT: 4.5 m
METRIC WEIGHT: 352.0 kg

POSSIBLE MOVES: Water Pulse, Scary Face, Body Slam, Muddy Water, Aqua Ring, Ice Beam, Ancient Power, Water Spout, Calm Mind, Aqua Tail, Sheer Cold, Double-Edge, Hydro Pump, Origin Pulse

PRIMAL KYOGRE
Sea Basin Pokémon

TYPE: WATER

IMPERIAL HEIGHT: 32'02"
IMPERIAL WEIGHT: 948.0 lbs.
METRIC HEIGHT: 9.8 m
METRIC WEIGHT: 430.0 kg

KYOGRE → PRIMAL KYOGRE

KYUREM

Boundary Pokémon

LEGENDARY POKÉMON

TYPE: DRAGON-ICE

This legendary ice Pokémon waits for a hero to fill in the missing parts of its body with truth or ideals.

It generates a powerful, freezing energy inside itself, but its body became frozen when the energy leaked out.

HOW TO SAY IT: KYOO-rem
IMPERIAL HEIGHT: 9'10" /
Black Kyurem: 10'10" /
White Kyurem: 11'10"
IMPERIAL WEIGHT: 716.5 lbs.
METRIC HEIGHT: 3.0 m /
Black Kyurem: 3.3m /
White Kyurem: 3.6m
METRIC WEIGHT: 325.0 kg

POSSIBLE MOVES: Icy Wind, Dragon Rage, Imprison, Ancient Power, Ice Beam, Dragon Breath, Slash, Scary Face, Glaciate, Dragon Pulse, Noble Roar, Endeavor, Blizzard, Outrage, Hyper Voice

BLACK KYUREM

WHITE KYUREM

DOES NOT EVOLVE

LAIRON
Iron Armor Pokémon

TYPE: STEEL-ROCK

Lairon tempers its steel body by drinking highly nutritious mineral springwater until it is bloated. This Pokémon makes its nest close to springs of delicious water.

Lairon feeds on iron contained in rocks and water. It makes its nest on mountains where iron ore is buried. As a result, the Pokémon often clashes with humans mining the iron ore.

HOW TO SAY IT: LAIR-ron   **METRIC HEIGHT:** 0.9 m
IMPERIAL HEIGHT: 2'11"   **METRIC WEIGHT:** 120.0 kg
IMPERIAL WEIGHT: 264.6 lbs.

POSSIBLE MOVES: Tackle, Harden, Mud-Slap, Headbutt, Metal Claw, Rock Tomb, Protect, Roar, Iron Head, Rock Slide, Take Down, Metal Sound, Iron Tail, Iron Defense, Double-Edge, Autotomize, Heavy Slam, Metal Burst

ARON   LAIRON   AGGRON   MEGA AGGRON

LAMPENT
Lamp Pokémon

TYPE: GHOST-FIRE

This Pokémon appears just before someone passes away, so it's feared as an emissary of death.

It lurks in cities, pretending to be a lamp. Once it finds someone whose death is near, it will trail quietly after them.

HOW TO SAY IT: LAM-pent   **METRIC HEIGHT:** 0.6 m
IMPERIAL HEIGHT: 2'00"   **METRIC WEIGHT:** 13.0 kg
IMPERIAL WEIGHT: 28.7 lbs.

POSSIBLE MOVES: Astonish, Confuse Ray, Curse, Ember, Fire Spin, Hex, Imprison, Inferno, Memento, Minimize, Night Shade, Overheat, Pain Split, Shadow Ball, Smog, Will-O-Wisp

LITWICK   LAMPENT   CHANDELURE

LANDORUS

Abundance Pokémon

LEGENDARY POKÉMON

TYPE: GROUND-FLYING

Lands visited by Landorus grant such bountiful crops that it has been hailed as "The Guardian of the Fields."

From the forces of lightning and wind, it creates energy to give nutrients to the soil and make the land abundant.

HOW TO SAY IT: LAN-duh-rus
IMPERIAL HEIGHT: Incarnate Forme: 4'11"
　　　　　　　　　　　Therian Forme: 4'03"
IMPERIAL WEIGHT: 149.9 lbs.
METRIC HEIGHT: Incarnate Forme: 1.5 m
　　　　　　　　　　Therian Forme: 1.3 m
METRIC WEIGHT: 68.0 kg

POSSIBLE MOVES: Block, Mud Shot, Rock Tomb, Imprison, Punishment, Bulldoze, Rock Throw, Extrasensory, Swords Dance, Earth Power, Rock Slide, Earthquake, Sandstorm, Fissure, Stone Edge, Hammer Arm, Outrage

INCARNATE FORME

THERIAN FORME

266

DOES NOT EVOLVE

TYPE: WATER-ELECTRIC

REGIONS:
ALOLA
GALAR
JOHTO
KALOS
(COASTAL)

LANTURN
Light Pokémon

The light it emits is so bright that it can illuminate the sea's surface from a depth of over three miles.

This Pokémon flashes a bright light that blinds its prey. This creates an opening for it to deliver an electrical attack.

HOW TO SAY IT: LAN-turn
IMPERIAL HEIGHT: 3'11"
IMPERIAL WEIGHT: 49.6 lbs.

METRIC HEIGHT: 1.2 m
METRIC WEIGHT: 22.5 kg

POSSIBLE MOVES: Aqua Ring, Bubble Beam, Charge, Confuse Ray, Discharge, Eerie Impulse, Electro Ball, Flail, Hydro Pump, Spark, Spit Up, Stockpile, Supersonic, Swallow, Take Down, Thunder Wave, Water Gun

CHINCHOU

LANTURN

LAPRAS

Transport Pokémon

REGIONS:
ALOLA
GALAR
KALOS
(COASTAL)
KANTO

TYPE: WATER-ICE

A smart and kindhearted Pokémon, it glides across the surface of the sea while its beautiful song echoes around it.

Crossing icy seas is no issue for this cold-resistant Pokémon. Its smooth skin is a little cool to the touch.

HOW TO SAY IT: LAP-rus
IMPERIAL HEIGHT: 8'02"
IMPERIAL WEIGHT: 485.0 lbs.
METRIC HEIGHT: 2.5 m
METRIC WEIGHT: 220.0 kg

POSSIBLE MOVES: Body Slam, Brine, Confuse Ray, Growl, Hydro Pump, Ice Beam, Ice Shard, Life Dew, Mist, Perish Song, Rain Dance, Sheer Cold, Sing, Water Gun, Water Pulse

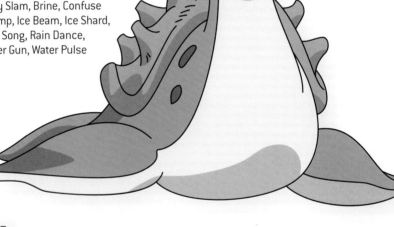

DOES NOT EVOLVE

Alternate Form:
GIGANTAMAX LAPRAS

Over 5,000 people can ride on its shell at once. And it's a very comfortable ride, without the slightest shaking or swaying.

It surrounds itself with a huge ring of gathered ice particles. It uses the ring to smash any icebergs that might impede its graceful swimming.

IMPERIAL HEIGHT: 78'09"+
IMPERIAL WEIGHT: ????.? lbs.
METRIC HEIGHT: 24.0+ m
METRIC WEIGHT: ???.? kg

LARVESTA
Torch Pokémon

TYPE: BUG-FIRE

The people of ancient times believed that Larvesta fell from the sun.

Larvesta's body is warm all over. It spouts fire from the tips of its horns to intimidate predators and scare prey.

HOW TO SAY IT: lar-VESS-tah
IMPERIAL HEIGHT: 3'07"
IMPERIAL WEIGHT: 63.5 lbs.
METRIC HEIGHT: 1.1 m
METRIC WEIGHT: 28.8 kg

POSSIBLE MOVES: Ember, String Shot, Absorb, Take Down, Flame Charge, Bug Bite, Double-Edge, Flame Wheel, Bug Buzz, Amnesia, Thrash, Flare Blitz

LARVESTA   VOLCARONA

LARVITAR
Rock Skin Pokémon

TYPE: ROCK-GROUND

Born deep underground, it comes aboveground and becomes a pupa once it has finished eating the surrounding soil.

It feeds on soil. After it has eaten a large mountain, it will fall asleep so it can grow.

HOW TO SAY IT: LAR-vuh-tar
IMPERIAL HEIGHT: 2'00"
IMPERIAL WEIGHT: 158.7 lbs.
METRIC HEIGHT: 0.6 m
METRIC WEIGHT: 72.0 kg

POSSIBLE MOVES: Bite, Crunch, Dark Pulse, Earthquake, Hyper Beam, Leer, Payback, Rock Slide, Rock Throw, Sandstorm, Scary Face, Screech, Stomping Tantrum, Stone Edge, Tackle, Thrash

LARVITAR   PUPITAR   TYRANITAR   MEGA TYRANITAR

TYPE: DRAGON-PSYCHIC

Latias is highly sensitive to the emotions of people. If it senses any hostility, this Pokémon ruffles the feathers all over its body and cries shrilly to intimidate the foe.

Latias is highly intelligent and capable of understanding human speech. It is covered with a glass-like down. The Pokémon enfolds its body with its down and refracts light to alter its appearance.

HOW TO SAY IT: LAT-ee-ahs
IMPERIAL HEIGHT: 4'07"
IMPERIAL WEIGHT: 88.2 lbs.
METRIC HEIGHT: 1.4 m
METRIC WEIGHT: 40.0 kg

POSSIBLE MOVES: Psywave, Wish, Helping Hand, Safeguard, Dragon Breath, Water Sport, Refresh, Mist Ball, Zen Headbutt, Recover, Psycho Shift, Charm, Psychic, Heal Pulse, Reflect Type, Guard Split, Dragon Pulse, Healing Wish, Stored Power

MEGA LATIAS
Eon Pokémon

TYPE: DRAGON-PSYCHIC

IMPERIAL HEIGHT: 5'11"
IMPERIAL WEIGHT: 114.6 lbs.
METRIC HEIGHT: 1.8 m
METRIC WEIGHT: 52.0 kg

LATIAS → **MEGA LATIAS**

TYPE: DRAGON-PSYCHIC

Latios has the ability to make others see an image of what it has seen or imagines in its head. This Pokémon is intelligent and understands human speech.

Latios will only open its heart to a Trainer with a compassionate spirit. This Pokémon can fly faster than a jet plane by folding its forelegs to minimize air resistance.

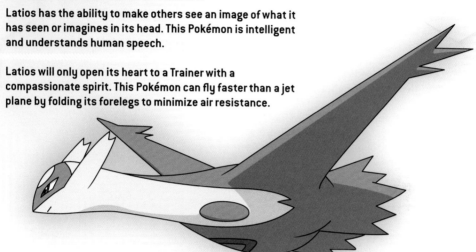

HOW TO SAY IT: LAT-ee-ose
IMPERIAL HEIGHT: 6'07"
IMPERIAL WEIGHT: 132.3 lbs.
METRIC HEIGHT: 2.0 m
METRIC WEIGHT: 60.0 kg

POSSIBLE MOVES: Memento, Helping Hand, Heal Block, Psywave, Safeguard, Protect, Dragon Dance, Stored Power, Refresh, Heal Pulse, Dragon Breath, Luster Purge, Psycho Shift, Recover, Telekinesis, Zen Headbutt, Power Split, Psychic, Dragon Pulse

MEGA LATIOS
Eon Pokémon

TYPE: DRAGON-PSYCHIC

IMPERIAL HEIGHT: 7'07"
IMPERIAL WEIGHT: 154.3 lbs.
METRIC HEIGHT: 2.3 m
METRIC WEIGHT: 70.0 kg

LATIOS   MEGA LATIOS

271

LEAFEON
Verdant Pokémon

REGIONS:
ALOLA
GALAR
KALOS
(COASTAL)
SINNOH

TYPE: GRASS

Galarians favor the distinctive aroma that drifts from this Pokémon's leaves. There's a popular perfume made using that scent.

This Pokémon's tail is blade sharp, with a fantastic cutting edge that can slice right though large trees.

HOW TO SAY IT: LEAF-ee-on **METRIC HEIGHT:** 1.0 m
IMPERIAL HEIGHT: 3'03" **METRIC WEIGHT:** 25.5 kg
IMPERIAL WEIGHT: 56.2 lbs.

POSSIBLE MOVES: Baby-Doll Eyes, Baton Pass, Bite, Charm, Copycat, Covet, Double-Edge, Giga Drain, Growl, Helping Hand, Last Resort, Leaf Blade, Leech Seed, Magical Leaf, Quick Attack, Razor Leaf, Sand Attack, Sunny Day, Swift, Swords Dance, Synthesis, Tackle, Tail Whip, Take Down

EEVEE　　**LEAFEON**

LEAVANNY
Nurturing Pokémon

TYPE: BUG-GRASS

Upon finding a small Pokémon, it weaves clothing for it from leaves by using the sticky silk secreted from its mouth.

It keeps its eggs warm with heat from fermenting leaves. It also uses leaves to make warm wrappings for Sewaddle.

HOW TO SAY IT: lee-VAN-nee **METRIC HEIGHT:** 1.2 m
IMPERIAL HEIGHT: 3'11" **METRIC WEIGHT:** 20.5 kg
IMPERIAL WEIGHT: 45.2 lbs.

POSSIBLE MOVES: Slash, False Swipe, Tackle, String Shot, Bug Bite, Razor Leaf, Struggle Bug, Fell Stinger, Helping Hand, Leaf Blade, X-Scissor, Entrainment, Swords Dance, Leaf Storm

SEWADDLE　　**SWADLOON**　　**LEAVANNY**

LEDIAN
Five Star Pokémon

TYPE: BUG-FLYING

It's said that the patterns on its back are related to the stars in the night sky, but the details of that relationship remain unclear.

It flies through the night sky, sprinkling sparkly dust. According to some, if that dust sticks to you, good things will happen to you.

HOW TO SAY IT: LEH-dee-an
IMPERIAL HEIGHT: 4'07"
IMPERIAL WEIGHT: 78.5 lbs.
METRIC HEIGHT: 1.4 m
METRIC WEIGHT: 35.6 kg

POSSIBLE MOVES: Tackle, Supersonic, Swift, Light Screen, Reflect, Safeguard, Mach Punch, Silver Wind, Comet Punch, Baton Pass, Agility, Bug Buzz, Air Slash, Double-Edge

LEDYBA   LEDIAN

LEDYBA
Five Star Pokémon

TYPE: BUG-FLYING

This Pokémon is very sensitive to cold. In the warmth of Alola, it appears quite lively.

These very cowardly Pokémon join together and use Reflect to protect their nest.

HOW TO SAY IT: LEH-dee-bah
IMPERIAL HEIGHT: 3'03"
IMPERIAL WEIGHT: 23.8 lbs.
METRIC HEIGHT: 1.0 m
METRIC WEIGHT: 10.8 kg

POSSIBLE MOVES: Tackle, Supersonic, Swift, Light Screen, Reflect, Safeguard, Mach Punch, Silver Wind, Comet Punch, Baton Pass, Agility, Bug Buzz, Air Slash, Double-Edge

LEDYBA   LEDIAN

LICKILICKY

Licking Pokémon

REGIONS:
ALOLA
KALOS
(MOUNTAIN)
SINNOH

TYPE: NORMAL

Lickilicky's strange tongue can stretch to many times the length of its body. No one has figured out how Lickilicky's tongue can stretch so far.

Lickilicky can do just about anything with its tongue, which is as dexterous as the human hand. In contrast, Lickilicky's use of its fingers is clumsy.

HOW TO SAY IT: LICK-ee-LICK-ee
IMPERIAL HEIGHT: 5'07"
IMPERIAL WEIGHT: 308.6 lbs.
METRIC HEIGHT: 1.7 m
METRIC WEIGHT: 140.0 kg

POSSIBLE MOVES: Wring Out, Power Whip, Lick, Supersonic, Defense Curl, Knock Off, Wrap, Stomp, Disable, Slam, Rollout, Chip Away, Me First, Refresh, Screech, Gyro Ball

LICKITUNG LICKILICKY

LICKITUNG

Licking Pokémon

REGIONS:
ALOLA
KALOS
(MOUNTAIN)
KANTO

TYPE: NORMAL

If this Pokémon's sticky saliva gets on you and you don't clean it off, an intense itch will set in. The itch won't go away, either.

Bug Pokémon are Lickitung's main food source. This Pokémon paralyzes its prey with a lick from its long tongue, then swallows the prey whole.

HOW TO SAY IT: LICK-it-tung
IMPERIAL HEIGHT: 3'11"
IMPERIAL WEIGHT: 144.4 lbs.
METRIC HEIGHT: 1.2 m
METRIC WEIGHT: 65.5 kg

POSSIBLE MOVES: Lick, Supersonic, Defense Curl, Knock Off, Wrap, Stomp, Disable, Slam, Rollout, Chip Away, Me First, Refresh, Screech, Power Whip, Wring Out

LICKITUNG LICKILICKY

LIEPARD
Cruel Pokémon

TYPE: DARK

Don't be fooled by its gorgeous fur and elegant figure. This is a moody and vicious Pokémon.

This stealthy Pokémon sneaks up behind prey without making any sound at all. It competes with Thievul for territory.

HOW TO SAY IT: LY-purd
IMPERIAL HEIGHT: 3'07"
IMPERIAL WEIGHT: 82.7 lbs.
METRIC HEIGHT: 1.1 m
METRIC WEIGHT: 37.5 kg

POSSIBLE MOVES: Assurance, Fake Out, Fury Swipes, Growl, Hone Claws, Nasty Plot, Night Slash, Play Rough, Sand Attack, Scratch, Sucker Punch, Torment

PURRLOIN **LIEPARD**

LILEEP
Sea Lily Pokémon

TYPE: ROCK-GRASS

In ancient times, it lived in warm seas. It disguised itself as seaweed to ambush its prey and devoured them whole when they got close.

It sticks to rocks with its powerful suckers and can't be washed away no matter how rough the surf gets.

HOW TO SAY IT: lil-LEEP
IMPERIAL HEIGHT: 3'03"
IMPERIAL WEIGHT: 52.5 lbs.
METRIC HEIGHT: 1.0 m
METRIC WEIGHT: 23.8 kg

POSSIBLE MOVES: Astonish, Constrict, Acid, Ingrain, Confuse Ray, Amnesia, Brine, Giga Drain, Gastro Acid, Ancient Power, Energy Ball, Stockpile, Spit Up, Swallow, Wring Out

LILEEP **CRADILY**

LILLIGANT

Flowering Pokémon

TYPE: GRASS

It's believed that even first-rate gardeners have a hard time getting the flower on a Lilligant's head to bloom.

Essential oils made from Lilligant flowers have a sublime scent, but they're also staggeringly expensive.

HOW TO SAY IT: LIL-lih-gunt **METRIC HEIGHT:** 1.1 m
IMPERIAL HEIGHT: 3'07" **METRIC WEIGHT:** 16.3 kg
IMPERIAL WEIGHT: 35.9 lbs.

POSSIBLE MOVES: Growth, Leech Seed, Mega Drain, Synthesis, Teeter Dance, Quiver Dance, Petal Dance, Petal Blizzard

PETILIL LILLIGANT

LILLIPUP

Puppy Pokémon

TYPE: NORMAL

This Pokémon is courageous but also cautious. It uses the soft fur covering its face to collect information about its surroundings.

This Pokémon is far brighter than the average child, and Lillipup won't forget the love it receives or any abuse it suffers.

HOW TO SAY IT: LIL-ee-pup **METRIC HEIGHT:** 0.4 m
IMPERIAL HEIGHT: 1'04" **METRIC WEIGHT:** 4.1 kg
IMPERIAL WEIGHT: 9.0 lbs.

POSSIBLE MOVES: Leer, Tackle, Odor Sleuth, Bite, Baby-Doll Eyes, Helping Hand, Take Down, Work Up, Crunch, Roar, Retaliate, Reversal, Last Resort, Giga Impact, Play Rough

LILLIPUP HERDIER STOUTLAND

REGIONS:
HOENN
KALOS
(CENTRAL)

LINOONE
Rushing Pokémon

TYPE: NORMAL

Its fur is strong and supple. Shaving brushes made with shed Linoone hairs are highly prized.

It uses its explosive speed and razor-sharp claws to bring down prey. Running along winding paths is not its strong suit.

HOW TO SAY IT: line-NOON **METRIC HEIGHT:** 0.5 m
IMPERIAL HEIGHT: 1'08" **METRIC WEIGHT:** 32.5 kg
IMPERIAL WEIGHT: 71.6 lbs.

POSSIBLE MOVES: Baby-Doll Eyes, Belly Drum, Covet, Double-Edge, Flail, Fling, Fury Swipes, Growl, Headbutt, Hone Claws, Pin Missile, Rest, Sand Attack, Slash, Switcheroo, Tackle, Tail Whip, Take Down

ZIGZAGOON   LINOONE

REGION:
GALAR

GALARIAN LINOONE
Rushing Pokémon

TYPE: DARK-NORMAL

It uses its long tongue to taunt opponents. Once the opposition is enraged, this Pokémon hurls itself at the opponent, tackling them forcefully.

This very aggressive Pokémon will recklessly challenge opponents stronger than itself.

HOW TO SAY IT: line-NOON **METRIC HEIGHT:** 0.5 m
IMPERIAL HEIGHT: 1'08" **METRIC WEIGHT:** 32.5 kg
IMPERIAL WEIGHT: 71.7 lbs.

POSSIBLE MOVES: Baby-Doll Eyes, Counter, Double-Edge, Fury Swipes, Headbutt, Hone Claws, Leer, Lick, Night Slash, Pin Missile, Rest, Sand Attack, Scary Face, Snarl, Switcheroo, Tackle, Take Down, Taunt

GALARIAN   GALARIAN   OBSTAGOON
ZIGZAGOON   LINOONE

LITLEO

Lion Cub Pokémon

LITLEO   PYROAR

REGIONS:
ALOLA
KALOS
(CENTRAL)

TYPE: FIRE-NORMAL

When they're young, they live with a pride. Once they're able to hunt prey on their own, they're kicked out and have to make their own way.

This hot-blooded Pokémon is filled with curiosity. When it gets angry or starts fighting, its short mane gets hot.

HOW TO SAY IT: LIT-lee-oh   **METRIC HEIGHT:** 0.6 m
IMPERIAL HEIGHT: 2'00"   **METRIC WEIGHT:** 13.5 kg
IMPERIAL WEIGHT: 29.8 lbs.

POSSIBLE MOVES: Tackle, Leer, Ember, Work Up, Headbutt, Noble Roar, Take Down, Fire Fang, Endeavor, Echoed Voice, Flamethrower, Crunch, Hyper Voice, Incinerate, Overheat

---

LITTEN

Fire Cat Pokémon

REGION:
ALOLA

TYPE: FIRE

If you try too hard to get close to it, it won't open up to you. Even if you do grow close, giving it too much affection is still a no-no.

Its coat regrows twice a year. When the time comes, Litten sets its own body on fire and burns away the old fur.

HOW TO SAY IT: LIT-n   **METRIC HEIGHT:** 0.4 m
IMPERIAL HEIGHT: 1'04"   **METRIC WEIGHT:** 4.3 kg
IMPERIAL WEIGHT: 9.5 lbs.

POSSIBLE MOVES: Scratch, Ember, Growl, Lick, Leer, Fire Fang, Double Kick, Roar, Bite, Swagger, Fury Swipes, Thrash, Flamethrower, Scary Face, Flare Blitz, Outrage

LITTEN   TORRACAT   INCINEROAR

LITWICK

Candle Pokémon

TYPE: GHOST-FIRE

The flame on its head keeps its body slightly warm. This Pokémon takes lost children by the hand to guide them to the spirit world.

The younger the life this Pokémon absorbs, the brighter and eerier the flame on its head burns.

HOW TO SAY IT: LIT-wik
IMPERIAL HEIGHT: 1'00"
IMPERIAL WEIGHT: 6.8 lbs.
METRIC HEIGHT: 0.3 m
METRIC WEIGHT: 3.1 kg

POSSIBLE MOVES: Astonish, Confuse Ray, Curse, Ember, Fire Spin, Hex, Imprison, Inferno, Memento, Minimize, Night Shade, Overheat, Pain Split, Shadow Ball, Smog, Will-O-Wisp

LITWICK   **LAMPENT**   **CHANDELURE**

LOMBRE

Jolly Pokémon

TYPE: WATER-GRASS

It is nocturnal and becomes active at nightfall. It feeds on aquatic mosses that grow in the riverbed.

It lives at the water's edge where it is sunny. It sleeps on a bed of water grass by day and becomes active at night.

HOW TO SAY IT: LOM-brey
IMPERIAL HEIGHT: 3'11"
IMPERIAL WEIGHT: 71.6 lbs.
METRIC HEIGHT: 1.2 m
METRIC WEIGHT: 32.5 kg

POSSIBLE MOVES: Absorb, Astonish, Bubble Beam, Energy Ball, Fake Out, Flail, Fury Swipes, Giga Drain, Growl, Hydro Pump, Knock Off, Mega Drain, Mist, Nature Power, Rain Dance, Teeter Dance, Water Gun, Zen Headbutt

LOTAD   **LOMBRE**   **LUDICOLO**

LOPUNNY

Rabbit Pokémon

TYPE: NORMAL

Lopunny is constantly monitoring its surroundings. If danger approaches, this Pokémon responds with superdestructive kicks.

Once hot seasons are over, Lopunny's coat will be replaced with fur that holds a lot of insulating air in preparation for colder weather.

HOW TO SAY IT: LAH-pun-nee
IMPERIAL HEIGHT: 3'11"
IMPERIAL WEIGHT: 73.4 lbs.
METRIC HEIGHT: 1.2 m
METRIC WEIGHT: 33.3 kg

POSSIBLE MOVES: Return, Healing Wish, Bounce, Rototiller, Mirror Coat, Magic Coat, Defense Curl, Splash, Pound, Endure, Baby-Doll Eyes, Quick Attack, Jump Kick, Baton Pass, Agility, Dizzy Punch, After You, Charm, Entrainment, High Jump Kick

MEGA LOPUNNY

Rabbit Pokémon

TYPE: NORMAL-FIGHTING

IMPERIAL HEIGHT: 4'03"
IMPERIAL WEIGHT: 62.4 lbs.
METRIC HEIGHT: 1.3 m
METRIC WEIGHT: 28.3 kg

BUNEARY → LOPUNNY → MEGA LOPUNNY

LOTAD
Water Weed Pokémon

TYPE: WATER-GRASS

It searches about for clean water. If it does not drink water for too long, the leaf on its head wilts.

Its leaf grew too large for it to live on land. That is how it began to live floating in the water.

HOW TO SAY IT: LOW-tad   **METRIC HEIGHT:** 0.5 m
IMPERIAL HEIGHT: 1'08"   **METRIC WEIGHT:** 2.6 kg
IMPERIAL WEIGHT: 5.7 lbs.

POSSIBLE MOVES: Absorb, Astonish, Bubble Beam, Energy Ball, Flail, Giga Drain, Growl, Mega Drain, Mist, Nature Power, Rain Dance, Water Gun, Zen Headbutt

LOTAD   LOMBRE   LUDICOLO

LOUDRED
Big Voice Pokémon

TYPE: NORMAL

Loudred's ears serve as speakers, and they can put out sound waves powerful enough to blow away a house.

The force of this Pokémon's loud voice isn't just the sound—it's also the wave of air pressure that blows opponents away and damages them.

HOW TO SAY IT: LOUD-red
IMPERIAL HEIGHT: 3'03"
IMPERIAL WEIGHT: 89.3 lbs.
METRIC HEIGHT: 1.0 m
METRIC WEIGHT: 40.5 kg

POSSIBLE MOVES: Bite, Pound, Echoed Voice, Astonish, Howl, Screech, Supersonic, Stomp, Uproar, Roar, Rest, Sleep Talk, Hyper Voice, Synchronoise

WHISMUR   LOUDRED   EXPLOUD

LUCARIO

Aura Pokémon

REGIONS:
ALOLA
GALAR
KALOS
(CENTRAL)
SINNOH

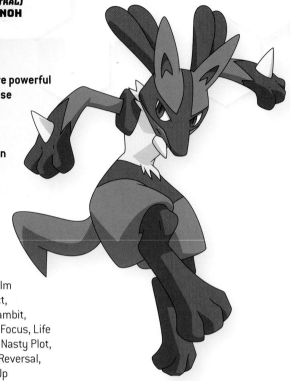

TYPE: FIGHTING-STEEL

It controls waves known as auras, which are powerful enough to pulverize huge rocks. It uses these waves to take down its prey.

It can tell what people are thinking. Only Trainers who have justice in their hearts can earn this Pokémon's trust.

HOW TO SAY IT: loo-CAR-ee-oh
IMPERIAL HEIGHT: 3'11"
IMPERIAL WEIGHT: 119.0 lbs.
METRIC HEIGHT: 1.2 m
METRIC WEIGHT: 54.0 kg

POSSIBLE MOVES: Aura Sphere, Bone Rush, Calm Mind, Close Combat, Copycat, Counter, Detect, Dragon Pulse, Extreme Speed, Feint, Final Gambit, Force Palm, Heal Pulse, Helping Hand, Laser Focus, Life Dew, Metal Claw, Metal Sound, Meteor Mash, Nasty Plot, Power-Up Punch, Quick Attack, Quick Guard, Reversal, Rock Smash, Screech, Swords Dance, Work Up

MEGA LUCARIO

Aura Pokémon

TYPE: FIGHTING-STEEL

IMPERIAL HEIGHT: 4'03"
IMPERIAL WEIGHT: 126.8 lbs.
METRIC HEIGHT: 1.3 m
METRIC WEIGHT: 57.5 kg

RIOLU   LUCARIO   MEGA LUCARIO

LUDICOLO
Carefree Pokémon

TYPE: WATER-GRASS

The rhythm of bright, festive music activates Ludicolo's cells, making it more powerful.

If it hears festive music, it begins moving in rhythm in order to amplify its power.

HOW TO SAY IT: LOO-dee-KO-low
IMPERIAL HEIGHT: 4'11"
IMPERIAL WEIGHT: 121.3 lbs.
METRIC HEIGHT: 1.5 m
METRIC WEIGHT: 55.0 kg

POSSIBLE MOVES: Absorb, Astonish, Bubble Beam, Energy Ball, Fake Out, Flail, Fury Swipes, Giga Drain, Growl, Hydro Pump, Knock Off, Mega Drain, Mist, Nature Power, Rain Dance, Teeter Dance, Water Gun, Zen Headbutt

LOTAD → LOMBRE → LUDICOLO

LEGENDARY POKÉMON

LUGIA
Diving Pokémon

TYPE: PSYCHIC-FLYING

Lugia's wings pack devastating power—a light fluttering of its wings can blow apart regular houses. As a result, this Pokémon chooses to live out of sight deep under the sea.

HOW TO SAY IT: LOO-gee-uh
IMPERIAL HEIGHT: 17'01"
IMPERIAL WEIGHT: 476.2 lbs.
METRIC HEIGHT: 5.2 m
METRIC WEIGHT: 216.0 kg

POSSIBLE MOVES: Whirlwind, Weather Ball, Gust, Dragon Rush, Extrasensory, Rain Dance, Hydro Pump, Aeroblast, Punishment, Ancient Power, Safeguard, Recover, Future Sight, Natural Gift, Calm Mind, Sky Attack

DOES NOT EVOLVE

LUMINEON

Neon Pokémon

TYPE: WATER

Deep down at the bottom of the ocean, prey is scarce. Lumineon get into fierce disputes with Lanturn over food.

They traverse the deep waters as if crawling over the seafloor. The fantastic lights of its fins shine like stars in the night sky.

HOW TO SAY IT: loo-MIN-ee-on **METRIC HEIGHT:** 1.2 m
IMPERIAL HEIGHT: 3'11" **METRIC WEIGHT:** 24.0 kg
IMPERIAL WEIGHT: 52.9 lbs.

POSSIBLE MOVES: Soak, Gust, Pound, Water Gun, Attract, Rain Dance, Water Pulse, Captivate, Safeguard, Aqua Ring, Whirlpool, U-turn, Bounce, Silver Wind

FINNEON **LUMINEON**

LUNALA

Moone Pokémon

LEGENDARY POKÉMON

TYPE: PSYCHIC-GHOST

Records of it exist in writings from long, long ago, where it was known by the name "the beast that calls the moon."

It sometimes summons unknown powers and life-forms here to this world from holes that lead to other worlds.

HOW TO SAY IT: loo-NAH-luh **METRIC HEIGHT:** 4.0 m
IMPERIAL HEIGHT: 13'01" **METRIC WEIGHT:** 120.0 kg
IMPERIAL WEIGHT: 264.6 lbs.

POSSIBLE MOVES: Moongeist Beam, Cosmic Power, Hypnosis, Teleport, Confusion, Night Shade, Confuse Ray, Air Slash, Shadow Ball, Moonlight, Night Daze, Magic Coat, Moonblast, Dream Eater, Phantom Force, Wide Guard, Hyper Beam

COSMOG **COSMOEM** **LUNALA**

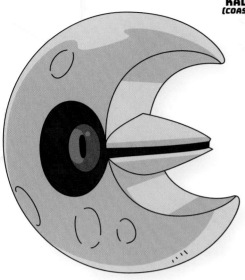

LUNATONE
Meteorite Pokémon

TYPE: ROCK-PSYCHIC

The phase of the moon apparently has some effect on its power. It's active on the night of a full moon.

It was discovered at the site of a meteor strike 40 years ago. Its stare can lull its foes to sleep.

HOW TO SAY IT: LOO-nuh-tone
IMPERIAL HEIGHT: 3'03"
IMPERIAL WEIGHT: 370.4 lbs.
METRIC HEIGHT: 1.0 m
METRIC WEIGHT: 168.0 kg

POSSIBLE MOVES: Confusion, Cosmic Power, Explosion, Future Sight, Harden, Hypnosis, Magic Room, Moonblast, Moonlight, Psychic, Psyshock, Rock Polish, Rock Slide, Rock Throw, Stone Edge, Tackle

DOES NOT EVOLVE

LURANTIS
Bloom Sickle Pokémon

TYPE: GRASS

This Pokémon resembles a beautiful flower. A properly raised Lurantis will have gorgeous, brilliant colors.

The petals on this Pokémon's arms are thin and super sharp, and they can fire laser beams if Lurantis gathers light first.

HOW TO SAY IT: loor-RAN-tis
IMPERIAL HEIGHT: 2'11"
IMPERIAL WEIGHT: 40.8 lbs.
METRIC HEIGHT: 0.9 m
METRIC WEIGHT: 18.5 kg

POSSIBLE MOVES: Petal Blizzard, X-Scissor, Night Slash, Fury Cutter, Leafage, Razor Leaf, Growth, Ingrain, Leaf Blade, Synthesis, Slash, Sweet Scent, Solar Blade, Sunny Day

FOMANTIS ⟶ LURANTIS

LUVDISC

Rendezvous Pokémon

REGIONS:
ALOLA
HOENN
KALOS
(COASTAL)

TYPE: WATER

There was an era when it was overfished due to the rumor that having one of its heart-shaped scales would enable you to find a sweetheart.

Luvdisc makes its home in coral reefs in warm seas. It especially likes sleeping in the space between Corsola's branches.

HOW TO SAY IT: LOVE-disk **METRIC HEIGHT:** 0.6 m
IMPERIAL HEIGHT: 2'00" **METRIC WEIGHT:** 8.7 kg
IMPERIAL WEIGHT: 19.2 lbs.

POSSIBLE MOVES: Tackle, Charm, Water Gun, Agility, Draining Kiss, Lucky Chant, Water Pulse, Attract, Heart Stamp, Flail, Sweet Kiss, Take Down, Captivate, Aqua Ring, Soak, Hydro Pump, Safeguard

DOES NOT EVOLVE

LUXIO

Spark Pokémon

REGION:
SINNOH

TYPE: ELECTRIC

By joining its tail with that of another Luxio, this Pokémon can receive some of the other Luxio's electricity and power up its own electric blasts.

Upon encountering an opponent, this Pokémon prepares for battle by extending its claws, which can put out 1,000,000 volts of electricity.

HOW TO SAY IT: LUCKS-ee-oh
IMPERIAL HEIGHT: 2'11"
IMPERIAL WEIGHT: 67.2 lbs.
METRIC HEIGHT: 0.9 m
METRIC WEIGHT: 30.5 kg

POSSIBLE MOVES: Tackle, Leer, Charge, Spark, Bite, Roar, Swagger, Thunder Fang, Crunch, Scary Face, Discharge, Wild Charge

SHINX

LUXIO

LUXRAY

LUXRAY
Gleam Eyes Pokémon

TYPE: ELECTRIC

Luxray can see through solid objects. It will instantly spot prey trying to hide behind walls, even if the walls are thick.

Seeing through solid objects uses up a lot of Luxray's electricity, so the Pokémon sleeps for long periods of time to store up energy.

HOW TO SAY IT: LUCKS-ray
IMPERIAL HEIGHT: 4'07"
IMPERIAL WEIGHT: 92.6 lbs.
METRIC HEIGHT: 1.4 m
METRIC WEIGHT: 42.0 kg

POSSIBLE MOVES: Electric Terrain, Tackle, Leer, Charge, Spark, Bite, Roar, Swagger, Thunder Fang, Crunch, Scary Face, Discharge, Wild Charge

SHINX **LUXIO** **LUXRAY**

LYCANROC

Wolf Pokémon

REGION: ALOLA

TYPE: ROCK

This Lycanroc is calm and cautious. The rocks jutting from its mane are razor sharp.

With swift movements, this Pokémon gradually backs its prey into a corner. Lycanroc's fangs are always aimed toward opponents' weak spots.

HOW TO SAY IT: LIE-can-rock
IMPERIAL HEIGHT: 2'07"
IMPERIAL WEIGHT: 55.1 lbs.
METRIC HEIGHT: 0.8 m
METRIC WEIGHT: 25.0 kg

POSSIBLE MOVES: Tackle, Leer, Sand Attack, Bite, Howl, Rock Throw, Odor Sleuth, Rock Tomb, Roar, Stealth Rock, Rock Slide, Scary Face, Crunch, Rock Climb, Stone Edge, Accelerock, Quick Guard, Quick Attack

MIDDAY FORM

DUSK FORM

MIDNIGHT FORM

ROCKRUFF

LYCANROC (MIDDAY FORM)

LYCANROC (DUSK FORM)

LYCANROC (MIDNIGHT FORM)

REGIONS:
ALOLA
GALAR
KALOS
(COASTAL)
KANTO

MACHAMP
Superpower Pokémon

TYPE: FIGHTING

It quickly swings its four arms to rock its opponents with ceaseless punches and chops from all angles.

With four arms that react more quickly than it can think, it can execute many punches at once.

HOW TO SAY IT: muh-CHAMP
IMPERIAL HEIGHT: 5'03"
IMPERIAL WEIGHT: 286.6 lbs.
METRIC HEIGHT: 1.6 m
METRIC WEIGHT: 130.0 kg

POSSIBLE MOVES: Bulk Up, Cross Chop, Double-Edge, Dual Chop, Dynamic Punch, Focus Energy, Knock Off, Leer, Low Kick, Low Sweep, Revenge, Scary Face, Seismic Toss, Strength, Vital Throw, Wide Guard

MACHOP   MACHOKE   MACHAMP

Alternate Form:
GIGANTAMAX MACHAMP

The Gigantamax energy coursing through its arms makes its punches hit as hard as bomb blasts.

One of these Pokémon once used its immeasurable strength to lift a large ship that was in trouble. It then carried the ship to port.

IMPERIAL HEIGHT: 82'00"+
IMPERIAL WEIGHT: ????.? lbs.
METRIC HEIGHT: 25.0+ m
METRIC WEIGHT: ???.? kg

MACHOKE
Superpower Pokémon

REGIONS:
ALOLA
GALAR
KALOS
(COASTAL)
KANTO

TYPE: FIGHTING

Its muscular body is so powerful, it must wear a power-save belt to be able to regulate its motions.

Its formidable body never gets tired. It helps people by doing work such as the moving of heavy goods.

HOW TO SAY IT: muh-CHOKE
IMPERIAL HEIGHT: 4'11"
IMPERIAL WEIGHT: 155.4 lbs.
METRIC HEIGHT: 1.5 m
METRIC WEIGHT: 70.5 kg

POSSIBLE MOVES: Bulk Up, Cross Chop, Double-Edge, Dual Chop, Dynamic Punch, Focus Energy, Knock Off, Leer, Low Kick, Low Sweep, Revenge, Scary Face, Seismic Toss, Strength, Vital Throw

MACHOP **MACHOKE** **MACHAMP**

REGIONS:
ALOLA
GALAR
KALOS
(COASTAL)
KANTO

MACHOP
Superpower Pokémon

TYPE: FIGHTING

Its whole body is composed of muscles. Even though it's the size of a human child, it can hurl 100 grown-ups.

Always brimming with power, it passes time by lifting boulders. Doing so makes it even stronger.

HOW TO SAY IT: muh-CHOP
IMPERIAL HEIGHT: 2'07"
IMPERIAL WEIGHT: 43.0 lbs.
METRIC HEIGHT: 0.8 m
METRIC WEIGHT: 19.5 kg

POSSIBLE MOVES: Bulk Up, Cross Chop, Double-Edge, Dual Chop, Dynamic Punch, Focus Energy, Knock Off, Leer, Low Kick, Low Sweep, Revenge, Scary Face, Seismic Toss, Strength, Vital Throw

MACHOP **MACHOKE** **MACHAMP**

MAGBY
Live Coal Pokémon

TYPE: FIRE

When flames drip from its nose, that means it has a cold. Have it lie down for a nice rest in some magma.

Its body temperature is always around 1,100 degrees Fahrenheit. If Magby falls into a small-enough pond, the whole thing will dry up.

HOW TO SAY IT: MAG-bee   **METRIC HEIGHT:** 0.7 m
IMPERIAL HEIGHT: 2'04"   **METRIC WEIGHT:** 21.4 kg
IMPERIAL WEIGHT: 47.2 lbs.

POSSIBLE MOVES: Smog, Leer, Ember, Smokescreen, Feint Attack, Fire Spin, Clear Smog, Flame Burst, Confuse Ray, Fire Punch, Lava Plume, Sunny Day, Flamethrower, Fire Blast

MAGBY   MAGMAR   MAGMORTAR

MAGCARGO
Lava Pokémon

REGIONS:
JOHTO
KALOS
(MOUNTAIN)

TYPE: FIRE-ROCK

Magcargo's shell is actually its skin that hardened as a result of cooling. Its shell is very brittle and fragile—just touching it causes it to crumble apart. This Pokémon returns to its original size by dipping itself in magma.

Magcargo's body temperature is approximately 18,000 degrees Fahrenheit. Water is vaporized on contact. If this Pokémon is caught in the rain, the raindrops instantly turn into steam, cloaking the area in a thick fog.

HOW TO SAY IT: mag-CAR-go   **METRIC HEIGHT:** 0.8 m
IMPERIAL HEIGHT: 2'07"   **METRIC WEIGHT:** 55.0 kg
IMPERIAL WEIGHT: 121.3 lbs.

POSSIBLE MOVES: Earth Power, Yawn, Smog, Ember, Rock Throw, Harden, Recover, Flame Burst, Ancient Power, Amnesia, Lava Plume, Shell Smash, Rock Slide, Body Slam, Flamethrower, Incinerate, Clear Smog

SLUGMA   MAGCARGO

MAGEARNA

Artificial Pokémon

MYTHICAL POKÉMON

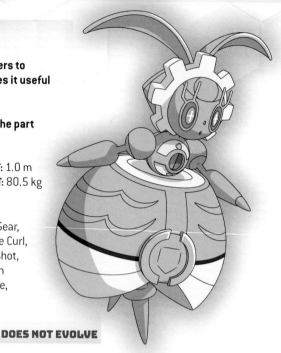

TYPE: STEEL-FAIRY

It synchronizes its consciousness with others to understand their feelings. This faculty makes it useful for taking care of people.

Built roughly 500 years ago by a scientist, the part called the Soul-Heart is the actual life-form.

HOW TO SAY IT: muh-GEER-nuh
IMPERIAL HEIGHT: 3'03"
IMPERIAL WEIGHT: 177.5 lbs.
METRIC HEIGHT: 1.0 m
METRIC WEIGHT: 80.5 kg

POSSIBLE MOVES: Crafty Shield, Gear Up, Shift Gear, Iron Head, Helping Hand, Sonic Boom, Defense Curl, Psybeam, Lucky Chant, Aurora Beam, Mirror Shot, Mind Reader, Flash Cannon, Fleur Cannon, Iron Defense, Pain Split, Synchronoise, Aura Sphere, Heart Swap, Trump Card

DOES NOT EVOLVE

REGIONS:
ALOLA
GALAR
KALOS
(CENTRAL)
KANTO

MAGIKARP

Fish Pokémon

TYPE: WATER

It is virtually worthless in terms of both power and speed. It is the most weak and pathetic Pokémon in the world.

This weak and pathetic Pokémon gets easily pushed along rivers when there are strong currents.

HOW TO SAY IT: MADGE-eh-karp
IMPERIAL HEIGHT: 2'11"
IMPERIAL WEIGHT: 22.0 lbs.
METRIC HEIGHT: 0.9 m
METRIC WEIGHT: 10.0 kg

POSSIBLE MOVES: Flail, Splash, Tackle

MAGIKARP   GYARADOS   MEGA GYARADOS

TYPE: FIRE

Born in an active volcano. Its body is always cloaked in flames, so it looks like a big ball of fire.

HOW TO SAY IT: MAG-marr
IMPERIAL HEIGHT: 4'03"
IMPERIAL WEIGHT: 98.1 lbs.
METRIC HEIGHT: 1.3 m
METRIC WEIGHT: 44.5 kg

POSSIBLE MOVES: Smog, Leer, Ember, Smokescreen, Feint Attack, Fire Spin, Clear Smog, Flame Burst, Confuse Ray, Fire Punch, Lava Plume, Sunny Day, Flamethrower, Fire Blast

MAGBY   MAGMAR   MAGMORTAR

MAGMORTAR
Blast Pokémon

TYPE: FIRE

There are still quite a few factories that rely on the flames provided by Magmortar to process metals.

Magmortar takes down its enemies by shooting fireballs, which burn them to a blackened crisp. It avoids this method when hunting prey.

HOW TO SAY IT: mag-MORT-ur
IMPERIAL HEIGHT: 5'03"
IMPERIAL WEIGHT: 149.9 lbs.
METRIC HEIGHT: 1.6 m
METRIC WEIGHT: 68.0 kg

POSSIBLE MOVES: Thunder Punch, Smog, Leer, Ember, Smokescreen, Feint Attack, Fire Spin, Clear Smog, Flame Burst, Confuse Ray, Fire Punch, Lava Plume, Sunny Day, Flamethrower, Fire Blast, Hyper Beam

MAGBY   MAGMAR   MAGMORTAR

MAGNEMITE

Magnet Pokémon

TYPE: ELECTRIC-STEEL

At times, Magnemite runs out of electricity and ends up on the ground. If you give batteries to a grounded Magnemite, it'll start moving again.

It subsists on electricity. As Magnemite flies, it emits electromagnetic waves from the units on each side of its body.

HOW TO SAY IT: MAG-ne-mite
IMPERIAL HEIGHT: 1'00"
IMPERIAL WEIGHT: 13.2 lbs.
METRIC HEIGHT: 0.3 m
METRIC WEIGHT: 6.0 kg

POSSIBLE MOVES: Tackle, Supersonic, Thunder Shock, Magnet Bomb, Thunder Wave, Light Screen, Sonic Boom, Spark, Mirror Shot, Metal Sound, Electro Ball, Flash Cannon, Screech, Discharge, Lock-On, Magnet Rise, Gyro Ball, Zap Cannon

MAGNEMITE　　**MAGNETON**　　**MAGNEZONE**

TYPE: ELECTRIC-STEEL

MAGNETON

Magnet Pokémon

This Pokémon is three Magnemite that have linked together. Magneton sends out powerful radio waves to study its surroundings.

This Pokémon is constantly putting out a powerful magnetic force. Most computers go haywire when a Magneton approaches.

HOW TO SAY IT: MAG-ne-ton
IMPERIAL HEIGHT: 3'03"
IMPERIAL WEIGHT: 132.3 lbs.
METRIC HEIGHT: 1.0 m
METRIC WEIGHT: 60.0 kg

POSSIBLE MOVES: Tri Attack, Zap Cannon, Electric Terrain, Tackle, Supersonic, Thunder Shock, Magnet Bomb, Thunder Wave, Light Screen, Sonic Boom, Spark, Mirror Shot, Metal Sound, Electro Ball, Flash Cannon, Screech, Discharge, Lock-On, Magnet Rise, Gyro Ball

MAGNEMITE　　**MAGNETON**　　**MAGNEZONE**

TYPE: ELECTRIC-STEEL

MAGNEZONE
Magnet Area Pokémon

Some say that Magnezone receives signals from space via the antenna on its head and that it's being controlled by some mysterious being.

It's thought that a special magnetic field changed the molecular structure of this Pokémon's body, and that's what caused the Pokémon's Evolution.

HOW TO SAY IT: MAG-nuh-zone
IMPERIAL HEIGHT: 3'11"
IMPERIAL WEIGHT: 396.8 lbs.
METRIC HEIGHT: 1.2 m
METRIC WEIGHT: 180.0 kg

POSSIBLE MOVES: Tri Attack, Zap Cannon, Magnetic Flux, Mirror Coat, Barrier, Electric Terrain, Tackle, Supersonic, Thunder Shock, Magnet Bomb, Thunder Wave, Light Screen, Sonic Boom, Spark, Mirror Shot, Metal Sound, Electro Ball, Flash Cannon, Screech, Discharge, Lock-On, Magnet Rise, Gyro Ball

MAGNEMITE   MAGNETON   MAGNEZONE

MAKUHITA
Guts Pokémon

TYPE: FIGHTING

It practices its slaps by repeatedly slapping tree trunks. It has been known to slap an Exeggutor and get flung away.

There's a rumor of a traditional recipe for stew that Trainers can use to raise strong Makuhita.

HOW TO SAY IT: MAK-oo-HEE-ta
IMPERIAL HEIGHT: 3'03"
IMPERIAL WEIGHT: 190.5 lbs.
METRIC HEIGHT: 1.0 m
METRIC WEIGHT: 86.4 kg

POSSIBLE MOVES: Tackle, Focus Energy, Sand Attack, Arm Thrust, Fake Out, Force Palm, Whirlwind, Knock Off, Vital Throw, Belly Drum, Smelling Salts, Seismic Toss, Wake-Up Slap, Endure, Close Combat, Reversal, Heavy Slam

MAKUHITA   HARIYAMA

MALAMAR

Overturning Pokémon

TYPE: DARK-PSYCHIC

Gazing at its luminescent spots will quickly induce a hypnotic state, putting the observer under Malamar's control.

It's said that Malamar's hypnotic powers played a role in certain history-changing events.

HOW TO SAY IT: MAL-uh-MAR
IMPERIAL HEIGHT: 4'11"
IMPERIAL WEIGHT: 103.6 lbs.
METRIC HEIGHT: 1.5 m
METRIC WEIGHT: 47.0 kg

POSSIBLE MOVES: Foul Play, Hypnosis, Night Slash, Payback, Peck, Pluck, Psybeam, Psycho Cut, Reversal, Slash, Superpower, Swagger, Switcheroo, Tackle, Topsy-Turvy, Wrap

INKAY   MALAMAR

MAMOSWINE

Twin Tusk Pokémon

REGIONS:
GALAR
KALOS
(MOUNTAIN)
SINNOH

TYPE: ICE-GROUND

This Pokémon can be spotted in wall paintings from as far back as 10,000 years ago. For a while, it was thought to have gone extinct.

It looks strong, and that's exactly what it is. As the weather grows colder, its ice tusks grow longer, thicker, and more impressive.

HOW TO SAY IT: MAM-oh-swine
IMPERIAL HEIGHT: 8'02"
IMPERIAL WEIGHT: 641.5 lbs.
METRIC HEIGHT: 2.5 m
METRIC WEIGHT: 291.0 kg

POSSIBLE MOVES: Amnesia, Ancient Power, Blizzard, Double Hit, Earthquake, Endure, Flail, Ice Fang, Ice Shard, Icy Wind, Mist, Mud-Slap, Powder Snow, Tackle, Take Down, Thrash

SWINUB   PILOSWINE   MAMOSWINE

REGION: SINNOH

MANAPHY
Seafaring Pokémon

TYPE: WATER

It is born with a wondrous power that lets it bond with any kind of Pokémon.

It starts its life with a wondrous power that permits it to bond with any kind of Pokémon.

HOW TO SAY IT: MAN-ah-fee
IMPERIAL HEIGHT: 1'00"
IMPERIAL WEIGHT: 3.1 lbs.
METRIC HEIGHT: 0.3 m
METRIC WEIGHT: 1.4 kg

POSSIBLE MOVES: Tail Glow, Bubble, Water Sport, Charm, Supersonic, Bubble Beam, Acid Armor, Whirlpool, Water Pulse, Aqua Ring, Dive, Rain Dance, Heart Swap

DOES NOT EVOLVE

REGIONS: ALOLA GALAR UNOVA

MANDIBUZZ
Bone Vulture Pokémon

TYPE: DARK-FLYING

Although it's a bit of a ruffian, this Pokémon will take lost Vullaby under its wing and care for them till they're ready to leave the nest.

They adorn themselves with bones. There seem to be fashion trends among them, as different bones come into and fall out of popularity.

HOW TO SAY IT: MAN-dih-buz
IMPERIAL HEIGHT: 3'11"
IMPERIAL WEIGHT: 87.1 lbs.
METRIC HEIGHT: 1.2 m
METRIC WEIGHT: 39.5 kg

POSSIBLE MOVES: Air Slash, Attract, Bone Rush, Brave Bird, Dark Pulse, Defog, Flatter, Gust, Iron Defense, Knock Off, Leer, Nasty Plot, Pluck, Sky Attack, Tailwind, Toxic, Whirlwind

VULLABY   **MANDIBUZZ**

MANECTRIC
Discharge Pokémon

REGIONS:
ALOLA
GALAR
HOENN
KALOS
(COASTAL)

TYPE: ELECTRIC

It stimulates its own muscles with electricity, so it can move quickly. It eases its soreness with electricity, too, so it can recover quickly as well.

It rarely appears before people. It is said to nest where lightning has fallen.

HOW TO SAY IT: mane-EK-trick
IMPERIAL HEIGHT: 4'11"
IMPERIAL WEIGHT: 88.6 lbs.
METRIC HEIGHT: 1.5 m
METRIC WEIGHT: 40.2 kg

POSSIBLE MOVES: Bite, Charge, Discharge, Electric Terrain, Fire Fang, Howl, Leer, Quick Attack, Roar, Shock Wave, Tackle, Thunder, Thunder Fang, Thunder Wave, Wild Charge

MEGA MANECTRIC
Discharge Pokémon

TYPE: ELECTRIC

IMPERIAL HEIGHT: 5'11"
IMPERIAL WEIGHT: 97.0 lbs.
METRIC HEIGHT: 1.8 m
METRIC WEIGHT: 44.0 kg

ELECTRIKE

MANECTRIC

MEGA MANECTRIC

MANKEY
Pig Monkey Pokémon

TYPE: FIGHTING

An agile Pokémon that lives in trees. It angers easily and will not hesitate to attack anything.

HOW TO SAY IT: MANG-key
IMPERIAL HEIGHT: 1'08"
IMPERIAL WEIGHT: 61.7 lbs.
METRIC HEIGHT: 0.5 m
METRIC WEIGHT: 28.0 kg

POSSIBLE MOVES: Covet, Scratch, Low Kick, Leer, Focus Energy, Fury Swipes, Karate Chop, Pursuit, Seismic Toss, Swagger, Cross Chop, Assurance, Punishment, Thrash, Close Combat, Screech, Stomping Tantrum, Outrage, Final Gambit

MANKEY → PRIMEAPE

MANTINE
Kite Pokémon

TYPE: WATER-FLYING

If it builds up enough speed swimming, it can jump out above the waves and glide for over 300 feet.

As it majestically swims, it doesn't care if Remoraid attach to it to scavenge for its leftovers.

HOW TO SAY IT: MAN-teen
IMPERIAL HEIGHT: 6'11"
IMPERIAL WEIGHT: 485.0 lbs.
METRIC HEIGHT: 2.1 m
METRIC WEIGHT: 220.0 kg

POSSIBLE MOVES: Agility, Air Slash, Aqua Ring, Bounce, Bubble Beam, Bullet Seed, Headbutt, Hydro Pump, Psybeam, Roost, Supersonic, Tackle, Take Down, Water Gun, Water Pulse, Wide Guard, Wing Attack

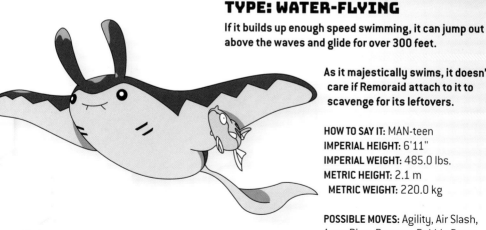

MANTYKE → MANTINE

MANTYKE
Kite Pokémon

REGIONS: ALOLA GALAR KALOS (COASTAL) SINNOH

TYPE: WATER-FLYING

Mantyke living in Galar seem to be somewhat sluggish. The colder waters of the seas in this region may be the cause.

It swims along with a school of Remoraid, and they'll all fight together to repel attackers.

HOW TO SAY IT: MAN-tike
IMPERIAL HEIGHT: 3'03"
IMPERIAL WEIGHT: 143.3 lbs.
METRIC HEIGHT: 1.0 m
METRIC WEIGHT: 65.0 kg

POSSIBLE MOVES: Agility, Air Slash, Aqua Ring, Bounce, Bubble Beam, Headbutt, Hydro Pump, Supersonic, Tackle, Take Down, Water Gun, Water Pulse, Wide Guard, Wing Attack

MANTYKE   MANTINE

MARACTUS
Cactus Pokémon

REGIONS: GALAR UNOVA

TYPE: GRASS

With noises that could be mistaken for the rattles of maracas, it creates an upbeat rhythm, startling bird Pokémon and making them fly off in a hurry.

Once each year, this Pokémon scatters its seeds. They're jam-packed with nutrients, making them a precious food source out in the desert.

HOW TO SAY IT: mah-RAK-tus
IMPERIAL HEIGHT: 3'03"
IMPERIAL WEIGHT: 61.7 lbs.
METRIC HEIGHT: 1.0 m
METRIC WEIGHT: 28.0 kg

POSSIBLE MOVES: Absorb, Acupressure, After You, Cotton Guard, Cotton Spore, Giga Drain, Growth, Ingrain, Leech Seed, Mega Drain, Peck, Petal Blizzard, Petal Dance, Pin Missile, Solar Beam, Spiky Shield, Sucker Punch, Sunny Day, Sweet Scent, Synthesis

DOES NOT EVOLVE

MAREANIE

Brutal Star Pokémon

TYPE: POISON-WATER

The first symptom of its sting is numbness. The next is an itching sensation so intense that it's impossible to resist the urge to claw at your skin.

Unlike their Alolan counterparts, the Mareanie of the Galar region have not yet figured out that the branches of Corsola are delicious.

HOW TO SAY IT: muh-REE-nee
IMPERIAL HEIGHT: 1'04"
IMPERIAL WEIGHT: 17.6 lbs.
METRIC HEIGHT: 0.4 m
METRIC WEIGHT: 8.0 kg

POSSIBLE MOVES: Bite, Liquidation, Peck, Pin Missile, Poison Jab, Poison Sting, Recover, Toxic, Toxic Spikes, Venom Drench, Venoshock, Wide Guard

MAREANIE   TOXAPEX

MAREEP
Wool Pokémon

REGIONS:
ALOLA
JOHTO
KALOS
(COASTAL)

TYPE: ELECTRIC

Clothing made from Mareep's fleece is easily charged with static electricity, so a special process is used on it.

Rubbing its fleece generates electricity. You'll want to pet it because it's cute, but if you use your bare hand, you'll get a painful shock.

HOW TO SAY IT: mah-REEP **METRIC HEIGHT:** 0.6 m
IMPERIAL HEIGHT: 2'00" **METRIC WEIGHT:** 7.8 kg
IMPERIAL WEIGHT: 17.2 lbs.

POSSIBLE MOVES: Tackle, Growl, Thunder Wave, Thunder Shock, Cotton Spore, Charge, Take Down, Electro Ball, Confuse Ray, Power Gem, Discharge, Cotton Guard, Signal Beam, Light Screen, Thunder

MAREEP   **FLAAFFY**   **AMPHAROS**   **MEGA AMPHAROS**

MARILL
Aqua Mouse Pokémon

REGIONS:
JOHTO
KALOS
(COASTAL)

TYPE: WATER-FAIRY

This Pokémon uses its round tail as a float. The ball of Marill's tail is filled with nutrients that have been turned into an oil.

Even after Marill swims in a cold sea, its water-repellent fur dries almost as soon as Marill leaves the water. That's why this Pokémon is never cold.

HOW TO SAY IT: MARE-rull **METRIC HEIGHT:** 0.4 m
IMPERIAL HEIGHT: 1'04" **METRIC WEIGHT:** 8.5 kg
IMPERIAL WEIGHT: 18.7 lbs.

POSSIBLE MOVES: Tackle, Water Gun, Tail Whip, Water Sport, Bubble, Defense Curl, Rollout, Bubble Beam, Helping Hand, Aqua Tail, Double-Edge, Aqua Ring, Rain Dance, Superpower, Hydro Pump, Play Rough

AZURILL   **MARILL**   **AZUMARILL**

MAROWAK
Bone Keeper Pokémon

TYPE: GROUND

This Pokémon overcame its sorrow to evolve a sturdy new body. Marowak faces its opponents bravely, using a bone as a weapon.

When this Pokémon evolved, the skull of its mother fused to it. Marowak's temperament also turned vicious at the same time.

HOW TO SAY IT: MARE-oh-wack
IMPERIAL HEIGHT: 3'03"
IMPERIAL WEIGHT: 99.2 lbs.
METRIC HEIGHT: 1.0 m
METRIC WEIGHT: 45.0 kg

POSSIBLE MOVES: Growl, Tail Whip, Bone Club, Headbutt, Leer, Focus Energy, Bonemerang, Rage, False Swipe, Thrash, Fling, Stomping Tantrum, Endeavor, Double-Edge, Retaliate, Bone Rush

CUBONE   MAROWAK

ALOLAN MAROWAK
Bone Keeper Pokémon

TYPE: FIRE-GHOST

This Pokémon sets the bone it holds on fire and dances through the night as a way to mourn its fallen allies.

The cursed flames that light up the bone carried by this Pokémon are said to cause both mental and physical pain that will never fade.

HOW TO SAY IT: MARE-oh-wack
IMPERIAL HEIGHT: 3'03"
IMPERIAL WEIGHT: 75.0 lbs.
METRIC HEIGHT: 1.0 m
METRIC WEIGHT: 34.0 kg

POSSIBLE MOVES: Growl, Tail Whip, Bone Club, Flame Wheel, Leer, Hex, Bonemerang, Will-O-Wisp, Shadow Bone, Thrash, Fling, Stomping Tantrum, Endeavor, Double-Edge, Retaliate, Bone Rush

CUBONE   ALOLAN MAROWAK

MARSHADOW

Gloomdweller Pokémon

MYTHICAL POKÉMON

TYPE: FIGHTING-GHOST

It slips into the shadows of others and mimics their powers and movements. As it improves, it becomes stronger than those it's imitating.

It sinks into the shadows of people and Pokémon, where it can understand their feelings and copy their capabilities.

HOW TO SAY IT: mar-SHAD-oh
IMPERIAL HEIGHT: 2'04'
IMPERIAL WEIGHT: 48.9 lbs.

METRIC HEIGHT: 0.7m
METRIC WEIGHT: 22.2 kg

POSSIBLE MOVES: Laser Focus, Assurance, Fire Punch, Thunder Punch, Ice Punch, Drain Punch, Counter, Pursuit, Shadow Sneak, Force Palm, Feint, Rolling Kick, Copycat, Shadow Punch, Role Play, Jump Kick, Psych Up, Spectral Thief, Close Combat, Sucker Punch, Endeavor

ZENITH MARSHADOW

DOES NOT EVOLVE

TYPE: WATER-GROUND

MARSHTOMP
Mud Fish Pokémon

The surface of Marshtomp's body is enveloped by a thin, sticky film that enables it to live on land. This Pokémon plays in mud on beaches when the ocean tide is low.

Marshtomp is much faster at traveling through mud than it is at swimming. This Pokémon's hindquarters exhibit obvious development, giving it the ability to walk on just its hind legs.

HOW TO SAY IT: MARSH-stomp
IMPERIAL HEIGHT: 2'04"
IMPERIAL WEIGHT: 61.7 lbs.
METRIC HEIGHT: 0.7 m
METRIC WEIGHT: 28.0 kg

POSSIBLE MOVES: Mud Shot, Tackle, Growl, Water Gun, Mud-Slap, Foresight, Bide, Mud Sport, Rock Slide, Protect, Muddy Water, Take Down, Earthquake, Endeavor

MUDKIP → MARSHTOMP → SWAMPERT → MEGA SWAMPERT

MASQUERAIN
Eyeball Pokémon

TYPE: BUG-FLYING

Masquerain intimidates enemies with the eyelike patterns of its eyespots. If that doesn't work, it deftly makes its escape on its set of four wings.

Its thin, winglike antennae are highly absorbent. It waits out rainy days in tree hollows.

HOW TO SAY IT: mas-ker-RAIN
IMPERIAL HEIGHT: 2'07"
IMPERIAL WEIGHT: 7.9 lbs.
METRIC HEIGHT: 0.8 m
METRIC WEIGHT: 3.6 kg

POSSIBLE MOVES: Quiver Dance, Whirlwind, Bug Buzz, Ominous Wind, Bubble, Quick Attack, Sweet Scent, Water Sport, Gust, Scary Face, Air Cutter, Stun Spore, Silver Wind, Air Slash

SURSKIT → MASQUERAIN

MAWILE
Deceiver Pokémon

REGIONS:
ALOLA
GALAR
HOENN
KALOS
(COASTAL)

TYPE: STEEL-FAIRY

It uses its docile-looking face to lull foes into complacency, then bites with its huge, relentless jaws.

It chomps with its gaping mouth. Its huge jaws are actually steel horns that have been transformed.

HOW TO SAY IT: MAW-while
IMPERIAL HEIGHT: 2'00"
IMPERIAL WEIGHT: 25.4 lbs.
METRIC HEIGHT: 0.6 m
METRIC WEIGHT: 11.5 kg

POSSIBLE MOVES:
Astonish, Baton Pass, Bite, Crunch, Fairy Wind, Fake Tears, Growl, Iron Defense, Iron Head, Play Rough, Spit Up, Stockpile, Sucker Punch, Swallow, Sweet Scent, Taunt

MEGA MAWILE
Deceiver Pokémon

TYPE: STEEL-FAIRY

IMPERIAL HEIGHT: 3'03"
IMPERIAL WEIGHT: 51.8 lbs.
METRIC HEIGHT: 1.0 m
METRIC WEIGHT: 23.5 kg

MAWILE → MEGA MAWILE

MEDICHAM
Meditate Pokémon

TYPE: FIGHTING-PSYCHIC

It is said that through meditation, Medicham heightens energy inside its body and sharpens its sixth sense. This Pokémon hides its presence by merging itself with fields and mountains.

Through the power of meditation, Medicham developed its sixth sense. It gained the ability to use psychokinetic powers. This Pokémon is known to meditate for a whole month without eating.

HOW TO SAY IT: MED-uh-cham
IMPERIAL HEIGHT: 4'03"
IMPERIAL WEIGHT: 69.4 lbs.
METRIC HEIGHT: 1.3 m
METRIC WEIGHT: 31.5 kg

POSSIBLE MOVES: Zen Headbutt, Fire Punch, Thunder Punch, Ice Punch, Bide, Meditate, Confusion, Detect, Endure, Hidden Power, Mind Reader, Feint, Calm Mind, Force Palm, High Jump Kick, Psych Up, Acupressure, Power Trick, Reversal, Recover, Counter

MEGA MEDICHAM
Meditate Pokémon

TYPE: FIGHTING-PSYCHIC

IMPERIAL HEIGHT: 4'03"
IMPERIAL WEIGHT: 69.4 lbs.
METRIC HEIGHT: 1.3 m
METRIC WEIGHT: 31.5 kg

MEDITITE ➡ MEDICHAM ➡ MEGA MEDICHAM

MEDITITE

Meditate Pokémon

TYPE: FIGHTING-PSYCHIC

Meditite undertakes rigorous mental training deep in the mountains. However, whenever it meditates, this Pokémon always loses its concentration and focus. As a result, its training never ends.

Meditite heightens its inner energy through meditation. It survives on just one berry a day. Minimal eating is another aspect of this Pokémon's training.

HOW TO SAY IT: MED-uh-tite
IMPERIAL HEIGHT: 2'00"
IMPERIAL WEIGHT: 24.7 lbs.
METRIC HEIGHT: 0.6 m
METRIC WEIGHT: 11.2 kg

POSSIBLE MOVES: Bide, Meditate, Confusion, Detect, Endure, Feint, Force Palm, Hidden Power, Calm Mind, Mind Reader, High Jump Kick, Psych Up, Acupressure, Power Trick, Reversal, Recover, Counter

MEDITITE   MEDICHAM   MEGA MEDICHAM

MEGANIUM

Herb Pokémon

REGION:
JOHTO

TYPE: GRASS

The fragrance of Meganium's flower soothes and calms emotions. In battle, this Pokémon gives off more of its becalming scent to blunt the foe's fighting spirit.

HOW TO SAY IT: meg-GAY-nee-um
IMPERIAL HEIGHT: 5'11"
IMPERIAL WEIGHT: 221.6 lbs.
METRIC HEIGHT: 1.8 m
METRIC WEIGHT: 100.5 kg

POSSIBLE MOVES: Petal Dance, Petal Blizzard, Tackle, Growl, Razor Leaf, Poison Powder, Synthesis, Reflect, Magical Leaf, Natural Gift, Petal Dance, Sweet Scent, Light Screen, Body Slam, Safeguard, Aromatherapy, Solar Beam

CHIKORITA   BAYLEEF   MEGANIUM

MELMETAL
Hex Nut Pokémon

TYPE: STEEL

Revered long ago for its capacity to create iron from nothing, for some reason it has come back to life after 3,000 years.

HOW TO SAY IT: MEL-metal
IMPERIAL HEIGHT: 8'02"
IMPERIAL WEIGHT: 1,763.7 lbs.
METRIC HEIGHT: 2.5 m
METRIC WEIGHT: 800.0 kg

POSSIBLE MOVES: Harden, Headbutt, Tail Whip, Thunder Punch, Thunder Shock, Thunder Wave, Acid Armor, Flash Cannon, Mega Punch, Protect, Discharge, Dynamic Punch, Superpower, Double Iron Bash, Hyper Beam

MELTAN   MELMETAL

Alternate Form:
GIGANTAMAX MELMETAL

In a distant land, there are legends about a cyclopean giant. In fact, the giant was a Melmetal that was flooded with Gigantamax energy.

It can send electric beams streaking out from the hole in its belly. The beams' tremendous energy can vaporize an opponent in one shot.

IMPERIAL HEIGHT: 82'00"+
IMPERIAL WEIGHT: ????.? lbs.
METRIC HEIGHT: 25.0+ m
METRIC WEIGHT: ???.? kg

MELOETTA
Melody Pokémon

MYTHICAL POKÉMON

TYPE: NORMAL-PSYCHIC

The melodies sung by Meloetta have the power to make Pokémon that hear them happy or sad.

Its melodies are sung with a special vocalization method that can control the feelings of those who hear it.

HOW TO SAY IT: mell-oh-ET-tuh
IMPERIAL HEIGHT: 2'00"
IMPERIAL WEIGHT: 14.3 lbs.
METRIC HEIGHT: 0.6 m
METRIC WEIGHT: 6.5 kg

POSSIBLE MOVES: Round, Quick Attack, Confusion, Sing, Teeter Dance, Acrobatics, Psybeam, Echoed Voice, U-turn, Wake-Up Slap, Psychic, Hyper Voice, Role Play, Close Combat, Perish Song

ARIA FORME

PIROUETTE FORME

DOES NOT EVOLVE

MELTAN
Hex Nut Pokémon

MYTHICAL POKÉMON

TYPE: STEEL

It melts particles of iron and other metals found in the subsoil, so it can absorb them into its body of molten steel.

HOW TO SAY IT: MEL-tan
IMPERIAL HEIGHT: 0'08"
IMPERIAL WEIGHT: 17.6 lbs.
METRIC HEIGHT: 0.2 m
METRIC WEIGHT: 8.0 kg

POSSIBLE MOVES: Harden, Thunder Shock, Tail Whip, Headbutt, Thunder Wave, Acid Armor, Flash Cannon

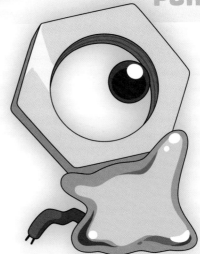

MELTAN MELMETAL

TYPE: PSYCHIC

Revealing the eyelike patterns on the insides of its ears will unleash its psychic powers. It normally keeps the patterns hidden, however.

The defensive instinct of the males is strong. It's when they're protecting themselves or their partners that they unleash their full power.

HOW TO SAY IT: MYOW-stik
IMPERIAL HEIGHT: 2'00"
IMPERIAL WEIGHT: 18.7 lbs.
METRIC HEIGHT: 0.6 m
METRIC WEIGHT: 8.5 kg

POSSIBLE MOVES: Charm, Confusion, Covet, Disarming Voice, Fake Out, Helping Hand, Imprison, Leer, Light Screen, Mean Look, Misty Terrain, Psybeam, Psychic, Psyshock, Quick Guard, Reflect, Role Play, Scratch, Sucker Punch

REGIONS:
GALAR
KALOS
(CENTRAL)

MEOWSTIC
Constraint Pokémon

MALE FORM

FEMALE FORM

MEOWSTIC
(MALE FORM)

ESPURR

MEOWSTIC
(FEMALE FORM)

MEOWTH
Scratch Cat Pokémon

REGION: KANTO

TYPE: NORMAL

It loves to collect shiny things. If it's in a good mood, it might even let its Trainer have a look at its hoard of treasures.

It washes its face regularly to keep the coin on its forehead spotless. It doesn't get along with Galarian Meowth.

HOW TO SAY IT: mee-OWTH
IMPERIAL HEIGHT: 1'04"
IMPERIAL WEIGHT: 9.3 lbs.
METRIC HEIGHT: 0.4 m
METRIC WEIGHT: 4.2 kg

POSSIBLE MOVES: Assurance, Bite, Fake Out, Feint, Fury Swipes, Growl, Nasty Plot, Pay Day, Play Rough, Scratch, Screech, Slash, Taunt

MEOWTH **PERSIAN**

Alternate Form:
GIGANTAMAX MEOWTH

The pattern that has appeared on its giant coin is thought to be the key to unlocking the secrets of the Dynamax phenomenon.

Its body has grown incredibly long and the coin on its forehead has grown incredibly large—all thanks to Gigantamax power.

IMPERIAL HEIGHT: 108'03"+
IMPERIAL WEIGHT: ????.? lbs.
METRIC HEIGHT: 33.0+ m
METRIC WEIGHT: ???.? kg

ALOLAN MEOWTH
Scratch Cat Pokémon

TYPE: DARK

It's accustomed to luxury because it used to live with Alolan royalty. As a result, it's very picky about food.

Deeply proud and keenly smart, this Pokémon moves with cunning during battle and relentlessly attacks enemies' weak points.

HOW TO SAY IT: mee-OWTH
IMPERIAL HEIGHT: 1'04"
IMPERIAL WEIGHT: 9.3 lbs.
METRIC HEIGHT: 0.4 m
METRIC WEIGHT: 4.2 kg

POSSIBLE MOVES: Assurance, Bite, Fake Out, Feint, Fury Swipes, Growl, Nasty Plot, Night Slash, Pay Day, Play Rough, Scratch, Screech, Taunt

ALOLAN MEOWTH → ALOLAN PERSIAN

GALARIAN MEOWTH
Scratch Cat Pokémon

TYPE: STEEL

Living with a savage, seafaring people has toughened this Pokémon's body so much that parts of it have turned to iron.

These daring Pokémon have coins on their foreheads. Darker coins are harder, and harder coins garner more respect among Meowth.

HOW TO SAY IT: mee-OWTH
IMPERIAL HEIGHT: 1'04"
IMPERIAL WEIGHT: 16.5 lbs.
METRIC HEIGHT: 0.4 m
METRIC WEIGHT: 7.5 kg

POSSIBLE MOVES: Fake Out, Fury Swipes, Growl, Hone Claws, Metal Claw, Metal Sound, Pay Day, Scratch, Screech, Slash, Swagger, Taunt, Thrash

GALARIAN MEOWTH   PERRSERKER

MESPRIT

Emotion Pokémon

REGION: SINNOH

TYPE: PSYCHIC

Known as "The Being of Emotion." It taught humans the nobility of sorrow, pain, and joy.

It sleeps at the bottom of a lake. Its spirit is said to leave its body to fly on the lake's surface.

HOW TO SAY IT: MES-sprit
IMPERIAL HEIGHT: 1'00"
IMPERIAL WEIGHT: 0.7 lbs.
METRIC HEIGHT: 0.3 m
METRIC WEIGHT: 0.3 kg

POSSIBLE MOVES: Rest, Confusion, Imprison, Protect, Swift, Lucky Chant, Future Sight, Charm, Extrasensory, Copycat, Natural Gift, Healing Wish

DOES NOT EVOLVE

METAGROSS

Iron Leg Pokémon

TYPE: STEEL-PSYCHIC

It boasts not only psychic powers but also fantastic strength. It grabs its prey with its four legs and holds them in place with its claws.

It analyzes its opponents with more accuracy than a supercomputer, which enables it to calmly back them into a corner.

HOW TO SAY IT: MET-uh-gross
IMPERIAL HEIGHT: 5'03"
IMPERIAL WEIGHT: 1,212.5 lbs.
METRIC HEIGHT: 1.6 m
METRIC WEIGHT: 550.0 kg

POSSIBLE MOVES: Hammer Arm, Confusion, Metal Claw, Magnet Rise, Take Down, Pursuit, Bullet Punch, Miracle Eye, Zen Headbutt, Scary Face, Psychic, Agility, Meteor Mash, Iron Defense, Hyper Beam

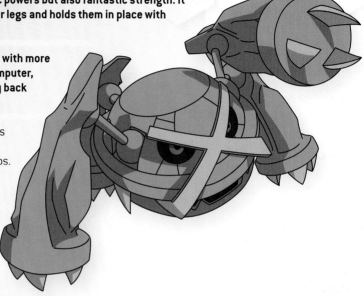

MEGA METAGROSS

Iron Leg Pokémon

TYPE: STEEL-PSYCHIC

IMPERIAL HEIGHT: 8'02"
IMPERIAL WEIGHT: 2,078.7 lbs.
METRIC HEIGHT: 2.5 m
METRIC WEIGHT: 942.9 kg

BELDUM

METANG

METAGROSS

MEGA METAGROSS

METANG

Iron Claw Pokémon

REGIONS:
ALOLA
HOENN

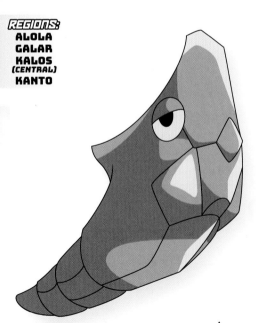

TYPE: STEEL-PSYCHIC

With its two brains, it fires powerful psychic energy to stop its prey in their tracks.

It flies at high speeds around the skies. When it finds its prey, Metang takes a firm grip with its sharp claws and never lets go.

HOW TO SAY IT: met-TANG
IMPERIAL HEIGHT: 3'11"
IMPERIAL WEIGHT: 446.4 lbs.
METRIC HEIGHT: 1.2 m
METRIC WEIGHT: 202.5 kg

POSSIBLE MOVES: Confusion, Metal Claw, Magnet Rise, Take Down, Pursuit, Bullet Punch, Miracle Eye, Zen Headbutt, Scary Face, Psychic, Agility, Meteor Mash, Iron Defense, Hyper Beam

BELDUM **METANG** **METAGROSS** **MEGA METAGROSS**

METAPOD

Cocoon Pokémon

REGIONS:
ALOLA
GALAR
KALOS
(CENTRAL)
KANTO

TYPE: BUG

It is waiting for the moment to evolve. At this stage, it can only harden, so it remains motionless to avoid attack.

Even though it is encased in a sturdy shell, the body inside is tender. It can't withstand a harsh attack.

HOW TO SAY IT: MET-uh-pod
IMPERIAL HEIGHT: 2'04"
IMPERIAL WEIGHT: 21.8 lbs.
METRIC HEIGHT: 0.7 m
METRIC WEIGHT: 9.9 kg

POSSIBLE MOVE: Harden

CATERPIE **METAPOD** **BUTTERFREE**

REGION: KANTO

MEW
New Species Pokémon

TYPE: PSYCHIC

When viewed through a microscope, this Pokémon's short, fine, delicate hair can be seen.

HOW TO SAY IT: MUE
IMPERIAL HEIGHT: 1'04"
IMPERIAL WEIGHT: 8.8 lbs.
METRIC HEIGHT: 0.4 m
METRIC WEIGHT: 4.0 kg

POSSIBLE MOVES: Pound, Reflect Type, Transform, Mega Punch, Metronome, Psychic, Barrier, Ancient Power, Amnesia, Me First, Baton Pass, Nasty Plot, Aura Sphere

DOES NOT EVOLVE

LEGENDARY POKÉMON

MEWTWO
Genetic Pokémon

TYPE: PSYCHIC

Its DNA is almost the same as Mew's. However, its size and disposition are vastly different.

HOW TO SAY IT: MUE-TOO **METRIC HEIGHT:** 2.0 m
IMPERIAL HEIGHT: 6'07" **METRIC WEIGHT:** 122.0 kg
IMPERIAL WEIGHT: 269.0 lbs.

POSSIBLE MOVES: Laser Focus, Psywave, Confusion, Disable, Safeguard, Swift, Future Sight, Psych Up, Miracle Eye, Psycho Cut, Power Swap, Guard Swap, Recover, Psychic, Barrier, Aura Sphere, Amnesia, Mist, Me First, Psystrike

MEGA MEWTWO X
Genetic Pokémon

TYPE: PSYCHIC-FIGHTING

IMPERIAL HEIGHT: 7'07"
IMPERIAL WEIGHT: 280.0 lbs.
METRIC HEIGHT: 2.3 m
METRIC WEIGHT: 127.0 kg

MEGA MEWTWO Y
Genetic Pokémon

TYPE: PSYCHIC

IMPERIAL HEIGHT: 4'11"
IMPERIAL WEIGHT: 72.8 lbs.
METRIC HEIGHT: 1.5 m
METRIC WEIGHT: 33.0 kg

MEGA MEWTWO X

MEWTWO

MEGA MEWTWO Y

MIENFOO
Martial Arts Pokémon

TYPE: FIGHTING

In one minute, a well-trained Mienfoo can chop with its arms more than 100 times.

Though small, Mienfoo's temperament is fierce. Any creature that approaches Mienfoo carelessly will be greeted with a flurry of graceful attacks.

HOW TO SAY IT: MEEN-FOO
IMPERIAL HEIGHT: 2'11"
IMPERIAL WEIGHT: 44.1 lbs.
METRIC HEIGHT: 0.9 m
METRIC WEIGHT: 20.0 kg

POSSIBLE MOVES: Pound, Meditate, Detect, Fake Out, Double Slap, Swift, Calm Mind, Force Palm, Drain Punch, Jump Kick, U-turn, Quick Guard, Bounce, High Jump Kick, Reversal, Aura Sphere

MIENFOO   MIENSHAO

MIENSHAO
Martial Arts Pokémon

TYPE: FIGHTING

When Mienshao comes across a truly challenging opponent, it will lighten itself by biting off the fur on its arms.

Delivered at blinding speeds, kicks from this Pokémon can shatter massive boulders into tiny pieces.

HOW TO SAY IT: MEEN-SHAU
IMPERIAL HEIGHT: 4'07"
IMPERIAL WEIGHT: 78.3 lbs.
METRIC HEIGHT: 1.4 m
METRIC WEIGHT: 35.5 kg

POSSIBLE MOVES: Aura Sphere, Reversal, Pound, Meditate, Detect, Fake Out, Double Slap, Swift, Calm Mind, Force Palm, Drain Punch, Jump Kick, U-turn, Wide Guard, Bounce, High Jump Kick

MIENFOO   MIENSHAO

MIGHTYENA

Bite Pokémon

TYPE: DARK

Mightyena gives obvious signals when it is preparing to attack. It starts to growl deeply and then flattens its body. This Pokémon will bite savagely with its sharply pointed fangs.

Mightyena travel and act as a pack in the wild. The memory of its life in the wild compels the Pokémon to obey only those Trainers that it recognizes to possess superior skill.

HOW TO SAY IT: MY-tee-EH-nah
IMPERIAL HEIGHT: 3'03"
IMPERIAL WEIGHT: 81.6 lbs.
METRIC HEIGHT: 1.0 m
METRIC WEIGHT: 37.0 kg

POSSIBLE MOVES: Snarl, Fire Fang, Thunder Fang, Ice Fang, Crunch, Thief, Tackle, Howl, Sand Attack, Bite, Odor Sleuth, Roar, Swagger, Assurance, Scary Face, Taunt, Yawn, Embargo, Take Down, Sucker Punch, Play Rough

POOCHYENA → MIGHTYENA

MILCERY

Cream Pokémon

TYPE: FAIRY

This Pokémon was born from sweet-smelling particles in the air. Its body is made of cream.

They say that any patisserie visited by Milcery is guaranteed success and good fortune.

HOW TO SAY IT: MIHL-suh-ree
IMPERIAL HEIGHT: 0'08"
IMPERIAL WEIGHT: 0.7 lbs.
METRIC HEIGHT: 0.2 m
METRIC WEIGHT: 0.3 kg

POSSIBLE MOVES: Acid Armor, Aromatherapy, Aromatic Mist, Attract, Dazzling Gleam, Draining Kiss, Entrainment, Misty Terrain, Recover, Sweet Kiss, Sweet Scent, Tackle

MILCERY → ALCREMIE

TYPE: WATER

Milotic has provided inspiration to many artists. It has even been referred to as the most beautiful Pokémon of all.

It's said that a glimpse of a Milotic and its beauty will calm any hostile emotions you're feeling.

HOW TO SAY IT: MY-low-tic   **METRIC HEIGHT:** 6.2 m
IMPERIAL HEIGHT: 20'04"   **METRIC WEIGHT:** 162.0 kg
IMPERIAL WEIGHT: 357.1 lbs.

POSSIBLE MOVES: Aqua Ring, Aqua Tail, Attract, Coil, Disarming Voice, Dragon Tail, Flail, Hydro Pump, Life Dew, Rain Dance, Recover, Safeguard, Splash, Surf, Tackle, Twister, Water Gun, Water Pulse, Wrap

FEEBAS → MILOTIC

MILTANK

Milk Cow Pokémon

REGIONS: ALOLA JOHTO KALOS (COASTAL)

TYPE: NORMAL

Miltank produces highly nutritious milk, so it's been supporting the lives of people and other Pokémon since ancient times.

This Pokémon needs to be milked every day, or else it will fall ill. The flavor of Miltank milk changes with the seasons.

HOW TO SAY IT: MILL-tank
IMPERIAL HEIGHT: 3'11"
IMPERIAL WEIGHT: 166.4 lbs.
METRIC HEIGHT: 1.2 m
METRIC WEIGHT: 75.5 kg

POSSIBLE MOVES: Tackle, Growl, Defense Curl, Stomp, Milk Drink, Bide, Rollout, Body Slam, Zen Headbutt, Captivate, Gyro Ball, Heal Bell, Wake-Up Slap

DOES NOT EVOLVE

MIME JR.

Mime Pokémon

REGIONS: ALOLA GALAR KALOS (COASTAL) SINNOH

TYPE: PSYCHIC-FAIRY

It mimics everyone it sees, but it puts extra effort into copying the graceful dance steps of Mr. Rime as practice.

It looks for a Mr. Rime that's a good dancer and carefully copies the Mr. Rime's steps like an apprentice.

HOW TO SAY IT: mime JOO-nyur
IMPERIAL HEIGHT: 2'00"
IMPERIAL WEIGHT: 28.7 lbs.
METRIC HEIGHT: 0.6 m
METRIC WEIGHT: 13.0 kg

POSSIBLE MOVES: Baton Pass, Confusion, Copycat, Dazzling Gleam, Encore, Light Screen, Mimic, Pound, Protect, Psybeam, Psychic, Recycle, Reflect, Role Play, Safeguard, Sucker Punch, Teeter Dance

MIME JR.

MR. MIME

GALARIAN MR. MIME

MR. RIME

TYPE: GHOST-FAIRY

It wears a rag fashioned into a Pikachu costume in an effort to look less scary. Unfortunately, the costume only makes it creepier.

There was a scientist who peeked under Mimikyu's old rag in the name of research. The scientist died of a mysterious disease.

MIMIKYU
Disguise Pokémon

HOW TO SAY IT: MEE-mee-kyoo
IMPERIAL HEIGHT: 0'08"
IMPERIAL WEIGHT: 1.5 lbs.
METRIC HEIGHT: 0.2 m
METRIC WEIGHT: 0.7 kg

POSSIBLE MOVES: Astonish, Baby-Doll Eyes, Charm, Copycat, Double Team, Hone Claws, Mimic, Pain Split, Play Rough, Scratch, Shadow Claw, Shadow Sneak, Slash, Splash, Wood Hammer

DOES NOT EVOLVE

MINCCINO
Chinchilla Pokémon

TYPE: NORMAL

The way it brushes away grime with its tail can be helpful when cleaning. But its focus on spotlessness can make cleaning more of a hassle.

They pet each other with their tails as a form of greeting. Of the two, the one whose tail is fluffier is a bit more boastful.

HOW TO SAY IT: min-CHEE-noh
IMPERIAL HEIGHT: 1'04"
IMPERIAL WEIGHT: 12.8 lbs.
METRIC HEIGHT: 0.4 m
METRIC WEIGHT: 5.8 kg

POSSIBLE MOVES: After You, Baby-Doll Eyes, Charm, Echoed Voice, Encore, Helping Hand, Hyper Voice, Last Resort, Pound, Sing, Slam, Swift, Tail Slap, Tickle

MINCCINO   CINCCINO

MINIOR

Meteor Pokémon

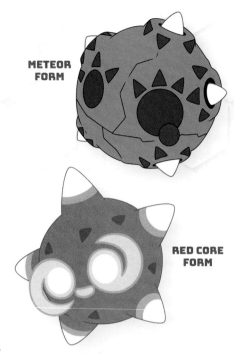

METEOR FORM

RED CORE FORM

TYPE: ROCK-FLYING

It lives in the ozone layer, where it becomes food for stronger Pokémon. When it tries to run away, it falls to the ground.

Although its outer shell is uncommonly durable, the shock of falling to the ground smashes the shell to smithereens.

HOW TO SAY IT: MIN-ee-or
IMPERIAL HEIGHT: 1'00"
IMPERIAL WEIGHT: 88.2 lbs.
METRIC HEIGHT: 0.3 m
METRIC WEIGHT: 40.0 kg

POSSIBLE MOVES: Tackle, Defense Curl, Rollout, Confuse Ray, Swift, Ancient Power, Self-Destruct, Stealth Rock, Take Down, Autotomize, Cosmic Power, Power Gem, Double-Edge, Shell Smash, Explosion

DOES NOT EVOLVE

MINUN

REGIONS: HOENN KALOS (CENTRAL)

Cheering Pokémon

TYPE: ELECTRIC

Minun is more concerned about cheering on its partners than its own safety. It shorts out the electricity in its body to create brilliant showers of sparks to cheer on its teammates.

Minun loves to cheer on its partner in battle. It gives off sparks from its body while it is doing so. If its partner is in trouble, this Pokémon gives off increasing amounts of sparks.

HOW TO SAY IT: MY-nun
IMPERIAL HEIGHT: 1'04"
IMPERIAL WEIGHT: 9.3 lbs.
METRIC HEIGHT: 0.4 m
METRIC WEIGHT: 4.2 kg

POSSIBLE MOVES: Nuzzle, Play Nice, Growl, Thunder Wave, Quick Attack, Helping Hand, Spark, Encore, Switcheroo, Swift, Electro Ball, Copycat, Fake Tears, Charge, Discharge, Baton Pass, Agility, Trump Card, Thunder, Nasty Plot, Entrainment

DOES NOT EVOLVE

MISDREAVUS
Screech Pokémon

TYPE: GHOST

What gives meaning to its life is surprising others. If you set your ear against the red orbs around its neck, you can hear shrieking.

What makes it happy is imitating the voices of weeping people and scaring everyone. It doesn't deal well with folks who aren't easily frightened.

HOW TO SAY IT: mis-DREE-vuss
IMPERIAL HEIGHT: 2'04"
IMPERIAL WEIGHT: 2.2 lbs.
METRIC HEIGHT: 0.7 m
METRIC WEIGHT: 1.0 kg

POSSIBLE MOVES: Growl, Psywave, Spite, Astonish, Confuse Ray, Mean Look, Hex, Psybeam, Pain Split, Payback, Shadow Ball, Perish Song, Grudge, Power Gem

MISDREAVUS   MISMAGIUS

MISMAGIUS
Magical Pokémon

TYPE: GHOST

Feared for its wrath and the curses it spreads, this Pokémon will also, on a whim, cast spells that help people.

Its muttered curses can cause awful headaches or terrifying visions that torment others.

HOW TO SAY IT: miss-MAG-ee-us
IMPERIAL HEIGHT: 2'11"
IMPERIAL WEIGHT: 9.7 lbs.
METRIC HEIGHT: 0.9 m
METRIC WEIGHT: 4.4 kg

POSSIBLE MOVES: Mystical Fire, Power Gem, Phantom Force, Lucky Chant, Magical Leaf, Growl, Psywave, Spite, Astonish

MISDREAVUS   MISMAGIUS

MOLTRES

Flame Pokémon

LEGENDARY POKÉMON

TYPE: FIRE-FLYING

A legendary bird Pokémon. As it flaps its flaming wings, even the night sky will turn red.

HOW TO SAY IT: MOHL-trace
IMPERIAL HEIGHT: 6'07"
IMPERIAL WEIGHT: 132.3 lbs.
METRIC HEIGHT: 2.0 m
METRIC WEIGHT: 60.0 kg

POSSIBLE MOVES: Roost, Hurricane, Sky Attack, Heat Wave, Wing Attack, Ember, Fire Spin, Agility, Endure, Ancient Power, Flamethrower, Safeguard, Air Slash, Sunny Day, Solar Beam, Burn Up

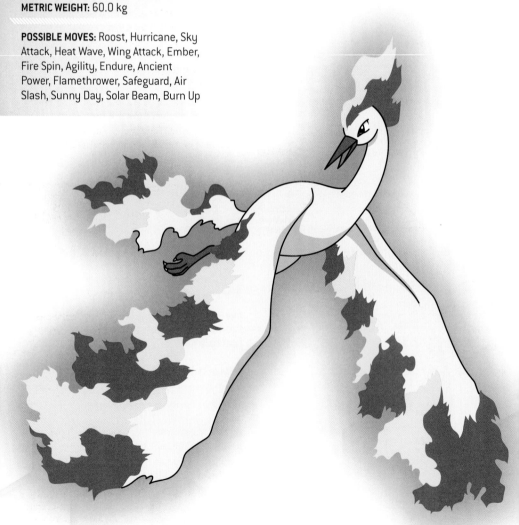

DOES NOT EVOLVE

MONFERNO
Playful Pokémon

TYPE: FIRE-FIGHTING

It skillfully controls the intensity of the fire on its tail to keep its foes at an ideal distance.

It uses ceilings and walls to launch aerial attacks. Its fiery tail is but one weapon.

HOW TO SAY IT: mon-FUR-no
IMPERIAL HEIGHT: 2'11"
IMPERIAL WEIGHT: 48.5 lbs.
METRIC HEIGHT: 0.9 m
METRIC WEIGHT: 22.0 kg

POSSIBLE MOVES: Scratch, Leer, Ember, Taunt, Mach Punch, Fury Swipes, Flame Wheel, Feint, Torment, Close Combat, Fire Spin, Acrobatics, Slack Off, Flare Blitz

CHIMCHAR → **MONFERNO** → **INFERNAPE**

REGIONS:
ALOLA
GALAR

MORELULL
Illuminating Pokémon

TYPE: GRASS-FAIRY

Pokémon living in the forest eat the delicious caps on Morelull's head. The caps regrow overnight.

Morelull live in forests that stay dark even during the day. They scatter flickering spores that put enemies to sleep.

HOW TO SAY IT: MORE-eh-lull
IMPERIAL HEIGHT: 0'08"
IMPERIAL WEIGHT: 3.3 lbs.
METRIC HEIGHT: 0.2 m
METRIC WEIGHT: 1.5 kg

POSSIBLE MOVES: Absorb, Astonish, Confuse Ray, Dazzling Gleam, Dream Eater, Giga Drain, Ingrain, Mega Drain, Moonblast, Moonlight, Sleep Powder, Spore, Strength Sap

MORELULL → **SHIINOTIC**

MORGREM

Devious Pokémon

REGION: GALAR

TYPE: DARK-FAIRY

When it gets down on all fours as if to beg for forgiveness, it's trying to lure opponents in so that it can stab them with its spear-like hair.

With sly cunning, it tries to lure people into the woods. Some believe it to have the power to make crops grow.

HOW TO SAY IT: MOHR-grehm
IMPERIAL HEIGHT: 2'07"
IMPERIAL WEIGHT: 27.6 lbs.
METRIC HEIGHT: 0.8 m
METRIC WEIGHT: 12.5 kg

POSSIBLE MOVES: Assurance, Bite, Confide, Dark Pulse, Fake Out, Fake Tears, False Surrender, Flatter, Foul Play, Nasty Plot, Play Rough, Sucker Punch, Swagger, Torment

IMPIDIMP   **MORGREM**   **GRIMMSNARL**

MORPEKO

Two-Sided Pokémon

REGION: GALAR

TYPE: ELECTRIC-DARK

As it eats the seeds stored up in its pocket-like pouches, this Pokémon is not just satisfying its constant hunger. It's also generating electricity.

It carries electrically roasted seeds with it as if they're precious treasures. No matter how much it eats, it always gets hungry again in short order.

HOW TO SAY IT: mohr-PEH-koh
IMPERIAL HEIGHT: 1'00"
IMPERIAL WEIGHT: 6.6 lbs.
METRIC HEIGHT: 0.3 m
METRIC WEIGHT: 3.0 kg

POSSIBLE MOVES: Agility, Aura Wheel, Bite, Bullet Seed, Crunch, Flatter, Leer, Power Trip, Quick Attack, Spark, Tail Whip, Thrash, Thunder Shock, Torment

FULL BELLY MODE

HANGRY MODE

DOES NOT EVOLVE

TYPE: BUG-FLYING

It loves the honey of flowers and steals honey collected by Combee.

It flutters around at night and steals honey from the Combee hive.

HOW TO SAY IT: MOTH-im
IMPERIAL HEIGHT: 2'11"
IMPERIAL WEIGHT: 51.4 lbs.
METRIC HEIGHT: 0.9 m
METRIC WEIGHT: 23.3 kg

POSSIBLE MOVES: Tackle, Protect, Bug Bite, Hidden Power, Confusion, Gust, Poison Powder, Psybeam, Camouflage, Silver Wind, Air Slash, Psychic, Lunge, Bug Buzz, Quiver Dance

REGIONS: KALOS (CENTRAL) SINNOH

MOTHIM
Moth Pokémon

BURMY ▶ MOTHIM

329

MR. MIME
Barrier Pokémon

TYPE: PSYCHIC-FAIRY

The broadness of its hands may be no coincidence—many scientists believe its palms became enlarged specifically for pantomiming.

It's known for its top-notch pantomime skills. It protects itself from all sorts of attacks by emitting auras from its fingers to create walls.

HOW TO SAY IT: MIS-ter MIME
IMPERIAL HEIGHT: 4'03"
IMPERIAL WEIGHT: 120.2 lbs.
METRIC HEIGHT: 1.3 m
METRIC WEIGHT: 54.5 kg

POSSIBLE MOVES: Baton Pass, Confusion, Copycat, Dazzling Gleam, Encore, Guard Swap, Light Screen, Mimic, Pound, Power Swap, Protect, Psybeam, Psychic, Quick Guard, Recycle, Reflect, Role Play, Safeguard, Sucker Punch, Teeter Dance, Wide Guard

MIME JR.   MR. MIME

GALARIAN MR. MIME
Dancing Pokémon

TYPE: ICE-PSYCHIC

Its talent is tap-dancing. It can also manipulate temperatures to create a floor of ice, which this Pokémon can kick up to use as a barrier.

It can radiate chilliness from the bottoms of its feet. It'll spend the whole day tap-dancing on a frozen floor.

HOW TO SAY IT: MIS-ter-MIME
IMPERIAL HEIGHT: 4'07"
IMPERIAL WEIGHT: 125.2 lbs.
METRIC HEIGHT: 1.4 m
METRIC WEIGHT: 56.8 kg

POSSIBLE MOVES: Ally Switch, Baton Pass, Confusion, Copycat, Dazzling Gleam, Double Kick, Encore, Freeze-Dry, Hypnosis, Ice Shard, Icy Wind, Light Screen, Mimic, Mirror Coat, Misty Terrain, Pound, Protect, Psybeam, Psychic, Rapid Spin, Recycle, Reflect, Role Play, Safeguard, Sucker Punch, Teeter Dance

MIME JR.   GALARIAN
MR. MIME   MR. RIME

TYPE: ICE-PSYCHIC

It's highly skilled at tap-dancing. It waves its cane of ice in time with its graceful movements.

Its amusing movements make it very popular. It releases its psychic power from the pattern on its belly.

REGION: GALAR

MR. RIME
Comedian Pokémon

HOW TO SAY IT: MIS-ter RYME
IMPERIAL HEIGHT: 4'11"
IMPERIAL WEIGHT: 128.3 lbs.

METRIC HEIGHT: 1.5 m
METRIC WEIGHT: 58.2 kg

POSSIBLE MOVES: After You, Ally Switch, Baton Pass, Block, Confusion, Copycat, Dazzling Gleam, Double Kick, Encore, Fake Tears, Freeze-Dry, Hypnosis, Ice Shard, Icy Wind, Light Screen, Mimic, Mirror Coat, Misty Terrain, Pound, Protect, Psybeam, Psychic, Rapid Spin, Recycle, Reflect, Role Play, Safeguard, Slack Off, Sucker Punch, Teeter Dance

MIME JR. → **GALARIAN MR. MIME** → **MR. RIME**

REGIONS: ALOLA GALAR

MUDBRAY
Donkey Pokémon

TYPE: GROUND

Loads weighing up to 50 times as much as its own body weight pose no issue for this Pokémon. It's skilled at making use of mud.

It eats dirt to create mud and smears this mud all over its feet, giving them the grip needed to walk on rough terrain without slipping.

HOW TO SAY IT: MUD-bray
IMPERIAL HEIGHT: 3'03"
IMPERIAL WEIGHT: 242.5 lbs.

METRIC HEIGHT: 1.0 m
METRIC WEIGHT: 110.0 kg

POSSIBLE MOVES: Bulldoze, Counter, Double Kick, Earthquake, Heavy Slam, High Horsepower, Iron Defense, Mega Kick, Mud-Slap, Rock Smash, Stomp, Strength, Superpower

MUDBRAY → **MUDSDALE**

MUDKIP

Mud Fish Pokémon

REGION:
HOENN

TYPE: WATER

The fin on Mudkip's head acts as a highly sensitive radar. Using this fin to sense movements of water and air, this Pokémon can determine what is taking place around it without using its eyes.

In water, Mudkip breathes using the gills on its cheeks. If it is faced with a tight situation in battle, this Pokémon will unleash its amazing power—it can crush rocks bigger than itself.

HOW TO SAY IT: MUD-kip **METRIC HEIGHT:** 0.4 m
IMPERIAL HEIGHT: 1'04" **METRIC WEIGHT:** 7.6 kg
IMPERIAL WEIGHT: 16.8 lbs.

POSSIBLE MOVES: Tackle, Growl, Mud-Slap, Water Gun, Bide, Foresight, Mud Sport, Take Down, Whirlpool, Protect, Hydro Pump, Endeavor, Rock Throw

 MUDKIP **MARSHTOMP** **SWAMPERT** **MEGA SWAMPERT**

MUDSDALE

Draft Horse Pokémon

REGIONS:
ALOLA
GALAR

TYPE: GROUND

Mud that hardens around a Mudsdale's legs sets harder than stone. It's so hard that it allows this Pokémon to scrap a truck with a single kick.

Mudsdale has so much stamina that it could carry over 10 tons across the Galar region without rest or sleep.

HOW TO SAY IT: MUDZ-dale **METRIC HEIGHT:** 2.5 m
IMPERIAL HEIGHT: 8'02" **METRIC WEIGHT:** 920.0 kg
IMPERIAL WEIGHT: 2,028.3 lbs.

POSSIBLE MOVES: Bulldoze, Counter, Double Kick, Earthquake, Heavy Slam, High Horsepower, Iron Defense, Mega Kick, Mud-Slap, Rock Smash, Stomp, Strength, Superpower

 MUDBRAY **MUDSDALE**

TYPE: POISON

Smells so awful, it can cause fainting. Through degeneration of its nose, it lost its sense of smell.

HOW TO SAY IT: MUCK
IMPERIAL HEIGHT: 3'11"
IMPERIAL WEIGHT: 66.1 lbs.
METRIC HEIGHT: 1.2 m
METRIC WEIGHT: 30.0 kg

POSSIBLE MOVES: Venom Drench, Pound, Poison Gas, Harden, Mud-Slap, Disable, Mud Bomb, Minimize, Fling, Sludge Bomb, Sludge Wave, Screech, Gunk Shot, Acid Armor, Memento

MUK
Sludge Pokémon

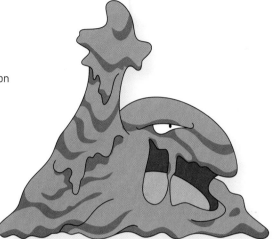

GRIMER **MUK**

TYPE: POISON-DARK

Muk's coloration becomes increasingly vivid the more it feasts on its favorite dish—trash.

ALOLAN MUK
Sludge Pokémon

HOW TO SAY IT: MUCK
IMPERIAL HEIGHT: 3'03"
IMPERIAL WEIGHT: 114.6 lbs.
METRIC HEIGHT: 1.0 m
METRIC WEIGHT: 52.0 kg

POSSIBLE MOVES: Venom Drench, Poison Gas, Pound, Harden, Bite, Disable, Acid Spray, Poison Fang, Minimize, Fling, Knock Off, Crunch, Screech, Gunk Shot, Acid Armor, Belch, Memento

ALOLAN GRIMER **ALOLAN MUK**

MUNCHLAX

Big Eater Pokémon

REGIONS:
ALOLA
GALAR
KALOS
(CENTRAL)
SINNOH

TYPE: NORMAL

Stuffing itself with vast amounts of food is its only concern. Whether the food is rotten or fresh, yummy or tasteless—it does not care.

It stores food beneath its fur. It might share just one bite, but only if it really trusts you.

HOW TO SAY IT: MUNCH-lax
IMPERIAL HEIGHT: 2'00"
IMPERIAL WEIGHT: 231.5 lbs.
METRIC HEIGHT: 0.6 m
METRIC WEIGHT: 105.0 kg

POSSIBLE MOVES: Amnesia, Belly Drum, Bite, Body Slam, Covet, Defense Curl, Flail, Fling, Last Resort, Lick, Metronome, Recycle, Screech, Stockpile, Swallow, Tackle

MUNCHLAX   SNORLAX

MUNNA

Dream Eater Pokémon

REGIONS:
GALAR
UNOVA

TYPE: PSYCHIC

Late at night, it appears beside people's pillows. As it feeds on dreams, the patterns on its body give off a faint glow.

It eats dreams and releases mist. The mist is pink when it's eating a good dream, and black when it's eating a nightmare.

HOW TO SAY IT: MOON-nuh
IMPERIAL HEIGHT: 2'00"
IMPERIAL WEIGHT: 51.4 lbs.
METRIC HEIGHT: 0.6 m
METRIC WEIGHT: 23.3 kg

POSSIBLE MOVES: Calm Mind, Defense Curl, Dream Eater, Future Sight, Hypnosis, Imprison, Magic Coat, Moonblast, Moonlight, Psybeam, Psychic, Stored Power, Wonder Room, Yawn, Zen Headbutt

MUNNA   MUSHARNA

TYPE: DARK-FLYING

It has a weakness for shiny things. It's been known to sneak into the nests of Gabite—noted collectors of jewels—in search of treasure.

It searches for shiny things for its boss. Murkrow's presence is said to be unlucky, so many people detest it.

HOW TO SAY IT: MUR-crow
IMPERIAL HEIGHT: 1'08"
IMPERIAL WEIGHT: 4.6 lbs.
METRIC HEIGHT: 0.5 m
METRIC WEIGHT: 2.1 kg

POSSIBLE MOVES: Peck, Astonish, Pursuit, Haze, Wing Attack, Night Shade, Assurance, Taunt, Feint Attack, Mean Look, Foul Play, Tailwind, Sucker Punch, Torment, Quash

MURKROW
Darkness Pokémon

MURKROW

HONCHKROW

TYPE: PSYCHIC

When dark mists emanate from its body, don't get too near. If you do, your nightmares will become reality.

It drowses and dreams all the time. It's best to leave it be if it's just woken up, as it's a terrible grump when freshly roused from sleep.

HOW TO SAY IT: moo-SHAHR-nuh
IMPERIAL HEIGHT: 3'07"
IMPERIAL WEIGHT: 133.4 lbs.
METRIC HEIGHT: 1.1 m
METRIC WEIGHT: 60.5 kg

POSSIBLE MOVES: Calm Mind, Defense Curl, Dream Eater, Future Sight, Hypnosis, Imprison, Magic Coat, Moonblast, Moonlight, Psybeam, Psychic, Psychic Terrain, Stored Power, Wonder Room, Yawn, Zen Headbutt

MUSHARNA
Drowsing Pokémon

MUNNA　**MUSHARNA**

NAGANADEL

Poison Pin Pokémon

TYPE: POISON-DRAGON

It stores hundreds of liters of poisonous liquid inside its body. It is one of the organisms known as UBs.

One kind of Ultra Beast, it fires a glowing, venomous liquid from its needles. This liquid is also immensely adhesive.

HOW TO SAY IT: NAW-guh-NAW-duhl
IMPERIAL HEIGHT: 11'10"
IMPERIAL WEIGHT: 330.7 lbs.
METRIC HEIGHT: 3.6 m
METRIC WEIGHT: 150.0 kg

POSSIBLE MOVES: Air Cutter, Dragon Pulse, Peck, Growl, Helping Hand, Acid, Fury Attack, Venoshock, Charm, Venom Drench, Nasty Plot, Poison Jab, Toxic, Fell Stinger, Air Slash, Dragon Pulse

POIPOLE   NAGANADEL

NATU

Tiny Bird Pokémon

TYPE: PSYCHIC-FLYING

It is extremely good at climbing tree trunks and likes to eat the new sprouts on the trees.

Because its wings aren't yet fully grown, it has to hop to get around. It is always staring at something.

HOW TO SAY IT: NAH-too
IMPERIAL HEIGHT: 0'08"
IMPERIAL WEIGHT: 4.4 lbs.
METRIC HEIGHT: 0.2 m
METRIC WEIGHT: 2.0 kg

POSSIBLE MOVES: Confuse Ray, Future Sight, Guard Swap, Leer, Night Shade, Peck, Power Swap, Psychic, Psycho Shift, Stored Power, Teleport, Wish

NATU   XATU

LEGENDARY POKÉMON

REGION: ALOLA

NECROZMA
Prism Pokémon

TYPE: PSYCHIC

It looks somehow pained as it rages around in search of light, which serves as its energy. It's apparently from another world.

Light is the source of its energy. If it isn't devouring light, impurities build up in it and on it, and Necrozma darkens and stops moving.

HOW TO SAY IT: neh-KROHZ-muh
IMPERIAL HEIGHT: 7'10"
IMPERIAL WEIGHT: 507.1 lbs.
METRIC HEIGHT: 2.4 m
METRIC WEIGHT: 230.0 kg

POSSIBLE MOVES: Moonlight, Morning Sun, Charge Beam, Mirror Shot, Metal Claw, Confusion, Slash, Stored Power, Rock Blast, Night Slash, Gravity, Psycho Cut, Power Gem, Autotomize, Photon Geyser, Stealth Rock, Iron Defense, Wring Out, Prismatic Laser

DUSK MANE NECROZMA

ULTRA NECROZMA

DAWN WINGS NECROZMA

DOES NOT EVOLVE

NICKIT

Fox Pokémon

TYPE: DARK

Aided by the soft pads on its feet, it silently raids the food stores of other Pokémon. It survives off its ill-gotten gains.

Cunning and cautious, this Pokémon survives by stealing food from others. It erases its tracks with swipes of its tail as it makes off with its plunder.

HOW TO SAY IT: NICK-it
IMPERIAL HEIGHT: 2'00"
METRIC HEIGHT: 0.6 m
IMPERIAL WEIGHT: 19.6 lbs.
METRIC WEIGHT: 8.9 kg

POSSIBLE MOVES: Assurance, Beat Up, Foul Play, Hone Claws, Nasty Plot, Night Slash, Quick Attack, Snarl, Sucker Punch, Tail Slap, Tail Whip

NICKIT → THIEVUL

NIDOKING
Drill Pokémon

TYPE: POISON-GROUND

Its steel-like hide adds to its powerful tackle. Its horns are so hard, they can pierce a diamond.

HOW TO SAY IT: NEE-do-king
IMPERIAL HEIGHT: 4'07"
IMPERIAL WEIGHT: 136.7 lbs.
METRIC HEIGHT: 1.4 m
METRIC WEIGHT: 62.0 kg

POSSIBLE MOVES: Megahorn, Peck, Focus Energy, Double Kick, Poison Sting, Chip Away, Thrash, Earth Power

NIDORAN ♂   **NIDORINO**   **NIDOKING**

TYPE: POISON-GROUND

Tough scales cover the sturdy body of this Pokémon. It appears that the scales grow in cycles.

HOW TO SAY IT: NEE-do-kween
IMPERIAL HEIGHT: 4'03"
IMPERIAL WEIGHT: 132.3 lbs.
METRIC HEIGHT: 1.3 m
METRIC WEIGHT: 60.0 kg

POSSIBLE MOVES: Superpower, Scratch, Tail Whip, Double Kick, Poison Sting, Chip Away, Body Slam, Earth Power

NIDOQUEEN
Drill Pokémon

NIDORAN ♀   **NIDORINA**   **NIDOQUEEN**

NIDORAN ♀

Poison Pin Pokémon

REGIONS:
KALOS
(COASTAL)
KANTO

TYPE: POISON

A mild-mannered Pokémon that does not like to fight. Beware—its small horn secretes venom.

HOW TO SAY IT: NEE-do-ran
IMPERIAL HEIGHT: 1'04"
IMPERIAL WEIGHT: 15.4 lbs.
METRIC HEIGHT: 0.4 m
METRIC WEIGHT: 7.0 kg

POSSIBLE MOVES: Growl, Scratch, Tail Whip, Double Kick, Poison Sting, Fury Swipes, Bite, Helping Hand, Toxic Spikes, Flatter, Crunch, Captivate, Poison Fang

NIDORAN ♀   NIDORINA   NIDOQUEEN

NIDORAN ♂

Poison Pin Pokémon

REGIONS:
KALOS
(COASTAL)
KANTO

TYPE: POISON

Its large ears are always kept upright. If it senses danger, it will attack with a poisonous sting.

HOW TO SAY IT: NEE-do-ran
IMPERIAL HEIGHT: 1'08"
IMPERIAL WEIGHT: 19.8 lbs.
METRIC HEIGHT: 0.5 m
METRIC WEIGHT: 9.0 kg

POSSIBLE MOVES: Leer, Peck, Focus Energy, Double Kick, Poison Sting, Fury Attack, Horn Attack, Helping Hand, Toxic Spikes, Flatter, Poison Jab, Captivate, Horn Drill

NIDORAN ♂   NIDORINO   NIDOKING

NIDORINA
Poison Pin Pokémon

TYPE: POISON

When resting deep in its burrow, its barbs always retract. This is proof that it is relaxed.

HOW TO SAY IT: NEE-do-REE-na
IMPERIAL HEIGHT: 2'07"
IMPERIAL WEIGHT: 44.1 lbs.
METRIC HEIGHT: 0.8 m
METRIC WEIGHT: 20.0 kg

POSSIBLE MOVES: Growl, Scratch, Tail Whip, Double Kick, Poison Sting, Fury Swipes, Bite, Helping Hand, Toxic Spikes, Flatter, Crunch, Captivate, Poison Fang

NIDORAN ♀ → NIDORINA → NIDOQUEEN

NIDORINO
Poison Pin Pokémon

TYPE: POISON

Its horn contains venom. If it stabs an enemy with the horn, the impact makes the poison leak out.

HOW TO SAY IT: NEE-do-REE-no
IMPERIAL HEIGHT: 2'11"
IMPERIAL WEIGHT: 43.0 lbs.
METRIC HEIGHT: 0.9 m
METRIC WEIGHT: 19.5 kg

POSSIBLE MOVES: Leer, Peck, Focus Energy, Double Kick, Poison Sting, Fury Attack, Horn Attack, Helping Hand, Toxic Spikes, Flatter, Poison Jab, Captivate, Horn Drill

NIDORAN ♂ → NIDORINO → NIDOKING

NIHILEGO

Parasite Pokémon

ULTRA BEAST

TYPE: ROCK-POISON

A life-form from another world, it was dubbed a UB and is thought to produce a strong neurotoxin.

It appeared in this world from an Ultra Wormhole. Nihilego appears to be a parasite that lives by feeding on people and Pokémon.

HOW TO SAY IT: NIE-uh-LEE-go
IMPERIAL HEIGHT: 3'11"
IMPERIAL WEIGHT: 122.4 lbs.
METRIC HEIGHT: 1.2 m
METRIC WEIGHT: 55.5 kg

POSSIBLE MOVES: Power Split, Guard Split, Tickle, Acid, Constrict, Pound, Clear Smog, Psywave, Headbutt, Venoshock, Toxic Spikes, Safeguard, Power Gem, Mirror Coat, Acid Spray, Venom Drench, Stealth Rock, Wonder Room, Head Smash

DOES NOT EVOLVE

NINCADA

Trainee Pokémon

REGIONS: GALAR HOENN KALOS (CENTRAL)

TYPE: BUG-GROUND

Because it lived almost entirely underground, it is nearly blind. It uses its antennae instead.

It can sometimes live underground for more than 10 years. It absorbs nutrients from the roots of trees.

HOW TO SAY IT: nin-KAH-da
IMPERIAL HEIGHT: 1'08"
IMPERIAL WEIGHT: 12.1 lbs.
METRIC HEIGHT: 0.5 m
METRIC WEIGHT: 5.5 kg

POSSIBLE MOVES: Absorb, Dig, False Swipe, Fury Swipes, Harden, Metal Claw, Mind Reader, Mud-Slap, Sand Attack, Scratch

NINJASK

NINCADA

SHEDINJA

TYPE: FIRE

It is said to live 1,000 years, and each of its tails is loaded with supernatural powers.

Very smart and very vengeful. Grabbing one of its many tails could result in a 1,000-year curse.

NINETALES
Fox Pokémon

HOW TO SAY IT: NINE-tails **METRIC HEIGHT:** 1.1 m
IMPERIAL HEIGHT: 3'07" **METRIC WEIGHT:** 19.9 kg
IMPERIAL WEIGHT: 43.9 lbs.

POSSIBLE MOVES: Confuse Ray, Disable, Ember, Extrasensory, Fire Blast, Fire Spin, Flamethrower, Grudge, Imprison, Incinerate, Inferno, Nasty Plot, Quick Attack, Safeguard, Spite, Tail Whip, Will-O-Wisp

VULPIX ➡ **NINETALES**

ALOLAN NINETALES
Fox Pokémon

TYPE: ICE-FAIRY

A deity resides in the snowy mountains where this Pokémon lives. In ancient times, it was worshiped as that deity's incarnation.

While it will guide travelers who get lost on a snowy mountain down to the mountain's base, it won't forgive anyone who harms nature.

HOW TO SAY IT: NINE-tails **METRIC HEIGHT:** 1.1 m
IMPERIAL HEIGHT: 3'07" **METRIC WEIGHT:** 19.9 kg
IMPERIAL WEIGHT: 43.9 lbs.

POSSIBLE MOVES: Aurora Beam, Aurora Veil, Blizzard, Confuse Ray, Dazzling Gleam, Disable, Extrasensory, Grudge, Ice Beam, Ice Shard, Icy Wind, Imprison, Mist, Nasty Plot, Powder Snow, Sheer Cold, Spite, Tail Whip

ALOLAN VULPIX ➡ **ALOLAN NINETALES**

NINJASK

Ninja Pokémon

TYPE: BUG-FLYING

Its cry leaves a lasting headache if heard for too long. It moves so quickly that it is almost invisible.

This Pokémon is so quick, it is said to be able to avoid any attack. It loves to feed on tree sap.

HOW TO SAY IT: NIN-jask
IMPERIAL HEIGHT: 2'07"
IMPERIAL WEIGHT: 26.5 lbs.
METRIC HEIGHT: 0.8 m
METRIC WEIGHT: 12.0 kg

POSSIBLE MOVES: Absorb, Aerial Ace, Agility, Baton Pass, Bug Bite, Dig, Double Team, False Swipe, Fury Cutter, Fury Swipes, Harden, Metal Claw, Mind Reader, Mud-Slap, Sand Attack, Scratch, Screech, Slash, Swords Dance, X-Scissor

NINCADA   NINJASK

NOCTOWL

Owl Pokémon

REGIONS:
ALOLA
GALAR
JOHTO
KALOS
(MOUNTAIN)

TYPE: NORMAL-FLYING

Its eyes are specially developed to enable it to see clearly even in murky darkness and minimal light.

When it needs to think, it rotates its head 180 degrees to sharpen its intellectual power.

HOW TO SAY IT: NAHK-towl
IMPERIAL HEIGHT: 5'03"
IMPERIAL WEIGHT: 89.9 lbs.
METRIC HEIGHT: 1.6 m
METRIC WEIGHT: 40.8 kg

POSSIBLE MOVES: Air Slash, Confusion, Dream Eater, Echoed Voice, Extrasensory, Growl, Hypnosis, Moonblast, Peck, Psycho Shift, Reflect, Roost, Sky Attack, Tackle, Take Down, Uproar

HOOTHOOT   NOCTOWL

NOIBAT
Sound Wave Pokémon

TYPE: FLYING-DRAGON

After nightfall, they emerge from the caves they nest in during the day. Using their ultrasonic waves, they go on the hunt for ripened fruit.

No wavelength of sound is beyond Noibat's ability to produce. The ultrasonic waves it generates can overcome much larger Pokémon.

HOW TO SAY IT: NOY-bat
IMPERIAL HEIGHT: 1'08"
IMPERIAL WEIGHT: 17.6 lbs.
METRIC HEIGHT: 0.5 m
METRIC WEIGHT: 8.0 kg

POSSIBLE MOVES: Absorb, Air Cutter, Air Slash, Bite, Double Team, Gust, Hurricane, Roost, Screech, Super Fang, Supersonic, Tackle, Tailwind, Whirlwind, Wing Attack

NOIBAT → NOIVERN

NOIVERN
Sound Wave Pokémon

TYPE: FLYING-DRAGON

Aggressive and cruel, this Pokémon will ruthlessly torment enemies that are helpless in the dark.

Flying through the darkness, it weakens enemies with ultrasonic waves that could crush stone. Its fangs finish the fight.

HOW TO SAY IT: NOY-vurn
IMPERIAL HEIGHT: 4'11"
IMPERIAL WEIGHT: 187.4 lbs.
METRIC HEIGHT: 1.5 m
METRIC WEIGHT: 85.0 kg

POSSIBLE MOVES: Absorb, Air Cutter, Air Slash, Bite, Boomburst, Double Team, Dragon Pulse, Gust, Hurricane, Moonlight, Roost, Screech, Super Fang, Supersonic, Tackle, Tailwind, Whirlwind, Wing Attack

NOIBAT → NOIVERN

NOSEPASS

Compass Pokémon

REGIONS:
ALOLA
HOENN
KALOS
(COASTAL)

TYPE: ROCK

It moves less than an inch a year, but when it's in a jam, it will spin and drill down into the ground in a split second.

It hunts without twitching a muscle by pulling in its prey with powerful magnetism. But sometimes it pulls natural enemies in close.

HOW TO SAY IT: NOSE-pass
IMPERIAL HEIGHT: 3'03"
IMPERIAL WEIGHT: 213.8 lbs.
METRIC HEIGHT: 1.0 m
METRIC WEIGHT: 97.0 kg

POSSIBLE MOVES: Tackle, Harden, Block, Rock Throw, Thunder Wave, Rest, Spark, Rock Slide, Power Gem, Rock Blast, Discharge, Sandstorm, Earth Power, Stone Edge, Lock-On, Zap Cannon

NOSEPASS ➡ **PROBOPASS**

NUMEL

Numb Pokémon

REGION:
HOENN

TYPE: FIRE-GROUND

Numel is extremely dull witted—it doesn't notice being hit. However, it can't stand hunger for even a second. This Pokémon's body is a seething cauldron of boiling magma.

Numel stores magma of almost 2,200 degrees Fahrenheit within its body. If it gets wet, the magma cools and hardens. In that event, the Pokémon's body grows heavy and its movements become sluggish.

HOW TO SAY IT: NUM-mull
IMPERIAL HEIGHT: 2'04"
IMPERIAL WEIGHT: 52.9 lbs.
METRIC HEIGHT: 0.7 m
METRIC WEIGHT: 24.0 kg

POSSIBLE MOVES: Growl, Tackle, Ember, Magnitude, Focus Energy, Flame Burst, Take Down, Amnesia, Lava Plume, Earth Power, Curse, Yawn, Earthquake, Flamethrower, Double-Edge

NUMEL ➡ **CAMERUPT** ➡ **MEGA CAMERUPT**

NUZLEAF
Wily Pokémon

TYPE: GRASS-DARK

It lives deep in forests. With the leaf on its head, it makes a flute whose song makes listeners uneasy.

They live in holes bored in large trees. The sound of Nuzleaf's grass flute fills listeners with dread.

HOW TO SAY IT: NUZ-leaf **METRIC HEIGHT:** 1.0 m
IMPERIAL HEIGHT: 3'03" **METRIC WEIGHT:** 28.0 kg
IMPERIAL WEIGHT: 61.7 lbs.

POSSIBLE MOVES: Absorb, Air Cutter, Astonish, Explosion, Extrasensory, Fake Out, Growth, Harden, Leaf Blade, Mega Drain, Nature Power, Payback, Razor Leaf, Rollout, Sucker Punch, Sunny Day, Swagger, Synthesis, Tackle, Torment

SEEDOT   **NUZLEAF**   **SHIFTRY**

OBSTAGOON
Blocking Pokémon

TYPE: DARK-NORMAL

Its voice is staggering in volume. Obstagoon has a tendency to take on a threatening posture and shout—this move is known as Obstruct.

It evolved after experiencing numerous fights. While crossing its arms, it lets out a shout that would make any opponent flinch.

HOW TO SAY IT: AHB-stuh-goon **METRIC HEIGHT:** 1.6 m
IMPERIAL HEIGHT: 5'03" **METRIC WEIGHT:** 46.0 kg
IMPERIAL WEIGHT: 101.4 lbs.

POSSIBLE MOVES: Baby-Doll Eyes, Counter, Cross Chop, Double-Edge, Fury Swipes, Headbutt, Hone Claws, Leer, Lick, Night Slash, Obstruct, Pin Missile, Rest, Sand Attack, Scary Face, Snarl, Submission, Switcheroo, Tackle, Take Down, Taunt

**GALARIAN
ZIGZAGOON**   **GALARIAN
LINOONE**   **OBSTAGOON**

OCTILLERY
Jet Pokémon

REGIONS:
ALOLA
GALAR
JOHTO
KALOS
(COASTAL)

TYPE: WATER

It has a tendency to want to be in holes. It prefers rock crags or pots and sprays ink from them before attacking.

It traps enemies with its suction-cupped tentacles, then smashes them with its rock-hard head.

HOW TO SAY IT: ock-TILL-er-ree
IMPERIAL HEIGHT: 2'11"
IMPERIAL WEIGHT: 62.8 lbs.
METRIC HEIGHT: 0.9 m
METRIC WEIGHT: 28.5 kg

POSSIBLE MOVES: Aurora Beam, Bubble Beam, Bullet Seed, Focus Energy, Gunk Shot, Helping Hand, Hydro Pump, Hyper Beam, Ice Beam, Lock-On, Octazooka, Psybeam, Rock Blast, Soak, Water Gun, Water Pulse, Wrap

REMORAID

OCTILLERY

ODDISH
Weed Pokémon

REGIONS:
GALAR
KALOS
(CENTRAL)
KANTO

TYPE: GRASS-POISON

If exposed to moonlight, it starts to move. It roams far and wide at night to scatter its seeds.

During the day, it stays in the cold underground to avoid the sun. It grows by bathing in moonlight.

HOW TO SAY IT: ODD-ish
IMPERIAL HEIGHT: 1'08"
IMPERIAL WEIGHT: 11.9 lbs.
METRIC HEIGHT: 0.5 m
METRIC WEIGHT: 5.4 kg

POSSIBLE MOVES: Absorb, Acid, Giga Drain, Grassy Terrain, Growth, Mega Drain, Moonblast, Moonlight, Petal Dance, Poison Powder, Sleep Powder, Stun Spore, Sweet Scent, Toxic

VILEPLUME

ODDISH   GLOOM

BELLOSSOM

OMANYTE
Spiral Pokémon

TYPE: ROCK-WATER

An ancient Pokémon that was recovered from a fossil. It swam by cleverly twisting its 10 tentacles about.

HOW TO SAY IT: AH-man-ite
IMPERIAL HEIGHT: 1'04"
IMPERIAL WEIGHT: 16.5 lbs.
METRIC HEIGHT: 0.4 m
METRIC WEIGHT: 7.5 kg

POSSIBLE MOVES: Constrict, Withdraw, Bite, Water Gun, Rollout, Leer, Mud Shot, Brine, Protect, Ancient Power, Tickle, Rock Blast, Shell Smash, Hydro Pump

OMANYTE → OMASTAR

OMASTAR
Spiral Pokémon

TYPE: ROCK-WATER

Its sharp beak rings its mouth. Its shell was too big for it to move freely, so it became extinct.

HOW TO SAY IT: AH-mah-star
IMPERIAL HEIGHT: 3'03"
IMPERIAL WEIGHT: 77.2 lbs.
METRIC HEIGHT: 1.0 m
METRIC WEIGHT: 35.0 kg

POSSIBLE MOVES: Constrict, Withdraw, Bite, Water Gun, Rollout, Leer, Mud Shot, Brine, Protect, Ancient Power, Spike Cannon, Tickle, Rock Blast, Shell Smash, Hydro Pump

OMANYTE → OMASTAR

ONIX
Rock Snake Pokémon

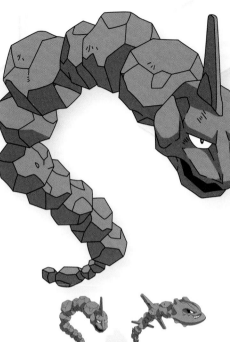

REGIONS: GALAR KALOS (COASTAL) KANTO

TYPE: ROCK-GROUND

As it digs through the ground, it absorbs many hard objects. This is what makes its body so solid.

It rapidly bores through the ground at 50 mph by squirming and twisting its massive, rugged body.

HOW TO SAY IT: ON-icks
METRIC HEIGHT: 8.8 m
IMPERIAL HEIGHT: 28'10"
METRIC WEIGHT: 210.0 kg
IMPERIAL WEIGHT: 463.0 lbs.

POSSIBLE MOVES: Bind, Curse, Dig, Double-Edge, Dragon Breath, Harden, Iron Tail, Rock Polish, Rock Slide, Rock Throw, Sand Tomb, Sandstorm, Screech, Slam, Smack Down, Stealth Rock, Stone Edge, Tackle

ONIX   STEELIX

ORANGURU
Sage Pokémon

REGIONS: ALOLA GALAR

TYPE: NORMAL-PSYCHIC

With waves of its fan—made from leaves and its own fur—Oranguru skillfully gives instructions to other Pokémon.

It knows the forest inside and out. If it comes across a wounded Pokémon, Oranguru will gather medicinal herbs to treat it.

HOW TO SAY IT: or-RANG-goo-roo
IMPERIAL HEIGHT: 4'11"
IMPERIAL WEIGHT: 167.6 lbs.
METRIC HEIGHT: 1.5 m
METRIC WEIGHT: 76.0 kg

POSSIBLE MOVES: After You, Calm Mind, Confusion, Foul Play, Future Sight, Instruct, Nasty Plot, Psych Up, Psychic, Quash, Stored Power, Taunt, Trick Room, Zen Headbutt

DOES NOT EVOLVE

REGION: GALAR

ORBEETLE
Seven Spot Pokémon

TYPE: BUG-PSYCHIC

It's famous for its high level of intelligence, and the large size of its brain is proof that it also possesses immense psychic power.

It emits psychic energy to observe and study what's around it—and what's around it can include things over six miles away.

HOW TO SAY IT: OR-BEE-del
IMPERIAL HEIGHT: 1'04"
IMPERIAL WEIGHT: 89.9 lbs.
METRIC HEIGHT: 0.4 m
METRIC WEIGHT: 40.8 kg

POSSIBLE MOVES: After You, Agility, Ally Switch, Bug Buzz, Calm Mind, Confuse Ray, Confusion, Hypnosis, Light Screen, Magic Coat, Mirror Coat, Psybeam, Psychic, Psychic Terrain, Reflect, Struggle Bug

BLIPBUG → **DOTTLER** → **ORBEETLE**

Alternate Form:
GIGANTAMAX ORBEETLE

Its brain has grown to a gargantuan size, as has the rest of its body. This Pokémon's intellect and psychic abilities are overpowering.

If it were to utilize every last bit of its power, it could control the minds of every living being in its vicinity.

IMPERIAL HEIGHT: 45'11"
IMPERIAL WEIGHT: ????.? lbs.
METRIC HEIGHT: 14.0 m
METRIC WEIGHT: ???.? kg

ORICORIO (BAILE STYLE)
Dancing Pokémon

TYPE: FIRE-FLYING

It wins the hearts of its enemies with its passionate dancing and then uses the opening it creates to burn them up with blazing flames.

This Oricorio has drunk red nectar. If its Trainer gives the wrong order, this passionate Pokémon becomes fiercely angry.

HOW TO SAY IT: or-ih-KOR-ee-oh
IMPERIAL HEIGHT: 2'00"
IMPERIAL WEIGHT: 7.5 lbs.
METRIC HEIGHT: 0.6 m
METRIC WEIGHT: 3.4 kg

POSSIBLE MOVES: Pound, Growl, Peck, Helping Hand, Air Cutter, Baton Pass, Feather Dance, Double Slap, Teeter Dance, Roost, Captivate, Air Slash, Revelation Dance, Mirror Move, Agility, Hurricane

DOES NOT EVOLVE

ORICORIO (PA'U STYLE)
Dancing Pokémon

TYPE: PSYCHIC-FLYING

It relaxes its opponents with its elegant dancing. When they let their guard down, it showers them with psychic energy.

This Oricorio has sipped pink nectar. It gets so caught up in its dancing that it sometimes doesn't hear its Trainer's orders.

HOW TO SAY IT: or-ih-KOR-ee-oh
IMPERIAL HEIGHT: 2'00"
IMPERIAL WEIGHT: 7.5 lbs.
METRIC HEIGHT: 0.6 m
METRIC WEIGHT: 3.4 kg

POSSIBLE MOVES: Pound, Growl, Peck, Helping Hand, Air Cutter, Baton Pass, Feather Dance, Double Slap, Teeter Dance, Roost, Captivate, Air Slash, Revelation Dance, Mirror Move, Agility, Hurricane

DOES NOT EVOLVE

ORICORIO (POM-POM STYLE)
Dancing Pokémon

TYPE: ELECTRIC-FLYING

It lifts its opponents' spirits with its cheerful dance moves. When they let their guard down, it electrocutes them with a jolt.

This Oricorio has drunk bright yellow nectar. When it sees someone looking glum, it will try to cheer them up with a dance.

HOW TO SAY IT: or-ih-KOR-ee-oh
IMPERIAL HEIGHT: 2'00"
IMPERIAL WEIGHT: 7.5 lbs.
METRIC HEIGHT: 0.6 m
METRIC WEIGHT: 3.4 kg

POSSIBLE MOVES: Pound, Growl, Peck, Helping Hand, Air Cutter, Baton Pass, Feather Dance, Double Slap, Teeter Dance, Roost, Captivate, Air Slash, Revelation Dance, Mirror Move, Agility, Hurricane

DOES NOT EVOLVE

ORICORIO (SENSU STYLE)
Dancing Pokémon

TYPE: GHOST-FLYING

It charms its opponents with its refined dancing. When they let their guard down, it places a curse on them that will bring on their demise.

This Oricorio has sipped purple nectar. Some dancers use its graceful, elegant dancing as inspiration.

HOW TO SAY IT: or-ih-KOR-ee-oh
IMPERIAL HEIGHT: 2'00"
IMPERIAL WEIGHT: 7.5 lbs.
METRIC HEIGHT: 0.6 m
METRIC WEIGHT: 3.4 kg

POSSIBLE MOVES: Pound, Growl, Peck, Helping Hand, Air Cutter, Baton Pass, Feather Dance, Double Slap, Teeter Dance, Roost, Captivate, Air Slash, Revelation Dance, Mirror Move, Agility, Hurricane

DOES NOT EVOLVE

OSHAWOTT
Sea Otter Pokémon

TYPE: WATER

The scalchop on its stomach isn't just used for battle—it can be used to break open hard berries as well.

It fights using the scalchop on its stomach. In response to an attack, it retaliates immediately by slashing.

HOW TO SAY IT: AH-shah-wot
IMPERIAL HEIGHT: 1'08"
IMPERIAL WEIGHT: 13.0 lbs.
METRIC HEIGHT: 0.5 m
METRIC WEIGHT: 5.9 kg

POSSIBLE MOVES: Tackle, Tail Whip, Water Gun, Water Sport, Focus Energy, Razor Shell, Fury Cutter, Water Pulse, Revenge, Aqua Jet, Encore, Aqua Tail, Retaliate, Swords Dance, Hydro Pump

OSHAWOTT   DEWOTT   SAMUROTT

PACHIRISU
EleSquirrel Pokémon

REGIONS: KALOS (COASTAL) SINNOH

TYPE: ELECTRIC

It makes fur balls that crackle with static electricity. It stores them with berries in tree holes.

A pair may be seen rubbing their cheek pouches together in an effort to share stored electricity.

HOW TO SAY IT: patch-ee-REE-sue
IMPERIAL HEIGHT: 1'04"
IMPERIAL WEIGHT: 8.6 lbs.
METRIC HEIGHT: 0.4 m
METRIC WEIGHT: 3.9 kg

POSSIBLE MOVES: Growl, Bide, Quick Attack, Charm, Spark, Endure, Nuzzle, Swift, Electro Ball, Sweet Kiss, Thunder Wave, Super Fang, Discharge, Last Resort, Hyper Fang

DOES NOT EVOLVE

TYPE: WATER-DRAGON

It is said to live in a gap in the spatial dimension parallel to ours. It appears in mythology.

It has the ability to distort space. It is described as a deity in Sinnoh-region mythology.

HOW TO SAY IT: PALL-kee-ah
IMPERIAL HEIGHT: 13'09"
IMPERIAL WEIGHT: 740.8 lbs.
METRIC HEIGHT: 4.2 m
METRIC WEIGHT: 336.0 kg

POSSIBLE MOVES: Dragon Breath, Scary Face, Water Pulse, Ancient Power, Slash, Power Gem, Aqua Ring, Dragon Claw, Earth Power, Aura Sphere, Aqua Tail, Spacial Rend, Hydro Pump

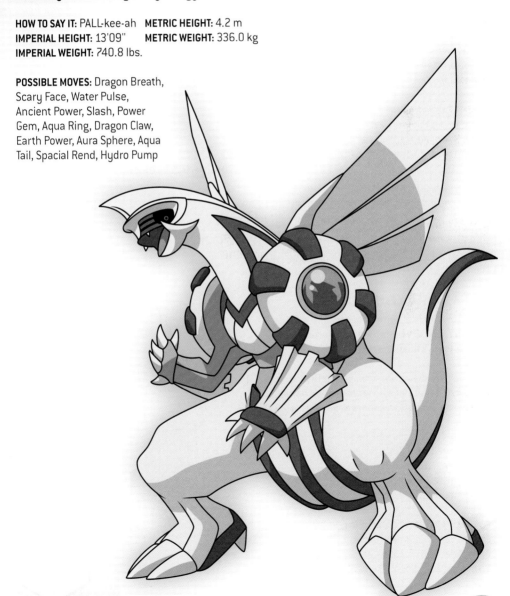

DOES NOT EVOLVE

PALOSSAND

Sand Castle Pokémon

REGION:
ALOLA

TYPE: GHOST-GROUND

Palossand is known as the Beach Nightmare. It pulls its prey down into the sand by controlling the sand itself, and then it sucks out their souls.

This Pokémon lives on beaches, but it hates water. Palossand can't maintain its castle-like shape if it gets drenched by a heavy rain.

HOW TO SAY IT: PAL-uh-sand
IMPERIAL HEIGHT: 4'03"
IMPERIAL WEIGHT: 551.2 lbs.
METRIC HEIGHT: 1.3 m
METRIC WEIGHT: 250.0 kg

POSSIBLE MOVES: Harden, Absorb, Astonish, Sand Attack, Sand Tomb, Mega Drain, Bulldoze, Hypnosis, Iron Defense, Giga Drain, Shadow Ball, Earth Power, Shore Up, Sandstorm

SANDYGAST   PALOSSAND

PALPITOAD

Vibration Pokémon

REGIONS:
GALAR
UNOVA

TYPE: WATER-GROUND

It weakens its prey with sound waves intense enough to cause headaches, then entangles them with its sticky tongue.

On occasion, their cries are sublimely pleasing to the ear. Palpitoad with larger lumps on their bodies can sing with a wider range of sounds.

HOW TO SAY IT: PAL-pih-tohd
IMPERIAL HEIGHT: 2'07"
IMPERIAL WEIGHT: 37.5 lbs.
METRIC HEIGHT: 0.8 m
METRIC WEIGHT: 17.0 kg

POSSIBLE MOVES: Acid, Aqua Ring, Bubble Beam, Echoed Voice, Flail, Growl, Hydro Pump, Hyper Voice, Mud Shot, Muddy Water, Rain Dance, Round, Supersonic, Uproar

TYMPOLE   PALPITOAD   SEISMITOAD

PANCHAM
Playful Pokémon

TYPE: FIGHTING

It chooses a Pangoro as its master and then imitates its master's actions. This is how it learns to battle and hunt for prey.

Wanting to make sure it's taken seriously, Pancham's always giving others a glare. But if it's not focusing, it ends up smiling.

HOW TO SAY IT: PAN-chum
IMPERIAL HEIGHT: 2'00"
IMPERIAL WEIGHT: 17.6 lbs.
METRIC HEIGHT: 0.6 m
METRIC WEIGHT: 8.0 kg

POSSIBLE MOVES: Arm Thrust, Body Slam, Circle Throw, Crunch, Entrainment, Leer, Low Sweep, Parting Shot, Slash, Tackle, Taunt, Vital Throw, Work Up

PANCHAM   PANGORO

TYPE: FIGHTING-DARK

This Pokémon is quick to anger, and it has no problem using its prodigious strength to get its way. It lives for duels against Obstagoon.

Using its leaf, Pangoro can predict the moves of its opponents. It strikes with punches that can turn a dump truck into scrap with just one hit.

PANGORO
Daunting Pokémon

HOW TO SAY IT: PAN-go-roh
IMPERIAL HEIGHT: 6'11"
IMPERIAL WEIGHT: 299.8 lbs.
METRIC HEIGHT: 2.1 m
METRIC WEIGHT: 136.0 kg

POSSIBLE MOVES: Arm Thrust, Body Slam, Bullet Punch, Circle Throw, Crunch, Entrainment, Hammer Arm, Leer, Low Sweep, Night Slash, Parting Shot, Slash, Tackle, Taunt, Vital Throw, Work Up

PANCHAM   PANGORO

PANPOUR
Spray Pokémon

TYPE: WATER

The water stored inside the tuft on its head is full of nutrients. It waters plants with it using its tail.

The water stored inside the tuft on its head is full of nutrients. Plants that receive its water grow large.

HOW TO SAY IT: PAN-por
IMPERIAL HEIGHT: 2'00"
IMPERIAL WEIGHT: 29.8 lbs.
METRIC HEIGHT: 0.6 m
METRIC WEIGHT: 13.5 kg

POSSIBLE MOVES: Scratch, Play Nice, Leer, Lick, Water Gun, Fury Swipes, Water Sport, Bite, Scald, Taunt, Fling, Acrobatics, Brine, Recycle, Natural Gift, Crunch

PANPOUR   SIMIPOUR

PANSAGE
Grass Monkey Pokémon

TYPE: GRASS

It shares the leaf on its head with weary-looking Pokémon. These leaves are known to relieve stress.

It's good at finding berries and gathers them from all over. It's kind enough to share them with friends.

HOW TO SAY IT: PAN-sayj
IMPERIAL HEIGHT: 2'00"
IMPERIAL WEIGHT: 23.1 lbs.
METRIC HEIGHT: 0.6 m
METRIC WEIGHT: 10.5 kg

POSSIBLE MOVES: Scratch, Play Nice, Leer, Lick, Vine Whip, Fury Swipes, Leech Seed, Bite, Seed Bomb, Torment, Fling, Acrobatics, Grass Knot, Recycle, Natural Gift, Crunch

PANSAGE   SIMISAGE

PANSEAR
High Temp Pokémon

TYPE: FIRE

Very intelligent, it roasts berries before eating them. It likes to help people.

This Pokémon lives in caves in volcanoes. The fire within the tuft on its head can reach 600 degrees Fahrenheit.

HOW TO SAY IT: PAN-seer
IMPERIAL HEIGHT: 2'00"
IMPERIAL WEIGHT: 24.3 lbs.
METRIC HEIGHT: 0.6 m
METRIC WEIGHT: 11.0 kg

POSSIBLE MOVES: Scratch, Play Nice, Leer, Lick, Incinerate, Fury Swipes, Yawn, Bite, Flame Burst, Amnesia, Fling, Acrobatics, Fire Blast, Recycle, Natural Gift, Crunch

PANSEAR   SIMISEAR

PARAS
Mushroom Pokémon

TYPE: BUG-GRASS

Burrows under the ground to gnaw on tree roots. The mushrooms on its back absorb most of the nutrition.

HOW TO SAY IT: PAIR-us (sounds like *Paris*)
IMPERIAL HEIGHT: 1'00"
IMPERIAL WEIGHT: 11.9 lbs.
METRIC HEIGHT: 0.3 m
METRIC WEIGHT: 5.4 kg

POSSIBLE MOVES: Scratch, Stun Spore, Poison Powder, Absorb, Fury Cutter, Spore, Slash, Growth, Giga Drain, Aromatherapy, Rage Powder, X-Scissor

PARAS   PARASECT

PARASECT
Mushroom Pokémon

TYPE: BUG-GRASS

The bug host is drained of energy by the mushroom on its back. The mushroom appears to do all the thinking.

HOW TO SAY IT: PARA-sekt
IMPERIAL HEIGHT: 3'03"
IMPERIAL WEIGHT: 65.0 lbs.
METRIC HEIGHT: 1.0 m
METRIC WEIGHT: 29.5 kg

POSSIBLE MOVES: Cross Poison, Scratch, Stun Spore, Poison Powder, Absorb, Fury Cutter, Spore, Slash, Growth, Giga Drain, Aromatherapy, Rage Powder, X-Scissor

PARAS   PARASECT

PASSIMIAN
Teamwork Pokémon

TYPE: FIGHTING

Displaying amazing teamwork, they follow the orders of their boss as they all help out in the search for their favorite berries.

Passimian live in groups of about 20, with each member performing an assigned role. Through cooperation, the group survives.

HOW TO SAY IT: pass-SIM-ee-uhn
IMPERIAL HEIGHT: 6'07"
IMPERIAL WEIGHT: 182.5 lbs.
METRIC HEIGHT: 2.0 m
METRIC WEIGHT: 82.8 kg

POSSIBLE MOVES: Beat Up, Bulk Up, Close Combat, Double-Edge, Fling, Focus Energy, Giga Impact, Leer, Reversal, Rock Smash, Scary Face, Tackle, Take Down, Thrash

DOES NOT EVOLVE

PATRAT
Scout Pokémon

TYPE: NORMAL

Using food stored in cheek pouches, they can keep watch for days. They use their tails to communicate with others.

Extremely cautious, one of them will always be on the lookout, but it won't notice a foe coming from behind.

HOW TO SAY IT: pat-RAT
IMPERIAL HEIGHT: 1'08"
IMPERIAL WEIGHT: 25.6 lbs.
METRIC HEIGHT: 0.5 m
METRIC WEIGHT: 11.6 kg

POSSIBLE MOVES: Tackle, Leer, Bite, Bide, Detect, Sand Attack, Crunch, Hypnosis, Super Fang, After You, Work Up, Hyper Fang, Mean Look, Baton Pass, Slam

PATRAT　　WATCHOG

REGIONS:
GALAR
ALOLA
KALOS
(MOUNTAIN)
UNOVA

PAWNIARD
Sharp Blade Pokémon

TYPE: DARK-STEEL

It uses river stones to maintain the cutting edges of the blades covering its body. These sharpened blades allow it to bring down opponents.

A pack of these Pokémon forms to serve a Bisharp boss. Each Pawniard trains diligently, dreaming of one day taking the lead.

HOW TO SAY IT: PAWN-yard　　**METRIC HEIGHT:** 0.5 m
IMPERIAL HEIGHT: 1'08"　　**METRIC WEIGHT:** 10.2 kg
IMPERIAL WEIGHT: 22.5 lbs.

POSSIBLE MOVES: Assurance, Fury Cutter, Guillotine, Iron Defense, Iron Head, Laser Focus, Leer, Metal Claw, Metal Sound, Night Slash, Scary Face, Scratch, Slash, Swords Dance, Torment

PAWNIARD　　BISHARP

PELIPPER

Water Bird Pokémon

REGIONS:
ALOLA
GALAR
HOENN
KALOS
(COASTAL)

TYPE: WATER-FLYING

It is a messenger of the skies, carrying small Pokémon and eggs to safety in its bill.

Skimming the water's surface, it dips its large bill in the sea, scoops up food and water, and carries it.

HOW TO SAY IT: PEL-ip-purr
IMPERIAL HEIGHT: 3'11"
IMPERIAL WEIGHT: 61.7 lbs.
METRIC HEIGHT: 1.2 m
METRIC WEIGHT: 28.0 kg

POSSIBLE MOVES: Agility, Air Slash, Fling, Growl, Hurricane, Hydro Pump, Mist, Protect, Quick Attack, Roost, Soak, Spit Up, Stockpile, Supersonic, Swallow, Tailwind, Water Gun, Water Pulse, Wing Attack

WINGULL   PELIPPER

PERRSERKER

Viking Pokémon

REGION:
GALAR

TYPE: STEEL

What appears to be an iron helmet is actually hardened hair. This Pokémon lives for the thrill of battle.

After many battles, it evolved dangerous claws that come together to form daggers when extended.

HOW TO SAY IT: purr-ZURR-kurr
IMPERIAL HEIGHT: 2'07"
IMPERIAL WEIGHT: 61.7 lbs.
METRIC HEIGHT: 0.8 m
METRIC WEIGHT: 28.0 kg

POSSIBLE MOVES: Fake Out, Fury Swipes, Growl, Hone Claws, Iron Defense, Iron Head, Metal Burst, Metal Claw, Metal Sound, Pay Day, Scratch, Screech, Slash, Swagger, Taunt, Thrash

GALARIAN MEOWTH   PERRSERKER

PERSIAN
Classy Cat Pokémon

TYPE: NORMAL

Getting this prideful Pokémon to warm up to you takes a lot of effort, and it will claw at you the moment it gets annoyed.

Its elegant and refined behavior clashes with that of the barbaric Perrserker. The relationship between the two is one of mutual disdain.

HOW TO SAY IT: PER-zhun
IMPERIAL HEIGHT: 3'03"
IMPERIAL WEIGHT: 70.5 lbs.
METRIC HEIGHT: 1.0 m
METRIC WEIGHT: 32.0 kg

POSSIBLE MOVES: Assurance, Bite, Fake Out, Feint, Fury Swipes, Growl, Nasty Plot, Pay Day, Play Rough, Power Gem, Scratch, Screech, Slash, Switcheroo, Taunt

MEOWTH   PERSIAN

ALOLAN PERSIAN
Classy Cat Pokémon

TYPE: DARK

The round face of Alolan Persian is considered to be a symbol of prosperity in the Alola region, so these Pokémon are very well cared for.

This Pokémon is one tough opponent. Not only does it have formidable physical abilities, but it's also not above fighting dirty.

HOW TO SAY IT: PER-zhun
IMPERIAL HEIGHT: 3'07"
IMPERIAL WEIGHT: 72.8 lbs.
METRIC HEIGHT: 1.1 m
METRIC WEIGHT: 33.0 kg

POSSIBLE MOVES: Assurance, Bite, Fake Out, Feint, Fury Swipes, Growl, Nasty Plot, Night Slash, Pay Day, Play Rough, Power Gem, Quash, Scratch, Screech, Switcheroo, Taunt

ALOLAN MEOWTH   ALOLAN PERSIAN

PETILIL

Bulb Pokémon

REGIONS:
ALOLA
UNOVA

TYPE: GRASS

Petilil appears around sources of clean water. Boiling leaves from this Pokémon's head results in a liquid that's sometimes used as a bug repellent.

The deeper the color of a Petilil's leaves, the healthier the Pokémon is. Petilil sometimes makes its home in a well-tended field or flowerbed.

HOW TO SAY IT: PEH-tuh-LIL **METRIC HEIGHT:** 0.5 m
IMPERIAL HEIGHT: 1'08" **METRIC WEIGHT:** 6.6 kg
IMPERIAL WEIGHT: 14.6 lbs.

POSSIBLE MOVES: Absorb, Growth, Leech Seed, Sleep Powder, Mega Drain, Synthesis, Magical Leaf, Stun Spore, Giga Drain, Aromatherapy, Helping Hand, Energy Ball, Entrainment, Sunny Day, After You, Leaf Storm

PETILIL   LILLIGANT

PHANPY

Long Nose Pokémon

REGION:
JOHTO

TYPE: GROUND

For its nest, Phanpy digs a vertical pit in the ground at the edge of a river. It marks the area around its nest with its trunk to let the others know that the area has been claimed.

Phanpy uses its long nose to shower itself. When others gather around, they thoroughly douse each other with water. These Pokémon can be seen drying their soaking-wet bodies at the edge of water.

HOW TO SAY IT: FAN-pee **METRIC HEIGHT:** 0.5 m
IMPERIAL HEIGHT: 1'08" **METRIC WEIGHT:** 33.5 kg
IMPERIAL WEIGHT: 73.9 lbs.

POSSIBLE MOVES: Odor Sleuth, Tackle, Growl, Defense Curl, Flail, Take Down, Rollout, Natural Gift, Slam, Endure, Charm, Last Resort, Double-Edge

PHANPY   DONPHAN

PHANTUMP
Stump Pokémon

TYPE: GHOST-GRASS

After a lost child perished in the forest, their spirit possessed a tree stump, causing the spirit's rebirth as this Pokémon.

With a voice like a human child's, it cries out to lure adults deep into the forest, getting them lost among the trees.

HOW TO SAY IT: FAN-tump
IMPERIAL HEIGHT: 1'04"
IMPERIAL WEIGHT: 15.4 lbs.
METRIC HEIGHT: 0.4 m
METRIC WEIGHT: 7.0 kg

POSSIBLE MOVES: Astonish, Branch Poke, Confuse Ray, Curse, Destiny Bond, Forest's Curse, Growth, Hex, Horn Leech, Ingrain, Leech Seed, Phantom Force, Tackle, Will-O-Wisp, Wood Hammer

PHANTUMP → **TREVENANT**

ULTRA BEAST

PHEROMOSA
Lissome Pokémon

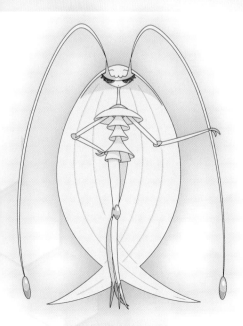

TYPE: BUG-FIGHTING

A life-form that lives in another world, its body is thin and supple, but it also possesses great power.

Although it's alien to this world and a danger here, it's apparently a common organism in the world where it normally lives.

HOW TO SAY IT: fair-uh-MO-suh
IMPERIAL HEIGHT: 5'11"
IMPERIAL WEIGHT: 55.1 lbs.
METRIC HEIGHT: 1.8 m
METRIC WEIGHT: 25.0 kg

POSSIBLE MOVES: Quiver Dance, Quick Guard, Low Kick, Rapid Spin, Leer, Double Kick, Swift, Stomp, Feint, Silver Wind, Bounce, Jump Kick, Agility, Triple Kick, Lunge, Bug Buzz, Me First, High Jump Kick, Speed Swap

DOES NOT EVOLVE

PHIONE

Sea Drifter Pokémon

REGION: SINNOH

MYTHICAL POKÉMON

TYPE: WATER

When the water warms, they inflate the flotation sac on their heads and drift languidly on the sea in packs.

It drifts in warm seas. It always returns to where it was born, no matter how far it may have drifted.

HOW TO SAY IT: fee-OH-nay
IMPERIAL HEIGHT: 1'04"
IMPERIAL WEIGHT: 6.8 lbs.
METRIC HEIGHT: 0.4 m
METRIC WEIGHT: 3.1 kg

POSSIBLE MOVES: Bubble, Water Sport, Charm, Supersonic, Bubble Beam, Acid Armor, Whirlpool, Water Pulse, Aqua Ring, Dive, Rain Dance

DOES NOT EVOLVE

PICHU

Tiny Mouse Pokémon

REGIONS: ALOLA GALAR JOHTO KALOS (CENTRAL)

TYPE: ELECTRIC

Despite its small size, it can zap even adult humans. However, if it does so, it also surprises itself.

The electric sacs in its cheeks are small. If even a little electricity leaks, it becomes shocked.

HOW TO SAY IT: PEE-choo
IMPERIAL HEIGHT: 1'00"
IMPERIAL WEIGHT: 4.4 lbs.
METRIC HEIGHT: 0.3 m
METRIC WEIGHT: 2.0 kg

POSSIBLE MOVES: Charm, Nasty Plot, Nuzzle, Play Nice, Sweet Kiss, Tail Whip, Thunder Shock

RAICHU

PICHU   PIKACHU

ALOLAN RAICH

PIDGEOT
Bird Pokémon

TYPE: NORMAL-FLYING

This Pokémon flies at Mach 2 speed, seeking prey. Its large talons are feared as wicked weapons.

HOW TO SAY IT: PIDG-ee-ott
IMPERIAL HEIGHT: 4'11"
IMPERIAL WEIGHT: 87.1 lbs.
METRIC HEIGHT: 1.5 m
METRIC WEIGHT: 39.5 kg

POSSIBLE MOVES: Hurricane, Tackle, Sand Attack, Gust, Quick Attack, Whirlwind, Twister, Feather Dance, Agility, Wing Attack, Roost, Tailwind, Mirror Move, Air Slash

MEGA PIDGEOT
Bird Pokémon

TYPE: NORMAL-FLYING

IMPERIAL HEIGHT: 7'03"
IMPERIAL WEIGHT: 111.3 lbs.
METRIC HEIGHT: 2.2 m
METRIC WEIGHT: 50.5 kg

PIDGEY

PIDGEOTTO

PIDGEOT

MEGA PIDGEOT

PIDGEOTTO

Bird Pokémon

REGIONS:
KALOS (CENTRAL)
KANTO

TYPE: NORMAL-FLYING

This Pokémon is full of vitality. It constantly flies around its large territory in search of prey.

HOW TO SAY IT: PIDG-ee-OH-toe
IMPERIAL HEIGHT: 3'07"
IMPERIAL WEIGHT: 66.1 lbs.
METRIC HEIGHT: 1.1 m
METRIC WEIGHT: 30.0 kg

POSSIBLE MOVES: Tackle, Sand Attack, Gust, Quick Attack, Whirlwind, Twister, Feather Dance, Agility, Wing Attack, Roost, Tailwind, Mirror Move, Air Slash, Hurricane

PIDGEY → PIDGEOTTO → PIDGEOT → MEGA PIDGEOT

PIDGEY

Tiny Bird Pokémon

REGIONS:
KALOS (CENTRAL)
KANTO

TYPE: NORMAL-FLYING

Very docile. If attacked, it will often kick up sand to protect itself rather than fight back.

HOW TO SAY IT: PIDG-ee
IMPERIAL HEIGHT: 1'00"
IMPERIAL WEIGHT: 4.0 lbs.
METRIC HEIGHT: 0.3 m
METRIC WEIGHT: 1.8 kg

POSSIBLE MOVES: Tackle, Sand Attack, Gust, Quick Attack, Whirlwind, Twister, Feather Dance, Agility, Wing Attack, Roost, Tailwind, Mirror Move, Air Slash, Hurricane

PIDGEY → PIDGEOTTO → PIDGEOT → MEGA PIDGEOT

PIDOVE

Tiny Pigeon Pokémon

TYPE: NORMAL-FLYING

Where people go, these Pokémon follow. If you're scattering food for them, be careful—several hundred of them can gather at once.

It's forgetful and not very bright, but many Trainers love it anyway for its friendliness and sincerity.

HOW TO SAY IT: pih-DUV
IMPERIAL HEIGHT: 1'00"
IMPERIAL WEIGHT: 4.6 lbs.
METRIC HEIGHT: 0.3 m
METRIC WEIGHT: 2.1 kg

POSSIBLE MOVES: Air Cutter, Air Slash, Detect, Feather Dance, Growl, Gust, Leer, Quick Attack, Roost, Sky Attack, Swagger, Tailwind, Taunt

PIDOVE **TRANQUILL** **UNFEZANT**

REGION: UNOVA

PIGNITE

Fire Pig Pokémon

TYPE: FIRE-FIGHTING

The more it eats, the more fuel it has to make the fire in its stomach stronger. This fills it with even more power.

When its internal fire flares up, its movements grow sharper and faster. When in trouble, it emits smoke.

HOW TO SAY IT: pig-NYTE
IMPERIAL HEIGHT: 3'03"
IMPERIAL WEIGHT: 122.4 lbs.
METRIC HEIGHT: 1.0 m
METRIC WEIGHT: 55.5 kg

POSSIBLE MOVES: Tackle, Tail Whip, Ember, Odor Sleuth, Defense Curl, Flame Charge, Arm Thrust, Smog, Rollout, Take Down, Heat Crash, Assurance, Flamethrower, Head Smash, Roar, Flare Blitz

TEPIG **PIGNITE** **EMBOAR**

PIKACHU
Mouse Pokémon

REGIONS:
ALOLA
GALAR
KALOS
(CENTRAL)
KANTO

TYPE: ELECTRIC

Pikachu that can generate powerful electricity have cheek sacs that are extra soft and super stretchy.

When Pikachu meet, they'll touch their tails together and exchange electricity through them as a form of greeting.

HOW TO SAY IT: PEE-ka-choo
IMPERIAL HEIGHT: 1'04"
IMPERIAL WEIGHT: 13.2 lbs.

METRIC HEIGHT: 0.4 m
METRIC WEIGHT: 6.0 kg

POSSIBLE MOVES: Agility, Charm, Discharge, Double Team, Electro Ball, Feint, Growl, Light Screen, Nasty Plot, Nuzzle, Play Nice, Quick Attack, Slam, Spark, Sweet Kiss, Tail Whip, Thunder, Thunder Shock, Thunder Wave, Thunderbolt

PICHU → PIKACHU → RAICHU
ALOLAN RAICHU

PIKACHU LIBRE

SPECIAL MOVE:
Flying Press

PIKACHU BELLE

SPECIAL MOVE:
Icicle Crash

PIKACHU PHD

SPECIAL MOVE:
Electric Terrain

PIKACHU POP STAR

SPECIAL MOVE:
Draining Kiss

PIKACHU ROCK STAR

SPECIAL MOVE:
Meteor Mash

DOES NOT EVOLVE

Alternate Form:
GIGANTAMAX PIKACHU

Its Gigantamax power expanded, forming its supersized body and towering tail.

When it smashes its opponents with its bolt-shaped tail, it delivers a surge of electricity equivalent to a lightning strike.

IMPERIAL HEIGHT: 68'11"+
IMPERIAL WEIGHT: ????.? lbs.
METRIC HEIGHT: 21.0+ m
METRIC WEIGHT: ???.? kg

PIKIPEK

Woodpecker Pokémon

TYPE: NORMAL-FLYING

It pecks at trees with its hard beak. You can get some idea of its mood or condition from the rhythm of its pecking.

It may look spindly, but its neck muscles are heavy-duty. It can peck at a tree 16 times per second!

HOW TO SAY IT: PICK-kee-peck
IMPERIAL HEIGHT: 1'00"
IMPERIAL WEIGHT: 2.6 lbs.
METRIC HEIGHT: 0.3 m
METRIC WEIGHT: 1.2 kg

POSSIBLE MOVES: Peck, Growl, Echoed Voice, Rock Smash, Supersonic, Pluck, Roost, Fury Attack, Screech, Drill Peck, Bullet Seed, Feather Dance, Hyper Voice

PIKIPEK　　**TRUMBEAK**　　**TOUCANNON**

PILOSWINE

Swine Pokémon

TYPE: ICE-GROUND

If it charges at an enemy, the hairs on its back stand up straight. It is very sensitive to sound.

Although its legs are short, its rugged hooves prevent it from slipping, even on icy ground.

HOW TO SAY IT: PILE-oh-swine
IMPERIAL HEIGHT: 3'07"
IMPERIAL WEIGHT: 123.0 lbs.
METRIC HEIGHT: 1.1 m
METRIC WEIGHT: 55.8 kg

POSSIBLE MOVES: Amnesia, Ancient Power, Blizzard, Earthquake, Endure, Flail, Ice Fang, Ice Shard, Icy Wind, Mist, Mud-Slap, Powder Snow, Tackle, Take Down, Thrash

SWINUB　　**PILOSWINE**　　**MAMOSWINE**

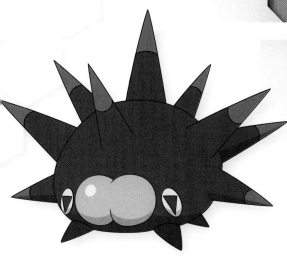

PINCURCHIN
Sea Urchin Pokémon

TYPE: ELECTRIC

It feeds on seaweed, using its teeth to scrape it off rocks. Electric current flows from the tips of its spines.

It stores electricity in each spine. Even if one gets broken off, it still continues to emit electricity for at least three hours.

HOW TO SAY IT: PIN-kur-chin
IMPERIAL HEIGHT: 1'00"
IMPERIAL WEIGHT: 2.2 lbs.
METRIC HEIGHT: 0.3 m
METRIC WEIGHT: 1.0 kg

POSSIBLE MOVES: Acupressure, Bubble Beam, Charge, Curse, Discharge, Electric Terrain, Fury Attack, Peck, Poison Jab, Recover, Spark, Thunder Shock, Water Gun, Zing Zap

DOES NOT EVOLVE

REGIONS: ALOLA JOHTO

PINECO
Bagworm Pokémon

TYPE: BUG

Motionless, it hangs from trees, waiting for its bug Pokémon prey to come to it. Its favorite in Alola is Cutiefly.

It sticks tree bark to itself with its saliva, making itself thicker and larger. Elderly Pineco are ridiculously huge.

HOW TO SAY IT: PINE-co
IMPERIAL HEIGHT: 2'00"
IMPERIAL WEIGHT: 15.9 lbs.
METRIC HEIGHT: 0.6 m
METRIC WEIGHT: 7.2 kg

POSSIBLE MOVES: Tackle, Protect, Self-Destruct, Bug Bite, Take Down, Rapid Spin, Bide, Natural Gift, Spikes, Payback, Explosion, Iron Defense, Gyro Ball, Double-Edge

PINECO   FORRETRESS

PINSIR

Stag Beetle Pokémon

REGIONS:
ALOLA
KALOS
(COASTAL)
KANTO

TYPE: BUG

These Pokémon judge one another based on pincers. Thicker, more impressive pincers make for more popularity with the opposite gender.

This Pokémon clamps its pincers down on its prey and then either splits the prey in half or flings it away.

HOW TO SAY IT: PIN-sir
IMPERIAL HEIGHT: 4'11"
IMPERIAL WEIGHT: 121.3 lbs.
METRIC HEIGHT: 1.5 m
METRIC WEIGHT: 55.0 kg

POSSIBLE MOVES: Vice Grip, Focus Energy, Bind, Seismic Toss, Harden, Revenge, Vital Throw, Double Hit, Brick Break, X-Scissor, Submission, Storm Throw, Swords Dance, Thrash, Superpower, Guillotine

MEGA PINSIR

Stag Beetle Pokémon

TYPE: BUG-FLYING

IMPERIAL HEIGHT: 5'07"
IMPERIAL WEIGHT: 130.1 lbs.
METRIC HEIGHT: 1.7 m
METRIC WEIGHT: 59.0 kg

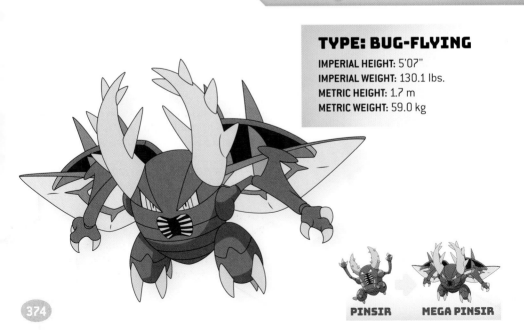

PINSIR → MEGA PINSIR

PIPLUP
Penguin Pokémon

TYPE: WATER

It doesn't like to be taken care of. It's difficult to bond with since it won't listen to its Trainer.

Because it is very proud, it hates accepting food from people. Its thick down guards it from cold.

HOW TO SAY IT: PIP-lup
IMPERIAL HEIGHT: 1'04"
IMPERIAL WEIGHT: 11.5 lbs.
METRIC HEIGHT: 0.4 m
METRIC WEIGHT: 5.2 kg

POSSIBLE MOVES: Pound, Growl, Bubble, Water Sport, Peck, Bubble Beam, Bide, Fury Attack, Brine, Whirlpool, Mist, Drill Peck, Hydro Pump

PIPLUP → **PRINPLUP** → **EMPOLEON**

PLUSLE
Cheering Pokémon

TYPE: ELECTRIC

Plusle always acts as a cheerleader for its partners. Whenever a teammate puts out a good effort in battle, this Pokémon shorts out its body to create the crackling noises of sparks to show its joy.

When Plusle is cheering on its partner, it flashes with electric sparks from all over its body. If its partner loses, this Pokémon cries loudly.

HOW TO SAY IT: PLUS-ull
IMPERIAL HEIGHT: 1'04"
IMPERIAL WEIGHT: 9.3 lbs.
METRIC HEIGHT: 0.4 m
METRIC WEIGHT: 4.2 kg

POSSIBLE MOVES: Nuzzle, Play Nice, Growl, Thunder Wave, Quick Attack, Helping Hand, Spark, Encore, Bestow, Swift, Electro Ball, Copycat, Charm, Charge, Discharge, Baton Pass, Agility, Last Resort, Thunder, Nasty Plot, Entrainment

DOES NOT EVOLVE

POIPOLE
Poison Pin Pokémon

REGION: ALOLA

ULTRA BEAST

TYPE: POISON

This Ultra Beast is well enough liked to be chosen as a first partner in its own world.

An Ultra Beast that lives in a different world, it cackles wildly as it sprays its opponents with poison from the needles on its head.

HOW TO SAY IT: POY-pull
IMPERIAL HEIGHT: 2'00"
IMPERIAL WEIGHT: 4.0 lbs.
METRIC HEIGHT: 0.6 m
METRIC WEIGHT: 1.8 kg

POSSIBLE MOVES: Dragon Pulse, Peck, Growl, Helping Hand, Acid, Fury Attack, Venoshock, Charm, Venom Drench, Nasty Plot, Poison Jab, Toxic, Fell Stinger

POIPOLE   NAGANADEL

POLITOED
Frog Pokémon

TYPE: WATER

At nightfall, these Pokémon appear on the shores of lakes. They announce their territorial claims by letting out cries that sound like shouting.

The cry of a male is louder than that of a female. Male Politoed with deep, menacing voices find more popularity with the opposite gender.

HOW TO SAY IT: PAUL-lee-TOED
IMPERIAL HEIGHT: 3'07"
IMPERIAL WEIGHT: 74.7 lbs.
METRIC HEIGHT: 1.1 m
METRIC WEIGHT: 33.9 kg

POSSIBLE MOVES: Bubble Beam, Hypnosis, Double Slap, Perish Song, Swagger, Bounce, Hyper Voice

POLIWAG   POLIWHIRL   POLITOED

POLIWAG
Tadpole Pokémon

TYPE: WATER

For Poliwag, swimming is easier than walking. The swirl pattern on its belly is actually part of the Pokémon's innards showing through the skin.

In rivers with fast-flowing water, this Pokémon will cling to a rock by using its thick lips, which act like a suction cup.

HOW TO SAY IT: PAUL-lee-wag
IMPERIAL HEIGHT: 2'00"
IMPERIAL WEIGHT: 27.3 lbs.
METRIC HEIGHT: 0.6 m
METRIC WEIGHT: 12.4 kg

POLIWRATH

POSSIBLE MOVES: Water Sport, Water Gun, Hypnosis, Bubble, Double Slap, Rain Dance, Body Slam, Bubble Beam, Mud Shot, Belly Drum, Wake-Up Slap, Hydro Pump, Mud Bomb

POLIWAG   POLIWHIRL   POLITOED

POLIWHIRL

Tadpole Pokémon

REGIONS:
ALOLA
KALOS
(MOUNTAIN)
KANTO

TYPE: WATER

Staring at the swirl on its belly causes drowsiness. This trait of Poliwhirl's has been used in place of lullabies to get children to go to sleep.

This Pokémon's sweat is a slimy mucus. When captured, Poliwhirl can slither from its enemies' grasp and escape.

HOW TO SAY IT: PAUL-lee-wirl
IMPERIAL HEIGHT: 3'03"
IMPERIAL WEIGHT: 44.1 lbs.
METRIC HEIGHT: 1.0 m
METRIC WEIGHT: 20.0 kg

POSSIBLE MOVES: Water Sport, Water Gun, Hypnosis, Bubble, Double Slap, Rain Dance, Body Slam, Bubble Beam, Mud Shot, Belly Drum, Wake-Up Slap, Hydro Pump, Mud Bomb

POLIWAG POLIWHIRL   POLIWRATH

POLITOED

POLIWRATH

Tadpole Pokémon

REGIONS:
ALOLA
KALOS
(MOUNTAIN)
KANTO

TYPE: WATER-FIGHTING

Its body is solid muscle. When swimming through cold seas, Poliwrath uses its impressive arms to smash through drift ice and plow forward.

Poliwrath is skilled at both swimming and martial arts. It uses its well-trained arms to dish out powerful punches.

HOW TO SAY IT: PAUL-lee-rath
IMPERIAL HEIGHT: 4'03"
IMPERIAL WEIGHT: 119.0 lbs.
METRIC HEIGHT: 1.3 m
METRIC WEIGHT: 54.0 kg

POSSIBLE MOVES: Circle Throw, Bubble Beam, Hypnosis, Double Slap, Submission, Dynamic Punch, Mind Reader

POLIWAG   POLIWHIRL   POLIWRATH

POLTEAGEIST
Black Tea Pokémon

TYPE: GHOST

This species lives in antique teapots. Most pots are forgeries, but on rare occasions, an authentic work is found.

Leaving leftover black tea unattended is asking for this Pokémon to come along and pour itself into it, turning the tea into a new Polteageist.

HOW TO SAY IT: POHL-tee-guyst
IMPERIAL HEIGHT: 0'08"
IMPERIAL WEIGHT: 0.9 lbs.
METRIC HEIGHT: 0.2 m
METRIC WEIGHT: 0.4 kg

POSSIBLE MOVES: Aromatherapy, Aromatic Mist, Astonish, Curse, Giga Drain, Mega Drain, Memento, Nasty Plot, Protect, Shadow Ball, Shell Smash, Strength Sap, Sucker Punch, Teatime, Withdraw

SINISTEA → POLTEAGEIST

PONYTA

Fire Horse Pokémon

TYPE: FIRE

It can't run properly when it's newly born. As it races around with others of its kind, its legs grow stronger.

If you've been accepted by Ponyta, its burning mane is mysteriously no longer hot to the touch.

HOW TO SAY IT: POH-nee-tah
IMPERIAL HEIGHT: 3'03"
IMPERIAL WEIGHT: 66.1 lbs.
METRIC HEIGHT: 1.0 m
METRIC WEIGHT: 30.0 kg

POSSIBLE MOVES: Agility, Ember, Fire Blast, Fire Spin, Flame Charge, Flame Wheel, Flare Blitz, Growl, Inferno, Stomp, Tackle, Tail Whip, Take Down

PONYTA   RAPIDASH

GALARIAN PONYTA

Unique Horn Pokémon

REGION: GALAR

TYPE: PSYCHIC

Its small horn hides a healing power. With a few rubs from this Pokémon's horn, any slight wound you have will be healed.

This Pokémon will look into your eyes and read the contents of your heart. If it finds evil there, it promptly hides away.

HOW TO SAY IT: POH-nee-tah
IMPERIAL HEIGHT: 2'07"
IMPERIAL WEIGHT: 52.9 lbs.
METRIC HEIGHT: 0.8 m
METRIC WEIGHT: 24.0 kg

POSSIBLE MOVES: Agility, Confusion, Dazzling Gleam, Fairy Wind, Growl, Heal Pulse, Healing Wish, Psybeam, Psychic, Stomp, Tackle, Tail Whip, Take Down

GALARIAN PONYTA   GALARIAN RAPIDASH

POOCHYENA
Bite Pokémon

TYPE: DARK

At first sight, Poochyena takes a bite at anything that moves. This Pokémon chases after prey until the victim becomes exhausted. However, it may turn tail if the prey strikes back.

Poochyena is an omnivore—it will eat anything. A distinguishing feature is how large its fangs are compared to its body. This Pokémon tries to intimidate its foes by making the hair on its tail bristle out.

HOW TO SAY IT: POO-chee-EH-nah **METRIC HEIGHT:** 0.5 m
IMPERIAL HEIGHT: 1'08" **METRIC WEIGHT:** 13.6 kg
IMPERIAL WEIGHT: 30.0 lbs.

POSSIBLE MOVES: Tackle, Howl, Sand Attack, Bite, Odor Sleuth, Roar, Swagger, Assurance, Scary Face, Taunt, Embargo, Take Down, Sucker Punch, Crunch, Yawn, Play Rough

POOCHYENA → MIGHTYENA

POPPLIO
Sea Lion Pokémon

TYPE: WATER

The balloons it inflates with its nose grow larger and larger as it practices day by day.

Popplio gets on top of its bouncy water balloons to jump higher. It's quite the acrobatic fighter!

HOW TO SAY IT: POP-lee-oh **METRIC HEIGHT:** 0.4 m
IMPERIAL HEIGHT: 1'04" **METRIC WEIGHT:** 7.5 kg
IMPERIAL WEIGHT: 16.5 lbs.

POSSIBLE MOVES: Pound, Water Gun, Growl, Disarming Voice, Baby-Doll Eyes, Aqua Jet, Icy Wind, Encore, Bubble Beam, Sing, Double Slap, Hyper Voice, Moonblast, Captivate, Hydro Pump, Misty Terrain

POPPLIO   BRIONNE   PRIMARINA

PORYGON

Virtual Pokémon

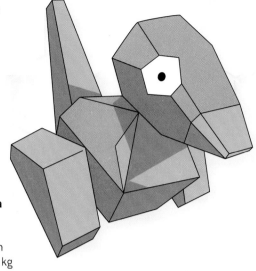

TYPE: NORMAL

State-of-the-art technology was used to create Porygon. It was the first artificial Pokémon to be created via computer programming.

In recent years, this species has been very helpful in cyberspace. These Pokémon will go around checking to make sure no suspicious data exists.

HOW TO SAY IT: PORE-ee-gon
IMPERIAL HEIGHT: 2'07"
IMPERIAL WEIGHT: 80.5 lbs.
METRIC HEIGHT: 0.8 m
METRIC WEIGHT: 36.5 kg

POSSIBLE MOVES: Conversion 2, Tackle, Conversion, Sharpen, Psybeam, Agility, Recover, Magnet Rise, Signal Beam, Recycle, Discharge, Lock-On, Tri Attack, Magic Coat, Zap Cannon

PORYGON   PORYGON2   PORYGON-Z

PORYGON2

Virtual Pokémon

TYPE: NORMAL

This is a Porygon that was updated with special data. Porygon2 develops itself by learning about many different subjects all on its own.

After artificial intelligence was implemented in Porygon2, the Pokémon began using a strange language that only other Porygon2 understand.

HOW TO SAY IT: PORE-ee-gon TWO
IMPERIAL HEIGHT: 2'00"
IMPERIAL WEIGHT: 71.6 lbs.
METRIC HEIGHT: 0.6 m
METRIC WEIGHT: 32.5 kg

POSSIBLE MOVES: Zap Cannon, Magic Coat, Conversion 2, Tackle, Conversion, Defense Curl, Psybeam, Agility, Recover, Magnet Rise, Signal Beam, Recycle, Discharge, Lock-On, Tri Attack, Magic Coat, Hyper Beam

PORYGON   PORYGON2   PORYGON-Z

PORYGON-Z
Virtual Pokémon

TYPE: NORMAL

Porygon-Z had a program installed to allow it to move between dimensions, but the program also caused instability in Porygon-Z's behavior.

Some say an additional program made this Pokémon evolve, but even academics can't agree on whether Porygon-Z is really an Evolution.

HOW TO SAY IT: PORE-ee-gon ZEE
IMPERIAL HEIGHT: 2'11"
IMPERIAL WEIGHT: 75.0 lbs.
METRIC HEIGHT: 0.9 m
METRIC WEIGHT: 34.0 kg

POSSIBLE MOVES: Trick Room, Zap Cannon, Magic Coat, Conversion 2, Tackle, Conversion, Nasty Plot, Psybeam, Agility, Recover, Magnet Rise, Signal Beam, Embargo, Discharge, Lock-On, Tri Attack, Hyper Beam

ORYGON **PORYGON2** **PORYGON-Z**

PRIMARINA
Soloist Pokémon

TYPE: WATER-FAIRY

To Primarina, every battle is a stage. It takes down its prey with beautiful singing and dancing.

Also known as a songstress, it has a fantastical look on moonlit nights when it leads its colony in song.

HOW TO SAY IT: PREE-muh-REE-nuh
IMPERIAL HEIGHT: 5'11"
IMPERIAL WEIGHT: 97.0 lbs.
METRIC HEIGHT: 1.8 m
METRIC WEIGHT: 44.0 kg

POSSIBLE MOVES: Sparkling Aria, Pound, Water Gun, Growl, Disarming Voice, Baby-Doll Eyes, Aqua Jet, Icy Wind, Encore, Bubble Beam, Sing, Double Slap, Hyper Voice, Moonblast, Captivate, Hydro Pump, Misty Terrain

POPPLIO **BRIONNE** **PRIMARINA**

PRIMEAPE

Pig Monkey Pokémon

TYPE: FIGHTING

It stops being angry only when nobody else is around. To view this moment is very difficult.

HOW TO SAY IT: PRIME-ape
IMPERIAL HEIGHT: 3'03"
IMPERIAL WEIGHT: 70.5 lbs.
METRIC HEIGHT: 1.0 m
METRIC WEIGHT: 32.0 kg

POSSIBLE MOVES: Rage, Final Gambit, Fling, Scratch, Low Kick, Leer, Focus Energy, Fury Swipes, Karate Chop, Pursuit, Seismic Toss, Swagger, Cross Chop, Assurance, Punishment, Thrash, Close Combat, Screech, Stomping Tantrum, Outrage

MANKEY   PRIMEAPE

PRINPLUP

Penguin Pokémon

TYPE: WATER

It lives alone, away from others. Apparently, every one of them believes it is the most important.

It lives a solitary life. Its wings deliver wicked blows that can snap even the thickest of trees.

HOW TO SAY IT: PRIN-plup   **METRIC HEIGHT:** 0.8 m
IMPERIAL HEIGHT: 2'07"   **METRIC WEIGHT:** 23.0 kg
IMPERIAL WEIGHT: 50.7 lbs.

POSSIBLE MOVES: Tackle, Growl, Bubble, Water Sport, Peck, Metal Claw, Bubble Beam, Bide, Fury Attack, Brine, Whirlpool, Mist, Drill Peck, Hydro Pump

PIPLUP   PRINPLUP   EMPOLEON

PROBOPASS
Compass Pokémon

TYPE: ROCK-STEEL

Although it can control its units known as Mini-Noses, they sometimes get lost and don't come back.

It uses three small units to catch prey and battle enemies. The main body mostly just gives orders.

HOW TO SAY IT: PRO-bow-pass
IMPERIAL HEIGHT: 4'07"
IMPERIAL WEIGHT: 749.6 lbs.
METRIC HEIGHT: 1.4 m
METRIC WEIGHT: 340.0 kg

POSSIBLE MOVES: Tri Attack, Magnetic Flux, Magnet Rise, Gravity, Wide Guard, Tackle, Iron Defense, Block, Magnet Bomb, Thunder Wave, Rest, Spark, Rock Slide, Power Gem, Rock Blast, Discharge, Sandstorm, Earth Power, Stone Edge, Lock-On, Zap Cannon

NOSEPASS   **PROBOPASS**

PSYDUCK
Duck Pokémon

TYPE: WATER

Psyduck is constantly beset by headaches. If the Pokémon lets its strange power erupt, apparently the pain subsides for a while.

As Psyduck gets stressed out, its headache gets progressively worse. It uses intense psychic energy to overwhelm those around it.

HOW TO SAY IT: SY-duck
IMPERIAL HEIGHT: 2'07"
IMPERIAL WEIGHT: 43.2 lbs.
METRIC HEIGHT: 0.8 m
METRIC WEIGHT: 19.6 kg

POSSIBLE MOVES: Water Sport, Scratch, Tail Whip, Water Gun, Confusion, Fury Swipes, Water Pulse, Disable, Screech, Zen Headbutt, Aqua Tail, Soak, Psych Up, Amnesia, Hydro Pump, Wonder Room

PSYDUCK   **GOLDUCK**

PUMPKABOO
Pumpkin Pokémon

TYPE: GHOST-GRASS

Spirits that wander this world are placed into Pumpkaboo's body. They're then moved on to the afterlife.

The light that streams out from the holes in the pumpkin can hypnotize and control the people and Pokémon that see it.

HOW TO SAY IT: PUMP-kuh-boo
IMPERIAL HEIGHT: 1'04"
IMPERIAL WEIGHT: 11.0 lbs.
METRIC HEIGHT: 0.4 m
METRIC WEIGHT: 5.0 kg

POSSIBLE MOVES: Astonish, Bullet Seed, Confuse Ray, Leech Seed, Pain Split, Razor Leaf, Scary Face, Seed Bomb, Shadow Ball, Shadow Sneak, Trick, Trick-or-Treat, Worry Seed

PUMPKABOO　　　GOURGEIST

PUPITAR
Hard Shell Pokémon

TYPE: ROCK-GROUND

Even sealed in its shell, it can move freely. Hard and fast, it has outstanding destructive power.

It will not stay still, even while it's a pupa. It already has arms and legs under its solid shell.

HOW TO SAY IT: PUE-puh-tar
IMPERIAL HEIGHT: 3'11"
IMPERIAL WEIGHT: 335.1 lbs.
METRIC HEIGHT: 1.2 m
METRIC WEIGHT: 152.0 kg

POSSIBLE MOVES: Bite, Crunch, Dark Pulse, Earthquake, Hyper Beam, Iron Defense, Leer, Payback, Rock Slide, Rock Throw, Sandstorm, Scary Face, Screech, Stomping Tantrum, Stone Edge, Tackle, Thrash

LARVITAR　　　PUPITAR　　　TYRANITAR　　　MEGA TYRANITAR

PURRLOIN
Devious Pokémon

TYPE: DARK

It steals things from people just to amuse itself with their frustration. A rivalry exists between this Pokémon and Nickit.

Opponents that get drawn in by its adorable behavior come away with stinging scratches from its claws and stinging pride from its laughter.

HOW TO SAY IT: PUR-loyn
IMPERIAL HEIGHT: 1'04"
IMPERIAL WEIGHT: 22.3 lbs.
METRIC HEIGHT: 0.4 m
METRIC WEIGHT: 10.1 kg

POSSIBLE MOVES: Assurance, Fake Out, Fury Swipes, Growl, Hone Claws, Nasty Plot, Night Slash, Play Rough, Sand Attack, Scratch, Sucker Punch, Torment

PURRLOIN LIEPARD

PURUGLY
Tiger Cat Pokémon

TYPE: NORMAL

It would claim another Pokémon's nest as its own if it finds a nest sufficiently comfortable.

To make itself appear intimidatingly beefy, it tightly cinches its waist with its twin tails.

HOW TO SAY IT: pur-UGG-lee
IMPERIAL HEIGHT: 3'03"
IMPERIAL WEIGHT: 96.6 lbs.
METRIC HEIGHT: 1.0 m
METRIC WEIGHT: 43.8 kg

POSSIBLE MOVES: Fake Out, Scratch, Growl, Hypnosis, Feint Attack, Fury Swipes, Charm, Assist, Captivate, Slash, Swagger, Body Slam, Attract, Hone Claws

GLAMEOW PURUGLY

PYROAR
Royal Pokémon

MALE FORM

TYPE: FIRE-NORMAL

The males are usually lazy, but when attacked by a strong foe, a male will protect its friends with no regard for its own safety.

The temperature of its breath is over 10,000 degrees Fahrenheit, but Pyroar doesn't use it on its prey. This Pokémon prefers to eat raw meat.

FEMALE FORM

HOW TO SAY IT: PIE-roar
METRIC HEIGHT: 1.5 m
IMPERIAL HEIGHT: 4'11"
METRIC WEIGHT: 81.5 kg
IMPERIAL WEIGHT: 179.7 lbs.

POSSIBLE MOVES: Hyper Beam, Tackle, Leer, Ember, Work Up, Headbutt, Noble Roar, Take Down, Fire Fang, Endeavor, Echoed Voice, Flamethrower, Crunch, Hyper Voice, Incinerate, Overheat

LITLEO

PYROAR

PYUKUMUKU
Sea Cucumber Pokémon

TYPE: WATER

It lives in warm, shallow waters. If it encounters a foe, it will spit out its internal organs as a means to punch them.

It's covered in a slime that keeps its skin moist, allowing it to stay on land for days without drying up.

HOW TO SAY IT: PYOO-koo-MOO-koo
IMPERIAL HEIGHT: 1'00"
IMPERIAL WEIGHT: 2.6 lbs.
METRIC HEIGHT: 0.3 m
METRIC WEIGHT: 1.2 kg

POSSIBLE MOVES: Baton Pass, Counter, Curse, Gastro Acid, Harden, Helping Hand, Memento, Pain Split, Purify, Recover, Safeguard, Soak, Taunt, Toxic

DOES NOT EVOLVE

REGIONS:
GALAR
JOHTO
KALOS
(MOUNTAIN)

QUAGSIRE
Water Fish Pokémon

TYPE: WATER-GROUND

It has an easygoing nature. It doesn't care if it bumps its head on boats and boulders while swimming.

Its body is always slimy. It often bangs its head on the river bottom as it swims but seems not to care.

HOW TO SAY IT: KWAG-sire **METRIC HEIGHT:** 1.4 m
IMPERIAL HEIGHT: 4'07" **METRIC WEIGHT:** 75.0 kg
IMPERIAL WEIGHT: 165.3 lbs.

POSSIBLE MOVES: Amnesia, Aqua Tail, Earthquake, Haze, Mist, Mud Shot, Muddy Water, Rain Dance, Slam, Tail Whip, Toxic, Water Gun, Yawn

WOOPER **QUAGSIRE**

TYPE: FIRE

Quilava keeps its foes at bay with the intensity of its flames and gusts of superheated air. This Pokémon applies its outstanding nimbleness to dodge attacks even while scorching the foe with flames.

REGION:
JOHTO

QUILAVA
Volcano Pokémon

HOW TO SAY IT: kwi-LAH-va
IMPERIAL HEIGHT: 2'11"
IMPERIAL WEIGHT: 41.9 lbs.
METRIC HEIGHT: 0.9 m
METRIC WEIGHT: 19.0 kg

POSSIBLE MOVES: Tackle, Leer, Smokescreen, Ember, Quick Attack, Flame Wheel, Defense Curl, Swift, Flame Charge, Lava Plume, Flamethrower, Inferno, Rollout, Double-Edge, Burn Up, Eruption

CYNDAQUIL **QUILAVA** **TYPHLOSION**

QUILLADIN
Spiny Armor Pokémon

REGION:
KALOS
(CENTRAL)

TYPE: GRASS

It relies on its sturdy shell to deflect predators' attacks. It counterattacks with its sharp quills.

They strengthen their lower bodies by running into one another. They are very kind and won't start fights.

HOW TO SAY IT: QUILL-uh-din
IMPERIAL HEIGHT: 2'04"
IMPERIAL WEIGHT: 63.9 lbs.
METRIC HEIGHT: 0.7 m
METRIC WEIGHT: 29.0 kg

POSSIBLE MOVES: Growl, Vine Whip, Rollout, Bite, Leech Seed, Pin Missile, Needle Arm, Take Down, Seed Bomb, Mud Shot, Bulk Up, Body Slam, Pain Split, Wood Hammer

CHESPIN   QUILLADIN   CHESNAUGHT

QWILFISH
Balloon Pokémon

REGIONS:
GALAR
JOHTO
KALOS
(COASTAL)

TYPE: WATER-POISON

When faced with a larger opponent, it swallows as much water as it can to match the opponent's size.

The small spikes covering its body developed from scales. They inject a toxin that causes fainting.

HOW TO SAY IT: KWILL-fish
IMPERIAL HEIGHT: 1'08"
IMPERIAL WEIGHT: 8.6 lbs.
METRIC HEIGHT: 0.5 m
METRIC WEIGHT: 3.9 kg

POSSIBLE MOVES: Acupressure, Aqua Tail, Brine, Destiny Bond, Fell Stinger, Harden, Minimize, Pin Missile, Poison Jab, Poison Sting, Revenge, Spikes, Spit Up, Stockpile, Tackle, Take Down, Toxic, Toxic Spikes, Water Gun

DOES NOT EVOLVE

TYPE: FIRE

Its thick and fluffy fur protects it from the cold and enables it to use hotter fire moves.

It kicks berries right off the branches of trees and then juggles them with its feet, practicing its footwork.

REGION: GALAR

RABOOT
Rabbit Pokémon

HOW TO SAY IT: RAB-boot   **METRIC HEIGHT:** 0.6 m
IMPERIAL HEIGHT: 2'00"   **METRIC WEIGHT:** 9.0 kg
IMPERIAL WEIGHT: 19.8 lbs.

POSSIBLE MOVES: Agility, Bounce, Counter, Double Kick, Double-Edge, Ember, Flame Charge, Growl, Headbutt, Quick Attack, Tackle

SCORBUNNY   **RABOOT**   **CINDERACE**

RAICHU
Mouse Pokémon

TYPE: ELECTRIC

Its long tail serves as a ground to protect itself from its own high-voltage power.

If its electric pouches run empty, it raises its tail to gather electricity from the atmosphere.

HOW TO SAY IT: RYE-choo
METRIC HEIGHT: 0.8 m
IMPERIAL HEIGHT: 2'07"
METRIC WEIGHT: 30.0 kg
IMPERIAL WEIGHT: 66.1 lbs.

POSSIBLE MOVES: Agility, Charm, Discharge, Double Team, Electro Ball, Feint, Growl, Light Screen, Nasty Plot, Nuzzle, Play Nice, Slam, Spark, Sweet Kiss, Tail Whip, Thunder, Thunder Punch, Thunder Shock, Thunder Wave, Thunderbolt

PICHU   **PIKACHU**   **RAICHU**

ALOLAN RAICHU
Mouse Pokémon

TYPE: ELECTRIC-PSYCHIC

It's believed that the weather, climate, and food of the Alola region all play a part in causing Pikachu to evolve into this form of Raichu.

This Pokémon rides on its tail while it uses its psychic powers to levitate. It attacks with star-shaped thunderbolts.

HOW TO SAY IT: RYE-choo
IMPERIAL HEIGHT: 2'04"
IMPERIAL WEIGHT: 46.3 lbs.
METRIC HEIGHT: 0.7 m
METRIC WEIGHT: 21.0 kg

POSSIBLE MOVES: Psychic, Speed Swap, Thunder Shock, Tail Whip, Quick Attack, Thunderbolt

PICHU   **PIKACHU**   **ALOLAN RAICHU**

LEGENDARY POKÉMON

RAIKOU
Thunder Pokémon

TYPE: ELECTRIC

Raikou embodies the speed of lightning. The roars of this Pokémon send shock waves shuddering through the air and shake the ground as if lightning bolts had come crashing down.

HOW TO SAY IT: RYE-coo
IMPERIAL HEIGHT: 6'03"
IMPERIAL WEIGHT: 392.4 lbs.
METRIC HEIGHT: 1.9 m
METRIC WEIGHT: 178.0 kg

POSSIBLE MOVES: Bite, Leer, Thunder Shock, Roar, Quick Attack, Spark, Reflect, Crunch, Thunder Fang, Discharge, Extrasensory, Rain Dance, Calm Mind, Thunder

DOES NOT EVOLVE

RALTS
Feeling Pokémon

REGIONS:
GALAR
HOENN
KALOS
(CENTRAL)

TYPE: PSYCHIC-FAIRY

It is highly attuned to the emotions of people and Pokémon. It hides if it senses hostility.

If its horns capture the warm feelings of people or Pokémon, its body warms up slightly.

HOW TO SAY IT: RALTS
IMPERIAL HEIGHT: 1'04"
IMPERIAL WEIGHT: 14.6 lbs.
METRIC HEIGHT: 0.4 m
METRIC WEIGHT: 6.6 kg

POSSIBLE MOVES: Calm Mind, Charm, Confusion, Disarming Voice, Double Team, Draining Kiss, Dream Eater, Future Sight, Growl, Heal Pulse, Hypnosis, Life Dew, Psybeam, Psychic, Teleport

GARDEVOIR   MEGA GARDEVOIR

RALTS   KIRLIA

GALLADE   MEGA GALLADE

RAMPARDOS
Head Butt Pokémon

REGIONS:
ALOLA
SINNOH

TYPE: ROCK

In ancient times, people would dig up fossils of this Pokémon and use its skull, which is harder than steel, to make helmets.

This ancient Pokémon used headbutts skillfully. Its brain was really small, so some theories suggest that its stupidity led to its extinction.

HOW TO SAY IT: ram-PAR-dose
IMPERIAL HEIGHT: 5'03"
IMPERIAL WEIGHT: 226.0 lbs.
METRIC HEIGHT: 1.6 m
METRIC WEIGHT: 102.5 kg

POSSIBLE MOVES: Endeavor, Headbutt, Leer, Focus Energy, Pursuit, Take Down, Scary Face, Assurance, Chip Away, Ancient Power, Zen Headbutt, Screech, Head Smash

CRANIDOS   RAMPARDOS

RAPIDASH
Fire Horse Pokémon

TYPE: FIRE

This Pokémon can be seen galloping through fields at speeds of up to 150 mph, its fiery mane fluttering in the wind.

The fastest runner becomes the leader, and it decides the herd's pace and direction of travel.

HOW TO SAY IT: RAP-id-dash
IMPERIAL HEIGHT: 5'07"
IMPERIAL WEIGHT: 209.4 lbs.
METRIC HEIGHT: 1.7 m
METRIC WEIGHT: 95.0 kg

POSSIBLE MOVES: Agility, Ember, Fire Blast, Fire Spin, Flame Charge, Flame Wheel, Flare Blitz, Growl, Inferno, Megahorn, Poison Jab, Quick Attack, Smart Strike, Stomp, Tackle, Tail Whip, Take Down

PONYTA → **RAPIDASH**

GALARIAN RAPIDASH
Unique Horn Pokémon

TYPE: PSYCHIC-FAIRY

Little can stand up to its Psycho Cut. Unleashed from this Pokémon's horn, the move will punch a hole right through a thick metal sheet.

Brave and prideful, this Pokémon dashes airily through the forest, its steps aided by the psychic power stored in the fur on its fetlocks.

HOW TO SAY IT: RAP-id-dash   **METRIC HEIGHT:** 1.7 m
IMPERIAL HEIGHT: 5'07"   **METRIC WEIGHT:** 80.0 kg
IMPERIAL WEIGHT: 176.4 lbs.

POSSIBLE MOVES: Agility, Confusion, Dazzling Gleam, Fairy Wind, Growl, Heal Pulse, Healing Wish, Megahorn, Psybeam, Psychic, Psycho Cut, Quick Attack, Stomp, Tackle, Tail Whip, Take Down

GALARIAN PONYTA → **GALARIAN RAPIDASH**

RATICATE

Mouse Pokémon

REGION: KANTO

TYPE: NORMAL

Its hind feet are webbed. They act as flippers, so it can swim in rivers and hunt for prey.

HOW TO SAY IT: RAT-ih-kate
IMPERIAL HEIGHT: 2'04"
IMPERIAL WEIGHT: 40.8 lbs.
METRIC HEIGHT: 0.7 m
METRIC WEIGHT: 18.5 kg

POSSIBLE MOVES: Scary Face, Swords Dance, Tackle, Tail Whip, Quick Attack, Focus Energy, Bite, Pursuit, Hyper Fang, Assurance, Crunch, Sucker Punch, Super Fang, Double-Edge, Endeavor

RATTATA   RATICATE

ALOLAN RATICATE

Mouse Pokémon

REGION: ALOLA

TYPE: DARK-NORMAL

It makes its Rattata underlings gather food for it, dining solely on the most nutritious and delicious fare.

HOW TO SAY IT: RAT-ih-kate
IMPERIAL HEIGHT: 2'04"
IMPERIAL WEIGHT: 56.2 lbs.
METRIC HEIGHT: 0.7 m
METRIC WEIGHT: 25.5 kg

POSSIBLE MOVES: Scary Face, Swords Dance, Tackle, Tail Whip, Focus Energy, Quick Attack, Bite, Pursuit, Hyper Fang, Assurance, Crunch, Sucker Punch, Super Fang, Double-Edge, Endeavor

ALOLAN RATTATA   ALOLAN RATICATE

RATTATA
Mouse Pokémon

TYPE: NORMAL

Will chew on anything with its fangs. If you see one, you can be certain that 40 more live in the area.

HOW TO SAY IT: RA-TAT-ta
IMPERIAL HEIGHT: 1'00"
IMPERIAL WEIGHT: 7.7 lbs.
METRIC HEIGHT: 0.3 m
METRIC WEIGHT: 3.5 kg

POSSIBLE MOVES: Tackle, Tail Whip, Quick Attack, Focus Energy, Bite, Pursuit, Hyper Fang, Assurance, Crunch, Sucker Punch, Super Fang, Double-Edge, Endeavor

RATTATA   RATICATE

ALOLAN RATTATA
Mouse Pokémon

TYPE: DARK-NORMAL

Its whiskers provide it with a keen sense of smell, enabling it to pick up the scent of hidden food and locate it instantly.

HOW TO SAY IT: RA-TAT-ta
IMPERIAL HEIGHT: 1'00"
IMPERIAL WEIGHT: 8.4 lbs.
METRIC HEIGHT: 0.3 m
METRIC WEIGHT: 3.8 kg

POSSIBLE MOVES: Tackle, Tail Whip, Quick Attack, Focus Energy, Bite, Pursuit, Hyper Fang, Assurance, Crunch, Sucker Punch, Super Fang, Double-Edge, Endeavor

ALOLAN RATTATA   ALOLAN RATICATE

RAYQUAZA

Sky High Pokémon

LEGENDARY POKÉMON

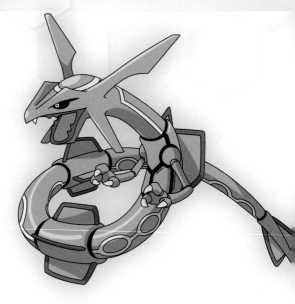

TYPE: DRAGON-FLYING

Rayquaza is said to have lived for hundreds of millions of years. Legends remain of how it put to rest the clash between Kyogre and Groudon.

It flies forever through the ozone layer, consuming meteoroids for sustenance. The many meteoroids in its body provide the energy it needs to Mega Evolve.

HOW TO SAY IT: ray-KWAY-zuh
IMPERIAL HEIGHT: 23'00"
IMPERIAL WEIGHT: 455.3 lbs.
METRIC HEIGHT: 7.0 m
METRIC WEIGHT: 206.5 kg

POSSIBLE MOVES: Twister, Scary Face, Crunch, Hyper Voice, Rest, Air Slash, Ancient Power, Outrage, Dragon Dance, Fly, Extreme Speed, Hyper Beam, Dragon Pulse, Rest

MEGA RAYQUAZA

Sky High Pokémon

TYPE: DRAGON-FLYING

IMPERIAL HEIGHT: 35'05"
IMPERIAL WEIGHT: 864.2 lbs.
METRIC HEIGHT: 10.8 m
METRIC WEIGHT: 392.0 kg

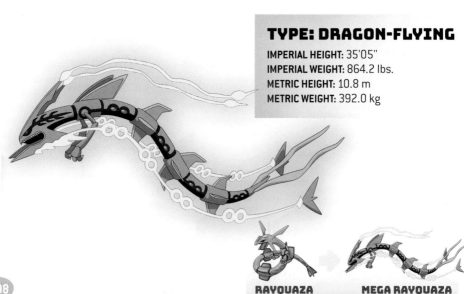

RAYQUAZA → MEGA RAYQUAZA

REGICE
Iceberg Pokémon

TYPE: ICE

Regice's body was made during an ice age. The deep-frozen body can't be melted, even by fire. This Pokémon controls frigid air of -328 degrees Fahrenheit.

Regice cloaks itself with frigid air of -328 degrees Fahrenheit. Things will freeze solid just by going near this Pokémon. Its icy body is so cold, it will not melt even if it is immersed in magma.

HOW TO SAY IT: REDGE-ice **METRIC HEIGHT:** 1.8 m
IMPERIAL HEIGHT: 5'11" **METRIC WEIGHT:** 175.0 kg
IMPERIAL WEIGHT: 385.8 lbs.

POSSIBLE MOVES: Explosion, Stomp, Icy Wind, Curse, Superpower, Ancient Power, Amnesia, Charge Beam, Lock-On, Zap Cannon, Ice Beam, Hammer Arm, Hyper Beam, Bulldoze

DOES NOT EVOLVE

REGIGIGAS
Colossal Pokémon

TYPE: NORMAL

It is said to have made Pokémon that look like itself from a special ice mountain, rocks, and magma.

There is an enduring legend that states this Pokémon towed continents with ropes.

HOW TO SAY IT: rej-jee-GIG-us
IMPERIAL HEIGHT: 12'02"
IMPERIAL WEIGHT: 925.9 lbs.
METRIC HEIGHT: 3.7 m
METRIC WEIGHT: 420.0 kg

POSSIBLE MOVES: Fire Punch, Ice Punch, Thunder Punch, Dizzy Punch, Knock Off, Confuse Ray, Foresight, Revenge, Wide Guard, Zen Headbutt, Payback, Crush Grip, Heavy Slam, Giga Impact

DOES NOT EVOLVE

REGION: HOENN

REGIROCK
Rock Peak Pokémon

TYPE: ROCK

Regirock was sealed away by people long ago. If this Pokémon's body is damaged in battle, it is said to seek out suitable rocks on its own to repair itself.

Regirock's body is composed entirely of rocks. Recently, a study made the startling discovery that the rocks were all unearthed from different locations.

HOW TO SAY IT: REDGE-ee-rock
IMPERIAL HEIGHT: 5'07"
IMPERIAL WEIGHT: 507.1 lbs.
METRIC HEIGHT: 1.7 m
METRIC WEIGHT: 230.0 k

POSSIBLE MOVES: Explosion, Stomp, Rock Throw, Curse, Superpower, Ancient Power, Iron Defense, Charge Beam, Lock-On, Zap Cannon, Stone Edge, Hammer Arm, Hyper Beam, Bulldoze

DOES NOT EVOLVE

REGION: HOENN

REGISTEEL
Iron Pokémon

TYPE: STEEL

Registeel has a body that is harder than any kind of metal. Its body is apparently hollow. No one has any idea what this Pokémon eats.

Registeel was imprisoned by people in ancient times. The metal composing its body is thought to be a curious substance that is not of this earth.

HOW TO SAY IT: REDGE-ee-steel
IMPERIAL HEIGHT: 6'03"
IMPERIAL WEIGHT: 451.9 lbs.
METRIC HEIGHT: 1.9 m
METRIC WEIGHT: 205.0 kg

POSSIBLE MOVES: Explosion, Stomp, Metal Claw, Curse, Superpower, Ancient Power, Iron Defense, Amnesia, Charge Beam, Lock-On, Zap Cannon, Iron Head, Flash Cannon, Hammer Arm, Hyper Beam, Bulldoze

DOES NOT EVOLVE

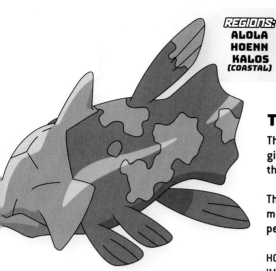

RELICANTH
Longevity Pokémon

TYPE: WATER-ROCK

Thought to have gone extinct, Relicanth was given a name that is a variation of the name of the person who discovered it.

The reason it hasn't changed at all in a hundred million years is that it's apparently already a perfect life-form.

HOW TO SAY IT: REL-uh-canth **METRIC HEIGHT:** 1.0 m
IMPERIAL HEIGHT: 3'03" **METRIC WEIGHT:** 23.4 kg
IMPERIAL WEIGHT: 51.6 lbs.

DOES NOT EVOLVE

POSSIBLE MOVES: Flail, Head Smash, Tackle, Harden, Mud Sport, Water Gun, Rock Tomb, Ancient Power, Dive, Take Down, Yawn, Rest, Hydro Pump, Double-Edge

REMORAID
Jet Pokémon

TYPE: WATER

The water they shoot from their mouths can hit moving prey from more than 300 feet away.

Using its dorsal fin as a suction pad, it clings to a Mantine's underside to scavenge for leftovers.

HOW TO SAY IT: REM-oh-raid
IMPERIAL HEIGHT: 2'00"
IMPERIAL WEIGHT: 26.5 lbs.
METRIC HEIGHT: 0.6 m
METRIC WEIGHT: 12.0 kg

POSSIBLE MOVES: Aurora Beam, Bubble Beam, Bullet Seed, Focus Energy, Helping Hand, Hydro Pump, Hyper Beam, Ice Beam, Lock-On, Psybeam, Soak, Water Gun, Water Pulse

REMORAID   OCTILLERY

LEGENDARY POKÉMON

REGION:
UNOVA

RESHIRAM
Vast White Pokémon

TYPE: DRAGON-FIRE

This legendary Pokémon can scorch the world with fire. It helps those who want to build a world of truth.

When Reshiram's tail flares, the heat energy moves the atmosphere and changes the world's weather.

HOW TO SAY IT: RESH-i-ram
IMPERIAL HEIGHT: 10'06"
IMPERIAL WEIGHT: 727.5 lbs.
METRIC HEIGHT: 3.2 m
METRIC WEIGHT: 330.0 kg

POSSIBLE MOVES: Fire Fang, Dragon Rage, Imprison, Ancient Power, Flamethrower, Dragon Breath, Slash, Extrasensory, Fusion Flare, Dragon Pulse, Noble Roar, Crunch, Fire Blast, Outrage, Hyper Voice, Blue Flare

OVERDRIVE MODE

DOES NOT EVOLVE

REUNICLUS
Multiplying Pokémon

TYPE: PSYCHIC

While it could use its psychic abilities in battle, this Pokémon prefers to swing its powerful arms around to beat opponents into submission.

It's said that drinking the liquid surrounding Reuniclus grants wisdom. Problem is, the liquid is highly toxic to anything besides Reuniclus itself.

HOW TO SAY IT: ree-yoo-NIH-klus
IMPERIAL HEIGHT: 3'03"
IMPERIAL WEIGHT: 44.3 lbs.
METRIC HEIGHT: 1.0 m
METRIC WEIGHT: 20.1 kg

POSSIBLE MOVES: Ally Switch, Charm, Confusion, Endeavor, Future Sight, Hammer Arm, Light Screen, Pain Split, Protect, Psybeam, Psychic, Psyshock, Recover, Reflect, Skill Swap, Wonder Room

SOLOSIS

DUOSION

REUNICLUS

RHYDON

Drill Pokémon

TYPE: GROUND-ROCK

It begins walking on its hind legs after Evolution. It can punch holes through boulders with its horn.

Protected by an armor-like hide, it is capable of living in molten lava of 3,600 degrees Fahrenheit.

HOW TO SAY IT: RYE-don **METRIC HEIGHT:** 1.9 m
IMPERIAL HEIGHT: 6'03" **METRIC WEIGHT:** 120.0 kg
IMPERIAL WEIGHT: 264.6 lbs.

POSSIBLE MOVES: Bulldoze, Drill Run, Earthquake, Hammer Arm, Horn Attack, Horn Drill, Megahorn, Rock Blast, Scary Face, Smack Down, Stomp, Stone Edge, Tackle, Tail Whip, Take Down

RHYHORN   RHYDON   RHYPERIOR

RHYHORN

Spikes Pokémon

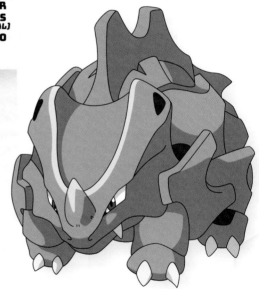

TYPE: GROUND-ROCK

Strong, but not too bright, this Pokémon can shatter even a skyscraper with its charging tackles.

It can remember only one thing at a time. Once it starts rushing, it forgets why it started.

HOW TO SAY IT: RYE-horn
IMPERIAL HEIGHT: 3'03"
IMPERIAL WEIGHT: 253.3 lbs.
METRIC HEIGHT: 1.0 m
METRIC WEIGHT: 115.0 kg

POSSIBLE MOVES: Bulldoze, Drill Run, Earthquake, Horn Attack, Horn Drill, Megahorn, Rock Blast, Scary Face, Smack Down, Stomp, Stone Edge, Tackle, Tail Whip, Take Down

RHYHORN   RHYDON   RHYPERIOR

RHYPERIOR
Drill Pokémon

TYPE: GROUND-ROCK

It can load up to three projectiles per arm into the holes in its hands. What launches out of those holes could be either rocks or Roggenrola.

It relies on its carapace to deflect incoming attacks and throw its enemy off balance. As soon as that happens, it drives its drill into the foe.

HOW TO SAY IT: rye-PEER-ee-or
IMPERIAL HEIGHT: 7'10"
IMPERIAL WEIGHT: 623.5 lbs.
METRIC HEIGHT: 2.4 m
METRIC WEIGHT: 282.8 kg

RHYHORN **RHYDON** **RHYPERIOR**

POSSIBLE MOVES: Bulldoze, Drill Run, Earthquake, Hammer Arm, Horn Attack, Horn Drill, Megahorn, Rock Blast, Rock Wrecker, Scary Face, Smack Down, Stomp, Stone Edge, Tackle, Tail Whip, Take Down

RIBOMBEE
Bee Fly Pokémon

TYPE: BUG-FAIRY

It makes pollen puffs from pollen and nectar. The puffs' effects depend on the type of ingredients and how much of each one is used.

Ribombee absolutely hate getting wet or rained on. In the cloudy Galar region, they are very seldom seen.

HOW TO SAY IT: rih-BOMB-bee
IMPERIAL HEIGHT: 0'08"
IMPERIAL WEIGHT: 1.1 lbs.
METRIC HEIGHT: 0.2 m
METRIC WEIGHT: 0.5 kg

POSSIBLE MOVES: Absorb, Aromatherapy, Bug Buzz, Covet, Dazzling Gleam, Draining Kiss, Fairy Wind, Pollen Puff, Quiver Dance, Struggle Bug, Stun Spore, Sweet Scent, Switcheroo

CUTIEFLY **RIBOMBEE**

RILLABOOM
Drumming Pokémon

TYPE: GRASS

By drumming, it taps into the power of its special tree stump. The roots of the stump follow its direction in battle.

The one with the best drumming techniques becomes the boss of the troop. It has a gentle disposition and values harmony among its group.

HOW TO SAY IT: RIL-uh-boom
IMPERIAL HEIGHT: 6'11"
IMPERIAL WEIGHT: 198.4 lbs.
METRIC HEIGHT: 2.1 m
METRIC WEIGHT: 90.0 kg

POSSIBLE MOVES: Boomburst, Branch Poke, Double Hit, Drum Beating, Endeavor, Grassy Terrain, Growl, Knock Off, Noble Roar, Razor Leaf, Scratch, Screech, Slam, Taunt, Uproar, Wood Hammer

GROOKEY ➡ THWACKEY ➡ RILLABOOM

Alternate Form:
GIGANTAMAX RILLABOOM

Gigantamax energy has caused Rillaboom's stump to grow into a drum set that resembles a forest.

Rillaboom has become one with its forest of drums and continues to lay down beats that shake all of Galar.

IMPERIAL HEIGHT: 91'10"+
IMPERIAL WEIGHT: ????.? lbs.
METRIC HEIGHT: 28.0+ m
METRIC WEIGHT: ???.? kg

REGIONS:
ALOLA
GALAR
KALOS
(CENTRAL)
SINNOH

RIOLU
Emanation Pokémon

TYPE: FIGHTING

It's exceedingly energetic, with enough stamina to keep running all through the night. Taking it for walks can be a challenging experience.

It can use waves called auras to gauge how others are feeling. These same waves can also tell this Pokémon about the state of the environment.

HOW TO SAY IT: ree-OH-loo **METRIC HEIGHT:** 0.7 m
IMPERIAL HEIGHT: 2'04" **METRIC WEIGHT:** 20.2 kg
IMPERIAL WEIGHT: 44.5 lbs.

POSSIBLE MOVES: Copycat, Counter, Endure, Feint, Final Gambit, Force Palm, Helping Hand, Metal Claw, Nasty Plot, Quick Attack, Quick Guard, Reversal, Rock Smash, Screech, Swords Dance, Work Up

RIOLU   LUCARIO   MEGA LUCARIO

ROCKRUFF
Puppy Pokémon

TYPE: ROCK

This Pokémon can bond very strongly with its Trainer, but it also has a habit of biting. Raising a Rockruff for a long time can be challenging.

This Pokémon intimidates opponents by striking the ground with the rocks on its neck. The moment an opponent flinches, Rockruff attacks.

HOW TO SAY IT: ROCK-ruff **METRIC HEIGHT:** 0.5 m
IMPERIAL HEIGHT: 1'08" **METRIC WEIGHT:** 9.2 kg
IMPERIAL WEIGHT: 20.3 lbs.

POSSIBLE MOVES: Tackle, Leer, Sand Attack, Bite, Howl, Rock Throw, Odor Sleuth, Rock Tomb, Roar, Stealth Rock, Rock Slide, Scary Face, Crunch, Rock Climb, Stone Edge

ROCKRUFF

LYCANROC
(MIDDAY FORM)

LYCANROC
(DUSK FORM)

LYCANROC
(MIDNIGHT FORM)

ROGGENROLA

Mantle Pokémon

REGIONS:
ALOLA
GALAR
KALOS
(COASTAL)
UNOVA

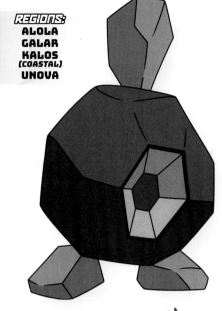

TYPE: ROCK

It's as hard as steel, but apparently a long soak in water will cause it to soften a bit.

When it detects a noise, it starts to move. The energy core inside it makes this Pokémon slightly warm to the touch.

HOW TO SAY IT: rah-gen-ROH-lah
IMPERIAL HEIGHT: 1'04"
IMPERIAL WEIGHT: 39.7 lbs.
METRIC HEIGHT: 0.4 m
METRIC WEIGHT: 18.0 kg

POSSIBLE MOVES: Explosion, Harden, Headbutt, Iron Defense, Mud-Slap, Rock Blast, Rock Slide, Sand Attack, Sandstorm, Smack Down, Stealth Rock, Stone Edge, Tackle

ROGGENROLA　　BOLDORE　　GIGALITH

ROLYCOLY

Coal Pokémon

TYPE: ROCK

Most of its body has the same composition as coal. Fittingly, this Pokémon was first discovered in coal mines about 400 years ago.

It can race around like a unicycle, even on rough, rocky terrain. Burning coal sustains it.

HOW TO SAY IT: ROH-lee-KOH-lee
IMPERIAL HEIGHT: 1'00"
IMPERIAL WEIGHT: 26.5 lbs.
METRIC HEIGHT: 0.3 m
METRIC WEIGHT: 12.0 kg

POSSIBLE MOVES: Ancient Power, Heat Crash, Incinerate, Rapid Spin, Rock Blast, Rock Polish, Smack Down, Smokescreen, Stealth Rock, Tackle

ROLYCOLY　　CARKOL　　COALOSSAL

ROOKIDEE
Tiny Bird Pokémon

TYPE: FLYING

It will bravely challenge any opponent, no matter how powerful. This Pokémon benefits from every battle—even a defeat increases its strength a bit.

Jumping nimbly about, this small-bodied Pokémon takes advantage of even the slightest opportunity to disorient larger opponents.

HOW TO SAY IT: ROOK-ih-dee
IMPERIAL HEIGHT: 0'08"
IMPERIAL WEIGHT: 4.0 lbs.
METRIC HEIGHT: 0.2 m
METRIC WEIGHT: 1.8 kg

POSSIBLE MOVES: Brave Bird, Drill Peck, Fury Attack, Hone Claws, Leer, Peck, Pluck, Power Trip, Scary Face, Swagger, Taunt

ROOKIDEE ➡ **CORVISQUIRE** ➡ **CORVIKNIGHT**

ROSELIA

Thorn Pokémon

TYPE: GRASS-POISON

Its flowers give off a relaxing fragrance. The stronger its aroma, the healthier the Roselia is.

It uses the different poisons in each hand separately when it attacks. The stronger its aroma, the healthier it is.

HOW TO SAY IT: roh-ZEH-lee-uh
IMPERIAL HEIGHT: 1'00"
IMPERIAL WEIGHT: 4.4 lbs.
METRIC HEIGHT: 0.3 m
METRIC WEIGHT: 2.0 kg

POSSIBLE MOVES: Absorb, Aromatherapy, Giga Drain, Growth, Ingrain, Leech Seed, Magical Leaf, Mega Drain, Petal Blizzard, Petal Dance, Poison Sting, Stun Spore, Sweet Scent, Synthesis, Toxic, Toxic Spikes, Worry Seed

BUDEW → ROSELIA → ROSERADE

ROSERADE

Bouquet Pokémon

TYPE: GRASS-POISON

After captivating opponents with its sweet scent, it lashes them with its thorny whips.

The poison in its right hand is quick acting. The poison in its left hand is slow acting. Both are life threatening.

HOW TO SAY IT: ROSE-raid
IMPERIAL HEIGHT: 2'11"
IMPERIAL WEIGHT: 32.0 lbs.
METRIC HEIGHT: 0.9 m
METRIC WEIGHT: 14.5 kg

POSSIBLE MOVES: Absorb, Aromatherapy, Giga Drain, Grassy Terrain, Growth, Ingrain, Leech Seed, Magical Leaf, Mega Drain, Petal Blizzard, Petal Dance, Poison Sting, Stun Spore, Sweet Scent, Synthesis, Toxic, Toxic Spikes, Venom Drench, Worry Seed

BUDEW → ROSELIA → ROSERADE

TYPE: ELECTRIC-GHOST

One boy's invention led to the development of many different machines that take advantage of Rotom's unique capabilities.

With a body made of plasma, it can inhabit all sorts of machines. It loves to surprise others.

HOW TO SAY IT: ROW-tom
IMPERIAL HEIGHT: 1'00"
IMPERIAL WEIGHT: 0.7 lbs.
METRIC HEIGHT: 0.3 m
METRIC WEIGHT: 0.3 kg

POSSIBLE MOVES:
Astonish, Charge, Confuse Ray, Discharge, Double Team, Electro Ball, Hex, Shock Wave, Substitute, Thunder Shock, Thunder Wave, Trick, Uproar

ROTOM
Plasma Pokémon

HEAT ROTOM

WASH ROTOM

FROST ROTOM

FAN ROTOM

MOW ROTOM

DOES NOT EVOLVE

ROWLET
Grass Quill Pokémon

TYPE: GRASS-FLYING

It sends its feathers, which are as sharp as blades, flying in attack. Its legs are strong, so its kicks are also formidable.

It feels relaxed in tight, dark places and has been known to use its Trainer's pocket or bag as a nest.

HOW TO SAY IT: ROW-let **METRIC HEIGHT:** 0.3 m
IMPERIAL HEIGHT: 1'00" **METRIC WEIGHT:** 1.5 kg
IMPERIAL WEIGHT: 3.3 lbs.

POSSIBLE MOVES: Tackle, Leafage, Growl, Peck, Astonish, Razor Leaf, Ominous Wind, Foresight, Pluck, Synthesis, Fury Attack, Sucker Punch, Leaf Blade, Feather Dance, Brave Bird, Nasty Plot

ROWLET   DARTRIX   DECIDUEYE

RUFFLET
Eaglet Pokémon

TYPE: NORMAL-FLYING

If it spies a strong Pokémon, Rufflet can't resist challenging it to a battle. But if Rufflet loses, it starts bawling.

A combative Pokémon, it's ready to pick a fight with anyone. It has talons that can crush hard berries.

HOW TO SAY IT: RUF-lit
IMPERIAL HEIGHT: 1'08"
IMPERIAL WEIGHT: 23.1 lbs.
METRIC HEIGHT: 0.5 m
METRIC WEIGHT: 10.5 kg

POSSIBLE MOVES: Aerial Ace, Air Slash, Brave Bird, Crush Claw, Defog, Hone Claws, Leer, Peck, Scary Face, Slash, Tailwind, Thrash, Whirlwind, Wing Attack

RUFFLET   BRAVIARY

RUNERIGUS
Grudge Pokémon

TYPE: GROUND-GHOST

A powerful curse was woven into an ancient painting. After absorbing the spirit of a Yamask, the painting began to move.

Never touch its shadowlike body, or you'll be shown the horrific memories behind the picture carved into it.

HOW TO SAY IT: ROON-uh-REE-gus
IMPERIAL HEIGHT: 5'03"
IMPERIAL WEIGHT: 146.8 lbs.
METRIC HEIGHT: 1.6 m
METRIC WEIGHT: 66.6 kg

POSSIBLE MOVES: Astonish, Brutal Swing, Crafty Shield, Curse, Destiny Bond, Disable, Earthquake, Guard Split, Haze, Hex, Mean Look, Night Shade, Power Split, Protect, Scary Face, Shadow Ball, Shadow Claw, Slam

GALARIAN VAMASK → RUNERIGUS

SABLEYE
Darkness Pokémon

REGIONS:
ALOLA
GALAR
HOENN
KALOS
(COASTAL)

DARK-GHOST

This Pokémon is feared. When its gemstone eyes begin to glow with a sinister shine, it's believed that Sableye will steal people's spirits away.

It feeds on gemstone crystals. In darkness, its eyes sparkle with the glitter of jewels.

HOW TO SAY IT: SAY-bull-eye
IMPERIAL HEIGHT: 1'08"
IMPERIAL WEIGHT: 24.3 lbs.
METRIC HEIGHT: 0.5 m
METRIC WEIGHT: 11.0 kg

POSSIBLE MOVES: Astonish, Confuse Ray, Detect, Disable, Fake Out, Foul Play, Fury Swipes, Knock Off, Leer, Mean Look, Night Shade, Power Gem, Quash, Scratch, Shadow Ball, Shadow Claw, Shadow Sneak, Zen Headbutt

MEGA SABLEYE
Darkness Pokémon

TYPE: DARK-GHOST

IMPERIAL HEIGHT: 1'08"
IMPERIAL WEIGHT: 354.9 lbs.
METRIC HEIGHT: 0.5 m
METRIC WEIGHT: 161.0 kg

SABLEYE ➡ MEGA SABLEYE

TYPE: DRAGON-FLYING

SALAMENCE
Dragon Pokémon

Overjoyed at finally being able to fly, it flies all over the place and usually doesn't land until it's completely exhausted and needs to sleep.

Thanks to its fervent wishes, the cells in its body finally mutated, and at last it has its heart's desire—wings.

HOW TO SAY IT: SAL-uh-mence
IMPERIAL HEIGHT: 4'11"
IMPERIAL WEIGHT: 226.2 lbs.
METRIC HEIGHT: 1.5 m
METRIC WEIGHT: 102.6 kg

POSSIBLE MOVES: Fly, Protect, Dragon Tail, Fire Fang, Thunder Fang, Rage, Ember, Leer, Bite, Dragon Breath, Headbutt, Focus Energy, Crunch, Dragon Claw, Zen Headbutt, Scary Face, Flamethrower, Double-Edge

MEGA SALAMENCE
Dragon Pokémon

TYPE: DRAGON-FLYING

IMPERIAL HEIGHT: 5'11"
IMPERIAL WEIGHT: 248.2 lbs.
METRIC HEIGHT: 1.8 m
METRIC WEIGHT: 112.6 kg

BAGON ➧ **SHELGON** ➧ **SALAMENCE** ➧ **MEGA SALAMENCE**

SALANDIT

Toxic Lizard Pokémon

REGIONS:
ALOLA
GALAR

TYPE: POISON-FIRE

Its venom sacs produce a fluid that this Pokémon then heats up with the flame in its tail. This process creates Salandit's poisonous gas.

This sneaky Pokémon will slink behind its prey and immobilize it with poisonous gas before the prey even realizes Salandit is there.

HOW TO SAY IT: suh-LAN-dit
IMPERIAL HEIGHT: 2'00"
IMPERIAL WEIGHT: 10.6 lbs.
METRIC HEIGHT: 0.6 m
METRIC WEIGHT: 4.8 kg

POSSIBLE MOVES: Dragon Pulse, Ember, Endeavor, Flamethrower, Incinerate, Nasty Plot, Poison Fang, Poison Gas, Scratch, Smog, Sweet Scent, Toxic, Venom Drench, Venoshock

SALANDIT   SALAZZLE

SALAZZLE

Toxic Lizard Pokémon

REGIONS:
ALOLA
GALAR

TYPE: POISON-FIRE

Only female Salazzle exist. They emit a gas laden with pheromones to captivate male Salandit.

The winner of competitions between Salazzle is decided by which one has the most male Salandit with it.

HOW TO SAY IT: suh-LAZ-zuhl
IMPERIAL HEIGHT: 3'11"
IMPERIAL WEIGHT: 48.9 lbs.
METRIC HEIGHT: 1.2 m
METRIC WEIGHT: 22.2 kg

POSSIBLE MOVES: Disable, Dragon Pulse, Ember, Encore, Endeavor, Fire Lash, Flamethrower, Incinerate, Knock Off, Nasty Plot, Poison Fang, Poison Gas, Pound, Scratch, Smog, Swagger, Sweet Scent, Torment, Toxic, Venom Drench, Venoshock

SALANDIT   SALAZZLE

TYPE: WATER

In the time it takes a foe to blink, it can draw and sheathe the seamitars attached to its front legs.

One swing of the sword incorporated in its armor can fell an opponent. A simple glare from one of them quiets everybody.

HOW TO SAY IT: SAM-uh-rot
IMPERIAL HEIGHT: 4'11"
IMPERIAL WEIGHT: 208.6 lbs.
METRIC HEIGHT: 1.5 m
METRIC WEIGHT: 94.6 kg

POSSIBLE MOVES: Megahorn, Tackle, Tail Whip, Water Gun, Water Sport, Focus Energy, Razor Shell, Fury Cutter, Water Pulse, Revenge, Aqua Jet, Slash, Encore, Aqua Tail, Retaliate, Swords Dance, Hydro Pump

REGION: UNOVA

SAMUROTT
Formidable Pokémon

OSHAWOTT

DEWOTT

SAMUROTT

SANDACONDA

Sand Snake Pokémon

TYPE: GROUND

When it contracts its body, over 220 pounds of sand sprays from its nose. If it ever runs out of sand, it becomes disheartened.

Its unique style of coiling allows it to blast sand out of its sand sac more efficiently.

HOW TO SAY IT: san-duh-KAHN-duh
IMPERIAL HEIGHT: 12'06"
IMPERIAL WEIGHT: 144.4 lbs.
METRIC HEIGHT: 3.8 m
METRIC WEIGHT: 65.5 kg

POSSIBLE MOVES: Brutal Swing, Bulldoze, Coil, Dig, Glare, Headbutt, Minimize, Sand Attack, Sand Tomb, Sandstorm, Skull Bash, Slam, Wrap

SILICOBRA → **SANDACONDA**

Alternate Form:
GIGANTAMAX SANDACONDA

Its sand pouch has grown to tremendous proportions. More than 1,000,000 tons of sand now swirl around its body.

Sand swirls around its body with such speed and power that it could pulverize a skyscraper.

IMPERIAL HEIGHT: 72'02"+
IMPERIAL WEIGHT: ????.? lbs.
METRIC HEIGHT: 22.0+ m
METRIC WEIGHT: ???.? kg

TYPE: GROUND-DARK

The desert gets cold at night, so when the sun sets, this Pokémon burrows deep into the sand and sleeps until sunrise.

Sandile is small, but its legs and lower body are powerful. Pushing sand aside as it goes, Sandile moves through the desert as if it's swimming.

HOW TO SAY IT: SAN-dyle
IMPERIAL HEIGHT: 2'04"
IMPERIAL WEIGHT: 33.5 lbs.
METRIC HEIGHT: 0.7 m
METRIC WEIGHT: 15.2 kg

POSSIBLE MOVES: Leer, Rage, Bite, Sand Attack, Torment, Sand Tomb, Assurance, Mud-Slap, Embargo, Swagger, Crunch, Dig, Scary Face, Foul Play, Sandstorm, Earthquake, Thrash

REGIONS:
ALOLA
KALOS
(COASTAL)
UNOVA

SANDILE
Desert Croc Pokémon

SANDILE

KROKOROK

KROOKODILE

SANDSHREW
Mouse Pokémon

REGIONS:
KALOS (MOUNTAIN)
KANTO

TYPE: GROUND

It loves to bathe in the grit of dry, sandy areas. By sand bathing, the Pokémon rids itself of dirt and moisture clinging to its body.

It burrows into the ground to create its nest. If hard stones impede its tunneling, it uses its sharp claws to shatter them and then carries on digging.

HOW TO SAY IT: SAND-shroo
IMPERIAL HEIGHT: 2'00"
IMPERIAL WEIGHT: 26.5 lbs.
METRIC HEIGHT: 0.6 m
METRIC WEIGHT: 12.0 kg

POSSIBLE MOVES: Scratch, Defense Curl, Sand Attack, Poison Sting, Rollout, Rapid Spin, Swift, Fury Cutter, Magnitude, Fury Swipes, Sand Tomb, Slash, Dig, Gyro Ball, Swords Dance, Sandstorm, Earthquake

SANDSHREW   **SANDSLASH**

ALOLAN SANDSHREW
Mouse Pokémon

REGION:
ALOLA

TYPE: ICE-STEEL

Life on mountains covered with deep snow has granted this Pokémon a body of ice that's as hard as steel.

It lives in snowy mountains on southern islands. When a blizzard rolls in, this Pokémon hunkers down in the snow to avoid getting blown away.

HOW TO SAY IT: SAND-shroo
IMPERIAL HEIGHT: 2'04"
IMPERIAL WEIGHT: 88.2 lbs.
METRIC HEIGHT: 0.7 m
METRIC WEIGHT: 40.0 kg

POSSIBLE MOVES: Scratch, Defense Curl, Bide, Powder Snow, Ice Ball, Rapid Spin, Fury Cutter, Metal Claw, Swift, Fury Swipes, Iron Defense, Slash, Magnitude, Iron Head, Gyro Ball, Swords Dance, Hail, Blizzard

ALOLAN SANDSHREW   **ALOLAN SANDSLASH**

REGIONS:
KALOS (MOUNTAIN)
KANTO

SANDSLASH
Mouse Pokémon

TYPE: GROUND

The drier the area Sandslash lives in, the harder and smoother the Pokémon's spikes will feel when touched.

It climbs trees by hooking on with its sharp claws. Sandslash shares the berries it gathers, dropping them down to Sandshrew waiting below the tree.

HOW TO SAY IT: SAND-slash
IMPERIAL HEIGHT: 3'03"
IMPERIAL WEIGHT: 65.0 lbs.
METRIC HEIGHT: 1.0 m
METRIC WEIGHT: 29.5 kg

POSSIBLE MOVES: Scratch, Defense Curl, Sand Attack, Poison Sting, Rollout, Rapid Spin, Swift, Fury Cutter, Magnitude, Fury Swipes, Crush Claw, Sand Tomb, Slash, Dig, Gyro Ball, Swords Dance, Sandstorm, Earthquake

SANDSHREW   SANDSLASH

ALOLAN SANDSLASH
Mouse Pokémon

REGION:
ALOLA

TYPE: ICE-STEEL

It uses large, hooked claws to cut a path through deep snow as it runs. On snowy mountains, this Sandslash is faster than any other Pokémon.

Many people climb snowy mountains, hoping to see the icy spikes of these Pokémon glistening in the light of dawn.

HOW TO SAY IT: SAND-slash
IMPERIAL HEIGHT: 3'11"
IMPERIAL WEIGHT: 121.3 lbs.
METRIC HEIGHT: 1.2 m
METRIC WEIGHT: 55.0 kg

POSSIBLE MOVES: Icicle Spear, Metal Burst, Icicle Crash, Slash, Defense Curl, Ice Ball, Metal Claw

ALOLAN SANDSHREW   ALOLAN SANDSLASH

SANDYGAST
Sand Heap Pokémon

TYPE: GHOST-GROUND

Grudges of the dead have possessed a mound of sand and become a Pokémon. Sandygast is fond of the shovel on its head.

Sandygast mainly inhabits beaches. It takes control of anyone who puts their hand into its mouth, forcing them to make its body bigger.

HOW TO SAY IT: SAN-dee-GAST
IMPERIAL HEIGHT: 1'08"
IMPERIAL WEIGHT: 154.3 lbs.
METRIC HEIGHT: 0.5 m
METRIC WEIGHT: 70.0 kg

POSSIBLE MOVES: Harden, Absorb, Astonish, Sand Attack, Sand Tomb, Mega Drain, Bulldoze, Hypnosis, Iron Defense, Giga Drain, Shadow Ball, Earth Power, Shore Up, Sandstorm

SANDYGAST   PALOSSAND

SAWK
Karate Pokémon

TYPE: FIGHTING

If you see a Sawk training in the mountains in its single-minded pursuit of strength, it's best to quietly pass by.

The karate chops of a Sawk that's trained itself to the limit can cleave the ocean itself.

HOW TO SAY IT: SAWK
IMPERIAL HEIGHT: 4'07"
IMPERIAL WEIGHT: 112.4 lbs.
METRIC HEIGHT: 1.4 m
METRIC WEIGHT: 51.0 kg

POSSIBLE MOVES: Brick Break, Bulk Up, Close Combat, Counter, Double Kick, Endure, Focus Energy, Leer, Low Sweep, Quick Guard, Retaliate, Reversal, Rock Smash

DOES NOT EVOLVE

TYPE: NORMAL-GRASS

They migrate according to the seasons. People can tell the season by looking at Sawsbuck's horns.

They migrate according to the seasons, so some people call Sawsbuck the harbingers of spring.

HOW TO SAY IT: SAWZ-buk **METRIC HEIGHT:** 1.9 m
IMPERIAL HEIGHT: 6'03" **METRIC WEIGHT:** 92.5 kg
IMPERIAL WEIGHT: 203.9 lbs.

POSSIBLE MOVES: Megahorn, Tackle, Camouflage, Growl, Sand Attack, Double Kick, Leech Seed, Feint Attack, Take Down, Jump Kick, Aromatherapy, Energy Ball, Charm, Horn Leech, Nature Power, Double-Edge, Solar Beam

REGION: UNOVA

SAWSBUCK
Season Pokémon

SPRING FORM

SUMMER FORM

AUTUMN FORM

WINTER FORM

DEERLING → SAWSBUCK

REGION: KALOS (COASTAL)

SCATTERBUG
Scatterdust Pokémon

TYPE: BUG

When under attack from bird Pokémon, it spews a poisonous black powder that causes paralysis on contact.

The powder that covers its body regulates its temperature, so it can live in any region or climate.

HOW TO SAY IT: SCAT-ter-BUG **METRIC HEIGHT:** 0.3 m
IMPERIAL HEIGHT: 1'00" **METRIC WEIGHT:** 2.5 kg
IMPERIAL WEIGHT: 5.5 lbs.

POSSIBLE MOVES: Tackle, String Shot, Stun Spore, Bug Bite

SCATTERBUG   SPEWPA   VIVILLON

SCEPTILE

Forest Pokémon

REGION: HOENN

TYPE: GRASS

The leaves growing on Sceptile's body are very sharp edged. This Pokémon is very agile—it leaps all over the branches of trees and jumps on its foe from above or behind.

Sceptile has seeds growing on its back. They are said to be bursting with nutrients that revitalize trees. This Pokémon raises the trees in a forest with loving care.

HOW TO SAY IT: SEP-tile
IMPERIAL HEIGHT: 5'07"
IMPERIAL WEIGHT: 115.1 lbs.
METRIC HEIGHT: 1.7 m
METRIC WEIGHT: 52.2 kg

POSSIBLE MOVES: Dual Chop, Fury Cutter, Leaf Storm, Night Slash, Pound, Leer, Absorb, Quick Attack, Mega Drain, Pursuit, Leaf Blade, Agility, Slam, Detect, X-Scissor, False Swipe, Quick Guard, Screech

MEGA SCEPTILE

Forest Pokémon

TYPE: GRASS-DRAGON

IMPERIAL HEIGHT: 6'03"
IMPERIAL WEIGHT: 121.7 lbs.
METRIC HEIGHT: 1.9 m
METRIC WEIGHT: 55.2 kg

TREECKO   GROVYLE   SCEPTILE   MEGA SCEPTILE

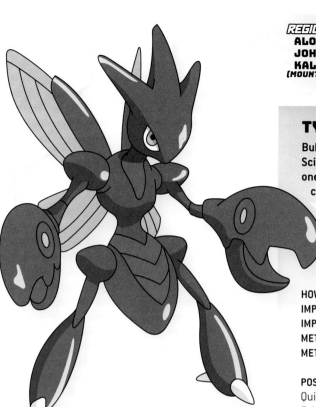

SCIZOR
Pincer Pokémon

TYPE: BUG-STEEL

Bulky pincers account for one third of Scizor's body weight. A single swing of one of these pincers will crush a boulder completely.

Though its body is slim, Scizor has tremendous attacking power. Even Scizor's muscles are made of metal.

HOW TO SAY IT: SIH-zor
IMPERIAL HEIGHT: 5'11"
IMPERIAL WEIGHT: 260.1 lbs.
METRIC HEIGHT: 1.8 m
METRIC WEIGHT: 118.0 kg

POSSIBLE MOVES: Feint, Bullet Punch, Quick Attack, Leer, Focus Energy, Pursuit, False Swipe, Agility, Metal Claw, Fury Cutter, Slash, Razor Wind, Iron Defense, X-Scissor, Night Slash, Double Hit, Iron Head, Swords Dance

MEGA SCIZOR
Pincer Pokémon

TYPE: BUG-STEEL

IMPERIAL HEIGHT: 6'07"
IMPERIAL WEIGHT: 275.6 lbs.
METRIC HEIGHT: 2.0 m
METRIC WEIGHT: 125.0 kg

SCYTHER → SCIZOR → MEGA SCIZOR

SCOLIPEDE
Megapede Pokémon

TYPE: BUG-POISON

Scolipede latches on to its prey with the claws on its neck before slamming them into the ground and jabbing them with its claws' toxic spikes.

Scolipede engage in fierce territorial battles with Centiskorch. At the end of one of these battles, the victor makes a meal of the loser.

HOW TO SAY IT: SKOH-lih-peed
IMPERIAL HEIGHT: 8'02"
IMPERIAL WEIGHT: 442.0 lbs.
METRIC HEIGHT: 2.5 m
METRIC WEIGHT: 200.5 kg

POSSIBLE MOVES: Iron Defense, Megahorn, Defense Curl, Rollout, Poison Sting, Screech, Pursuit, Protect, Poison Tail, Bug Bite, Venoshock, Baton Pass, Agility, Steamroller, Toxic, Venom Drench, Rock Climb, Double-Edge

VENIPEDE　　WHIRLIPEDE　　SCOLIPEDE

SCORBUNNY
Rabbit Pokémon

TYPE: FIRE

A warm-up of running around gets fire energy coursing through this Pokémon's body. Once that happens, it's ready to fight at full power.

It has special pads on the backs of its feet, and one on its nose. Once it's raring to fight, these pads radiate tremendous heat.

HOW TO SAY IT: SKOHR-buh-nee
IMPERIAL HEIGHT: 1'00"
IMPERIAL WEIGHT: 9.9 lbs.
METRIC HEIGHT: 0.3 m
METRIC WEIGHT: 4.5 kg

POSSIBLE MOVES: Agility, Bounce, Counter, Double Kick, Double-Edge, Ember, Flame Charge, Growl, Headbutt, Quick Attack, Tackle

SCORBUNNY　　RABOOT　　CINDERACE

SCRAFTY

Hoodlum Pokémon

REGIONS:
ALOLA
GALAR
KALOS
(CENTRAL)
UNOVA

TYPE: DARK-FIGHTING

As halfhearted as this Pokémon's kicks may seem, they pack enough power to shatter Conkeldurr's concrete pillars.

While mostly known for having the temperament of an aggressive ruffian, this Pokémon takes very good care of its family, friends, and territory.

HOW TO SAY IT: SKRAF-tee
IMPERIAL HEIGHT: 3'07"
IMPERIAL WEIGHT: 66.1 lbs.
METRIC HEIGHT: 1.1 m
METRIC WEIGHT: 30.0 kg

POSSIBLE MOVES: Beat Up, Brick Break, Crunch, Facade, Focus Punch, Head Smash, Headbutt, High Jump Kick, Leer, Low Kick, Payback, Protect, Sand Attack, Scary Face, Swagger

SCRAGGY   SCRAFTY

REGIONS:
ALOLA
GALAR
KALOS
(CENTRAL)
UNOVA

SCRAGGY

Shedding Pokémon

TYPE: DARK-FIGHTING

If it locks eyes with you, watch out! Nothing and no one is safe from the reckless headbutts of this troublesome Pokémon.

It protects itself with its durable skin. It's thought that this Pokémon will evolve once its skin has completely stretched out.

HOW TO SAY IT: SKRAG-ee
IMPERIAL HEIGHT: 2'00"
IMPERIAL WEIGHT: 26.0 lbs.
METRIC HEIGHT: 0.6 m
METRIC WEIGHT: 11.8 kg

POSSIBLE MOVES: Beat Up, Brick Break, Crunch, Facade, Focus Punch, Head Smash, Headbutt, High Jump Kick, Leer, Low Kick, Payback, Protect, Sand Attack, Scary Face, Swagger

SCRAGGY   SCRAFTY

SCYTHER

Mantis Pokémon

TYPE: BUG-FLYING

As Scyther fights more and more battles, its scythes become sharper and sharper. With a single slice, Scyther can fell a massive tree.

If you come across an area in a forest where a lot of the trees have been cut down, what you've found is a Scyther's territory.

HOW TO SAY IT: SY-thur
IMPERIAL HEIGHT: 4'11"
IMPERIAL WEIGHT: 123.5 lbs.
METRIC HEIGHT: 1.5 m
METRIC WEIGHT: 56.0 kg

POSSIBLE MOVES: Vacuum Wave, Quick Attack, Leer, Focus Energy, Pursuit, False Swipe, Agility, Wing Attack, Fury Cutter, Slash, Razor Wind, Double Team, X-Scissor, Night Slash, Double Hit, Air Slash, Swords Dance, Feint

SCYTHER　　**SCIZOR**　　**MEGA SCIZOR**

SEADRA

Dragon Pokémon

TYPE: WATER

It's the males that raise the offspring. While Seadra are raising young, the spines on their backs secrete thicker and stronger poison.

Seadra's mouth is slender, but its suction power is strong. In an instant, Seadra can suck in food that's larger than the opening of its mouth.

HOW TO SAY IT: SEE-dra
IMPERIAL HEIGHT: 3'11"
IMPERIAL WEIGHT: 55.1 lbs.
METRIC HEIGHT: 1.2 m
METRIC WEIGHT: 25.0 kg

POSSIBLE MOVES: Water Gun, Smokescreen, Leer, Bubble, Focus Energy, Bubble Beam, Agility, Twister, Brine, Hydro Pump, Dragon Dance, Dragon Pulse

HORSEA　　**SEADRA**　　**KINGDRA**

REGIONS:
ALOLA
GALAR
KALOS
(COASTAL)
KANTO

SEAKING

Goldfish Pokémon

TYPE: WATER

In autumn, its body becomes more fatty in preparing to propose to a mate. It takes on beautiful colors.

Using its horn, it bores holes in riverbed boulders, making nests to prevent its eggs from washing away.

HOW TO SAY IT: SEE-king   **METRIC HEIGHT:** 1.3 m
IMPERIAL HEIGHT: 4'03"   **METRIC WEIGHT:** 39.0 kg
IMPERIAL WEIGHT: 86.0 lbs.

POSSIBLE MOVES: Agility, Aqua Ring, Flail, Horn Attack, Horn Drill, Megahorn, Peck, Soak, Supersonic, Tail Whip, Water Pulse, Waterfall

GOLDEEN   SEAKING

SEALEO

Ball Roll Pokémon

TYPE: ICE-WATER

Sealeo has the habit of always juggling on the tip of its nose anything it sees for the first time. This Pokémon occasionally entertains itself by balancing and rolling a Spheal on its nose.

Sealeo often balances and rolls things on the tip of its nose. While the Pokémon is rolling something, it checks the object's aroma and texture to determine whether it likes the object or not.

HOW TO SAY IT: SEEL-ee-oh   **METRIC HEIGHT:** 1.1 m
IMPERIAL HEIGHT: 3'07"   **METRIC WEIGHT:** 87.6 kg
IMPERIAL WEIGHT: 193.1 lbs.

POSSIBLE MOVES: Powder Snow, Growl, Water Gun, Encore, Ice Ball, Body Slam, Aurora Beam, Hail, Swagger, Rest, Snore, Blizzard, Sheer Cold, Defense Curl, Rollout, Brine

SPHEAL   SEALEO   WALREIN

SEEDOT

Acorn Pokémon

REGIONS:
GALAR
HOENN

TYPE: GRASS

If it remains still, it looks just like a real nut. It delights in surprising foraging Pokémon.

It attaches itself to a tree branch using the top of its head. Strong winds can sometimes make it fall.

HOW TO SAY IT: SEE-dot
IMPERIAL HEIGHT: 1'08"
IMPERIAL WEIGHT: 8.8 lbs.
METRIC HEIGHT: 0.5 m
METRIC WEIGHT: 4.0 kg

POSSIBLE MOVES: Absorb, Astonish, Explosion, Growth, Harden, Mega Drain, Nature Power, Payback, Rollout, Sucker Punch, Sunny Day, Synthesis, Tackle

SEEDOT   NUZLEAF   SHIFTRY

SEEL

Seal Lion Pokémon

REGIONS:
ALOLA
KANTO

TYPE: WATER

Loves freezing-cold conditions. Relishes swimming in a frigid climate of around 14 degrees Fahrenheit.

HOW TO SAY IT: SEEL
IMPERIAL HEIGHT: 3'07"
IMPERIAL WEIGHT: 198.4 lbs.
METRIC HEIGHT: 1.1 m
METRIC WEIGHT: 90.0 kg

POSSIBLE MOVES: Headbutt, Growl, Water Sport, Icy Wind, Encore, Ice Shard, Rest, Aqua Ring, Aurora Beam, Aqua Jet, Brine, Take Down, Dive, Aqua Tail, Ice Beam, Safeguard, Hail

SEEL   DEWGONG

SEISMITOAD
Vibration Pokémon

TYPE: WATER-GROUND

The vibrating of the bumps all over its body causes earthquake-like tremors. Seismitoad and Croagunk are similar species.

This Pokémon is popular among the elderly, who say the vibrations of its lumps are great for massages.

HOW TO SAY IT: SYZ-mih-tohd
IMPERIAL HEIGHT: 4'11"
IMPERIAL WEIGHT: 136.7 lbs.
METRIC HEIGHT: 1.5 m
METRIC WEIGHT: 62.0 kg

POSSIBLE MOVES: Acid, Aqua Ring, Bubble Beam, Drain Punch, Echoed Voice, Flail, Gastro Acid, Growl, Hydro Pump, Hyper Voice, Mud Shot, Muddy Water, Rain Dance, Round, Supersonic, Uproar

TYMPOLE　**PALPITOAD**　**SEISMITOAD**

SENTRET
Scout Pokémon

TYPE: NORMAL

When Sentret sleeps, it does so while another stands guard. The sentry wakes the others at the first sign of danger. When this Pokémon becomes separated from its pack, it becomes incapable of sleep due to fear.

HOW TO SAY IT: SEN-tret
IMPERIAL HEIGHT: 2'07"
IMPERIAL WEIGHT: 13.2 lbs.
METRIC HEIGHT: 0.8 m
METRIC WEIGHT: 6.0 kg

POSSIBLE MOVES: Scratch, Foresight, Defense Curl, Quick Attack, Fury Swipes, Helping Hand, Follow Me, Slam, Rest, Sucker Punch, Amnesia, Baton Pass, Me First, Hyper Voice

SENTRET　**FURRET**

SERPERIOR

Regal Pokémon

TYPE: GRASS

It only gives its all against strong opponents who are not fazed by the glare from Serperior's noble eyes.

It can stop its opponents' movements with just a glare. It takes in solar energy and boosts it internally.

HOW TO SAY IT: sur-PEER-ee-ur
IMPERIAL HEIGHT: 10'10"
IMPERIAL WEIGHT: 138.9 lbs.
METRIC HEIGHT: 3.3 m
METRIC WEIGHT: 63.0 kg

POSSIBLE MOVES: Tackle, Leer, Vine Whip, Wrap, Growth, Leaf Tornado, Leech Seed, Mega Drain, Slam, Leaf Blade, Coil, Giga Drain, Wring Out, Gastro Acid, Leaf Storm

SNIVY → **SERVINE** → **SERPERIOR**

SERVINE

Grass Snake Pokémon

TYPE: GRASS

It moves along the ground as if sliding. Its swift movements befuddle its foes, and it then attacks with a vine whip.

When it gets dirty, its leaves can't be used in photosynthesis, so it always keeps itself clean.

HOW TO SAY IT: SUR-vine
IMPERIAL HEIGHT: 2'07"
IMPERIAL WEIGHT: 35.3 lbs.
METRIC HEIGHT: 0.8 m
METRIC WEIGHT: 16.0 kg

POSSIBLE MOVES: Tackle, Leer, Vine Whip, Wrap, Growth, Leaf Tornado, Leech Seed, Mega Drain, Slam, Leaf Blade, Coil, Giga Drain, Wring Out, Gastro Acid, Leaf Storm

SNIVY → **SERVINE** → **SERPERIOR**

SEVIPER
Fang Snake Pokémon

TYPE: POISON

Seviper shares a generations-long feud with Zangoose. The scars on its body are evidence of vicious battles. This Pokémon attacks using its sword-edged tail.

Seviper's swordlike tail serves two purposes—it slashes foes and douses them with secreted poison. This Pokémon will not give up its long-running blood feud with Zangoose.

HOW TO SAY IT: seh-VY-per
IMPERIAL HEIGHT: 8'10"
IMPERIAL WEIGHT: 115.7 lbs.
METRIC HEIGHT: 2.7 m
METRIC WEIGHT: 52.5 kg

DOES NOT EVOLVE

POSSIBLE MOVES: Wrap, Swagger, Bite, Lick, Poison Tail, Feint, Screech, Venoshock, Glare, Poison Fang, Venom Drench, Night Slash, Gastro Acid, Haze, Poison Jab, Crunch, Belch, Coil, Wring Out, Swords Dance

SEWADDLE
Sewing Pokémon

TYPE: BUG-GRASS

This Pokémon makes clothes for itself. It chews up leaves and sews them with sticky thread extruded from its mouth.

Since this Pokémon makes its own clothes out of leaves, it is a popular mascot for fashion designers.

HOW TO SAY IT: seh-WAH-dul
IMPERIAL HEIGHT: 1'00"
IMPERIAL WEIGHT: 5.5 lbs.
METRIC HEIGHT: 0.3 m
METRIC WEIGHT: 2.5 kg

POSSIBLE MOVES: Tackle, String Shot, Bug Bite, Razor Leaf, Struggle Bug, Endure, Sticky Web, Bug Buzz, Flail

SEWADDLE SWADLOON LEAVANNY

SHARPEDO

Brutal Pokémon

TYPE: WATER-DARK

As soon as it catches the scent of prey, Sharpedo will jet seawater from its backside, hurtling toward the target to attack at 75 mph.

This Pokémon is known as the Bully of the Sea. Any ship entering the waters Sharpedo calls home will be attacked—no exceptions.

HOW TO SAY IT: shar-PEE-do
IMPERIAL HEIGHT: 5'11"
IMPERIAL WEIGHT: 195.8 lbs.
METRIC HEIGHT: 1.8 m
METRIC WEIGHT: 88.8 kg

POSSIBLE MOVES: Slash, Night Slash, Feint, Leer, Bite, Rage, Focus Energy, Aqua Jet, Assurance, Screech, Swagger, Ice Fang, Scary Face, Poison Fang, Crunch, Agility, Skull Bash, Taunt

MEGA SHARPEDO

Brutal Pokémon

TYPE: WATER-DARK

IMPERIAL HEIGHT: 8'02"
IMPERIAL WEIGHT: 287.3 lbs.
METRIC HEIGHT: 2.5 m
METRIC WEIGHT: 130.3 kg

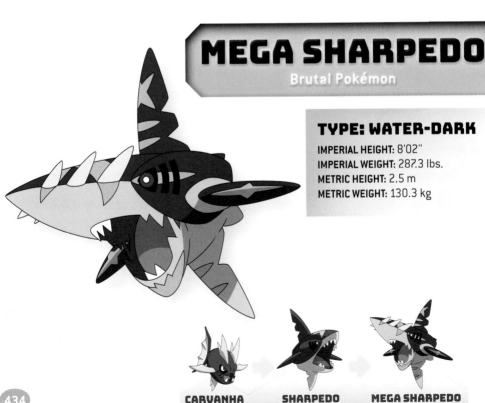

CARVANHA → SHARPEDO → MEGA SHARPEDO

MYTHICAL POKÉMON

REGION: SINNOH

SHAYMIN LAND FORME
Gratitude Pokémon

TYPE: GRASS

It can dissolve toxins in the air to instantly transform ruined land into a lush field of flowers.

The blooming of Gracidea flowers confers the power of flight upon it. Feelings of gratitude are the message it delivers.

HOW TO SAY IT: SHAY-min
IMPERIAL HEIGHT: 0'08"
IMPERIAL WEIGHT: 4.6 lbs.
METRIC HEIGHT: 0.2 m
METRIC WEIGHT: 2.1 kg

POSSIBLE MOVES: Growth, Magical Leaf, Leech Seed, Synthesis, Sweet Scent, Natural Gift, Worry Seed, Aromatherapy, Energy Ball, Sweet Kiss, Healing Wish, Seed Flare

SHAYMIN SKY FORME
Gratitude Pokémon

TYPE: GRASS

IMPERIAL HEIGHT: 1'04"
IMPERIAL WEIGHT: 11.5 lbs.
METRIC HEIGHT: 0.4 m
METRIC WEIGHT: 5.2 kg

DOES NOT EVOLVE

SHEDINJA

Shed Pokémon

TYPE: BUG-GHOST

A most peculiar Pokémon that somehow appears in a Poké Ball when a Nincada evolves.

A strange Pokémon—it flies without moving its wings, has a hollow shell for a body, and does not breathe.

HOW TO SAY IT: sheh-DIN-ja
IMPERIAL HEIGHT: 2'07"
IMPERIAL WEIGHT: 2.6 lbs.
METRIC HEIGHT: 0.8 m
METRIC WEIGHT: 1.2 kg

POSSIBLE MOVES: Absorb, Confuse Ray, Dig, False Swipe, Fury Swipes, Grudge, Harden, Metal Claw, Mind Reader, Mud-Slap, Phantom Force, Sand Attack, Scratch, Shadow Ball, Shadow Claw, Shadow Sneak, Spite

NINCADA → SHEDINJA

SHELGON

Endurance Pokémon

TYPE: DRAGON

The cells within its body are changing at a bewildering pace. Its hard shell is made from the same substance as bone.

Shelgon lives deep within caves. It stays shut up in its hard shell, dreaming of the day it will be able to fly.

HOW TO SAY IT: SHELL-gon
IMPERIAL HEIGHT: 3'07"
IMPERIAL WEIGHT: 243.6 lbs.
METRIC HEIGHT: 1.1 m
METRIC WEIGHT: 110.5 kg

POSSIBLE MOVES: Protect, Rage, Ember, Leer, Bite, Dragon Breath, Headbutt, Focus Energy, Crunch, Dragon Claw, Zen Headbutt, Scary Face, Flamethrower, Double-Edge

BAGON → SHELGON → SALAMENCE → MEGA SALAMENCE

TYPE: WATER

It swims facing backward by opening and closing its two-piece shell. It is surprisingly fast.

Its hard shell repels any kind of attack. It is vulnerable only when its shell is open.

REGIONS:
ALOLA
GALAR
KALOS
(COASTAL)
KANTO

SHELLDER
Bivalve Pokémon

HOW TO SAY IT: SHELL-der **METRIC HEIGHT:** 0.3 m
IMPERIAL HEIGHT: 1'00" **METRIC WEIGHT:** 4.0 kg
IMPERIAL WEIGHT: 8.8 lbs.

POSSIBLE MOVES: Aurora Beam, Hydro Pump, Ice Beam, Ice Shard, Iron Defense, Leer, Protect, Razor Shell, Shell Smash, Supersonic, Tackle, Water Gun, Whirlpool, Withdraw

SHELLDER   CLOYSTER

REGIONS:
ALOLA
GALAR
SINNOH

SHELLOS (EAST SEA)
Sea Slug Pokémon

TYPE: WATER

There's speculation that its appearance is determined by what it eats, but the truth remains elusive.

Its appearance changes depending on the environment. One theory suggests that living in cold seas causes Shellos to take on this form.

HOW TO SAY IT: SHELL-loss **METRIC HEIGHT:** 0.3 m
IMPERIAL HEIGHT: 1'00" **METRIC WEIGHT:** 6.3 kg
IMPERIAL WEIGHT: 13.9 lbs.

POSSIBLE MOVES: Ancient Power, Body Slam, Earth Power, Harden, Memento, Muddy Water, Mud-Slap, Rain Dance, Recover, Water Gun, Water Pulse

SHELLOS
(EAST SEA)

GASTRODON
(EAST SEA)

SHELLOS (WEST SEA)

Sea Slug Pokémon

REGIONS:
ALOLA
SINNOH

TYPE: WATER

This Pokémon's habitat shapes its physique. According to some theories, life in warm ocean waters causes this variation to develop.

Subjecting this Pokémon to a strong force causes it to secrete a strange purple fluid. Though harmless, the fluid is awfully sticky.

HOW TO SAY IT: SHELL-loss
IMPERIAL HEIGHT: 1'00"
IMPERIAL WEIGHT: 13.9 lbs.
METRIC HEIGHT: 0.3 m
METRIC WEIGHT: 6.3 kg

POSSIBLE MOVES: Ancient Power, Body Slam, Earth Power, Harden, Memento, Muddy Water, Mud-Slap, Rain Dance, Recover, Water Gun, Water Pulse

SHELLOS (WEST SEA) → **GASTRODON (WEST SEA)**

SHELMET

Snail Pokémon

REGIONS:
GALAR
KALOS (MOUNTAIN)
UNOVA

TYPE: BUG

When attacked, it tightly shuts the lid of its shell. This reaction fails to protect it from Karrablast, however, because they can still get into the shell.

It has a strange physiology that responds to electricity. When together with Karrablast, Shelmet evolves for some reason.

HOW TO SAY IT: SHELL-meht
IMPERIAL HEIGHT: 1'04"
IMPERIAL WEIGHT: 17.0 lbs.
METRIC HEIGHT: 0.4 m
METRIC WEIGHT: 7.7 kg

POSSIBLE MOVES: Absorb, Acid, Acid Armor, Body Slam, Bug Buzz, Curse, Final Gambit, Giga Drain, Guard Swap, Mega Drain, Protect, Recover, Struggle Bug, Yawn

SHELMET → **ACCELGOR**

TYPE: ROCK-STEEL

A mild-mannered, herbivorous Pokémon, it used its face to dig up tree roots to eat. The skin on its face was plenty tough.

Although its fossils can be found in layers of primeval rock, nothing but its face has ever been discovered.

HOW TO SAY IT: SHEEL-don
IMPERIAL HEIGHT: 1'08"
IMPERIAL WEIGHT: 125.7 lbs.
METRIC HEIGHT: 0.5 m
METRIC WEIGHT: 57.0 kg

POSSIBLE MOVES: Tackle, Protect, Taunt, Metal Sound, Take Down, Iron Defense, Swagger, Ancient Power, Endure, Metal Burst, Iron Head, Heavy Slam

SHIELDON
Shield Pokémon

SHIELDON → BASTIODON

SHIFTRY
Wicked Pokémon

TYPE: GRASS-DARK

A Pokémon that was feared as a forest guardian. It can read the foe's mind and take preemptive action.

It lives quietly in the deep forest. It is said to create chilly winter winds with the fans it holds.

HOW TO SAY IT: SHIFF-tree
IMPERIAL HEIGHT: 4'03"
IMPERIAL WEIGHT: 131.4 lbs.
METRIC HEIGHT: 1.3 m
METRIC WEIGHT: 59.6 kg

POSSIBLE MOVES: Air Cutter, Explosion, Extrasensory, Fake Out, Growth, Hurricane, Leaf Blade, Leaf Tornado, Mega Drain, Nature Power, Payback, Razor Leaf, Rollout, Sucker Punch, Sunny Day, Swagger, Synthesis, Tackle, Torment, Whirlwind

SEEDOT → NUZLEAF → SHIFTRY

SHIINOTIC

Illuminating Pokémon

TYPE: GRASS-FAIRY

Its flickering spores lure in prey and put them to sleep. Once this Pokémon has its prey snoozing, it drains their vitality with its fingertips.

If you see a light deep in a forest at night, don't go near. Shiinotic will make you fall fast asleep.

HOW TO SAY IT: shee-NAH-tick
IMPERIAL HEIGHT: 3'03"
IMPERIAL WEIGHT: 25.4 lbs.
METRIC HEIGHT: 1.0 m
METRIC WEIGHT: 11.5 kg

POSSIBLE MOVES: Absorb, Astonish, Confuse Ray, Dazzling Gleam, Dream Eater, Giga Drain, Ingrain, Mega Drain, Moonblast, Moonlight, Sleep Powder, Spore, Strength Sap

MORELULL   SHIINOTIC

SHINX

Flash Pokémon

TYPE: ELECTRIC

This Pokémon generates electricity by contracting its muscles. Excited trembling is a sign that Shinx is generating a tremendous amount of electricity.

Electricity makes this Pokémon's fur glow. Shinx sends signals to others of its kind by shaking the tip of its tail while the tail tip is shining brightly.

HOW TO SAY IT: SHINKS
IMPERIAL HEIGHT: 1'08"
IMPERIAL WEIGHT: 20.9 lbs.
METRIC HEIGHT: 0.5 m
METRIC WEIGHT: 9.5 kg

POSSIBLE MOVES: Tackle, Leer, Charge, Baby-Doll Eyes, Spark, Bite, Roar, Swagger, Thunder Fang, Crunch, Scary Face, Discharge, Wild Charge

SHINX   LUXIO   LUXRAY

SHROOMISH
Mushroom Pokémon

TYPE: GRASS

Shroomish live in damp soil in the dark depths of forests. They are often found keeping still under fallen leaves. This Pokémon feeds on compost that is made up of fallen, rotted leaves.

If Shroomish senses danger, it shakes its body and scatters spores from the top of its head. This Pokémon's spores are so toxic, they make trees and weeds wilt.

HOW TO SAY IT: SHROOM-ish
IMPERIAL HEIGHT: 1'04"
IMPERIAL WEIGHT: 9.9 lbs.
METRIC HEIGHT: 0.4 m
METRIC WEIGHT: 4.5 kg

POSSIBLE MOVES: Absorb, Tackle, Stun Spore, Leech Seed, Mega Drain, Headbutt, Poison Powder, Worry Seed, Growth, Giga Drain, Seed Bomb, Spore, Toxic

SHROOMISH   BRELOOM

SHUCKLE
Mold Pokémon

TYPE: BUG-ROCK

It stores berries inside its shell. To avoid attacks, it hides beneath rocks and remains completely still.

The berries stored in its vaselike shell eventually become a thick, pulpy juice.

HOW TO SAY IT: SHUCK-kull
IMPERIAL HEIGHT: 2'00"
IMPERIAL WEIGHT: 45.2 lbs.
METRIC HEIGHT: 0.6 m
METRIC WEIGHT: 20.5 kg

POSSIBLE MOVES: Bug Bite, Gastro Acid, Guard Split, Power Split, Power Trick, Rest, Rock Slide, Rock Throw, Rollout, Safeguard, Shell Smash, Sticky Web, Stone Edge, Struggle Bug, Withdraw, Wrap

DOES NOT EVOLVE

SHUPPET

Puppet Pokémon

REGIONS:
ALOLA
HOENN
KALOS
(MOUNTAIN)

TYPE: GHOST

It eats up emotions like malice, jealousy, and resentment, so some people are grateful for its presence.

There's a proverb that says, "Shun the house where Shuppet gather in the growing dusk."

HOW TO SAY IT: SHUP-pett
IMPERIAL HEIGHT: 2'00"
IMPERIAL WEIGHT: 5.1 lbs.
METRIC HEIGHT: 0.6 m
METRIC WEIGHT: 2.3 kg

POSSIBLE MOVES: Knock Off, Screech, Night Shade, Spite, Will-O-Wisp, Shadow Sneak, Curse, Feint Attack, Hex, Shadow Ball, Sucker Punch, Embargo, Snatch, Grudge, Trick, Phantom Force

SHUPPET   BANETTE   MEGA BANETTE

SIGILYPH

Avianoid Pokémon

REGIONS:
GALAR
KALOS
(COASTAL)
UNOVA

TYPE: PSYCHIC-FLYING

Psychic power allows these Pokémon to fly. Some say they were the guardians of an ancient city. Others say they were the guardians' emissaries.

A discovery was made in the desert where Sigilyph fly. The ruins of what may have been an ancient city were found beneath the sands.

HOW TO SAY IT: SIH-jih-liff
IMPERIAL HEIGHT: 4'07"
IMPERIAL WEIGHT: 30.9 lbs.
METRIC HEIGHT: 1.4 m
METRIC WEIGHT: 14.0 kg

POSSIBLE MOVES: Air Cutter, Air Slash, Confusion, Cosmic Power, Gravity, Gust, Hypnosis, Light Screen, Psybeam, Psychic, Reflect, Skill Swap, Sky Attack, Tailwind, Whirlwind

DOES NOT EVOLVE

SILCOON
Cocoon Pokémon

TYPE: BUG

Silcoon tethers itself to a tree branch using silk to keep from falling. There, this Pokémon hangs quietly while it awaits Evolution. It peers out of the silk cocoon through a small hole.

Silcoon was thought to endure hunger and not consume anything before its Evolution. However, it is now thought that this Pokémon slakes its thirst by drinking rainwater that collects on its silk.

HOW TO SAY IT: sill-COON **METRIC HEIGHT:** 0.6 m
IMPERIAL HEIGHT: 2'00" **METRIC WEIGHT:** 10.0 kg
IMPERIAL WEIGHT: 22.0 lbs.

POSSIBLE MOVE: Harden

WURMPLE ➤ **SILCOON** ➤ **BEAUTIFLY**

SILICOBRA
Sand Snake Pokémon

TYPE: GROUND

As it digs, it swallows sand and stores it in its neck pouch. The pouch can hold more than 17 pounds of sand.

It spews sand from its nostrils. While the enemy is blinded, it burrows into the ground to hide.

HOW TO SAY IT: sih-lih-KOH-bruh
IMPERIAL HEIGHT: 7'03"
IMPERIAL WEIGHT: 16.8 lbs.
METRIC HEIGHT: 2.2 m
METRIC WEIGHT: 7.6 kg

POSSIBLE MOVES: Brutal Swing, Bulldoze, Coil, Dig, Glare, Headbutt, Minimize, Sand Attack, Sand Tomb, Sandstorm, Slam, Wrap

SILICOBRA ➤ **SANDACONDA**

SILVALLY

Synthetic Pokémon

LEGENDARY POKÉMON

TYPE: NORMAL

A solid bond of trust between this Pokémon and its Trainer awakened the strength hidden within Silvally. It can change its type at will.

The final factor needed to release this Pokémon's true power was a strong bond with a Trainer it trusts.

HOW TO SAY IT: sill-VAL-lie
IMPERIAL HEIGHT: 7'07"
IMPERIAL WEIGHT: 221.6 lbs.
METRIC HEIGHT: 2.3 m
METRIC WEIGHT: 100.5 kg

POSSIBLE MOVES: Aerial Ace, Air Slash, Bite, Crunch, Crush Claw, Double Hit, Double-Edge, Explosion, Fire Fang, Ice Fang, Imprison, Iron Head, Metal Sound, Multi-Attack, Parting Shot, Poison Fang, Scary Face, Tackle, Take Down, Thunder Fang, Tri Attack, X-Scissor

TYPE: NULL SILVALLY

SIMIPOUR

Geyser Pokémon

TYPE: WATER

The high-pressure water expelled from its tail is so powerful, it can destroy a concrete wall.

It prefers places with clean water. When its tuft runs low, it replenishes it by siphoning up water with its tail.

HOW TO SAY IT: SIH-mee-por
IMPERIAL HEIGHT: 3'03"
IMPERIAL WEIGHT: 63.9 lbs.
METRIC HEIGHT: 1.0 m
METRIC WEIGHT: 29.0 kg

POSSIBLE MOVES: Leer, Lick, Fury Swipes, Scald

PANPOUR SIMIPOUR

TYPE: GRASS

It attacks enemies with strikes of its thorn-covered tail. This Pokémon is wild tempered.

Ill tempered, it fights by swinging its barbed tail around wildly. The leaf growing on its head is very bitter.

HOW TO SAY IT: SIH-mee-sayj
IMPERIAL HEIGHT: 3'07"
IMPERIAL WEIGHT: 67.2 lbs.
METRIC HEIGHT: 1.1 m
METRIC WEIGHT: 30.5 kg

POSSIBLE MOVES: Leer, Lick, Fury Swipes, Seed Bomb

SIMISAGE
Thorn Monkey Pokémon

PANSAGE → SIMISAGE

SIMISEAR
Ember Pokémon

TYPE: FIRE

A flame burns inside its body. It scatters embers from its head and tail to sear its opponents.

When it gets excited, embers rise from its head and tail and it gets hot. For some reason, it loves sweets.

HOW TO SAY IT: SIH-mee-seer
IMPERIAL HEIGHT: 3'03"
IMPERIAL WEIGHT: 67.1 lbs.
METRIC HEIGHT: 1.0 m
METRIC WEIGHT: 28.0 kg

POSSIBLE MOVES: Leer, Lick, Fury Swipes, Flame Burst

PANSEAR → SIMISEAR

SINISTEA

Black Tea Pokémon

TYPE: GHOST

This Pokémon is said to have been born when a lonely spirit possessed a cold, leftover cup of tea.

The teacup in which this Pokémon makes its home is a famous piece of antique tableware. Many forgeries are in circulation.

HOW TO SAY IT: SIH-nis-tee
IMPERIAL HEIGHT: 0'04"
IMPERIAL WEIGHT: 0.4 lbs.
METRIC HEIGHT: 0.1 m
METRIC WEIGHT: 0.2 kg

POSSIBLE MOVES: Aromatherapy, Aromatic Mist, Astonish, Giga Drain, Mega Drain, Memento, Nasty Plot, Protect, Shadow Ball, Shell Smash, Sucker Punch, Withdraw

SINISTEA   POLTEAGEIST

SIRFETCH'D

Wild Duck Pokémon

TYPE: FIGHTING

Only Farfetch'd that have survived many battles can attain this Evolution. When this Pokémon's leek withers, it will retire from combat.

After deflecting attacks with its hard leaf shield, it strikes back with its sharp leek stalk. The leek stalk is both weapon and food.

HOW TO SAY IT: sir-fehcht
IMPERIAL HEIGHT: 2'07"
IMPERIAL WEIGHT: 257.9 lbs.
METRIC HEIGHT: 0.8 m
METRIC WEIGHT: 117.0 kg

POSSIBLE MOVES: Brave Bird, Brick Break, Brutal Swing, Defog, Detect, Final Gambit, First Impression, Fury Cutter, Iron Defense, Knock Off, Leaf Blade, Leer, Meteor Assault, Peck, Rock Smash, Sand Attack, Slam, Swords Dance

GALARIAN FARFETCH'D   SIRFETCH'D

TYPE: FIRE-BUG

It stores flammable gas in its body and uses it to generate heat. The yellow sections on its belly get particularly hot.

It wraps prey up with its heated body, cooking them in its coils. Once they're well-done, it will voraciously nibble them down to the last morsel.

REGION: GALAR

SIZZLIPEDE
Radiator Pokémon

HOW TO SAY IT: SIZ-lih-peed
IMPERIAL HEIGHT: 2'04"
IMPERIAL WEIGHT: 2.2 lbs.
METRIC HEIGHT: 0.7 m
METRIC WEIGHT: 1.0 kg

POSSIBLE MOVES: Bite, Bug Bite, Burn Up, Coil, Crunch, Ember, Fire Lash, Fire Spin, Flame Wheel, Lunge, Slam, Smokescreen, Wrap

SIZZLIPEDE   CENTISKORCH

REGIONS: ALOLA JOHTO KALOS (MOUNTAIN)

SKARMORY
Armor Bird Pokémon

TYPE: STEEL-FLYING

The pointed feathers of these Pokémon are sharper than swords. Skarmory and Corviknight fight viciously over territory.

People fashion swords from Skarmory's shed feathers, so this Pokémon is a popular element in heraldic designs.

HOW TO SAY IT: SKAR-more-ree
IMPERIAL HEIGHT: 5'07"
IMPERIAL WEIGHT: 111.3 lbs.
METRIC HEIGHT: 1.7 m
METRIC WEIGHT: 50.5 kg

POSSIBLE MOVES: Leer, Peck, Sand Attack, Metal Claw, Air Cutter, Fury Attack, Feint, Swift, Spikes, Agility, Steel Wing, Slash, Metal Sound, Air Slash, Autotomize, Night Slash

DOES NOT EVOLVE

SKIDDO
Mount Pokémon

TYPE: GRASS

Thought to be one of the first Pokémon to live in harmony with humans, it has a placid disposition.

If it has sunshine and water, it doesn't need to eat, because it can generate energy from the leaves on its back.

HOW TO SAY IT: skid-OO
IMPERIAL HEIGHT: 2'11"
IMPERIAL WEIGHT: 68.3 lbs.
METRIC HEIGHT: 0.9 m
METRIC WEIGHT: 31.0 kg

POSSIBLE MOVES: Tackle, Growth, Vine Whip, Tail Whip, Leech Seed, Razor Leaf, Worry Seed, Synthesis, Take Down, Bulldoze, Seed Bomb, Bulk Up, Double-Edge, Horn Leech, Leaf Blade, Milk Drink

SKIDDO   GOGOAT

SKIPLOOM
Cottonweed Pokémon

TYPE: GRASS-FLYING

Skiploom's flower blossoms when the temperature rises above 64 degrees Fahrenheit. How much the flower opens depends on the temperature. For that reason, this Pokémon is sometimes used as a thermometer.

HOW TO SAY IT: SKIP-loom
IMPERIAL HEIGHT: 2'00"
IMPERIAL WEIGHT: 2.2 lbs.
METRIC HEIGHT: 0.6 m
METRIC WEIGHT: 1.0 kg

POSSIBLE MOVES: Splash, Absorb, Synthesis, Tail Whip, Tackle, Fairy Wind, Poison Powder, Stun Spore, Sleep Powder, Bullet Seed, Leech Seed, Mega Drain, Acrobatics, Rage Powder, Cotton Spore, U-turn, Worry Seed, Giga Drain, Bounce, Memento

HOPPIP   SKIPLOOM   JUMPLUFF

SKITTY
Kitten Pokémon

TYPE: NORMAL

Skitty has the habit of becoming fascinated by moving objects and chasing them around. This Pokémon is known to chase after its own tail and become dizzy.

Skitty is known to chase around playfully after its own tail. In the wild, this Pokémon lives in holes in the trees of forests. It is very popular as a pet because of its adorable looks.

HOW TO SAY IT: SKIT-tee
IMPERIAL HEIGHT: 2'00"
IMPERIAL WEIGHT: 24.3 lbs.
METRIC HEIGHT: 0.6 m
METRIC WEIGHT: 11.0 kg

POSSIBLE MOVES: Fake Out, Growl, Tail Whip, Tackle, Foresight, Attract, Sing, Disarming Voice, Double Slap, Copycat, Assist, Charm, Feint Attack, Wake-Up Slap, Covet, Heal Bell, Double-Edge, Captivate, Play Rough

SKITTY   DELCATTY

TYPE: POISON-BUG

After burrowing into the sand, it waits patiently for prey to come near. This Pokémon and Sizzlipede share common descent.

It attacks using the claws on its tail. Once locked in its grip, its prey is unable to move as this Pokémon's poison seeps in.

HOW TO SAY IT: skor-ROOP-ee
IMPERIAL HEIGHT: 2'07"
IMPERIAL WEIGHT: 26.5 lbs.
METRIC HEIGHT: 0.8 m
METRIC WEIGHT: 12.0 kg

POSSIBLE MOVES: Acupressure, Bite, Bug Bite, Cross Poison, Crunch, Fell Stinger, Hone Claws, Knock Off, Leer, Night Slash, Pin Missile, Poison Fang, Poison Sting, Scary Face, Toxic, Toxic Spikes, Venoshock, X-Scissor

SKORUPI
Scorpion Pokémon

SKORUPI

DRAPION

SKRELP

Mock Kelp Pokémon

TYPE: POISON-WATER

It drifts in the ocean, blending in with floating seaweed. When other Pokémon come to feast on the seaweed, Skrelp feasts on them instead.

Skrelp looks like a piece of rotten seaweed, so it can blend in with seaweed drifting on the ocean and avoid being detected by enemies.

HOW TO SAY IT: SKRELP
IMPERIAL HEIGHT: 1'08"
IMPERIAL WEIGHT: 16.1 lbs.
METRIC HEIGHT: 0.5 m
METRIC WEIGHT: 7.3 kg

POSSIBLE MOVES: Tackle, Smokescreen, Water Gun, Feint Attack, Tail Whip, Bubble, Acid, Camouflage, Poison Tail, Water Pulse, Double Team, Toxic, Aqua Tail, Sludge Bomb, Hydro Pump, Dragon Pulse

SKRELP → DRAGALGE

SKUNTANK

Skunk Pokémon

TYPE: POISON-DARK

In its belly, it reserves stinky fluid that it shoots from its tail during battle. As this Pokémon's diet varies, so does the stench of its fluid.

It digs holes in the ground to make its nest. The stench of the fluid it lets fly from the tip of its tail is extremely potent.

HOW TO SAY IT: SKUN-tank
IMPERIAL HEIGHT: 3'03"
IMPERIAL WEIGHT: 83.8 lbs.
METRIC HEIGHT: 1.0 m
METRIC WEIGHT: 38.0 kg

POSSIBLE MOVES: Acid Spray, Belch, Bite, Explosion, Feint, Flamethrower, Focus Energy, Fury Swipes, Memento, Night Slash, Poison Gas, Scratch, Screech, Smokescreen, Sucker Punch, Toxic, Venom Drench, Venoshock

STUNKY →

SKUNTANK

SKWOVET
Cheeky Pokémon

TYPE: NORMAL

Found throughout the Galar region, this Pokémon becomes uneasy if its cheeks are ever completely empty of berries.

It eats berries nonstop—a habit that has made it more resilient than it looks. It'll show up on farms, searching for yet more berries.

HOW TO SAY IT: SKWUH-vet
IMPERIAL HEIGHT: 1'00"
IMPERIAL WEIGHT: 5.5 lbs.
METRIC HEIGHT: 0.3 m
METRIC WEIGHT: 2.5 kg

POSSIBLE MOVES: Belch, Bite, Body Slam, Bullet Seed, Counter, Rest, Spit Up, Stockpile, Stuff Cheeks, Super Fang, Swallow, Tackle, Tail Whip

SKWOVET → GREEDENT

TYPE: NORMAL

Slaking spends all day lying down and lolling about. It eats grass growing within its reach. If it eats all the grass it can reach, this Pokémon reluctantly moves to another spot.

Wherever Slaking live, rings of over a yard in diameter appear in grassy fields. They are made by the Pokémon as it eats all the grass within reach while lying prone on the ground.

HOW TO SAY IT: SLACK-ing
IMPERIAL HEIGHT: 6'07"
IMPERIAL WEIGHT: 287.7 lbs.
METRIC HEIGHT: 2.0 m
METRIC WEIGHT: 130.5 kg

POSSIBLE MOVES: Scratch, Yawn, Encore, Slack Off, Feint Attack, Amnesia, Covet, Swagger, Chip Away, Counter, Flail, Fling, Punishment, Hammer Arm

SLAKING
Lazy Pokémon

SLAKOTH

VIGOROTH

SLAKING

451

SLAKOTH

Slacker Pokémon

TYPE: NORMAL

Slakoth lolls around for over 20 hours every day. Because it moves so little, it does not need much food. This Pokémon's sole daily meal consists of just three leaves.

Slakoth's heart beats just once a minute. Whatever happens, it is content to loaf around motionless. It is rare to see this Pokémon in motion.

HOW TO SAY IT: SLACK-oth
IMPERIAL HEIGHT: 2'07"
IMPERIAL WEIGHT: 52.9 lbs.
METRIC HEIGHT: 0.8 m
METRIC WEIGHT: 24.0 kg

POSSIBLE MOVES: Scratch, Yawn, Encore, Slack Off, Feint Attack, Amnesia, Covet, Chip Away, Counter, Flail, Play Rough

SLAKOTH **VIGOROTH** **SLAKING**

SLIGGOO

Soft Tissue Pokémon

TYPE: DRAGON

Although this Pokémon isn't very strong, its body is coated in a caustic slime that can melt through anything, so predators steer clear of it.

The lump on its back contains its tiny brain. It thinks only of food and escaping its enemies.

HOW TO SAY IT: SLIH-goo
IMPERIAL HEIGHT: 2'07"
IMPERIAL WEIGHT: 38.6 lbs.
METRIC HEIGHT: 0.8 m
METRIC WEIGHT: 17.5 kg

POSSIBLE MOVES: Absorb, Acid Spray, Body Slam, Curse, Dragon Breath, Dragon Pulse, Flail, Muddy Water, Protect, Rain Dance, Tackle, Water Gun, Water Pulse

GOOMY **SLIGGOO** **GOODRA**

SLOWBRO
Hermit Crab Pokémon

TYPE: WATER-PSYCHIC

Slowpoke became Slowbro when a Shellder bit on to its tail. Sweet flavors seeping from the tail make the Shellder feel as if its life is a dream.

Being bitten by a Shellder shocked this Pokémon into standing on two legs. If the Shellder lets go, it seems Slowbro will turn back into a Slowpoke.

HOW TO SAY IT: SLOW-bro
IMPERIAL HEIGHT: 5'03"
IMPERIAL WEIGHT: 173.1 lbs.
METRIC HEIGHT: 1.6 m
METRIC WEIGHT: 78.5 kg

POSSIBLE MOVES: Withdraw, Heal Pulse, Curse, Yawn, Tackle, Growl, Water Gun, Confusion, Disable, Headbutt, Water Pulse, Zen Headbutt, Slack Off, Amnesia, Psychic, Rain Dance, Psych Up

MEGA SLOWBRO
Hermit Crab Pokémon

TYPE: WATER-PSYCHIC

IMPERIAL HEIGHT: 6'07"
IMPERIAL WEIGHT: 264.6 lbs.
METRIC HEIGHT: 2.0 m
METRIC WEIGHT: 120.0 kg

SLOWPOKE   SLOWBRO   MEGA SLOWBRO

SLOWKING

Royal Pokémon

TYPE: WATER-PSYCHIC

Miraculously, this former Slowpoke's latent intelligence was drawn out when Shellder poison raced through its brain.

Slowking can solve any problem presented to it, but no one can understand a thing Slowking says.

HOW TO SAY IT: SLOW-king
IMPERIAL HEIGHT: 6'07"
IMPERIAL WEIGHT: 175.3 lbs.
METRIC HEIGHT: 2.0 m
METRIC WEIGHT: 79.5 kg

POSSIBLE MOVES: Heal Pulse, Power Gem, Hidden Power, Curse, Yawn, Tackle, Growl, Water Gun, Confusion, Disable, Headbutt, Water Pulse, Zen Headbutt, Nasty Plot, Swagger, Psychic, Trump Card, Psych Up

SLOWPOKE   SLOWKING

SLOWPOKE

Dopey Pokémon

TYPE: WATER-PSYCHIC

Slow-witted and oblivious, this Pokémon won't feel any pain if its tail gets eaten. It won't notice when its tail grows back, either.

When this Pokémon's tail is soaked in water, sweetness seeps from it. Slowpoke uses this trait to lure in and fish up other Pokémon.

HOW TO SAY IT: SLOW-poke
IMPERIAL HEIGHT: 3'11"
IMPERIAL WEIGHT: 79.4 lbs.
METRIC HEIGHT: 1.2 m
METRIC WEIGHT: 36.0 kg

POSSIBLE MOVES: Curse, Yawn, Tackle, Growl, Water Gun, Confusion, Disable, Headbutt, Water Pulse, Zen Headbutt, Slack Off, Amnesia, Psychic, Rain Dance, Psych Up, Heal Pulse

SLOWBRO   MEGA SLOWBR

SLOWPOKE

SLOWKING

SLUGMA
Lava Pokémon

TYPE: FIRE

Molten magma courses throughout Slugma's circulatory system. If this Pokémon is chilled, the magma cools and hardens. Its body turns brittle and chunks fall off, reducing its size.

Slugma does not have any blood in its body. Instead, intensely hot magma circulates throughout this Pokémon's body, carrying essential nutrients and oxygen to its organs.

HOW TO SAY IT: SLUG-ma
IMPERIAL HEIGHT: 2'04"
IMPERIAL WEIGHT: 77.2 lbs.
METRIC HEIGHT: 0.7 m
METRIC WEIGHT: 35.0 kg

POSSIBLE MOVES: Yawn, Smog, Ember, Rock Throw, Harden, Incinerate, Clear Smog, Recover, Flame Burst, Ancient Power, Amnesia, Lava Plume, Rock Slide, Body Slam, Flamethrower, Earth Power

SLUGMA → MAGCARGO

SLURPUFF
Meringue Pokémon

TYPE: FAIRY

By taking in a person's scent, it can sniff out their mental and physical condition. It's hoped that this skill will have many medical applications.

Slurpuff's fur contains a lot of air, making it soft to the touch and lighter than it looks.

HOW TO SAY IT: SLUR-puff
IMPERIAL HEIGHT: 2'07"
IMPERIAL WEIGHT: 11.0 lbs.
METRIC HEIGHT: 0.8 m
METRIC WEIGHT: 5.0 kg

POSSIBLE MOVES: Aromatherapy, Cotton Guard, Cotton Spore, Draining Kiss, Endeavor, Energy Ball, Fairy Wind, Fake Tears, Play Nice, Play Rough, Round, Sticky Web, String Shot, Sweet Scent, Tackle, Wish

SWIRLIX → SLURPUFF

SMEARGLE

Painter Pokémon

TYPE: NORMAL

The fluid of Smeargle's tail secretions changes in the intensity of its hue as the Pokémon's emotions change.

It draws symbols with the fluid that oozes from the tip of its tail. Depending on the symbol, Smeargle fanatics will pay big money for them.

HOW TO SAY IT: SMEAR-gull
IMPERIAL HEIGHT: 3'11"
IMPERIAL WEIGHT: 127.9 lbs.
METRIC HEIGHT: 1.2 m
METRIC WEIGHT: 58.0 kg

POSSIBLE MOVE: Sketch

DOES NOT EVOLVE

SMOOCHUM

Kiss Pokémon

TYPE: ICE-PSYCHIC

When it examines things, before touching them with its hands, it makes lip contact and then diligently licks all the dirt off its lips.

Highly perceptive sensors, Smoochum's lips are kept moist by its daily application of tree sap.

HOW TO SAY IT: SMOO-chum
IMPERIAL HEIGHT: 1'04"
IMPERIAL WEIGHT: 13.2 lbs.
METRIC HEIGHT: 0.4 m
METRIC WEIGHT: 6.0 kg

POSSIBLE MOVES: Pound, Lick, Sweet Kiss, Powder Snow, Confusion, Sing, Heart Stamp, Mean Look, Fake Tears, Lucky Chant, Avalanche, Psychic, Copycat, Perish Song, Blizzard

SMOOCHUM   JYNX

REGIONS:
ALOLA
GALAR
JOHTO
KALOS
(MOUNTAIN)

SNEASEL
Sharp Claw Pokémon

TYPE: DARK-ICE

Its paws conceal sharp claws. If attacked, it suddenly extends the claws and startles its enemy.

It has a cunning yet savage disposition. It waits for parents to leave their nests, and then it sneaks in to steal their eggs.

HOW TO SAY IT: SNEE-zul
METRIC HEIGHT: 0.9 m
IMPERIAL HEIGHT: 2'11"
METRIC WEIGHT: 28.0 kg
IMPERIAL WEIGHT: 61.7 lbs.

POSSIBLE MOVES: Agility, Beat Up, Fury Swipes, Hone Claws, Icy Wind, Leer, Metal Claw, Quick Attack, Scratch, Screech, Slash, Taunt

SNEASEL → WEAVILE

SNIVY
Grass Snake Pokémon

TYPE: GRASS

Being exposed to sunlight makes its movements swifter. It uses vines more adeptly than its hands.

They photosynthesize by bathing their tails in sunlight. When they are not feeling well, their tails droop.

HOW TO SAY IT: SNY-vee
METRIC HEIGHT: 0.6 m
IMPERIAL HEIGHT: 2'00"
METRIC WEIGHT: 8.1 kg
IMPERIAL WEIGHT: 17.9 lbs.

POSSIBLE MOVES: Tackle, Leer, Vine Whip, Wrap, Growth, Leaf Tornado, Leech Seed, Mega Drain, Slam, Leaf Blade, Coil, Giga Drain, Wring Out, Gastro Acid, Leaf Storm

SNIVY → SERVINE → SERPERIOR

SNOM

Worm Pokémon

REGION: GALAR

TYPE: ICE-BUG

It spits out thread imbued with a frigid sort of energy and uses it to tie its body to branches, disguising itself as an icicle while it sleeps.

It eats snow that piles up on the ground. The more snow it eats, the bigger and more impressive the spikes on its back grow.

HOW TO SAY IT: snahm
IMPERIAL HEIGHT: 1'00"
IMPERIAL WEIGHT: 8.4 lbs.
METRIC HEIGHT: 0.3 m
METRIC WEIGHT: 3.8 kg

POSSIBLE MOVES: Powder Snow, Struggle Bug

SNOM

FROSMOTH

REGIONS:
ALOLA
GALAR
KALOS
(CENTRAL)
KANTO

SNORLAX

Sleeping Pokémon

TYPE: NORMAL

It is not satisfied unless it eats over 880 pounds of food every day. When it is done eating, it goes promptly to sleep.

This Pokémon's stomach is so strong, even eating moldy or rotten food will not affect it.

HOW TO SAY IT: SNOR-lacks
IMPERIAL HEIGHT: 6'11"
IMPERIAL WEIGHT: 1,014.1 lbs.
METRIC HEIGHT: 2.1 m
METRIC WEIGHT: 460.0 kg

POSSIBLE MOVES: Amnesia, Belch, Belly Drum, Bite, Block, Body Slam, Covet, Crunch, Defense Curl, Flail, Fling, Giga Impact, Hammer Arm, Heavy Slam, High Horsepower, Last Resort, Lick, Metronome, Recycle, Rest, Screech, Sleep Talk, Snore, Stockpile, Swallow, Tackle, Yawn

MUNCHLAX **SNORLAX**

Alternate Form:
GIGANTAMAX SNORLAX

Gigantamax energy has affected stray seeds and even pebbles that got stuck to Snorlax, making them grow to a huge size.

Terrifyingly strong, this Pokémon is the size of a mountain—and moves about as much as one as well.

IMPERIAL HEIGHT: 114'10"+
IMPERIAL WEIGHT: ????.? lbs.
METRIC HEIGHT: 35.0 + m
METRIC WEIGHT: ???.? kg

SNORUNT

Snow Hat Pokémon

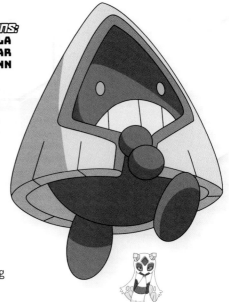

TYPE: ICE

It's said that if they are seen at midnight, they'll cause heavy snow. They eat snow and ice to survive.

It can only survive in cold areas. It bounces happily around, even in environments as cold as -150 degrees Fahrenheit.

HOW TO SAY IT: SNOW-runt
IMPERIAL HEIGHT: 2'04"
IMPERIAL WEIGHT: 37.0 lbs.
METRIC HEIGHT: 0.7 m
METRIC WEIGHT: 16.8 kg

POSSIBLE MOVES: Astonish, Bite, Blizzard, Crunch, Double Team, Frost Breath, Hail, Headbutt, Ice Fang, Ice Shard, Icy Wind, Leer, Powder Snow, Protect

SNORUNT

GLALIE

FROSLASS

MEGA GLALIE

SNOVER

Frost Tree Pokémon

TYPE: GRASS-ICE

It lives on snowy mountains. It sinks its legs into the snow to absorb water and keep its own temperature down.

The berries that grow around its belly are like ice pops. Galarian Darumaka absolutely love these berries.

HOW TO SAY IT: SNOW-vur
IMPERIAL HEIGHT: 3'03"
IMPERIAL WEIGHT: 111.3 lbs.
METRIC HEIGHT: 1.0 m
METRIC WEIGHT: 50.5 kg

POSSIBLE MOVES: Blizzard, Ice Shard, Icy Wind, Ingrain, Leafage, Leer, Mist, Powder Snow, Razor Leaf, Sheer Cold, Swagger, Wood Hammer

SNOVER

ABOMASNOW

MEGA ABOMASNOW

SNUBBULL

Fairy Pokémon

TYPE: FAIRY

It grows close to others easily and is also easily spoiled. The disparity between its face and its actions makes many young people wild about it.

In contrast to its appearance, it's quite timid. When playing with other puppy Pokémon, it sometimes gets bullied.

HOW TO SAY IT: SNUB-bull
IMPERIAL HEIGHT: 2'00"
IMPERIAL WEIGHT: 17.2 lbs.
METRIC HEIGHT: 0.6 m
METRIC WEIGHT: 7.8 kg

POSSIBLE MOVES: Ice Fang, Fire Fang, Thunder Fang, Tackle, Scary Face, Tail Whip, Charm, Bite, Lick, Headbutt, Roar, Rage, Play Rough, Payback, Crunch

SNUBBULL   GRANBULL

SOBBLE

Water Lizard Pokémon

TYPE: WATER

When scared, this Pokémon cries. Its tears pack the chemical punch of 100 onions, and attackers won't be able to resist weeping.

When it gets wet, its skin changes color, and this Pokémon becomes invisible as if it were camouflaged.

HOW TO SAY IT: SAH-bull
IMPERIAL HEIGHT: 1'00"
IMPERIAL WEIGHT: 8.8 lbs.
METRIC HEIGHT: 0.3 m
METRIC WEIGHT: 4.0 kg

POSSIBLE MOVES: Bind, Growl, Liquidation, Pound, Rain Dance, Soak, Sucker Punch, Tearful Look, U-turn, Water Gun, Water Pulse

SOBBLE   DRIZZILE   INTELEON

SOLGALEO

Sunne Pokémon

LEGENDARY POKÉMON

TYPE: PSYCHIC-STEEL

Sometimes the result of its opening an Ultra Wormhole is that energy and life-forms from other worlds are called here to this world. In writings from the distant past, it's called by the name "the beast that devours the sun."

HOW TO SAY IT: SOUL-gah-LAY-oh
IMPERIAL HEIGHT: 11'02"
IMPERIAL WEIGHT: 507.1 lbs.
METRIC HEIGHT: 3.4 m
METRIC WEIGHT: 230.0 kg

POSSIBLE MOVES: Sunsteel Strike, Cosmic Power, Wake-Up Slap, Teleport, Metal Claw, Iron Head, Metal Sound, Zen Headbutt, Flash Cannon, Morning Sun, Crunch, Metal Burst, Solar Beam, Noble Roar, Flare Blitz, Wide Guard, Giga Impact

COSMOG

COSMOEM

SOLGALEO

SOLOSIS
Cell Pokémon

TYPE: PSYCHIC

It communicates with others telepathically. Its body is encapsulated in liquid, but if it takes a heavy blow, the liquid will leak out.

Many say that the special liquid covering this Pokémon's body would allow it to survive in the vacuum of space.

HOW TO SAY IT: soh-LOH-sis
IMPERIAL HEIGHT: 1'00"
IMPERIAL WEIGHT: 2.2 lbs.
METRIC HEIGHT: 0.3 m
METRIC WEIGHT: 1.0 kg

POSSIBLE MOVES: Ally Switch, Charm, Confusion, Endeavor, Future Sight, Light Screen, Pain Split, Protect, Psybeam, Psychic, Psyshock, Recover, Reflect, Skill Swap, Wonder Room

| SOLOSIS | DUOSION | REUNICLUS |

SOLROCK
Meteorite Pokémon

TYPE: ROCK-PSYCHIC

When it rotates itself, it gives off light similar to the sun, thus blinding its foes.

Solar energy is the source of its power, so it is strong during the daytime. When it spins, its body shines.

HOW TO SAY IT: SOLE-rock
IMPERIAL HEIGHT: 3'11"
IMPERIAL WEIGHT: 339.5 lbs.
METRIC HEIGHT: 1.2 m
METRIC WEIGHT: 154.0 kg

POSSIBLE MOVES: Confusion, Cosmic Power, Explosion, Flare Blitz, Harden, Hypnosis, Morning Sun, Psychic, Rock Polish, Rock Slide, Rock Throw, Solar Beam, Stone Edge, Tackle, Wonder Room, Zen Headbutt

DOES NOT EVOLVE

SPEAROW

Tiny Bird Pokémon

TYPE: NORMAL-FLYING

Inept at flying high. However, it can fly around very fast to protect its territory.

HOW TO SAY IT: SPEER-oh
IMPERIAL HEIGHT: 1'00"
IMPERIAL WEIGHT: 4.4 lbs.
METRIC HEIGHT: 0.3 m
METRIC WEIGHT: 2.0 kg

POSSIBLE MOVES: Peck, Growl, Leer, Pursuit, Fury Attack, Aerial Ace, Mirror Move, Assurance, Agility, Focus Energy, Roost, Drill Peck

SPEAROW   FEAROW

SPEWPA

Scatterdust Pokémon

TYPE: BUG

It lives hidden within thicket shadows. When predators attack, it quickly bristles the fur covering its body in an effort to threaten them.

The beaks of bird Pokémon can't begin to scratch its stalwart body. To defend itself, it spews powder.

HOW TO SAY IT: SPEW-puh
IMPERIAL HEIGHT: 1'00"
IMPERIAL WEIGHT: 18.5 lbs.
METRIC HEIGHT: 0.3 m
METRIC WEIGHT: 8.4 kg

POSSIBLE MOVES: Harden, Protect

SCATTERBUG   SPEWPA   VIVILLON

SPHEAL

Clap Pokémon

TYPE: ICE-WATER

Spheal is much faster rolling than walking to get around. When groups of this Pokémon eat, they all clap at once to show their pleasure. Because of this, their mealtimes are noisy.

Spheal always travels by rolling around on its ball-like body. When the season for ice floes arrives, this Pokémon can be seen rolling about on ice and crossing the sea.

HOW TO SAY IT: SFEEL
IMPERIAL HEIGHT: 2'07"
IMPERIAL WEIGHT: 87.1 lbs.
METRIC HEIGHT: 0.8 m
METRIC WEIGHT: 39.5 kg

POSSIBLE MOVES: Defense Curl, Powder Snow, Growl, Water Gun, Rollout, Encore, Ice Ball, Body Slam, Aurora Beam, Hail, Rest, Snore, Blizzard, Sheer Cold, Brine

SPHEAL   SEALEO   WALREIN

SPINARAK

String Spit Pokémon

TYPE: BUG-POISON

With threads from its mouth, it fashions sturdy webs that won't break even if you set a rock on them.

Although the poison from its fangs isn't that strong, it's potent enough to weaken prey that gets caught in its web.

HOW TO SAY IT: SPIN-uh-rack
IMPERIAL HEIGHT: 1'08"
IMPERIAL WEIGHT: 18.7 lbs.
METRIC HEIGHT: 0.5 m
METRIC WEIGHT: 8.5 kg

POSSIBLE MOVES: Poison Sting, String Shot, Constrict, Absorb, Infestation, Scary Face, Night Shade, Shadow Sneak, Fury Swipes, Sucker Punch, Spider Web, Agility, Pin Missile, Psychic, Poison Jab, Cross Poison, Sticky Web, Toxic Thread

SPINARAK   ARIADOS

SPINDA

Spot Panda Pokémon

TYPE: NORMAL

Its steps are shaky and stumbling. Walking for a long time makes it feel sick.

Each Spinda's spot pattern is different. With its stumbling movements, it evades opponents' attacks brilliantly!

HOW TO SAY IT: SPIN-dah
IMPERIAL HEIGHT: 3'07"
IMPERIAL WEIGHT: 11.0 lbs.
METRIC HEIGHT: 1.1 m
METRIC WEIGHT: 5.0 kg

POSSIBLE MOVES: Tackle, Copycat, Feint Attack, Psybeam, Hypnosis, Dizzy Punch, Sucker Punch, Teeter Dance, Uproar, Psych Up, Double-Edge, Flail, Thrash

DOES NOT EVOLVE

SPIRITOMB

Forbidden Pokémon

TYPE: GHOST-DARK

A Pokémon that was formed by 108 spirits. It is bound to a fissure in an odd keystone.

It was bound to a fissure in an odd keystone as punishment for misdeeds 500 years ago.

HOW TO SAY IT: SPIR-it-tomb
IMPERIAL HEIGHT: 3'03"
IMPERIAL WEIGHT: 238.1 lbs.
METRIC HEIGHT: 1.0 m
METRIC WEIGHT: 108.0 kg

POSSIBLE MOVES: Curse, Pursuit, Confuse Ray. Spite, Shadow Sneak, Feint Attack, Hypnosis, Dream Eater, Ominous Wind, Sucker Punch, Nasty Plot, Memento, Dark Pulse

DOES NOT EVOLVE

SPOINK

Bounce Pokémon

TYPE: PSYCHIC

Spoink bounces around on its tail. The shock of its bouncing makes its heart pump. As a result, this Pokémon cannot afford to stop bouncing—if it stops, its heart will stop.

Spoink keeps a pearl on top of its head. The pearl functions to amplify this Pokémon's psychokinetic powers. It is therefore on a constant search for a bigger pearl.

HOW TO SAY IT: SPOINK   **METRIC HEIGHT:** 0.7 m
IMPERIAL HEIGHT: 2'04"   **METRIC WEIGHT:** 30.6 kg
IMPERIAL WEIGHT: 67.5 lbs.

POSSIBLE MOVES: Splash, Psywave, Odor Sleuth, Psybeam, Psych Up, Confuse Ray, Magic Coat, Zen Headbutt, Rest, Snore, Power Gem, Psyshock, Payback, Psychic, Bounce

SPOINK   GRUMPIG

SPRITZEE

Perfume Pokémon

TYPE: FAIRY

A scent pouch within this Pokémon's body allows it to create various scents. A change in its diet will alter the fragrance it produces.

The scent its body gives off enraptures those who smell it. Noble ladies had no shortage of love for Spritzee.

HOW TO SAY IT: SPRIT-zee   **METRIC HEIGHT:** 0.2 m
IMPERIAL HEIGHT: 0'08"   **METRIC WEIGHT:** 0.5 kg
IMPERIAL WEIGHT: 1.1 lbs.

POSSIBLE MOVES: Aromatherapy, Attract, Calm Mind, Charm, Draining Kiss, Echoed Voice, Fairy Wind, Flail, Misty Terrain, Moonblast, Psychic, Skill Swap, Sweet Kiss, Sweet Scent

SPRITZEE   AROMATISSE

SQUIRTLE
Tiny Turtle Pokémon

REGIONS:
KALOS
(CENTRAL)
KANTO

TYPE: WATER

When it retracts its long neck into its shell, it squirts out water with vigorous force.

When it feels threatened, it draws its limbs inside its shell and sprays water from its mouth.

HOW TO SAY IT: SKWIR-tul
IMPERIAL HEIGHT: 1'08"
IMPERIAL WEIGHT: 19.8 lbs.
METRIC HEIGHT: 0.5 m
METRIC WEIGHT: 9.0 kg

POSSIBLE MOVES: Tackle, Tail Whip, Water Gun, Withdraw, Bubble, Bite, Rapid Spin, Protect, Water Pulse, Aqua Tail, Skull Bash, Iron Defense, Rain Dance, Hydro Pump

SQUIRTLE   **WARTORTLE**   **BLASTOISE**   **MEGA BLASTOISE**

STAKATAKA
Rampart Pokémon

REGION:
ALOLA

ULTRA BEAST

TYPE: ROCK-STEEL

It appeared from an Ultra Wormhole. Each one appears to be made up of many life-forms stacked one on top of each other.

When stone walls started moving and attacking, the brute's true identity was this mysterious life-form, which brings to mind an Ultra Beast.

HOW TO SAY IT: STACK-uh-TACK-uh
IMPERIAL HEIGHT: 18'01"
IMPERIAL WEIGHT: 1,807.8 lbs.
METRIC HEIGHT: 5.5 m
METRIC WEIGHT: 820.0 kg

POSSIBLE MOVES: Protect, Tackle, Rock Slide, Stealth Rock, Bide, Take Down, Rock Throw, Autotomize, Iron Defense, Iron Head, Rock Blast, Wide Guard, Double-Edge

DOES NOT EVOLVE

STANTLER
Big Horn Pokémon

TYPE: NORMAL

Stantler's magnificent antlers were traded at high prices as works of art. As a result, this Pokémon was hunted close to extinction by those who were after the priceless antlers.

HOW TO SAY IT: STAN-tler
IMPERIAL HEIGHT: 4'07"
IMPERIAL WEIGHT: 157.0 lbs.
METRIC HEIGHT: 1.4 m
METRIC WEIGHT: 71.2 kg

POSSIBLE MOVES: Tackle, Leer, Astonish, Hypnosis, Stomp, Sand Attack, Take Down, Confuse Ray, Calm Mind, Role Play, Zen Headbutt, Jump Kick, Imprison, Captivate, Me First

DOES NOT EVOLVE

TYPE: NORMAL-FLYING

The muscles in its wings and legs are strong. It can easily fly while gripping a small Pokémon.

When Staravia evolve into Staraptor, they leave the flock to live alone. They have sturdy wings.

STARAPTOR
Predator Pokémon

HOW TO SAY IT: star-RAP-tor
IMPERIAL HEIGHT: 3'11"
IMPERIAL WEIGHT: 54.9 lbs.
METRIC HEIGHT: 1.2 m
METRIC WEIGHT: 24.9 kg

POSSIBLE MOVES: Tackle, Growl, Quick Attack, Wing Attack, Double Team, Endeavor, Whirlwind, Aerial Ace, Take Down, Close Combat, Agility, Brave Bird, Final Gambit

STARLY → **STARAVIA** → **STARAPTOR**

STARAVIA
Starling Pokémon

TYPE: NORMAL-FLYING

They maintain huge flocks, although fierce scuffles break out between various flocks.

It lives in forests and fields. Squabbles over territory occur when flocks collide.

HOW TO SAY IT: star-EY-vee-a
IMPERIAL HEIGHT: 2'00"
IMPERIAL WEIGHT: 34.2 lbs.
METRIC HEIGHT: 0.6 m
METRIC WEIGHT: 15.5 kg

POSSIBLE MOVES: Tackle, Growl, Quick Attack, Wing Attack, Double Team, Endeavor, Whirlwind, Aerial Ace, Take Down, Agility, Brave Bird, Final Gambit

STARLY → STARAVIA → STARAPTOR

STARLY
Starling Pokémon

TYPE: NORMAL-FLYING

They flock in great numbers. Though small, they flap their wings with great power.

They flock around mountains and fields, chasing after bug Pokémon. Their singing is noisy and annoying.

HOW TO SAY IT: STAR-lee
IMPERIAL HEIGHT: 1'00"
IMPERIAL WEIGHT: 4.4 lbs.
METRIC HEIGHT: 0.3 m
METRIC WEIGHT: 2.0 kg

POSSIBLE MOVES: Tackle, Growl, Quick Attack, Wing Attack, Double Team, Endeavor, Whirlwind, Aerial Ace, Take Down, Agility, Brave Bird, Final Gambit

STARLY → STARAVIA → STARAPTOR

STARMIE
Mysterious Pokémon

TYPE: WATER-PSYCHIC

This Pokémon has an organ known as its core. The organ glows in seven colors when Starmie is unleashing its potent psychic powers.

Starmie swims by spinning its body at high speed. As this Pokémon cruises through the ocean, it absorbs tiny plankton.

HOW TO SAY IT: STAR-mee   **METRIC HEIGHT:** 1.1 m
IMPERIAL HEIGHT: 3'07"   **METRIC WEIGHT:** 80.0 kg
IMPERIAL WEIGHT: 176.4 lbs.

POSSIBLE MOVES: Hydro Pump, Spotlight, Water Gun, Rapid Spin, Recover, Swift, Confuse Ray

STARYU   STARMIE

STARYU
Star Shape Pokémon

TYPE: WATER

If you visit a beach at the end of summer, you'll be able to see groups of Staryu lighting up in a steady rhythm.

Fish Pokémon nibble at it, but Staryu isn't bothered. Its body regenerates quickly, even if part of it is completely torn off.

HOW TO SAY IT: STAR-you   **METRIC HEIGHT:** 0.8 m
IMPERIAL HEIGHT: 2'07"   **METRIC WEIGHT:** 34.5 kg
IMPERIAL WEIGHT: 76.1 lbs.

POSSIBLE MOVES: Tackle, Harden, Water Gun, Rapid Spin, Recover, Psywave, Swift, Bubble Beam, Camouflage, Gyro Ball, Brine, Minimize, Reflect Type, Power Gem, Confuse Ray, Psychic, Light Screen, Cosmic Power, Hydro Pump

STARYU   STARMIE

STEELIX

Iron Snake Pokémon

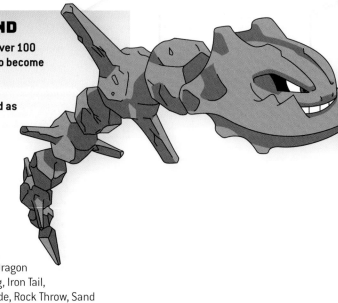

TYPE: STEEL-GROUND

It is said that if an Onix lives for over 100 years, its composition changes to become diamond-like.

It is thought its body transformed as a result of iron accumulating internally from swallowing soil.

HOW TO SAY IT: STEE-licks
IMPERIAL HEIGHT: 30'02"
IMPERIAL WEIGHT: 881.8 lbs.
METRIC HEIGHT: 9.2 m
METRIC WEIGHT: 400.0 kg

POSSIBLE MOVES: Autotomize, Bind, Crunch, Curse, Dig, Double-Edge, Dragon Breath, Fire Fang, Harden, Ice Fang, Iron Tail, Magnet Rise, Rock Polish, Rock Slide, Rock Throw, Sand Tomb, Sandstorm, Screech, Slam, Smack Down, Stealth Rock, Stone Edge, Tackle, Thunder Fang

MEGA STEELIX

Iron Snake Pokémon

TYPE: STEEL-GROUND

IMPERIAL HEIGHT: 34'05"
IMPERIAL WEIGHT: 1,631.4 lbs.
METRIC HEIGHT: 10.5 m
METRIC WEIGHT: 740.0 kg

ONIX → STEELIX → MEGA STEELIX

STEENEE
Fruit Pokémon

TYPE: GRASS

As it twirls like a dancer, a sweet smell spreads out around it. Anyone who inhales the scent will feel a surge of happiness.

Any Corvisquire that pecks at this Pokémon will be greeted with a smack from its sepals followed by a sharp kick.

HOW TO SAY IT: STEE-nee
IMPERIAL HEIGHT: 2'04"
IMPERIAL WEIGHT: 18.1 lbs.
METRIC HEIGHT: 0.7 m
METRIC WEIGHT: 8.2 kg

POSSIBLE MOVES: Aromatherapy, Aromatic Mist, Flail, Leaf Storm, Magical Leaf, Play Nice, Rapid Spin, Razor Leaf, Splash, Stomp, Sweet Scent, Teeter Dance

BOUNSWEET   STEENEE   TSAREENA

STONJOURNER
Big Rock Pokémon

REGION:
GALAR

TYPE: ROCK

It stands in grasslands, watching the sun's descent from zenith to horizon. This Pokémon has a talent for delivering dynamic kicks.

Once a year, on a specific date and at a specific time, they gather out of nowhere and form up in a circle.

HOW TO SAY IT: STONE-jer-ner
IMPERIAL HEIGHT: 8'02"
IMPERIAL WEIGHT: 1146.4 lbs.
METRIC HEIGHT: 2.5 m
METRIC WEIGHT: 520.0 kg

POSSIBLE MOVES: Block, Body Slam, Gravity, Heavy Slam, Mega Kick, Rock Polish, Rock Slide, Rock Throw, Rock Tomb, Stealth Rock, Stomp, Stone Edge, Wide Guard

DOES NOT EVOLVE

STOUTLAND

Big-Hearted Pokémon

TYPE: NORMAL

These Pokémon seem to enjoy living with humans. Even a Stoutland caught in the wild will warm up to people in about three days.

Stoutland is immensely proud of its impressive mustache. It's said that mustache length is what determines social standing among this species.

HOW TO SAY IT: STOWT-lund
IMPERIAL HEIGHT: 3'11"
IMPERIAL WEIGHT: 134.5 lbs.
METRIC HEIGHT: 1.2 m
METRIC WEIGHT: 61.0 kg

POSSIBLE MOVES: Ice Fang, Fire Fang, Thunder Fang, Leer, Tackle, Odor Sleuth, Bite, Helping Hand, Take Down, Work Up, Crunch, Roar, Retaliate, Reversal, Last Resort, Giga Impact, Play Rough

LILLIPUP ➡ HERDIER ➡ STOUTLAND

STUFFUL

Flailing Pokémon

TYPE: NORMAL-FIGHTING

Its fluffy fur is a delight to pet, but carelessly reaching out to touch this Pokémon could result in painful retaliation.

The way it protects itself by flailing its arms may be an adorable sight, but stay well away. This is flailing that can snap thick tree trunks.

HOW TO SAY IT: STUFF-fuhl
IMPERIAL HEIGHT: 1'08"
IMPERIAL WEIGHT: 15.0 lbs.
METRIC HEIGHT: 0.5 m
METRIC WEIGHT: 6.8 kg

POSSIBLE MOVES: Baby-Doll Eyes, Brutal Swing, Double-Edge, Endure, Flail, Hammer Arm, Leer, Pain Split, Payback, Strength, Superpower, Tackle, Take Down, Thrash

STUFFUL ➡ BEWEAR

STUNFISK
Trap Pokémon

TYPE: GROUND-ELECTRIC

Thanks to bacteria that lived in the mud flats with it, this Pokémon developed the organs it uses to generate electricity.

For some reason, this Pokémon smiles slightly when it emits a strong electric current from the yellow markings on its body.

HOW TO SAY IT: STUN-fisk **METRIC HEIGHT:** 0.7 m
IMPERIAL HEIGHT: 2'04" **METRIC WEIGHT:** 11.0 kg
IMPERIAL WEIGHT: 24.3 lbs.

POSSIBLE MOVES: Bounce, Charge, Discharge, Electric Terrain, Endure, Fissure, Flail, Mud Shot, Muddy Water, Mud-Slap, Revenge, Sucker Punch, Tackle, Thunder Shock, Water Gun

DOES NOT EVOLVE

GALARIAN STUNFISK
Trap Pokémon

TYPE: GROUND-STEEL

Living in mud with a high iron content has given it a strong steel body.

Its conspicuous lips lure prey in as it lies in wait in the mud. When prey gets close, Stunfisk clamps its jagged steel fins down on them.

HOW TO SAY IT: STUN-fisk
IMPERIAL HEIGHT: 2'04"
IMPERIAL WEIGHT: 45.2 lbs.
METRIC HEIGHT: 0.7 m
METRIC WEIGHT: 20.5 kg

POSSIBLE MOVES: Bounce, Endure, Fissure, Flail, Iron Defense, Metal Claw, Metal Sound, Mud Shot, Muddy Water, Mud-Slap, Revenge, Snap Trap, Sucker Punch, Tackle, Water Gun

DOES NOT EVOLVE

STUNKY

Skunk Pokémon

REGIONS:
GALAR
KALOS
(COASTAL)
SINNOH

TYPE: POISON-DARK

From its rear, it sprays a foul-smelling liquid at opponents. It aims for their faces, and it can hit them from over 16 feet away.

If it lifts its tail and points its rear at you, beware. It's about to spray you with a fluid stinky enough to make you faint.

HOW TO SAY IT: STUNK-ee
IMPERIAL HEIGHT: 1'04"
IMPERIAL WEIGHT: 42.3 lbs.
METRIC HEIGHT: 0.4 m
METRIC WEIGHT: 19.2 kg

POSSIBLE MOVES: Acid Spray, Belch, Bite, Explosion, Feint, Focus Energy, Fury Swipes, Memento, Night Slash, Poison Gas, Scratch, Screech, Smokescreen, Sucker Punch, Toxic, Venom Drench, Venoshock

STUNKY → SKUNTANK

SUDOWOODO

Imitation Pokémon

REGIONS:
ALOLA
GALAR
JOHTO
KALOS
(MOUNTAIN)

TYPE: ROCK

If a tree branch shakes when there is no wind, it's a Sudowoodo, not a tree. It hides from the rain.

It disguises itself as a tree to avoid attack. It hates water, so it will disappear if it starts raining.

HOW TO SAY IT: SOO-doe-WOO-doe
IMPERIAL HEIGHT: 3'11"
IMPERIAL WEIGHT: 83.8 lbs.
METRIC HEIGHT: 1.2 m
METRIC WEIGHT: 38.0 kg

POSSIBLE MOVES: Block, Copycat, Counter, Double-Edge, Fake Tears, Flail, Hammer Arm, Head Smash, Low Kick, Mimic, Rock Slide, Rock Throw, Rock Tomb, Slam, Stone Edge, Sucker Punch, Tearful Look, Wood Hammer

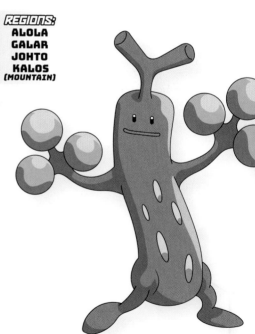

BONSLY   SUDOWOODO

SUICUNE
Aurora Pokémon

TYPE: WATER

Suicune embodies the compassion of a pure spring of water. It runs across the land with gracefulness. This Pokémon has the power to purify dirty water.

HOW TO SAY IT: SWEE-koon
IMPERIAL HEIGHT: 6'07"
IMPERIAL WEIGHT: 412.3 lbs.
METRIC HEIGHT: 2.0 m
METRIC WEIGHT: 187.0 kg

POSSIBLE MOVES: Sheer Cold, Bite, Leer, Bubble Beam, Rain Dance, Gust, Aurora Beam, Mist, Mirror Coat, Ice Fang, Tailwind, Extrasensory, Hydro Pump, Calm Mind, Blizzard

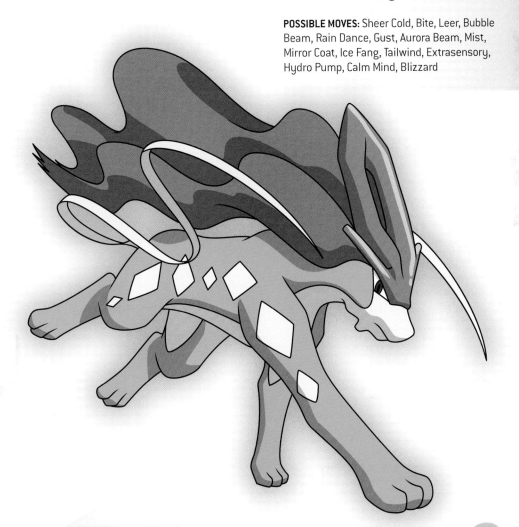

DOES NOT EVOLVE

SUNFLORA

Sun Pokémon

TYPE: GRASS

Sunflora converts solar energy into nutrition. It moves around actively in the daytime when it is warm. It stops moving as soon as the sun goes down for the night.

HOW TO SAY IT: SUN-FLOR-uh
IMPERIAL HEIGHT: 2'07"
IMPERIAL WEIGHT: 18.7 lbs.
METRIC HEIGHT: 0.8 m
METRIC WEIGHT: 8.5 kg

POSSIBLE MOVES: Flower Shield, Absorb, Pound, Growth, Ingrain, Grass Whistle, Mega Drain, Leech Seed, Razor Leaf, Worry Seed, Giga Drain, Bullet Seed, Petal Dance, Natural Gift, Solar Beam, Double-Edge, Sunny Day, Leaf Storm, Petal Blizzard

SUNKERN   SUNFLORA

SUNKERN

Seed Pokémon

TYPE: GRASS

Sunkern tries to move as little as it possibly can. It does so because it tries to conserve all the nutrients it has stored in its body for its Evolution. It will not eat a thing, subsisting only on morning dew.

HOW TO SAY IT: SUN-kurn
IMPERIAL HEIGHT: 1'00"
IMPERIAL WEIGHT: 4.0 lbs.
METRIC HEIGHT: 0.3 m
METRIC WEIGHT: 1.8 kg

POSSIBLE MOVES: Absorb, Growth, Mega Drain, Ingrain, Grass Whistle, Leech Seed, Endeavor, Worry Seed, Razor Leaf, Synthesis, Sunny Day, Giga Drain, Seed Bomb, Natural Gift, Double-Edge, Solar Beam

SUNKERN   SUNFLORA

TYPE: BUG-WATER

SURSKIT
Pond Skater Pokémon

If it's in a pinch, it will secrete a sweet liquid from the tip of its head. Syrup made from gathering that liquid is tasty on bread.

It lives in ponds and marshes that feature lots of plant life. It often fights with Dewpider, whose habitat and diet are similar.

HOW TO SAY IT: SUR-skit
IMPERIAL HEIGHT: 1'08"
IMPERIAL WEIGHT: 3.7 lbs.
METRIC HEIGHT: 0.5 m
METRIC WEIGHT: 1.7 kg

POSSIBLE MOVES: Bubble, Quick Attack, Sweet Scent, Water Sport, Bubble Beam, Agility, Mist, Haze, Aqua Jet, Baton Pass, Sticky Web

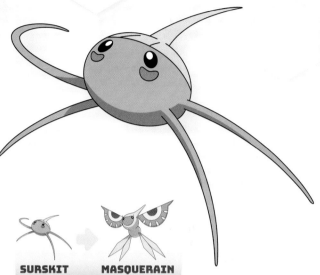

SURSKIT → MASQUERAIN

TYPE: NORMAL-FLYING

SWABLU
Cotton Bird Pokémon

Swablu has light and fluffy wings that are like cottony clouds. This Pokémon is not frightened of people. It lands on the heads of people and sits there like a cotton-fluff hat.

Swablu loves to make things clean. If it spots something dirty, it will wipe and polish it with its cottony wings. If its wings become dirty, this Pokémon finds a stream and showers itself.

HOW TO SAY IT: swah-BLUE
IMPERIAL HEIGHT: 1'04"
IMPERIAL WEIGHT: 2.6 lbs.
METRIC HEIGHT: 0.4 m
METRIC WEIGHT: 1.2 kg

POSSIBLE MOVES: Peck, Growl, Astonish, Sing, Fury Attack, Safeguard, Disarming Voice, Mist, Round, Natural Gift, Take Down, Refresh, Mirror Move, Cotton Guard, Dragon Pulse, Perish Song, Moonblast

SWABLU → ALTARIA → MEGA ALTARIA

SWADLOON

Leaf-Wrapped Pokémon

REGION:
UNOVA

TYPE: BUG-GRASS

Forests where Swadloon live have superb foliage because the nutrients they make from fallen leaves nourish the plant life.

It protects itself from the cold by wrapping up in leaves. It stays on the move, eating leaves in forests.

HOW TO SAY IT: SWAHD-loon
IMPERIAL HEIGHT: 1'08"
IMPERIAL WEIGHT: 16.1 lbs.
METRIC HEIGHT: 0.5 m
METRIC WEIGHT: 7.3 kg

POSSIBLE MOVES: Grass Whistle, Tackle, String Shot, Bug Bite, Razor Leaf, Protect

SEWADDLE   SWADLOON   LEAVANNY

SWALOT

Poison Bag Pokémon

REGIONS:
HOENN
KALOS
(COASTAL)

TYPE: POISON

When Swalot spots prey, it spurts out a hideously toxic fluid from its pores and sprays the target. Once the prey has weakened, this Pokémon gulps it down whole with its cavernous mouth.

Swalot has no teeth, so what it eats, it swallows whole, no matter what. Its cavernous mouth yawns widely. An automobile tire could easily fit inside this Pokémon's mouth.

HOW TO SAY IT: SWAH-lot   **METRIC HEIGHT:** 1.7 m
IMPERIAL HEIGHT: 5'07"   **METRIC WEIGHT:** 80.0 kg
IMPERIAL WEIGHT: 176.4 lbs.

POSSIBLE MOVES: Body Slam, Venom Drench, Gunk Shot, Wring Out, Pound, Yawn, Poison Gas, Sludge, Amnesia, Acid Spray, Encore, Toxic, Stockpile, Spit Up, Swallow, Sludge Bomb, Gastro Acid, Belch

GULPIN   SWALOT

TYPE: WATER-GROUND

Swampert is very strong. It has enough power to easily drag a boulder weighing more than a ton. This Pokémon also has powerful vision that lets it see even in murky water.

Swampert predicts storms by sensing subtle differences in the sounds of waves and tidal winds with its fins. If a storm is approaching, it piles up boulders to protect itself.

HOW TO SAY IT: SWAM-pert
IMPERIAL HEIGHT: 4'11"
IMPERIAL WEIGHT: 180.6 lbs.
METRIC HEIGHT: 1.5 m
METRIC WEIGHT: 81.9 kg

POSSIBLE MOVES: Mud Shot, Hammer Arm, Tackle, Growl, Water Gun, Mud-Slap, Foresight, Bide, Mud Bomb, Rock Slide, Protect, Muddy Water, Take Down, Earthquake, Endeavor

SWAMPERT
Mud Fish Pokémon

MEGA SWAMPERT
Mud Fish Pokémon

TYPE: WATER-GROUND

IMPERIAL HEIGHT: 6'03"
IMPERIAL WEIGHT: 224.9 lbs.
METRIC HEIGHT: 1.9 m
METRIC WEIGHT: 102.0 kg

MUDKIP → **MARSHTOMP** → **SWAMPERT** → **MEGA SWAMPERT**

SWANNA

White Bird Pokémon

TYPE: WATER-FLYING

Despite their elegant appearance, they can flap their wings strongly and fly for thousands of miles.

Swanna start to dance at dusk. The one dancing in the middle is the leader of the flock.

HOW TO SAY IT: SWAH-nuh
IMPERIAL HEIGHT: 4'03"
IMPERIAL WEIGHT: 53.4 lbs.
METRIC HEIGHT: 1.3 m
METRIC WEIGHT: 24.2 kg

POSSIBLE MOVES: Water Gun, Water Sport, Defog, Wing Attack, Water Pulse, Aerial Ace, Bubble Beam, Feather Dance, Aqua Ring, Air Slash, Roost, Rain Dance, Tailwind, Brave Bird, Hurricane

DUCKLETT → **SWANNA**

SWELLOW

Swallow Pokémon

TYPE: NORMAL-FLYING

Swellow flies high above our heads, making graceful arcs in the sky. This Pokémon dives at a steep angle as soon as it spots its prey. The hapless prey is tightly grasped by Swellow's clawed feet, preventing escape.

Swellow is very conscientious about the upkeep of its glossy wings. Once two Swellow are gathered, they diligently take care of cleaning each other's wings.

HOW TO SAY IT: SWELL-low
IMPERIAL HEIGHT: 2'04"
IMPERIAL WEIGHT: 43.7 lbs.
METRIC HEIGHT: 0.7 m
METRIC WEIGHT: 19.8 kg

POSSIBLE MOVES: Air Slash, Pluck, Peck, Growl, Focus Energy, Quick Attack, Wing Attack, Double Team, Endeavor, Aerial Ace, Agility, Quick Guard, Brave Bird, Reversal

TAILLOW → **SWELLOW**

TYPE: ICE-GROUND

It rubs its snout on the ground to find and dig up food. It sometimes discovers hot springs.

If it smells something enticing, it dashes off headlong to find the source of the aroma.

HOW TO SAY IT: SWY-nub
IMPERIAL HEIGHT: 1'04"
IMPERIAL WEIGHT: 14.3 lbs.
METRIC HEIGHT: 0.4 m
METRIC WEIGHT: 6.5 kg

POSSIBLE MOVES: Amnesia, Blizzard, Earthquake, Endure, Flail, Ice Shard, Icy Wind, Mist, Mud-Slap, Powder Snow, Tackle, Take Down

REGIONS:
GALAR
JOHTO
KALOS
(MOUNTAIN)

SWINUB
Pig Pokémon

SWINUB ➡ **PILOSWINE** ➡ **MAMOSWINE**

REGIONS:
GALAR
KALOS
(CENTRAL)

SWIRLIX
Cotton Candy Pokémon

TYPE: FAIRY

It eats its own weight in sugar every day. If it doesn't get enough sugar, it becomes incredibly grumpy.

The sweet smell of cotton candy perfumes Swirlix's fluffy fur. This Pokémon spits out sticky string to tangle up its enemies.

HOW TO SAY IT: SWUR-licks
IMPERIAL HEIGHT: 1'04"
IMPERIAL WEIGHT: 7.7 lbs.
METRIC HEIGHT: 0.4 m
METRIC WEIGHT: 3.5 kg

POSSIBLE MOVES: Aromatherapy, Cotton Guard, Cotton Spore, Draining Kiss, Endeavor, Energy Ball, Fairy Wind, Fake Tears, Play Nice, Play Rough, Round, String Shot, Sweet Scent, Tackle, Wish

SWIRLIX **SLURPUFF**

SWOOBAT

Courting Pokémon

TYPE: PSYCHIC-FLYING

Emitting powerful sound waves tires it out. Afterward, it won't be able to fly for a little while.

The auspicious shape of this Pokémon's nose apparently led some regions to consider Swoobat a symbol of good luck.

HOW TO SAY IT: SWOO-bat
IMPERIAL HEIGHT: 2'11"
IMPERIAL WEIGHT: 23.1 lbs.
METRIC HEIGHT: 0.9 m
METRIC WEIGHT: 10.5 kg

POSSIBLE MOVES: Air Cutter, Air Slash, Amnesia, Assurance, Attract, Calm Mind, Confusion, Endeavor, Future Sight, Gust, Imprison, Psychic, Simple Beam

WOOBAT → SWOOBAT

SYLVEON

Intertwining Pokémon

TYPE: FAIRY

By releasing enmity-erasing waves from its ribbonlike feelers, Sylveon stops any conflict.

There's a Galarian fairy tale that describes a beautiful Sylveon vanquishing a dreadful dragon Pokémon.

HOW TO SAY IT: SIL-vee-on
IMPERIAL HEIGHT: 3'03"
IMPERIAL WEIGHT: 51.8 lbs.
METRIC HEIGHT: 1.0 m
METRIC WEIGHT: 23.5 kg

POSSIBLE MOVES: Baby-Doll Eyes, Baton Pass, Bite, Charm, Copycat, Covet, Disarming Voice, Double-Edge, Draining Kiss, Growl, Helping Hand, Last Resort, Light Screen, Misty Terrain, Moonblast, Psych Up, Quick Attack, Sand Attack, Skill Swap, Swift, Tackle, Tail Whip, Take Down

EEVEE → SYLVEON

TYPE: NORMAL-FLYING

TAILLOW
Tiny Swallow Pokémon

Taillow courageously stands its ground against foes, however strong they may be. This gutsy Pokémon will remain defiant even after a loss. On the other hand, it cries loudly if it becomes hungry.

Taillow is young—it has only just left its nest. As a result, it sometimes becomes lonesome and cries at night. This Pokémon feeds on Wurmple that live in forests.

HOW TO SAY IT: TAY-low
IMPERIAL HEIGHT: 1'00"
IMPERIAL WEIGHT: 5.1 lbs.
METRIC HEIGHT: 0.3 m
METRIC WEIGHT: 2.3 kg

POSSIBLE MOVES: Peck, Growl, Focus Energy, Quick Attack, Wing Attack, Double Team, Endeavor, Aerial Ace, Agility, Air Slash, Brave Bird, Reversal

TAILLOW   SWELLOW

TYPE:
FIRE-FLYING

TALONFLAME
Scorching Pokémon

Talonflame mainly preys upon other bird Pokémon. To intimidate opponents, it sends embers spewing from gaps between its feathers.

Talonflame dives toward prey at speeds of up to 310 mph and assaults them with powerful kicks, giving the prey no chance to escape.

HOW TO SAY IT: TAL-un-flame
IMPERIAL HEIGHT: 3'11"
IMPERIAL WEIGHT: 54.0 lbs.
METRIC HEIGHT: 1.2 m
METRIC WEIGHT: 24.5 kg

POSSIBLE MOVES: Ember, Brave Bird, Flare Blitz, Tackle, Growl, Quick Attack, Peck, Agility, Flail, Roost, Razor Wind, Natural Gift, Flame Charge, Acrobatics, Me First, Tailwind, Steel Wing

FLETCHLING   FLETCHINDER   TALONFLAME

TANGELA

Vine Pokémon

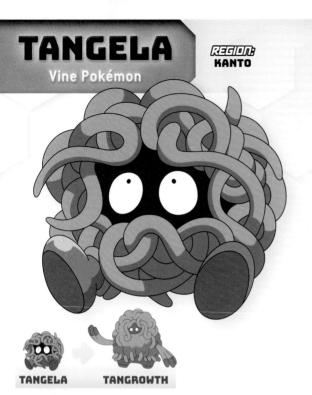

TYPE: GRASS

Hidden beneath a tangle of vines that grows nonstop even if the vines are torn off, this Pokémon's true appearance remains a mystery.

The vines of a Tangela have a distinct scent. In some parts of Galar, Tangela vines are used as herbs.

HOW TO SAY IT: TANG-ghel-a
IMPERIAL HEIGHT: 3'03"
IMPERIAL WEIGHT: 77.2 lbs.
METRIC HEIGHT: 1.0 m
METRIC WEIGHT: 35.0 kg

POSSIBLE MOVES: Ingrain, Constrict, Sleep Powder, Absorb, Growth, Poison Powder, Vine Whip, Bind, Mega Drain, Stun Spore, Knock Off, Ancient Power, Natural Gift, Slam, Tickle, Wring Out, Power Whip, Grassy Terrain, Giga Drain

TANGELA   TANGROWTH

TANGROWTH

Vine Pokémon

TYPE: GRASS

Tangrowth has two arms that it can extend as it pleases. Recent research has shown that these arms are, in fact, bundles of vines.

Vine growth is accelerated for Tangrowth living in warm climates. If the vines grow long, Tangrowth shortens them by tearing parts of them off.

HOW TO SAY IT: TANG-growth
IMPERIAL HEIGHT: 6'07"
IMPERIAL WEIGHT: 283.5 lbs.
METRIC HEIGHT: 2.0 m
METRIC WEIGHT: 128.6 kg

POSSIBLE MOVES: Block, Ingrain, Constrict, Sleep Powder, Vine Whip, Absorb, Poison Powder, Bind, Growth, Mega Drain, Knock Off, Stun Spore, Natural Gift, Giga Drain, Ancient Power, Slam, Tickle, Wring Out, Grassy Terrain, Power Whip

TANGELA   TANGROWTH

REGION:
ALOLA

TAPU BULU
Land Spirit Pokémon

TYPE: GRASS-FAIRY

Although it's called a guardian deity, it's violent enough to crush anyone it sees as an enemy.

It makes ringing sounds with its tail to let others know where it is, avoiding unneeded conflicts. This guardian deity of Ula'ula controls plants.

HOW TO SAY IT: TAH-poo BOO-loo
IMPERIAL HEIGHT: 6'03"
IMPERIAL WEIGHT: 100.3 lbs.
METRIC HEIGHT: 1.9 m
METRIC WEIGHT: 45.5 kg

POSSIBLE MOVES: Grassy Terrain, Wood Hammer, Superpower, Mean Look, Disable, Whirlwind, Withdraw, Leafage, Horn Attack, Giga Drain, Scary Face, Leech Seed, Horn Leech, Rototiller, Nature's Madness, Zen Headbutt, Megahorn, Skull Bash

DOES NOT EVOLVE

REGION:
ALOLA

TAPU FINI
Land Spirit Pokémon

TYPE: WATER-FAIRY

This guardian deity of Poni Island manipulates water. Because it lives deep within a thick fog, it came to be both feared and revered.

Although it's called a guardian deity, terrible calamities sometimes befall those who recklessly approach Tapu Fini.

HOW TO SAY IT: TAH-poo FEE-nee   **METRIC HEIGHT:** 1.3 m
IMPERIAL HEIGHT: 4'03"   **METRIC WEIGHT:** 21.2 kg
IMPERIAL WEIGHT: 46.7 lbs.

POSSIBLE MOVES: Misty Terrain, Moonblast, Heal Pulse, Mean Look, Haze, Mist, Withdraw, Water Gun, Water Pulse, Whirlpool, Soak, Refresh, Brine, Defog, Nature's Madness, Muddy Water, Aqua Ring, Hydro Pump

DOES NOT EVOLVE

TAPU KOKO
Land Spirit Pokémon

LEGENDARY POKÉMON

TYPE: ELECTRIC-FAIRY

Although it's called a guardian deity, if a person or Pokémon puts it in a bad mood, it will become a malevolent deity and attack.

The lightning-wielding guardian deity of Melemele, Tapu Koko is brimming with curiosity and appears before people from time to time.

HOW TO SAY IT: TAH-poo KO-ko
IMPERIAL HEIGHT: 5'11"
IMPERIAL WEIGHT: 45.2 lbs.
METRIC HEIGHT: 1.8 m
METRIC WEIGHT: 20.5 kg

POSSIBLE MOVES: Electric Terrain, Brave Bird, Power Swap, Mean Look, Quick Attack, False Swipe, Withdraw, Thunder Shock, Spark, Shock Wave, Screech, Charge, Wild Charge, Mirror Move, Nature's Madness, Discharge, Agility, Electro Ball

DOES NOT EVOLVE

LEGENDARY POKÉMON

TAPU LELE
Land Spirit Pokémon

TYPE: PSYCHIC-FAIRY

It heals the wounds of people and Pokémon by sprinkling them with its sparkling scales. This guardian deity is worshiped on Akala.

Although called a guardian deity, Tapu Lele is devoid of guilt about its cruel disposition and can be described as nature incarnate.

HOW TO SAY IT: TAH-poo LEH-leh
IMPERIAL HEIGHT: 3'11"
IMPERIAL WEIGHT: 41.0 lbs.
METRIC HEIGHT: 1.2 m
METRIC WEIGHT: 18.6 kg

POSSIBLE MOVES: Psychic Terrain, Aromatic Mist, Aromatherapy, Mean Look, Draining Kiss, Astonish, Withdraw, Confusion, Psywave, Psybeam, Sweet Scent, Skill Swap, Psyshock, Tickle, Nature's Madness, Extrasensory, Flatter, Moonblast

DOES NOT EVOLVE

TAUROS
Wild Bull Pokémon

TYPE: NORMAL

When Tauros begins whipping itself with its tails, it's a warning that the Pokémon is about to charge with astounding speed.

The Tauros of the Galar region are volatile in nature, and they won't allow people to ride on their backs.

HOW TO SAY IT: TORE-ros **METRIC HEIGHT:** 1.4 m
IMPERIAL HEIGHT: 4'07" **METRIC WEIGHT:** 88.4 kg
IMPERIAL WEIGHT: 194.9 lbs.

POSSIBLE MOVES: Tackle, Tail Whip, Rage, Horn Attack, Scary Face, Pursuit, Rest, Payback, Work Up, Zen Headbutt, Take Down, Swagger, Thrash, Giga Impact, Double-Edge

DOES NOT EVOLVE

TEDDIURSA
Little Bear Pokémon

TYPE: NORMAL

This Pokémon likes to lick its palms that are sweetened by being soaked in honey.

Teddiursa concocts its own honey by blending fruits and pollen collected by Beedrill.

HOW TO SAY IT: TED-dy-UR-sa **METRIC HEIGHT:** 0.6 m
IMPERIAL HEIGHT: 2'00" **METRIC WEIGHT:** 8.8 kg
IMPERIAL WEIGHT: 19.4 lbs.

POSSIBLE MOVES: Fling, Covet, Scratch, Baby-Doll Eyes, Lick, Fake Tears, Fury Swipes, Feint Attack, Sweet Scent, Play Nice, Slash, Charm, Rest, Snore, Thrash

TEDDIURSA   URSARING

TENTACOOL

Jellyfish Pokémon

TYPE: WATER-POISON

Tentacool is not a particularly strong swimmer. It drifts across the surface of shallow seas as it searches for prey.

This Pokémon is mostly made of water. A Tentacool out in the ocean is very hard to spot, because its body blends in with the sea.

HOW TO SAY IT: TEN-ta-cool
IMPERIAL HEIGHT: 2'11"
IMPERIAL WEIGHT: 100.3 lbs.
METRIC HEIGHT: 0.9 m
METRIC WEIGHT: 45.5 kg

POSSIBLE MOVES: Poison Sting, Supersonic, Constrict, Acid, Toxic Spikes, Water Pulse, Wrap, Acid Spray, Bubble Beam, Barrier, Poison Jab, Brine, Screech, Hex, Sludge Wave, Hydro Pump, Wring Out

TENTACOOL → TENTACRUEL

TENTACRUEL

Jellyfish Pokémon

TYPE: WATER-POISON

When the red orbs on Tentacruel's head glow brightly, watch out. The Pokémon is about to fire off a burst of ultrasonic waves.

Its 80 tentacles can stretch and shrink freely. Tentacruel ensnares prey in a net of spread-out tentacles, delivering venomous stings to its catch.

HOW TO SAY IT: TEN-ta-crool
IMPERIAL HEIGHT: 5'03"
IMPERIAL WEIGHT: 121.3 lbs.
METRIC HEIGHT: 1.6 m
METRIC WEIGHT: 55.0 kg

POSSIBLE MOVES: Reflect Type, Wring Out, Poison Sting, Supersonic, Constrict, Acid, Toxic Spikes, Water Pulse, Wrap, Acid Spray, Bubble Beam, Barrier, Poison Jab, Brine, Screech, Hex, Sludge Wave, Hydro Pump

TENTACOOL → TENTACRUEL

TYPE: FIRE

TEPIG
Fire Pig Pokémon

It can deftly dodge its foe's attacks while shooting fireballs from its nose. It roasts berries before it eats them.

It loves to eat roasted berries, but sometimes it gets too excited and burns them to a crisp.

HOW TO SAY IT: TEH-pig
IMPERIAL HEIGHT: 1'08"
IMPERIAL WEIGHT: 21.8 lbs.
METRIC HEIGHT: 0.5 m
METRIC WEIGHT: 9.9 kg

POSSIBLE MOVES: Tackle, Tail Whip, Ember, Odor Sleuth, Defense Curl, Flame Charge, Smog, Rollout, Take Down, Heat Crash, Assurance, Flamethrower, Head Smash, Roar, Flare Blitz

TEPIG   **PIGNITE**   **EMBOAR**

TERRAKION
Cavern Pokémon

LEGENDARY POKÉMON

TYPE: ROCK-FIGHTING

Its charge is strong enough to break through a giant castle wall in one blow. This Pokémon is spoken of in legends.

Spoken of in legend, this Pokémon used its phenomenal power to destroy a castle in its effort to protect Pokémon.

HOW TO SAY IT: tur-RAK-ee-un
IMPERIAL HEIGHT: 6'03"
IMPERIAL WEIGHT: 573.2 lbs.
METRIC HEIGHT: 1.9 m
METRIC WEIGHT: 260.0 kg

POSSIBLE MOVES: Quick Attack, Leer, Double Kick, Smack Down, Take Down, Helping Hand, Retaliate, Rock Slide, Sacred Sword, Swords Dance, Quick Guard, Work Up, Stone Edge, Close Combat

DOES NOT EVOLVE

THIEVUL

Fox Pokémon

TYPE: DARK

It secretly marks potential targets with a scent. By following the scent, it stalks its targets and steals from them when they least expect it.

With a lithe body and sharp claws, it goes around stealing food and eggs. Boltund is its natural enemy.

HOW TO SAY IT: THEEV-ull
IMPERIAL HEIGHT: 3'11"
IMPERIAL WEIGHT: 43.9 lbs.
METRIC HEIGHT: 1.2 m
METRIC WEIGHT: 19.9 kg

POSSIBLE MOVES: Assurance, Beat Up, Foul Play, Hone Claws, Nasty Plot, Night Slash, Parting Shot, Quick Attack, Snarl, Sucker Punch, Tail Slap, Tail Whip, Thief

NICKIT   **THIEVUL**

THROH

Judo Pokémon

TYPE: FIGHTING

It performs throwing moves with first-rate skill. Over the course of many battles, Throh's belt grows darker as it absorbs its wearer's sweat.

They train in groups of five. Any member that can't keep up will discard its belt and leave the group.

HOW TO SAY IT: THROH
IMPERIAL HEIGHT: 4'03"
IMPERIAL WEIGHT: 122.4 lbs.
METRIC HEIGHT: 1.3 m
METRIC WEIGHT: 55.5 kg

POSSIBLE MOVES: Bind, Bulk Up, Circle Throw, Endure, Focus Energy, Leer, Revenge, Reversal, Seismic Toss, Storm Throw, Superpower, Vital Throw, Wide Guard

DOES NOT EVOLVE

THUNDURUS
Bolt Strike Pokémon

INCARNATE FORME

TYPE: ELECTRIC-FLYING

The spikes on its tail discharge immense bolts of lightning. It flies around the Unova region firing off lightning bolts.

As it flies around, it shoots lightning all over the place and causes forest fires. It is therefore disliked.

HOW TO SAY IT: THUN-duh-rus
IMPERIAL HEIGHT: Incarnate Forme: 4'11" /
                     Therian Forme: 9'10"
IMPERIAL WEIGHT: 134.5 lbs.
METRIC HEIGHT: Incarnate Forme: 1.5 m /
                     Therian Forme: 3.0m
METRIC WEIGHT: 61.0 kg

POSSIBLE MOVES: Uproar, Astonish, Thunder Shock, Swagger, Bite, Revenge, Shock Wave, Heal Block, Agility, Discharge, Crunch, Charge, Nasty Plot, Thunder, Dark Pulse, Hammer Arm, Thrash

THERIAN FORME

DOES NOT EVOLVE

THWACKEY
Beat Pokémon

TYPE: GRASS

The faster a Thwackey can beat out a rhythm with its two sticks, the more respect it wins from its peers.

When it's drumming out rapid beats in battle, it gets so caught up in the rhythm that it won't even notice that it's already knocked out its opponent.

HOW TO SAY IT: THWAK-ee
IMPERIAL HEIGHT: 2'04"
IMPERIAL WEIGHT: 30.9 lbs.
METRIC HEIGHT: 0.7 m
METRIC WEIGHT: 14.0 kg

POSSIBLE MOVES: Branch Poke, Double Hit, Endeavor, Growl, Knock Off, Razor Leaf, Scratch, Screech, Slam, Taunt, Uproar, Wood Hammer

GROOKEY ⟶ THWACKEY ⟶ RILLABOOM

TIMBURR

Muscular Pokémon

TYPE: FIGHTING

It loves helping out with construction projects. It loves it so much that if rain causes work to halt, it swings its log around and throws a tantrum.

Timburr that have started carrying logs that are about three times their size are nearly ready to evolve.

HOW TO SAY IT: TIM-bur
IMPERIAL HEIGHT: 2'00"
IMPERIAL WEIGHT: 27.6 lbs.
METRIC HEIGHT: 0.6 m
METRIC WEIGHT: 12.5 kg

POSSIBLE MOVES: Bulk Up, Dynamic Punch, Focus Energy, Focus Punch, Hammer Arm, Leer, Low Kick, Pound, Rock Slide, Rock Throw, Scary Face, Slam, Stone Edge, Superpower

TIMBURR   GURDURR   CONKELDURR

TIRTOUGA

Prototurtle Pokémon

TYPE: WATER-ROCK

It was restored from an ancient fossil. Tirtouga lived in the sea but came up onto the land to search for prey.

Its hunting grounds encompassed a broad area, from the land to more than half a mile deep in the ocean.

HOW TO SAY IT: teer-TOO-gah
IMPERIAL HEIGHT: 2'04"
IMPERIAL WEIGHT: 36.4 lbs.
METRIC HEIGHT: 0.7 m
METRIC WEIGHT: 16.5 kg

POSSIBLE MOVES: Bide, Withdraw, Water Gun, Rollout, Bite, Protect, Aqua Jet, Ancient Power, Crunch, Wide Guard, Brine, Smack Down, Curse, Shell Smash, Aqua Tail, Rock Slide, Rain Dance, Hydro Pump

TIRTOUGA   CARRACOSTA

TOGEDEMARU
Roly-Poly Pokémon

REGIONS:
ALOLA
GALAR

TYPE: ELECTRIC-STEEL

With the long hairs on its back, this Pokémon takes in electricity from other electric Pokémon. It stores what it absorbs in an electric sac.

When it's in trouble, it curls up into a ball, makes its fur spikes stand on end, and then discharges electricity indiscriminately.

HOW TO SAY IT: TOH-geh-deh-MAH-roo
IMPERIAL HEIGHT: 1'00"
IMPERIAL WEIGHT: 7.3 lbs.
METRIC HEIGHT: 0.3 m
METRIC WEIGHT: 3.3 kg

POSSIBLE MOVES: Charge, Defense Curl, Discharge, Electric Terrain, Fell Stinger, Magnet Rise, Nuzzle, Pin Missile, Spark, Spiky Shield, Tackle, Thunder Shock, Wild Charge, Zing Zap

DOES NOT EVOLVE

TOGEKISS
Jubilee Pokémon

REGIONS:
GALAR
SINNOH

TYPE: FAIRY-FLYING

These Pokémon are never seen anywhere near conflict or turmoil. In recent times, they've hardly been seen at all.

Known as a bringer of blessings, it's been depicted on good-luck charms since ancient times.

HOW TO SAY IT: TOE-geh-kiss
IMPERIAL HEIGHT: 4'11"
IMPERIAL WEIGHT: 83.8 lbs.
METRIC HEIGHT: 1.5 m
METRIC WEIGHT: 38.0 kg

POSSIBLE MOVES: After You, Air Slash, Ancient Power, Aura Sphere, Baton Pass, Charm, Double-Edge, Extreme Speed, Fairy Wind, Follow Me, Growl, Last Resort, Metronome, Pound, Safeguard, Sky Attack, Sweet Kiss, Tri Attack, Wish, Yawn

TOGEPI **TOGETIC** **TOGEKISS**

TOGEPI
Spike Ball Pokémon

TYPE: FAIRY

The shell seems to be filled with joy. It is said that it will share good luck when treated kindly.

It is considered to be a symbol of good luck. Its shell is said to be filled with happiness.

HOW TO SAY IT: TOE-ghep-pee
IMPERIAL HEIGHT: 1'00"
IMPERIAL WEIGHT: 3.3 lbs.
METRIC HEIGHT: 0.3 m
METRIC WEIGHT: 1.5 kg

POSSIBLE MOVES: After You, Ancient Power, Baton Pass, Charm, Double-Edge, Follow Me, Growl, Last Resort, Life Dew, Metronome, Pound, Safeguard, Sweet Kiss, Wish, Yawn

TOGETIC
Happiness Pokémon

TYPE: FAIRY-FLYING

They say that it will appear before kindhearted, caring people and shower them with happiness.

It grows dispirited if it is not with kind people. It can float in midair without moving its wings.

HOW TO SAY IT: TOE-ghet-tic
IMPERIAL HEIGHT: 2'00"
IMPERIAL WEIGHT: 7.1 lbs.
METRIC HEIGHT: 0.6 m
METRIC WEIGHT: 3.2 kg

POSSIBLE MOVES: After You, Ancient Power, Baton Pass, Charm, Double-Edge, Fairy Wind, Follow Me, Growl, Last Resort, Life Dew, Metronome, Pound, Safeguard, Sweet Kiss, Wish, Yawn

TORCHIC
Chick Pokémon

REGION: HOENN

TYPE: FIRE

Torchic sticks with its Trainer, following behind with unsteady steps. This Pokémon breathes fire of over 1,800 degrees Fahrenheit, including fireballs that leave the foe scorched black.

Torchic has a place inside its body where it keeps its flame. Give it a hug—it will be glowing with warmth. This Pokémon is covered all over by a fluffy coat of down.

HOW TO SAY IT: TOR-chick
IMPERIAL HEIGHT: 1'04"
IMPERIAL WEIGHT: 5.5 lbs.
METRIC HEIGHT: 0.4 m
METRIC WEIGHT: 2.5 kg

POSSIBLE MOVES: Scratch, Growl, Focus Energy, Ember, Peck, Sand Attack, Fire Spin, Quick Attack, Slash, Mirror Move, Flamethrower, Flame Burst

TORCHIC **COMBUSKEN** **BLAZIKEN** **MEGA BLAZIKEN**

TORKOAL
Coal Pokémon

REGIONS: ALOLA GALAR HOENN KALOS (MOUNTAIN)

TYPE: FIRE

It burns coal inside its shell for energy. It blows out black soot if it is endangered.

You find abandoned coal mines full of them. They dig tirelessly in search of coal.

HOW TO SAY IT: TOR-coal
IMPERIAL HEIGHT: 1'08"
IMPERIAL WEIGHT: 177.2 lbs.
METRIC HEIGHT: 0.5 m
METRIC WEIGHT: 80.4 kg

POSSIBLE MOVES: Amnesia, Body Slam, Clear Smog, Curse, Ember, Eruption, Flame Wheel, Flamethrower, Heat Wave, Inferno, Iron Defense, Lava Plume, Protect, Rapid Spin, Shell Smash, Smog, Smokescreen, Withdraw

DOES NOT EVOLVE

REGION: UNOVA

TORNADUS
Cyclone Pokémon

TYPE: FLYING

The lower half of its body is wrapped in a cloud of energy. It zooms through the sky at 200 mph.

Tornadus expels massive energy from its tail, causing severe storms. Its power is great enough to blow houses away.

HOW TO SAY IT: tohr-NAY-dus
IMPERIAL HEIGHT: Incarnate Forme: 4'11" /
Therian Forme: 4'07"
IMPERIAL WEIGHT: 138.9 lbs.
METRIC HEIGHT: Incarnate Forme: 1.5 m /
Therian Forme: 1.4m
METRIC WEIGHT: 63.0 kg

POSSIBLE MOVES: Uproar, Astonish, Gust, Swagger, Bite, Revenge, Air Cutter, Extrasensory, Agility, Air Slash, Crunch, Tailwind, Rain Dance, Hurricane, Dark Pulse, Hammer Arm, Thrash

INCARNATE FORME

THERIAN FORME

DOES NOT EVOLVE

TORRACAT
Fire Cat Pokémon

REGION: ALOLA

TYPE: FIRE

It can act spoiled if it grows close to its Trainer. A powerful Pokémon, its sharp claws can leave its Trainer's whole body covered in scratches.

When its mane is standing on end, you can tell it's feeling good. When it isn't feeling well, its fur will lie down flat.

HOW TO SAY IT: TOR-ruh-cat
IMPERIAL HEIGHT: 2'04"
IMPERIAL WEIGHT: 55.1 lbs.
METRIC HEIGHT: 0.7 m
METRIC WEIGHT: 25.0 kg

POSSIBLE MOVES: Scratch, Ember, Growl, Lick, Leer, Fire Fang, Roar, Bite, Swagger, Fury Swipes, Thrash, Flamethrower, Scary Face, Flare Blitz, Outrage, Double Kick

LITTEN → TORRACAT → INCINEROAR

TORTERRA
Continent Pokémon

REGION: SINNOH

TYPE: GRASS-GROUND

Ancient people imagined that beneath the ground, a gigantic Torterra dwelled.

Small Pokémon occasionally gather on its unmoving back to begin building their nests.

HOW TO SAY IT: tor-TER-ra
IMPERIAL HEIGHT: 7'03"
IMPERIAL WEIGHT: 683.4 lbs.
METRIC HEIGHT: 2.2 m
METRIC WEIGHT: 310.0 kg

POSSIBLE MOVES: Wood Hammer, Tackle, Withdraw, Absorb, Razor Leaf, Curse, Bite, Mega Drain, Earthquake, Leech Seed, Synthesis, Crunch, Giga Drain, Leaf Storm

TURTWIG → GROTLE → TORTERRA

REGION: JOHTO

TOTODILE
Big Jaw Pokémon

TYPE: WATER

Despite the smallness of its body, Totodile's jaws are very powerful. While the Pokémon may think it is just playfully nipping, its bite has enough power to cause serious injury.

HOW TO SAY IT: TOE-toe-dyle
IMPERIAL HEIGHT: 2'00"
IMPERIAL WEIGHT: 20.9 lbs.
METRIC HEIGHT: 0.6 m
METRIC WEIGHT: 9.5 kg

POSSIBLE MOVES: Scratch, Leer, Water Gun, Rage, Bite, Scary Face, Ice Fang, Flail, Crunch, Chip Away, Slash, Screech, Thrash, Aqua Tail, Superpower, Hydro Pump

TOTODILE	CROCONAW	FERALIGATR

REGION: ALOLA

TOUCANNON
Cannon Pokémon

TYPE: NORMAL-FLYING

They smack beaks with others of their kind to communicate. The strength and number of hits tell each other how they feel.

Known for forming harmonious couples, this Pokémon is brought to wedding ceremonies as a good-luck charm.

HOW TO SAY IT: too-CAN-nun
IMPERIAL HEIGHT: 3'07"
IMPERIAL WEIGHT: 57.3 lbs.
METRIC HEIGHT: 1.1 m
METRIC WEIGHT: 26.0 kg

POSSIBLE MOVES: Beak Blast, Rock Blast, Peck, Growl, Echoed Voice, Rock Smash, Supersonic, Pluck, Roost, Fury Attack, Screech, Drill Peck, Bullet Seed, Feather Dance, Hyper Voice

PIKIPEK	TRUMBEAK	TOUCANNON

TOXAPEX

Brutal Star Pokémon

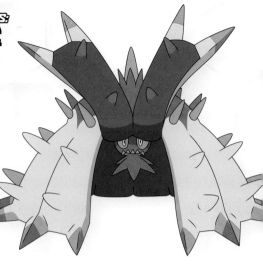

TYPE: POISON-WATER

To survive in the cold waters of Galar, this Pokémon forms a dome with its legs, enclosing its body so it can capture its own body heat.

Within the poison sac in its body is a poison so toxic that Pokémon as large as Wailord will still be suffering three days after it first takes effect.

HOW TO SAY IT: TOX-uh-pex
IMPERIAL HEIGHT: 2'04"
IMPERIAL WEIGHT: 32.0 lbs.
METRIC HEIGHT: 0.7 m
METRIC WEIGHT: 14.5 kg

POSSIBLE MOVES: Baneful Bunker, Bite, Liquidation, Peck, Pin Missile, Poison Jab, Poison Sting, Recover, Toxic, Toxic Spikes, Venom Drench, Venoshock, Wide Guard

MAREANIE   TOXAPEX

TOXEL

Baby Pokémon

TYPE: ELECTRIC-POISON

It stores poison in an internal poison sac and secretes that poison through its skin. If you touch this Pokémon, a tingling sensation follows.

It manipulates the chemical makeup of its poison to produce electricity. The voltage is weak, but it can cause a tingling paralysis.

HOW TO SAY IT: TAHKS-ull
IMPERIAL HEIGHT: 1'04"
IMPERIAL WEIGHT: 24.3 lbs.
METRIC HEIGHT: 0.4 m
METRIC WEIGHT: 11.0 kg

POSSIBLE MOVES: Acid, Belch, Flail, Growl, Nuzzle, Tearful Look

TOXEL   TOXTRICITY

TOXICROAK
Toxic Mouth Pokémon

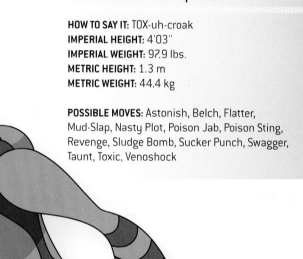

TYPE: POISON-FIGHTING

It bounces toward opponents and gouges them with poisonous claws. No more than a scratch is needed to knock out its adversaries.

It booms out a victory croak when its prey goes down in defeat. This Pokémon and Seismitoad are related species.

HOW TO SAY IT: TOX-uh-croak
IMPERIAL HEIGHT: 4'03"
IMPERIAL WEIGHT: 97.9 lbs.
METRIC HEIGHT: 1.3 m
METRIC WEIGHT: 44.4 kg

POSSIBLE MOVES: Astonish, Belch, Flatter, Mud-Slap, Nasty Plot, Poison Jab, Poison Sting, Revenge, Sludge Bomb, Sucker Punch, Swagger, Taunt, Toxic, Venoshock

CROAGUNK

TOXICROAK

TOXTRICITY

Punk Pokémon

LOW KEY FORM

TYPE: ELECTRIC-POISON

Capable of generating 15,000 volts of electricity, this Pokémon looks down on all that would challenge it.

It has an electrical organ on its chest. While generating electricity, it fills its surroundings with what sounds like the strumming of a bass guitar.

HOW TO SAY IT: tahks-TRIS-ih-tee
IMPERIAL HEIGHT: 5'03"
IMPERIAL WEIGHT: 88.2 lbs.
METRIC HEIGHT: 1.6 m
METRIC WEIGHT: 40.0 kg

POSSIBLE MOVES: Acid, Acid Spray, Belch, Boomburst, Charge, Discharge, Eerie Impulse, Flail, Growl, Leer, Magnetic Flux, Noble Roar, Nuzzle, Overdrive, Poison Jab, Scary Face, Screech, Shock Wave, Spark, Swagger, Taunt, Tearful Look, Thunder Shock, Toxic, Venom Drench

AMPED FORM

TOXEL ➡ TOXTRICITY

Alternate Form:
GIGANTAMAX TOXTRICITY

Its excessive electric energy is its weapon. This Pokémon can build up more electricity than any thundercloud.

Out of control after its own poison penetrated its brain, it tears across the land in a rampage, contaminating the earth with toxic sweat.

IMPERIAL HEIGHT: 78'09"+
IMPERIAL WEIGHT: ????.? lbs.
METRIC HEIGHT: 24.0+ m
METRIC WEIGHT: ???.? kg

TRANQUILL

Wild Pigeon Pokémon

TYPE: NORMAL-FLYING

It can fly moderately quickly. No matter how far it travels, it can always find its way back to its master and its nest.

These bright Pokémon have acute memories. Apparently delivery workers often choose them as their partners.

HOW TO SAY IT: TRAN-kwil
IMPERIAL HEIGHT: 2'00"
IMPERIAL WEIGHT: 33.1 lbs.
METRIC HEIGHT: 0.6 m
METRIC WEIGHT: 15.0 kg

POSSIBLE MOVES: Air Cutter, Air Slash, Detect, Feather Dance, Growl, Gust, Leer, Quick Attack, Roost, Sky Attack, Swagger, Tailwind, Taunt

PIDOVE → **TRANQUILL** → **UNFEZANT**

REGIONS:
ALOLA
GALAR
HOENN
KALOS
(MOUNTAIN)

TRAPINCH

Ant Pit Pokémon

TYPE: GROUND

Its nest is a sloped, bowl-like pit in the desert. Once something has fallen in, there is no escape.

It makes an inescapable conical pit and lies in wait at the bottom for prey to come tumbling down.

HOW TO SAY IT: TRAP-inch
IMPERIAL HEIGHT: 2'04"
IMPERIAL WEIGHT: 33.1 lbs.
METRIC HEIGHT: 0.7 m
METRIC WEIGHT: 15.0 kg

POSSIBLE MOVES: Astonish, Bite, Bulldoze, Crunch, Dig, Earth Power, Earthquake, Fissure, Laser Focus, Mud-Slap, Sand Attack, Sand Tomb, Sandstorm, Superpower

TRAPINCH → **VIBRAVA** → **FLYGON**

TREECKO

Wood Gecko Pokémon

REGION: HOENN

TYPE: GRASS

Treecko has small hooks on the bottom of its feet that enable it to scale vertical walls. This Pokémon attacks by slamming foes with its thick tail.

Treecko is cool, calm, and collected—it never panics under any situation. If a bigger foe were to glare at this Pokémon, it would glare right back without conceding an inch of ground.

HOW TO SAY IT: TREE-ko **METRIC HEIGHT:** 0.5 m
IMPERIAL HEIGHT: 1'08" **METRIC WEIGHT:** 5.0 kg
IMPERIAL WEIGHT: 11.0 lbs.

POSSIBLE MOVES: Pound, Leer, Absorb, Quick Attack, Pursuit, Screech, Mega Drain, Agility, Slam, Detect, Giga Drain, Energy Ball, Quick Guard, Endeavor

TREECKO → GROVYLE → SCEPTILE → MEGA SCEPTILE

TREVENANT

Elder Tree Pokémon

**REGIONS:
ALOLA
GALAR
KALOS
(MOUNTAIN)**

TYPE: GHOST-GRASS

People fear it due to a belief that it devours any who try to cut down trees in its forest, but to the Pokémon it shares its woods with, it's kind.

Small roots that extend from the tips of this Pokémon's feet can tie into the trees of the forest and give Trevenant control over them.

HOW TO SAY IT: TREV-uh-nunt
IMPERIAL HEIGHT: 4'11"
IMPERIAL WEIGHT: 156.5 lbs.
METRIC HEIGHT: 1.5 m
METRIC WEIGHT: 71.0 kg

POSSIBLE MOVES: Astonish, Branch Poke, Confuse Ray, Curse, Destiny Bond, Forest's Curse, Growth, Hex, Horn Leech, Ingrain, Leech Seed, Phantom Force, Shadow Claw, Tackle, Will-O-Wisp, Wood Hammer

PHANTUMP → TREVENANT

TROPIUS
Fruit Pokémon

TYPE: GRASS-FLYING

The bunches of fruit growing around the necks of Tropius in Alola are especially sweet compared to those in other regions.

Bunches of delicious fruit grow around its neck. In warm areas, many ranches raise Tropius.

HOW TO SAY IT: TROP-ee-us
IMPERIAL HEIGHT: 6'07"
IMPERIAL WEIGHT: 220.5 lbs.
METRIC HEIGHT: 2.0 m
METRIC WEIGHT: 100.0 kg

POSSIBLE MOVES: Leer, Gust, Growth, Razor Leaf, Stomp, Sweet Scent, Whirlwind, Magical Leaf, Body Slam, Synthesis, Leaf Tornado, Air Slash, Bestow, Solar Beam, Natural Gift, Leaf Storm

DOES NOT EVOLVE

REGIONS:
ALOLA
GALAR
KALOS
(MOUNTAIN)
UNOVA

TRUBBISH
Trash Bag Pokémon

TYPE: POISON

Its favorite places are unsanitary ones. If you leave trash lying around, you could even find one of these Pokémon living in your room.

This Pokémon was born from a bag stuffed with trash. Galarian Weezing relish the fumes belched by Trubbish.

HOW TO SAY IT: TRUB-bish
IMPERIAL HEIGHT: 2'00"
IMPERIAL WEIGHT: 68.3 lbs.
METRIC HEIGHT: 0.6 m
METRIC WEIGHT: 31.0 kg

POSSIBLE MOVES: Acid Spray, Amnesia, Belch, Clear Smog, Explosion, Gunk Shot, Pain Split, Poison Gas, Pound, Recycle, Sludge, Sludge Bomb, Stockpile, Swallow, Take Down, Toxic, Toxic Spikes

TRUBBISH → GARBODOR

TRUMBEAK

Bugle Beak Pokémon

TYPE: NORMAL-FLYING

It can bend the tip of its beak to produce over a hundred different cries at will.

From its mouth, it fires the seeds of berries it has eaten. The scattered seeds give rise to new plants.

HOW TO SAY IT: TRUM-beak
IMPERIAL HEIGHT: 2'00"
IMPERIAL WEIGHT: 32.6 lbs.
METRIC HEIGHT: 0.6 m
METRIC WEIGHT: 14.8 kg

POSSIBLE MOVES: Rock Blast, Peck, Growl, Echoed Voice, Rock Smash, Supersonic, Pluck, Roost, Fury Attack, Screech, Drill Peck, Bullet Seed, Feather Dance, Hyper Voice

PIKIPEK → TRUMBEAK → TOUCANNON

TSAREENA

Fruit Pokémon

TYPE: GRASS

This feared Pokémon has long, slender legs and a cruel heart. It shows no mercy as it stomps on its opponents.

A kick from the hardened tips of this Pokémon's legs leaves a wound in the opponent's body and soul that will never heal.

HOW TO SAY IT: zar-EE-nuh
IMPERIAL HEIGHT: 3'11"
IMPERIAL WEIGHT: 47.2 lbs.
METRIC HEIGHT: 1.2 m
METRIC WEIGHT: 21.4 kg

POSSIBLE MOVES: Aromatherapy, Aromatic Mist, Flail, High Jump Kick, Leaf Storm, Magical Leaf, Play Nice, Power Whip, Rapid Spin, Razor Leaf, Splash, Stomp, Swagger, Sweet Scent, Teeter Dance, Trop Kick

BOUNSWEET → STEENEE → TSAREENA

TURTONATOR
Blast Turtle Pokémon

TYPE: FIRE-DRAGON

Explosive substances coat the shell on its back. Enemies that dare attack it will be blown away by an immense detonation.

Eating sulfur in its volcanic habitat is what causes explosive compounds to develop in its shell. Its droppings are also dangerously explosive.

HOW TO SAY IT: TURT-nay-ter **METRIC HEIGHT:** 2.0 m
IMPERIAL HEIGHT: 6'07" **METRIC WEIGHT:** 212.0 kg
IMPERIAL WEIGHT: 467.4 lbs.

POSSIBLE MOVES: Body Slam, Dragon Pulse, Ember, Endure, Explosion, Flail, Flamethrower, Incinerate, Iron Defense, Overheat, Protect, Shell Smash, Shell Trap, Smog, Tackle

DOES NOT EVOLVE

TURTWIG
Tiny Leaf Pokémon

TYPE: GRASS

Photosynthesis occurs across its body under the sun. The shell on its back is actually hardened soil.

It undertakes photosynthesis with its body, making oxygen. The leaf on its head wilts if it is thirsty.

HOW TO SAY IT: TUR-twig
IMPERIAL HEIGHT: 1'04"
IMPERIAL WEIGHT: 22.5 lbs.
METRIC HEIGHT: 0.4 m
METRIC WEIGHT: 10.2 kg

POSSIBLE MOVES: Tackle, Withdraw, Absorb, Razor Leaf, Curse, Bite, Mega Drain, Leech Seed, Synthesis, Crunch, Giga Drain, Leaf Storm

TURTWIG **GROTLE** **TORTERRA**

TYMPOLE

Tadpole Pokémon

TYPE: WATER

Graceful ripples running across the water's surface are a sure sign that Tympole are singing in high-pitched voices below.

It uses sound waves to communicate with others of its kind. People and other Pokémon species can't hear its cries of warning.

HOW TO SAY IT: TIM-pohl
IMPERIAL HEIGHT: 1'08"
IMPERIAL WEIGHT: 9.9 lbs.
METRIC HEIGHT: 0.5 m
METRIC WEIGHT: 4.5 kg

POSSIBLE MOVES: Acid, Aqua Ring, Bubble Beam, Echoed Voice, Flail, Growl, Hydro Pump, Hyper Voice, Mud Shot, Muddy Water, Rain Dance, Round, Supersonic, Uproar

TYMPOLE   PALPITOAD   SEISMITOAD

TYNAMO

EleFish Pokémon

TYPE: ELECTRIC

While one alone doesn't have much power, a chain of many Tynamo can be as powerful as lightning.

One alone can emit only a trickle of electricity, so a group of them gathers to unleash a powerful electric shock.

HOW TO SAY IT: TIE-nah-moh
IMPERIAL HEIGHT: 0'08"
IMPERIAL WEIGHT: 0.7 lbs.
METRIC HEIGHT: 0.2 m
METRIC WEIGHT: 0.3 kg

POSSIBLE MOVES: Tackle, Thunder Wave, Spark, Charge Beam

TYNAMO   EELEKTRIK   EELEKTROSS

TYPE: NULL
Synthetic Pokémon

TYPE: NORMAL

Rumor has it that the theft of top-secret research notes led to a new instance of this Pokémon being created in the Galar region.

It was modeled after a mighty Pokémon of myth. The mask placed upon it limits its power in order to keep it under control.

HOW TO SAY IT: TYPE NULL
IMPERIAL HEIGHT: 6'03"
IMPERIAL WEIGHT: 265.7 lbs.
METRIC HEIGHT: 1.9 m
METRIC WEIGHT: 120.5 kg

POSSIBLE MOVES: Aerial Ace, Air Slash, Crush Claw, Double Hit, Double-Edge, Imprison, Iron Head, Metal Sound, Scary Face, Tackle, Take Down, Tri Attack, X-Scissor

TYPE: NULL → SILVALLY

REGION:
JOHTO

TYPHLOSION
Volcano Pokémon

TYPE: FIRE

Typhlosion obscures itself behind a shimmering heat haze that it creates using its intensely hot flames. This Pokémon creates blazing explosive blasts that burn everything to cinders.

HOW TO SAY IT: tie-FLOW-zhun
IMPERIAL HEIGHT: 5'07"
IMPERIAL WEIGHT: 175.3 lbs.
METRIC HEIGHT: 1.7 m
METRIC WEIGHT: 79.5 kg

POSSIBLE MOVES: Gyro Ball, Tackle, Leer, Smokescreen, Ember, Quick Attack, Flame Wheel, Defense Curl, Swift, Flame Charge, Lava Plume, Flamethrower, Inferno, Rollout, Double-Edge, Eruption, Burn Up

CYNDAQUIL → QUILAVA → TYPHLOSION

TYRANITAR

Armor Pokémon

REGIONS:
ALOLA
GALAR
JOHTO
KALOS
(MOUNTAIN)

TYPE: ROCK-DARK

Its body can't be harmed by any sort of attack, so it is very eager to make challenges against enemies.

The quakes caused when it walks make even great mountains crumble and change the surrounding terrain.

HOW TO SAY IT: tie-RAN-uh-tar
IMPERIAL HEIGHT: 6'07"
IMPERIAL WEIGHT: 445.3 lbs.
METRIC HEIGHT: 2.0 m
METRIC WEIGHT: 202.0 kg

POSSIBLE MOVES: Bite, Crunch, Dark Pulse, Earthquake, Fire Fang, Giga Impact, Hyper Beam, Ice Fang, Iron Defense, Leer, Payback, Rock Slide, Rock Throw, Sandstorm, Scary Face, Screech, Stomping Tantrum, Stone Edge, Tackle, Thrash, Thunder Fang

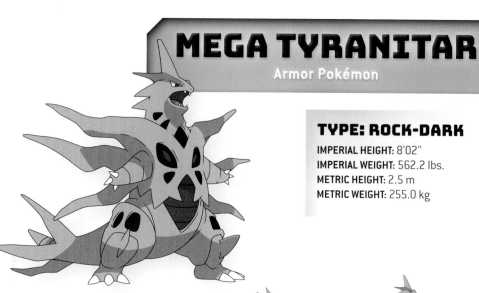

MEGA TYRANITAR

Armor Pokémon

TYPE: ROCK-DARK

IMPERIAL HEIGHT: 8'02"
IMPERIAL WEIGHT: 562.2 lbs.
METRIC HEIGHT: 2.5 m
METRIC WEIGHT: 255.0 kg

LARVITAR ➡ PUPITAR ➡ TYRANITAR ➡ MEGA TYRANITAR

TYPE: ROCK-DRAGON

Complete restoration is impossible, allowing room for theories that its entire body was once covered in a feather-like coat.

The king of the ancient world, it can easily crunch a car with the devastating strength of its enormous jaws.

HOW TO SAY IT: tie-RAN-trum
IMPERIAL HEIGHT: 8'02"
IMPERIAL WEIGHT: 595.2 lbs.
METRIC HEIGHT: 2.5 m
METRIC WEIGHT: 270.0 kg

POSSIBLE MOVES: Head Smash, Tail Whip, Tackle, Roar, Stomp, Bide, Stealth Rock, Bite, Charm, Ancient Power, Dragon Tail, Crunch, Dragon Claw, Thrash, Earthquake, Horn Drill, Rock Slide, Giga Impact

REGION: ALOLA KALOS (COASTAL)

TYRANTRUM
Despot Pokémon

TYRUNT

TYRANTRUM

513

TYROGUE
Scuffle Pokémon

REGIONS:
GALAR
JOHTO

TYPE: FIGHTING

It is always bursting with energy. To make itself stronger, it keeps on fighting even if it loses.

Even though it is small, it can't be ignored because it will slug any handy target without warning.

HOW TO SAY IT: tie-ROAG
IMPERIAL HEIGHT: 2'04"
IMPERIAL WEIGHT: 46.3 lbs.
METRIC HEIGHT: 0.7 m
METRIC WEIGHT: 21.0 kg

POSSIBLE MOVES: Fake Out, Focus Energy, Helping Hand, Tackle

TYROGUE

HITMONLEE

HITMONCHAN

HITMONTOP

TYRUNT
Royal Heir Pokémon

REGIONS:
ALOLA
KALOS
(COASTAL)

TYPE: ROCK-DRAGON

Its large jaw has incredible destructive power. Some theories suggest that its restored form is different from its form of long ago.

Tyrunt is spoiled and selfish. It may just be trying to frolic, but sometimes the ones it's trying to frolic with are gravely injured.

HOW TO SAY IT: TIE-runt
IMPERIAL HEIGHT: 2'07"
IMPERIAL WEIGHT: 57.3 lbs.

POSSIBLE MOVES: Tail Whip, Tackle, Roar, Stomp, Bide, Stealth Rock, Bite, Charm, Ancient Power, Dragon Tail, Crunch, Dragon Claw, Thrash, Earthquake, Horn Drill

TYRUNT

TYRANTRUM

TYPE: DARK

When this Pokémon becomes angry, its pores secrete a poisonous sweat, which it sprays at its opponent's eyes.

On the night of a full moon, or when it gets excited, the ring patterns on its body glow yellow.

REGIONS:
ALOLA
GALAR
JOHTO
KALOS
(COASTAL)

UMBREON
Moonlight Pokémon

HOW TO SAY IT: UM-bree-on
IMPERIAL HEIGHT: 3'03"
IMPERIAL WEIGHT: 59.5 lbs.
METRIC HEIGHT: 1.0 m
METRIC WEIGHT: 27.0 kg

POSSIBLE MOVES: Assurance, Baby-Doll Eyes, Baton Pass, Bite, Charm, Confuse Ray, Copycat, Covet, Dark Pulse, Double-Edge, Growl, Guard Swap, Helping Hand, Last Resort, Mean Look, Moonlight, Quick Attack, Sand Attack, Screech, Snarl, Swift, Tackle, Tail Whip, Take Down

EEVEE → UMBREON

MALE FORM

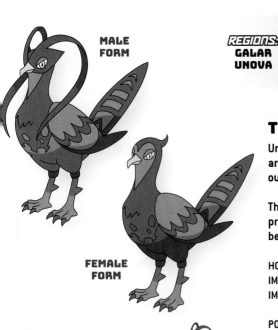

FEMALE FORM

PIDOVE → TRANQUILL → UNFEZANT

REGIONS:
GALAR
UNOVA

UNFEZANT
Proud Pokémon

TYPE: NORMAL-FLYING

Unfezant are exceptional fliers. The females are known for their stamina, while the males outclass them in terms of speed.

This Pokémon is intelligent and intensely proud. People will sit up and take notice if you become the Trainer of one.

HOW TO SAY IT: un-FEZ-ent
IMPERIAL HEIGHT: 3'11"
IMPERIAL WEIGHT: 63.9 lbs.
METRIC HEIGHT: 0.8 m
METRIC WEIGHT: 26.0 kg

POSSIBLE MOVES: Air Cutter, Air Slash, Detect, Feather Dance, Growl, Gust, Leer, Quick Attack, Roost, Sky Attack, Swagger, Tailwind, Taunt

UNOWN
Symbol Pokémon

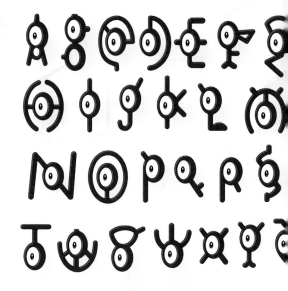

REGION: JOHTO

TYPE: PSYCHIC

This Pokémon is shaped like ancient writing. It is a mystery as to which came first, the ancient writings or the various Unown. Research into this topic is ongoing but nothing is known.

HOW TO SAY IT: un-KNOWN
IMPERIAL HEIGHT: 1'08"
IMPERIAL WEIGHT: 11.0 lbs.
METRIC HEIGHT: 0.5 m
METRIC WEIGHT: 5.0 kg

POSSIBLE MOVE: Hidden Power

DOES NOT EVOLVE

URSARING
Hibernator Pokémon

REGIONS: JOHTO KALOS (MOUNTAIN)

TYPE: NORMAL

In the forests inhabited by Ursaring, it is said that there are many streams and towering trees where they gather food. This Pokémon walks through its forest gathering food every day.

HOW TO SAY IT: UR-sa-ring
IMPERIAL HEIGHT: 5'11"
IMPERIAL WEIGHT: 277.3 lbs.
METRIC HEIGHT: 1.8 m
METRIC WEIGHT: 125.8 kg

POSSIBLE MOVES: Hammer Arm, Covet, Scratch, Leer, Lick, Fake Tears, Fury Swipes, Feint Attack, Sweet Scent, Play Nice, Slash, Scary Face, Rest, Snore, Thrash

TEDDIURSA   URSARING

UXIE
Knowledge Pokémon

TYPE: PSYCHIC

Known as "The Being of Knowledge." It is said that it can wipe out the memory of those who see its eyes.

It is said that its emergence gave humans the intelligence to improve their quality of life.

HOW TO SAY IT: YOOK-zee
IMPERIAL HEIGHT: 1'00"
IMPERIAL WEIGHT: 0.7 lbs.
METRIC HEIGHT: 0.3 m
METRIC WEIGHT: 0.3 kg

POSSIBLE MOVES: Rest, Confusion, Imprison, Endure, Swift, Yawn, Future Sight, Amnesia, Extrasensory, Flail, Natural Gift, Memento

DOES NOT EVOLVE

VANILLISH
Icy Snow Pokémon

REGIONS:
ALOLA
GALAR
KALOS
(MOUNTAIN)
UNOVA

TYPE: ICE

By drinking pure water, it grows its icy body. This Pokémon can be hard to find on days with warm, sunny weather.

It blasts enemies with cold air reaching -148 degrees Fahrenheit, freezing them solid. But it spares their lives afterward—it's a kind Pokémon.

HOW TO SAY IT: vuh-NIHL-lish
IMPERIAL HEIGHT: 3'07"
IMPERIAL WEIGHT: 90.4 lbs.
METRIC HEIGHT: 1.1 m
METRIC WEIGHT: 41.0 kg

POSSIBLE MOVES: Acid Armor, Astonish, Avalanche, Blizzard, Hail, Harden, Ice Beam, Icicle Spear, Icy Wind, Mirror Coat, Mist, Sheer Cold, Taunt, Uproar

VANILLITE   VANILLISH   VANILLUXE

VANILLITE
Fresh Snow Pokémon

REGIONS:
ALOLA
GALAR
KALOS
(MOUNTAIN)
UNOVA

TYPE: ICE

Unable to survive in hot areas, it makes itself comfortable by breathing out air cold enough to cause snow. It burrows into the snow to sleep.

Supposedly, this Pokémon was born from an icicle. It spews out freezing air at -58 degrees Fahrenheit to make itself more comfortable.

HOW TO SAY IT: vuh-NIHL-lyte
IMPERIAL HEIGHT: 1'04"
IMPERIAL WEIGHT: 12.6 lbs.
METRIC HEIGHT: 0.4 m
METRIC WEIGHT: 5.7 kg

POSSIBLE MOVES: Acid Armor, Astonish, Avalanche, Blizzard, Hail, Harden, Ice Beam, Icicle Spear, Icy Wind, Mirror Coat, Mist, Sheer Cold, Taunt, Uproar

VANILLITE   VANILLISH   VANILLUXE

REGIONS:
ALOLA
GALAR
KALOS
(MOUNTAIN)
UNOVA

VANILLUXE
Snowstorm Pokémon

TYPE: ICE

When its anger reaches a breaking point, this Pokémon unleashes a fierce blizzard that freezes every creature around it, be they friend or foe.

People believe this Pokémon formed when two Vanillish stuck together. Its body temperature is roughly 21 degrees Fahrenheit.

HOW TO SAY IT: vuh-NIHL-lux
IMPERIAL HEIGHT: 4'03"
IMPERIAL WEIGHT: 126.8 lbs.
METRIC HEIGHT: 1.3 m
METRIC WEIGHT: 57.5 kg

POSSIBLE MOVES: Acid Armor, Astonish, Avalanche, Blizzard, Freeze-Dry, Hail, Harden, Ice Beam, Icicle Crash, Icicle Spear, Icy Wind, Mirror Coat, Mist, Sheer Cold, Taunt, Uproar, Weather Ball

VANILLITE → VANILLISH → VANILLUXE

VAPOREON

Bubble Jet Pokémon

REGIONS:
ALOLA
GALAR
KALOS
(COASTAL)
KANTO

TYPE: WATER

When Vaporeon's fins begin to vibrate, it is a sign that rain will come within a few hours.

Its body's cellular structure is similar to the molecular composition of water. It can melt invisibly in water.

HOW TO SAY IT: vay-POUR-ree-on
IMPERIAL HEIGHT: 3'03"
IMPERIAL WEIGHT: 63.9 lbs.
METRIC HEIGHT: 1.0 m
METRIC WEIGHT: 29.0 kg

POSSIBLE MOVES: Acid Armor, Aqua Ring, Aurora Beam, Baby-Doll Eyes, Baton Pass, Bite, Charm, Copycat, Covet, Double-Edge, Growl, Haze, Helping Hand, Hydro Pump, Last Resort, Muddy Water, Quick Attack, Sand Attack, Swift, Tackle, Tail Whip, Take Down, Water Gun, Water Pulse

EEVEE   VAPOREON

VENIPEDE

Centipede Pokémon

REGIONS:
KALOS
(CENTRAL)
UNOVA

TYPE: BUG-POISON

Venipede and Sizzlipede are similar species, but when the two meet, a huge fight ensues.

Its fangs are highly venomous. If this Pokémon finds prey it thinks it can eat, it leaps for them without any thought of how things might turn out.

HOW TO SAY IT: VEHN-ih-peed
IMPERIAL HEIGHT: 1'04"
IMPERIAL WEIGHT: 11.7 lbs.
METRIC HEIGHT: 0.4 m
METRIC WEIGHT: 5.3 kg

POSSIBLE MOVES: Defense Curl, Rollout, Poison Sting, Screech, Pursuit, Protect, Poison Tail, Bug Bite, Venoshock, Agility, Steamroller, Toxic, Venom Drench, Rock Climb, Double-Edge

VENIPEDE   WHIRLIPEDE   SCOLIPEDE

TYPE: BUG-POISON

The powdery scales on its wings are hard to remove from skin. They also contain poison that leaks out on contact.

REGION: KANTO

VENOMOTH
Poison Moth Pokémon

HOW TO SAY IT: VEH-no-moth
IMPERIAL HEIGHT: 4'11"
IMPERIAL WEIGHT: 27.6 lbs.
METRIC HEIGHT: 1.5 m
METRIC WEIGHT: 12.5 kg

POSSIBLE MOVES: Silver Wind, Tackle, Disable, Foresight, Supersonic, Confusion, Poison Powder, Leech Life, Stun Spore, Psybeam, Sleep Powder, Gust, Signal Beam, Zen Headbutt, Poison Fang, Psychic, Bug Buzz, Quiver Dance

VENONAT → VENOMOTH

REGION: KANTO

VENONAT
Insect Pokémon

TYPE: BUG-POISON

Its large eyes act as radar. In a bright place, you can see that they are clusters of many tiny eyes.

HOW TO SAY IT: VEH-no-nat
IMPERIAL HEIGHT: 3'03"
IMPERIAL WEIGHT: 66.1 lbs.
METRIC HEIGHT: 1.0 m
METRIC WEIGHT: 30.0 kg

POSSIBLE MOVES: Tackle, Disable, Foresight, Supersonic, Confusion, Poison Powder, Leech Life, Stun Spore, Psybeam, Sleep Powder, Signal Beam, Zen Headbutt, Poison Fang, Psychic

VENONAT → VENOMOTH

VENUSAUR

Seed Pokémon

TYPE: GRASS-POISON

Its plant blooms when it is absorbing solar energy. It stays on the move to seek sunlight.

A bewitching aroma wafts from its flower. The fragrance becalms those engaged in a battle.

HOW TO SAY IT: VEE-nuh-sore
IMPERIAL HEIGHT: 6'07"
IMPERIAL WEIGHT: 220.5 lbs.
METRIC HEIGHT: 2.0 m
METRIC WEIGHT: 100.0 kg

POSSIBLE MOVES: Tackle, Growl, Vine Whip, Leech Seed, Poison Powder, Sleep Powder, Take Down, Razor Leaf, Sweet Scent, Growth, Double-Edge, Petal Dance, Worry Seed, Synthesis, Petal Blizzard, Solar Beam

MEGA VENUSAUR
Seed Pokémon

TYPE: GRASS-POISON

IMPERIAL HEIGHT: 7'10"
IMPERIAL WEIGHT: 342.8 lbs.
METRIC HEIGHT: 2.4 m
METRIC WEIGHT: 155.5 kg

BULBASAUR → **IVYSAUR** → **VENUSAUR** → **MEGA VENUSAUR**

Alternate Form:
GIGANTAMAX VENUSAUR

In battle, this Pokémon swings around two thick vines. If these vines slammed into a 10-story building, they could easily topple it.

Huge amounts of pollen burst from it with the force of a volcanic eruption. Breathing in too much of the pollen can cause fainting.

IMPERIAL HEIGHT: 78'09"+
IMPERIAL WEIGHT: ????.? lbs.
METRIC HEIGHT: 24.0+ m
METRIC WEIGHT: ???.? kg

VESPIQUEN

Beehive Pokémon

TYPE: BUG-FLYING

It skillfully commands its grubs in battles with its enemies. The grubs are willing to risk their lives to defend Vespiquen.

Vespiquen that give off more pheromones have larger swarms of Combee attendants.

HOW TO SAY IT: VES-pih-kwen
IMPERIAL HEIGHT: 3'11"
IMPERIAL WEIGHT: 84.9 lbs.
METRIC HEIGHT: 1.2 m
METRIC WEIGHT: 38.5 kg

POSSIBLE MOVES: Air Slash, Aromatherapy, Aromatic Mist, Attack Order, Bug Bite, Confuse Ray, Defend Order, Destiny Bond, Fell Stinger, Fury Cutter, Fury Swipes, Gust, Poison Sting, Power Gem, Slash, Struggle Bug, Swagger, Sweet Scent, Toxic

COMBEE   **VESPIQUEN**

VIBRAVA

Vibration Pokémon

TYPE: GROUND-DRAGON

The ultrasonic waves it generates by rubbing its two wings together cause severe headaches.

To help make its wings grow, it dissolves quantities of prey in its digestive juices and guzzles them down every day.

HOW TO SAY IT: VY-BRAH-va
IMPERIAL HEIGHT: 3'07"
IMPERIAL WEIGHT: 33.7 lbs.
METRIC HEIGHT: 1.1 m
METRIC WEIGHT: 15.3 kg

POSSIBLE MOVES: Astonish, Bite, Boomburst, Bug Buzz, Bulldoze, Crunch, Dig, Dragon Breath, Dragon Rush, Dragon Tail, Earth Power, Earthquake, Fissure, Laser Focus, Mud-Slap, Sand Attack, Sand Tomb, Sandstorm, Screech, Superpower, Supersonic, Uproar

TRAPINCH   **VIBRAVA**   **FLYGON**

MYTHICAL POKÉMON

VICTINI
Victory Pokémon

TYPE: PSYCHIC-FIRE

This Pokémon brings victory. It is said that Trainers with Victini always win, regardless of the type of encounter.

When it shares the infinite energy it creates, that being's entire body will be overflowing with power.

HOW TO SAY IT: vik-TEE-nee
IMPERIAL HEIGHT: 1'04"
IMPERIAL WEIGHT: 8.8 lbs.
METRIC HEIGHT: 0.4 m
METRIC WEIGHT: 4.0 kg

POSSIBLE MOVES: Searing Shot, Focus Energy, Confusion, Incinerate, Quick Attack, Endure, Headbutt, Flame Charge, Reversal, Flame Burst, Zen Headbutt, Inferno, Double-Edge, Flare Blitz, Final Gambit, Stored Power, Overheat

DOES NOT EVOLVE

VICTREEBEL
Flycatcher Pokémon

TYPE: GRASS-POISON

Lures prey with the sweet aroma of honey. Swallowed whole, the prey is dissolved in a day, bones and all.

HOW TO SAY IT: VICK-tree-bell
IMPERIAL HEIGHT: 5'07"
IMPERIAL WEIGHT: 34.2 lbs.
METRIC HEIGHT: 1.7 m
METRIC WEIGHT: 15.5 kg

POSSIBLE MOVES: Stockpile, Swallow, Spit Up, Vine Whip, Sleep Powder, Sweet Scent, Razor Leaf, Leaf Tornado, Leaf Storm, Leaf Blade

BELLSPROUT   WEEPINBELL   VICTREEBEL

VIGOROTH

Wild Monkey Pokémon

REGION: HOENN

TYPE: NORMAL

Vigoroth is always itching and agitated to go on a wild rampage. It simply can't tolerate sitting still for even a minute. This Pokémon's stress level rises if it can't be moving constantly.

Vigoroth is simply incapable of remaining still. Even when it tries to sleep, the blood in its veins grows agitated, compelling this Pokémon to run wild throughout the jungle before it can settle down.

HOW TO SAY IT: VIG-er-roth **METRIC HEIGHT:** 1.4 m
IMPERIAL HEIGHT: 4'07" **METRIC WEIGHT:** 46.5 kg
IMPERIAL WEIGHT: 102.5 lbs.

POSSIBLE MOVES: Scratch, Focus Energy, Encore, Uproar, Fury Swipes, Endure, Slash, Counter, Chip Away, Focus Punch, Reversal

SLAKOTH VIGOROTH SLAKING

VIKAVOLT

Stag Beetle Pokémon

REGIONS: ALOLA GALAR

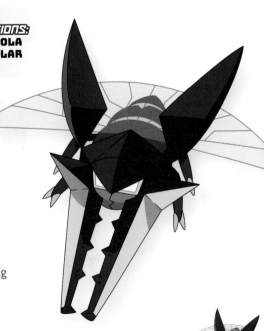

TYPE: BUG-ELECTRIC

It builds up electricity in its abdomen, focuses it through its jaws, and then fires the electricity off in concentrated beams.

If it carries a Charjabug to use as a spare battery, a flying Vikavolt can rapidly fire high-powered beams of electricity.

HOW TO SAY IT: VIE-kuh-volt **METRIC HEIGHT:** 1.5 m
IMPERIAL HEIGHT: 4'11" **METRIC WEIGHT:** 45.0 kg
IMPERIAL WEIGHT: 99.2 lbs.

POSSIBLE MOVES: Agility, Bite, Bug Bite, Bug Buzz, Charge, Crunch, Dig, Discharge, Fly, Guillotine, Iron Defense, Mud-Slap, Spark, Sticky Web, String Shot, Thunderbolt, Vise Grip, X-Scissor, Zap Cannon

GRUBBIN CHARJABUG VIKAVOLT

TYPE: GRASS-POISON

It has the world's largest petals. With every step, the petals shake out heavy clouds of toxic pollen.

The larger its petals, the more toxic pollen it contains. Its big head is heavy and hard to hold up.

HOW TO SAY IT: VILE-ploom
IMPERIAL HEIGHT: 3'11"
IMPERIAL WEIGHT: 41.0 lbs.
METRIC HEIGHT: 1.2 m
METRIC WEIGHT: 18.6 kg

POSSIBLE MOVES: Absorb, Acid, Aromatherapy, Giga Drain, Grassy Terrain, Growth, Mega Drain, Moonblast, Moonlight, Petal Blizzard, Petal Dance, Poison Powder, Sleep Powder, Stun Spore, Sweet Scent, Toxic

REGIONS:
GALAR
KALOS (CENTRAL)
KANTO

VILEPLUME
Flower Pokémon

ODDISH   GLOOM   VILEPLUME

LEGENDARY POKÉMON

REGION:
UNOVA

VIRIZION
Grassland Pokémon

TYPE: GRASS-FIGHTING

Its head sprouts horns as sharp as blades. Using whirlwind-like movements, it confounds and swiftly cuts opponents.

Legends say this Pokémon confounded opponents with its swift movements.

HOW TO SAY IT: vih-RY-zee-un
IMPERIAL HEIGHT: 6'07"
IMPERIAL WEIGHT: 440.9 lbs.
METRIC HEIGHT: 2.0 m
METRIC WEIGHT: 200.0 kg

POSSIBLE MOVES: Quick Attack, Leer, Double Kick, Magical Leaf, Take Down, Helping Hand, Retaliate, Giga Drain, Sacred Sword, Swords Dance, Quick Guard, Work Up, Leaf Blade, Close Combat

DOES NOT EVOLVE

VIVILLON
Scale Pokémon

TYPE: BUG-FLYING

Vivillon with many different patterns are found all over the world. These patterns are affected by the climate of their habitat.

The patterns on this Pokémon's wings depend on the climate and topography of its habitat. It scatters colorful scales.

HOW TO SAY IT: VIH-vee-yon
IMPERIAL HEIGHT: 3'11"
IMPERIAL WEIGHT: 37.5 lbs.
METRIC HEIGHT: 1.2 m
METRIC WEIGHT: 17.0 kg

POSSIBLE MOVES: Powder, Sleep Powder, Poison Powder, Stun Spore, Gust, Light Screen, Struggle Bug, Psybeam, Supersonic, Draining Kiss, Aromatherapy, Bug Buzz, Safeguard, Quiver Dance, Hurricane

SCATTERBUG ➡ SPEWPA ➡ VIVILLON

VOLBEAT
Firefly Pokémon

TYPE: BUG

With the arrival of night, Volbeat emits light from its tail. It communicates with others by adjusting the intensity and flashing of its light. This Pokémon is attracted by the sweet aroma of Illumise.

Volbeat's tail glows like a lightbulb. With other Volbeat, it uses its tail to draw geometric shapes in the night sky. This Pokémon loves the sweet aroma given off by Illumise.

HOW TO SAY IT: VOLL-beat
IMPERIAL HEIGHT: 2'04"
IMPERIAL WEIGHT: 39.0 lbs.
METRIC HEIGHT: 0.7 m
METRIC WEIGHT: 17.7 kg

POSSIBLE MOVES: Flash, Tackle, Double Team, Confuse Ray, Moonlight, Quick Attack, Tail Glow, Signal Beam, Protect, Helping Hand, Zen Headbutt, Bug Buzz, Double-Edge, Struggle Bug, Play Rough, Infestation

DOES NOT EVOLVE

REGION: KALOS

VOLCANION
Steam Pokémon

DOES NOT EVOLVE

TYPE: FIRE-WATER

It lets out billows of steam and disappears into the dense fog. It's said to live in mountains where humans do not tread.

It expels its internal steam from the arms on its back. It has enough power to blow away a mountain.

HOW TO SAY IT: vol-KAY-nee-un
IMPERIAL HEIGHT: 5'07"
IMPERIAL WEIGHT: 429.9 lbs.
METRIC HEIGHT: 1.7 m
METRIC WEIGHT: 195.0 kg

POSSIBLE MOVES: Steam Eruption, Flare Blitz, Take Down, Mist, Haze, Flame Charge, Water Pulse, Stomp, Scald, Weather Ball, Body Slam, Hydro Pump, Overheat, Explosion

---

REGION: ALOLA UNOVA

VOLCARONA
Sun Pokémon

TYPE: BUG-FIRE

Volcarona scatters burning scales. Some say it does this to start fires. Others say it's trying to rescue those that suffer in the cold.

This Pokémon emerges from a cocoon formed of raging flames. Ancient murals depict Volcarona as a deity of fire.

HOW TO SAY IT: vol-kah-ROH-nah
IMPERIAL HEIGHT: 5'03"
IMPERIAL WEIGHT: 101.4 lbs.
METRIC HEIGHT: 1.6 m
METRIC WEIGHT: 46.0 kg

POSSIBLE MOVES: Gust, Fire Spin, Whirlwind, Silver Wind, Quiver Dance, Heat Wave, Bug Buzz, Rage Powder, Hurricane, Fiery Dance, Flare Blitz, Thrash, Amnesia, Absorb, Flame Wheel, Ember, String Shot

LARVESTA

VOLCARONA

VOLTORB

Ball Pokémon

REGIONS:
KALOS
(MOUNTAIN)
KANTO

TYPE: ELECTRIC

It is said to camouflage itself as a Poké Ball. It will self-destruct with very little stimulus.

HOW TO SAY IT: VOLT-orb
IMPERIAL HEIGHT: 1'08"
IMPERIAL WEIGHT: 22.9 lbs.
METRIC HEIGHT: 0.5 m
METRIC WEIGHT: 10.4 kg

POSSIBLE MOVES: Charge, Tackle, Sonic Boom, Eerie Impulse, Spark, Rollout, Screech, Charge Beam, Light Screen, Electro Ball, Self-Destruct, Swift, Magnet Rise, Gyro Ball, Explosion, Mirror Coat, Discharge

VOLTORB   ELECTRODE

VULLABY

Diapered Pokémon

REGIONS:
ALOLA
GALAR
UNOVA

TYPE: DARK-FLYING

It wears a bone to protect its rear. It often squabbles with others of its kind over particularly comfy bones.

Vullaby grow quickly. Bones that have gotten too small for older Vullaby to wear often get passed down to younger ones in the nest.

HOW TO SAY IT: VUL-luh-bye
IMPERIAL HEIGHT: 1'08"
IMPERIAL WEIGHT: 19.8 lbs.
METRIC HEIGHT: 0.5 m
METRIC WEIGHT: 9.0 kg

POSSIBLE MOVES: Air Slash, Attract, Brave Bird, Dark Pulse, Defog, Flatter, Gust, Iron Defense, Knock Off, Leer, Nasty Plot, Pluck, Tailwind, Whirlwind

VULLABY   MANDIBUZZ

TYPE: FIRE

While young, it has six gorgeous tails. When it grows, several new tails are sprouted.

As each tail grows, its fur becomes more lustrous. When held, it feels slightly warm.

HOW TO SAY IT: VULL-picks
IMPERIAL HEIGHT: 2'00"
IMPERIAL WEIGHT: 21.8 lbs.
METRIC HEIGHT: 0.6 m
METRIC WEIGHT: 9.9 kg

POSSIBLE MOVES: Confuse Ray, Disable, Ember, Extrasensory, Fire Blast, Fire Spin, Flamethrower, Grudge, Imprison, Incinerate, Inferno, Quick Attack, Safeguard, Spite, Tail Whip, Will-O-Wisp

REGIONS:
GALAR
KANTO

VULPIX
Fox Pokémon

VULPIX → **NINETALES**

REGION:
ALOLA

ALOLAN VULPIX
Fox Pokémon

TYPE: ICE

After long years in the ever-snowcapped mountains of Alola, this Vulpix has gained power over ice.

If you observe its curly hairs through a microscope, you'll see small ice particles springing up.

HOW TO SAY IT: VULL-picks
IMPERIAL HEIGHT: 2'00"
IMPERIAL WEIGHT: 21.8 lbs.
METRIC HEIGHT: 0.6 m
METRIC WEIGHT: 9.9 kg

POSSIBLE MOVES: Aurora Beam, Aurora Veil, Blizzard, Confuse Ray, Disable, Extrasensory, Grudge, Ice Beam, Ice Shard, Icy Wind, Imprison, Mist, Powder Snow, Sheer Cold, Spite, Tail Whip

ALOLAN VULPIX **ALOLAN NINETALES**

WAILMER
Ball Whale Pokémon

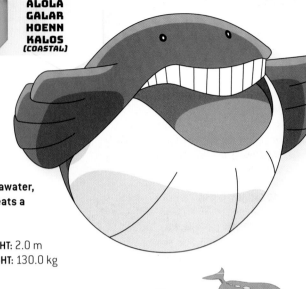

TYPE: WATER

It shows off by spraying jets of seawater from the nostrils above its eyes. It eats a solid ton of Wishiwashi every day.

When it sucks in a large volume of seawater, it becomes like a big, bouncy ball. It eats a ton of food daily.

HOW TO SAY IT: WAIL-murr   **METRIC HEIGHT:** 2.0 m
IMPERIAL HEIGHT: 6'07"   **METRIC WEIGHT:** 130.0 kg
IMPERIAL WEIGHT: 286.6 lbs.

POSSIBLE MOVES: Amnesia, Astonish, Body Slam, Bounce, Brine, Dive, Growl, Heavy Slam, Hydro Pump, Mist, Rest, Splash, Water Gun, Water Pulse, Water Spout, Whirlpool

WAILMER   WAILORD

WAILORD
Float Whale Pokémon

TYPE: WATER

It can sometimes knock out opponents with the shock created by breaching and crashing its big body onto the water.

Its immense size is the reason for its popularity. Wailord watching is a favorite sightseeing activity in various parts of the world.

HOW TO SAY IT: WAIL-ord
IMPERIAL HEIGHT: 47'07"
IMPERIAL WEIGHT: 877.4 lbs.
METRIC HEIGHT: 14.5 m
METRIC WEIGHT: 398.0 kg

POSSIBLE MOVES: Amnesia, Astonish, Body Slam, Bounce, Brine, Dive, Growl, Heavy Slam, Hydro Pump, Mist, Noble Roar, Rest, Soak, Splash, Water Gun, Water Pulse, Water Spout, Whirlpool

WAILMER   WAILORD

TYPE: ICE-WATER

Walrein's two massively developed tusks can totally shatter blocks of ice weighing 10 tons with one blow. This Pokémon's thick coat of blubber insulates it from subzero temperatures.

Walrein swims all over in frigid seawater while crushing icebergs with its grand, imposing tusks. Its thick layer of blubber makes enemy attacks bounce off harmlessly.

REGION: HOENN

WALREIN
Ice Break Pokémon

HOW TO SAY IT: WAL-rain
IMPERIAL HEIGHT: 4'07"
IMPERIAL WEIGHT: 332.0 lbs.
METRIC HEIGHT: 1.4 m
METRIC WEIGHT: 150.6 kg

POSSIBLE MOVES: Crunch, Powder Snow, Growl, Water Gun, Encore, Ice Ball, Body Slam, Aurora Beam, Hail, Swagger, Rest, Snore, Ice Fang, Blizzard, Sheer Cold, Defense Curl, Rollout, Brine

SPHEAL ➡ SEALEO ➡ WALREIN

TYPE: WATER

It is recognized as a symbol of longevity. If its shell has algae on it, that Wartortle is very old.

It cleverly controls its furry ears and tail to maintain its balance while swimming.

REGIONS: KALOS (CENTRAL) KANTO

WARTORTLE
Turtle Pokémon

HOW TO SAY IT: WOR-TORE-tul
IMPERIAL HEIGHT: 3'03"
IMPERIAL WEIGHT: 49.6 lbs.
METRIC HEIGHT: 1.0 m
METRIC WEIGHT: 22.5 kg

POSSIBLE MOVES: Tackle, Tail Whip, Water Gun, Tail Whip, Water Gun, Withdraw, Bubble, Bite, Rapid Spin, Protect, Water Pulse, Aqua Tail, Skull Bash, Iron Defense, Rain Dance, Hydro Pump

SQUIRTLE ➡ WARTORTLE ➡ BLASTOISE ➡ MEGA BLASTOISE

WATCHOG
Lookout Pokémon

TYPE: NORMAL

Using luminescent matter, it makes its eyes and body glow and stuns attacking opponents.

When they see an enemy, their tails stand high, and they spit the seeds of berries stored in their cheek pouches.

HOW TO SAY IT: WAH-chawg
IMPERIAL HEIGHT: 3'07"
IMPERIAL WEIGHT: 59.5 lbs.
METRIC HEIGHT: 1.1 m
METRIC WEIGHT: 27.0 kg

POSSIBLE MOVES: Rototiller, Tackle, Leer, Bite, Low Kick, Bide, Detect, Sand Attack, Crunch, Hypnosis, Confuse Ray, Super Fang, After You, Psych Up, Hyper Fang, Mean Look, Baton Pass, Slam, Nasty Plot, Focus Energy

PATRAT → WATCHOG

WEAVILE
Sharp Claw Pokémon

REGIONS:
ALOLA
GALAR
KALOS
(MOUNTAIN)
SINNOH

TYPE: DARK-ICE

They attack their quarry in packs. Prey as large as Mamoswine easily fall to the teamwork of a group of Weavile.

With its claws, it leaves behind signs for its friends to find. The number of distinct signs is said to be over 500.

HOW TO SAY IT: WEE-vile
IMPERIAL HEIGHT: 3'07"
IMPERIAL WEIGHT: 75.0 lbs.
METRIC HEIGHT: 1.1 m
METRIC WEIGHT: 34.0 kg

POSSIBLE MOVES: Agility, Assurance, Beat Up, Dark Pulse, Fling, Fury Swipes, Hone Claws, Ice Shard, Icy Wind, Leer, Metal Claw, Nasty Plot, Night Slash, Quick Attack, Revenge, Scratch, Screech, Slash, Taunt

SNEASEL → WEAVILE

WEEDLE

Hairy Bug Pokémon

TYPE: BUG-POISON

Beware of the sharp stinger on its head. It hides in grass and bushes where it eats leaves.

HOW TO SAY IT: WEE-dull
IMPERIAL HEIGHT: 1'00"
IMPERIAL WEIGHT: 7.1 lbs.
METRIC HEIGHT: 0.3 m
METRIC WEIGHT: 3.2 kg

POSSIBLE MOVES: Poison Sting, String Shot, Bug Bite

WEEDLE **KAKUNA** **BEEDRILL** **MEGA BEEDRILL**

WEEPINBELL

Flycatcher Pokémon

TYPE: GRASS-POISON

When hungry, it swallows anything that moves. Its hapless prey is dissolved by strong acids.

HOW TO SAY IT: WEE-pin-bell
IMPERIAL HEIGHT: 3'03"
IMPERIAL WEIGHT: 14.1 lbs.
METRIC HEIGHT: 1.0 m
METRIC WEIGHT: 6.4 kg

POSSIBLE MOVES: Vine Whip, Growth, Wrap, Sleep Powder, Poison Powder, Stun Spore, Acid, Knock Off, Sweet Scent, Gastro Acid, Razor Leaf, Poison Jab, Slam, Wring Out

BELLSPROUT **WEEPINBELL** **VICTREEBEL**

WEEZING

Poison Gas Pokémon

TYPE: POISON

It mixes gases between its two bodies. It's said that these Pokémon were seen all over the Galar region back in the day.

It can't suck in air quite as well as a Galarian Weezing, but the toxins it creates are more potent than those of its counterpart.

HOW TO SAY IT: WEEZ-ing **METRIC HEIGHT:** 1.2 m
IMPERIAL HEIGHT: 3'11" **METRIC WEIGHT:** 9.5 kg
IMPERIAL WEIGHT: 20.9 lbs.

POSSIBLE MOVES: Assurance, Belch, Clear Smog, Destiny Bond, Double Hit, Explosion, Haze, Heat Wave, Memento, Poison Gas, Self-Destruct, Sludge, Sludge Bomb, Smog, Smokescreen, Tackle, Toxic

KOFFING   WEEZING

GALARIAN WEEZING

Poison Gas Pokémon

TYPE: POISON-FAIRY

This Pokémon consumes particles that contaminate the air. Instead of leaving droppings, it expels clean air.

Long ago, during a time when droves of factories fouled the air with pollution, Weezing changed into this form for some reason.

HOW TO SAY IT: WEEZ-ing **METRIC HEIGHT:** 3.0 m
IMPERIAL HEIGHT: 9'10" **METRIC WEIGHT:** 16.0 kg
IMPERIAL WEIGHT: 35.3 lbs.

POSSIBLE MOVES: Aromatherapy, Aromatic Mist, Assurance, Belch, Clear Smog, Defog, Destiny Bond, Double Hit, Explosion, Fairy Wind, Haze, Heat Wave, Memento, Misty Terrain, Poison Gas, Self-Destruct, Sludge, Sludge Bomb, Smog, Smokescreen, Strange Steam, Tackle, Toxic

KOFFING

GALARIAN WEEZING

WHIMSICOTT
Windveiled Pokémon

TYPE: GRASS-FAIRY

It scatters cotton all over the place as a prank. If it gets wet, it'll become too heavy to move and have no choice but to answer for its mischief.

As long as this Pokémon bathes in sunlight, its cotton keeps growing. If too much cotton fluff builds up, Whimsicott tears it off and scatters it.

HOW TO SAY IT: WHIM-sih-kot **METRIC HEIGHT:** 0.7 m
IMPERIAL HEIGHT: 2'04" **METRIC WEIGHT:** 6.6 kg
IMPERIAL WEIGHT: 14.6 lbs.

POSSIBLE MOVES: Absorb, Charm, Cotton Guard, Cotton Spore, Endeavor, Energy Ball, Giga Drain, Growth, Gust, Helping Hand, Hurricane, Leech Seed, Mega Drain, Memento, Moonblast, Poison Powder, Razor Leaf, Solar Beam, Sunny Day, Tailwind

COTTONEE   WHIMSICOTT

WHIRLIPEDE
Curlipede Pokémon

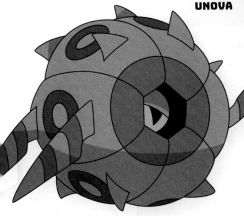

TYPE: BUG-POISON

This Pokémon spins itself rapidly and charges into its opponents. Its top speed is just over 60 mph.

Whirlipede protects itself with a sturdy shell and poisonous spikes while it stores up the energy it'll need for Evolution.

HOW TO SAY IT: WHIR-lih-peed **METRIC HEIGHT:** 1.2 m
IMPERIAL HEIGHT: 3'11" **METRIC WEIGHT:** 58.5 kg
IMPERIAL WEIGHT: 129.0 lbs.

POSSIBLE MOVES: Defense Curl, Rollout, Poison Sting, Screech, Pursuit, Protect, Poison Tail, Iron Defense, Bug Bite, Venoshock, Agility, Steamroller, Toxic, Venom Drench, Rock Climb, Double-Edge

VENIPEDE   WHIRLIPEDE   SCOLIPEDE

WHISCASH
Whiskers Pokémon

REGIONS:
ALOLA
GALAR
HOENN
KALOS
(MOUNTAIN)

TYPE: WATER-GROUND

It makes its nest at the bottom of swamps. It will eat anything—if it is alive, Whiscash will eat it.

It claims a large swamp to itself. If a foe comes near it, it sets off tremors by thrashing around.

HOW TO SAY IT: WISS-cash
IMPERIAL HEIGHT: 2'11"
IMPERIAL WEIGHT: 52.0 lbs.
METRIC HEIGHT: 0.9 m
METRIC WEIGHT: 23.6 kg

POSSIBLE MOVES: Amnesia, Aqua Tail, Belch, Earthquake, Fissure, Future Sight, Muddy Water, Mud-Slap, Rest, Snore, Thrash, Tickle, Water Gun, Water Pulse, Zen Headbutt

BARBOACH   WHISCASH

WHISMUR
Whisper Pokémon

TYPE: NORMAL

The cry of a Whismur is over 100 decibels. If you're close to a Whismur when it lets out a cry, you'll be stuck with an all-day headache.

When Whismur cries, the sound of its own voice startles it, making the Pokémon cry even louder. It cries until it's exhausted, and then it falls asleep.

HOW TO SAY IT: WHIS-mur
IMPERIAL HEIGHT: 2'00"
IMPERIAL WEIGHT: 35.9 lbs.
METRIC HEIGHT: 0.6 m
METRIC WEIGHT: 16.3 kg

POSSIBLE MOVES: Pound, Uproar, Astonish, Howl, Supersonic, Stomp, Screech, Roar, Synchronoise, Rest, Sleep Talk, Hyper Voice, Echoed Voice

WHISMUR   LOUDRED   EXPLOUD

WIGGLYTUFF
Balloon Pokémon

TYPE: NORMAL-FAIRY

When the weather gets warm, Wigglytuff shed their fur, which can be spun into delightfully soft yarn. As these Pokémon breathe in, their bodies expand to hold more air—sometimes they make a game of how much they can inflate.

HOW TO SAY IT: WIG-lee-tuff
IMPERIAL HEIGHT: 3'03"
IMPERIAL WEIGHT: 26.5 lbs.
METRIC HEIGHT: 1.0 m
METRIC WEIGHT: 12.0 kg

POSSIBLE MOVES: Double-Edge, Play Rough, Sing, Defense Curl, Disable, Double Slap

IGGLYBUFF ➡ JIGGLYPUFF ➡ WIGGLYTUFF

WIMPOD
Turn Tail Pokémon

TYPE: BUG-WATER

It's nature's cleaner—it eats anything and everything, including garbage and rotten things. The ground near its nest is always clean.

Wimpod gather in swarms, constantly on the lookout for danger. They scatter the moment they detect an enemy's presence.

HOW TO SAY IT: WIM-pod   **METRIC HEIGHT:** 0.5 m
IMPERIAL HEIGHT: 1'08"   **METRIC WEIGHT:** 12.0 kg
IMPERIAL WEIGHT: 26.5 lbs.

POSSIBLE MOVES: Defense Curl, Sand Attack, Struggle Bug

WIMPOD   GOLISOPOD

WINGULL

Seagull Pokémon

REGIONS:
ALOLA
GALAR
HOENN
KALOS
(COASTAL)

TYPE: WATER-FLYING

It makes its nest on sheer cliffs. Riding the sea breeze, it glides up into the expansive skies.

It soars on updrafts without flapping its wings. It makes a nest on sheer cliffs at the sea's edge.

HOW TO SAY IT: WING-gull
IMPERIAL HEIGHT: 2'00"
IMPERIAL WEIGHT: 20.9 lbs.
METRIC HEIGHT: 0.6 m
METRIC WEIGHT: 9.5 kg

POSSIBLE MOVES: Agility, Air Slash, Growl, Hurricane, Mist, Quick Attack, Roost, Supersonic, Water Gun, Water Pulse, Wing Attack

WINGULL　　PELIPPER

WISHIWASHI

Small Fry Pokémon

SOLO FORM

TYPE: WATER

Individually, they're incredibly weak. It's by gathering up into schools that they're able to confront opponents.

When it senses danger, its eyes tear up. The sparkle of its tears signals other Wishiwashi to gather.

HOW TO SAY IT: WISH-ee-WASH-ee
IMPERIAL HEIGHT: Solo Form: 0'08" / School Form: 26'11"
IMPERIAL WEIGHT: Solo Form: 0.7 lbs. /
　　　　　　　　　School Form: 173.3 lbs.
METRIC HEIGHT: Solo Form: 0.2 m / School Form: 8.2 m
METRIC WEIGHT: Solo Form: 0.3 kg /
　　　　　　　　　School Form: 78.6 kg

SCHOOL FORM

POSSIBLE MOVES: Aqua Ring, Aqua Tail, Beat Up, Brine, Dive, Double-Edge, Endeavor, Growl, Helping Hand, Hydro Pump, Soak, Tearful Look, Uproar, Water Gun

DOES NOT EVOLVE

TYPE: PSYCHIC

It hates light and shock. If attacked, it inflates its body to pump up its counterstrike.

To keep its pitch-black tail hidden, it lives quietly in the darkness. It is never first to attack.

WOBBUFFET
Patient Pokémon

REGIONS:
GALAR
JOHTO
KALOS
(COASTAL)

HOW TO SAY IT: WAH-buf-fett
IMPERIAL HEIGHT: 4'03"
IMPERIAL WEIGHT: 62.8 lbs.
METRIC HEIGHT: 1.3 m
METRIC WEIGHT: 28.5 kg

POSSIBLE MOVES: Amnesia, Charm, Counter, Destiny Bond, Encore, Mirror Coat, Safeguard, Splash

WYNAUT   WOBBUFFET

WOOBAT
Bat Pokémon

REGIONS:
GALAR
KALOS
(COASTAL)
UNOVA

TYPE: PSYCHIC-FLYING

While inside a cave, if you look up and see lots of heart-shaped marks lining the walls, it's evidence that Woobat live there.

It emits ultrasonic waves as it flutters about, searching for its prey—bug Pokémon.

HOW TO SAY IT: WOO-bat
IMPERIAL HEIGHT: 1'04"
IMPERIAL WEIGHT: 4.6 lbs.
METRIC HEIGHT: 0.4 m
METRIC WEIGHT: 2.1 kg

POSSIBLE MOVES: Air Cutter, Air Slash, Amnesia, Assurance, Attract, Calm Mind, Confusion, Endeavor, Future Sight, Gust, Imprison, Psychic, Simple Beam

WOOBAT   SWOOBAT

WOOLOO
Sheep Pokémon

REGION: GALAR

TYPE: NORMAL

Its curly fleece is such an effective cushion that this Pokémon could fall off a cliff and stand right back up at the bottom, unharmed.

If its fleece grows too long, Wooloo won't be able to move. Cloth made with the wool of this Pokémon is surprisingly strong.

HOW TO SAY IT: WOO-loo
IMPERIAL HEIGHT: 2'00"
IMPERIAL WEIGHT: 13.2 lbs.
METRIC HEIGHT: 0.6 m
METRIC WEIGHT: 6.0 kg

POSSIBLE MOVES: Copycat, Cotton Guard, Defense Curl, Double Kick, Double-Edge, Growl, Guard Split, Guard Swap, Headbutt, Reversal, Tackle, Take Down

WOOLOO → DUBWOOL

WOOPER
Water Fish Pokémon

REGIONS: GALAR JOHTO KALOS (MOUNTAIN)

TYPE: WATER-GROUND

This Pokémon lives in cold water. It will leave the water to search for food when it gets cold outside.

When walking on land, it covers its body with a poisonous film that keeps its skin from dehydrating.

HOW TO SAY IT: WOOP-pur
IMPERIAL HEIGHT: 1'04"
IMPERIAL WEIGHT: 18.7 lbs.
METRIC HEIGHT: 0.4 m
METRIC WEIGHT: 8.5 kg

POSSIBLE MOVES: Amnesia, Aqua Tail, Earthquake, Haze, Mist, Mud Shot, Muddy Water, Rain Dance, Slam, Tail Whip, Toxic, Water Gun, Yawn

WOOPER → QUAGSIRE

WORMADAM

Bagworm Pokémon

PLANT CLOAK

SANDY CLOAK

PLANT CLOAK TYPE: BUG-GRASS
SANDY CLOAK TYPE: BUG-GROUND
TRASH CLOAK TYPE: BUG-STEEL

Its appearance changes depending on where it evolved. The materials on hand become a part of its body.

When Burmy evolved, its cloak became a part of this Pokémon's body. The cloak is never shed.

HOW TO SAY IT: WUR-muh-dam
IMPERIAL HEIGHT: 1'08"
IMPERIAL WEIGHT: 14.3 lbs.
METRIC HEIGHT: 0.5 m
METRIC WEIGHT: 6.5 kg

POSSIBLE MOVES: Quiver Dance, Sucker Punch, Tackle, Protect, Bug Bite, Hidden Power, Confusion, Razor Leaf, Growth, Psybeam, Captivate, Flail, Attract, Psychic, Leaf Storm, Bug Buzz

TRASH CLOAK

BURMY → **WORMADAM**

WURMPLE
Worm Pokémon

TYPE: BUG

Using the spikes on its rear end, Wurmple peels the bark off trees and feeds on the sap that oozes out. This Pokémon's feet are tipped with suction pads that allow it to cling to glass without slipping.

Wurmple is targeted by Swellow as prey. This Pokémon will try to resist by pointing the spikes on its rear at the attacking predator. It will weaken the foe by leaking poison from the spikes.

HOW TO SAY IT: WERM-pull
IMPERIAL HEIGHT: 1'00"
IMPERIAL WEIGHT: 7.9 lbs.
METRIC HEIGHT: 0.3 m
METRIC WEIGHT: 3.6 kg

POSSIBLE MOVES: Tackle, String Shot, Poison Sting, Bug Bite

SILCOON

BEAUTIFLY

WURMPLE

CASCOON

DUSTOX

WYNAUT
Bright Pokémon

TYPE: PSYCHIC

It tends to move in a pack. Individuals squash against one another to toughen their spirits.

It tends to move in a pack with others. They cluster in a tight group to sleep in a cave.

HOW TO SAY IT: WHY-not
IMPERIAL HEIGHT: 2'00"
IMPERIAL WEIGHT: 30.9 lbs.
METRIC HEIGHT: 0.6 m
METRIC WEIGHT: 14.0 kg

POSSIBLE MOVES: Amnesia, Charm, Counter, Destiny Bond, Encore, Mirror Coat, Safeguard, Splash

WYNAUT

WOBBUFFET

XATU
Mystic Pokémon

TYPE: PSYCHIC-FLYING

They say that it stays still and quiet because it is seeing both the past and future at the same time.

This odd Pokémon can see both the past and the future. It eyes the sun's movement all day.

HOW TO SAY IT: ZAH-too
IMPERIAL HEIGHT: 4'11"
IMPERIAL WEIGHT: 33.1 lbs.
METRIC HEIGHT: 1.5 m
METRIC WEIGHT: 15.0 kg

POSSIBLE MOVES: Air Slash, Confuse Ray, Future Sight, Guard Swap, Leer, Night Shade, Peck, Power Swap, Psychic, Psycho Shift, Stored Power, Tailwind, Teleport, Wish

NATU   **XATU**

LEGENDARY POKÉMON

XERNEAS
Life Pokémon

TYPE: FAIRY

Legends say it can share eternal life. It slept for a thousand years in the form of a tree before its revival.

When the horns on its head shine in seven colors, it is said to be sharing everlasting life.

HOW TO SAY IT: ZURR-nee-us
IMPERIAL HEIGHT: 9'10"
IMPERIAL WEIGHT: 474.0 lbs.
METRIC HEIGHT: 3.0 m
METRIC WEIGHT: 215.0 kg

POSSIBLE MOVES: Heal Pulse, Aromatherapy, Ingrain, Take Down, Light Screen, Aurora Beam, Gravity, Geomancy, Moonblast, Megahorn, Night Slash, Horn Leech, Psych Up, Misty Terrain, Nature Power, Close Combat, Giga Impact, Outrage

DOES NOT EVOLVE

XURKITREE
Glowing Pokémon

ULTRA BEAST

TYPE: ELECTRIC

Although it's alien to this world and a danger here, it's apparently a common organism in the world where it normally lives.

They've been dubbed Ultra Beasts. Some of them stand unmoving, like trees, with their arms and legs stuck into the ground.

HOW TO SAY IT: ZURK-ih-tree
IMPERIAL HEIGHT: 12'06"
IMPERIAL WEIGHT: 220.5 lbs.
METRIC HEIGHT: 3.8 m
METRIC WEIGHT: 100.0 kg

POSSIBLE MOVES: Tail Glow, Spark, Charge, Wrap, Thunder Shock, Thunder Wave, Shock Wave, Ingrain, Thunder Punch, Eerie Impulse, Signal Beam, Thunderbolt, Hypnosis, Discharge, Electric Terrain, Power Whip, Ion Deluge, Zap Cannon

DOES NOT EVOLVE

YAMASK
Spirit Pokémon

TYPE: GHOST

It wanders through ruins by night, carrying a mask that's said to have been the face it had when it was still human.

The spirit of a person from a bygone age became this Pokémon. It rambles through ruins, searching for someone who knows its face.

HOW TO SAY IT: YAH-mask
IMPERIAL HEIGHT: 1'08"
IMPERIAL WEIGHT: 3.3 lbs.
METRIC HEIGHT: 0.5 m
METRIC WEIGHT: 1.5 kg

POSSIBLE MOVES: Astonish, Crafty Shield, Curse, Dark Pulse, Destiny Bond, Disable, Grudge, Guard Split, Haze, Hex, Mean Look, Night Shade, Power Split, Protect, Shadow Ball, Will-O-Wisp

YAMASK → COFAGRIGUS

GALARIAN YAMASK
Spirit Pokémon

TYPE: GROUND-GHOST

A clay slab with cursed engravings took possession of a Yamask. The slab is said to be absorbing the Yamask's dark power.

It's said that this Pokémon was formed when an ancient clay tablet was drawn to a vengeful spirit.

HOW TO SAY IT: YAH-mask
IMPERIAL HEIGHT: 1'08"
IMPERIAL WEIGHT: 3.3 lbs.
METRIC HEIGHT: 0.5 m
METRIC WEIGHT: 15. kg

POSSIBLE MOVES: Astonish, Brutal Swing, Crafty Shield, Curse, Destiny Bond, Disable, Earthquake, Guard Split, Haze, Hex, Mean Look, Night Shade, Power Split, Protect, Shadow Ball, Slam

GALARIAN
YAMASK → RUNERIGUS

YAMPER

Puppy Pokémon

TYPE: ELECTRIC

This Pokémon is very popular as a herding dog in the Galar region. As it runs, it generates electricity from the base of its tail.

This gluttonous Pokémon only assists people with their work because it wants treats. As it runs, it crackles with electricity.

HOW TO SAY IT: YAM-per
IMPERIAL HEIGHT: 1'00"
IMPERIAL WEIGHT: 29.8 lbs.
METRIC HEIGHT: 0.3 m
METRIC WEIGHT: 13.5 kg

POSSIBLE MOVES: Bite, Charge, Charm, Crunch, Nuzzle, Play Rough, Roar, Spark, Tackle, Tail Whip, Wild Charge

VAMPER   **BOLTUND**

YANMA

Clear Wing Pokémon

TYPE: BUG-FLYING

Yanma is capable of seeing 360 degrees without having to move its eyes. It is a great flier that is adept at making sudden stops and turning midair. This Pokémon uses its flying ability to quickly chase down targeted prey.

HOW TO SAY IT: YAN-ma
IMPERIAL HEIGHT: 3'11"
IMPERIAL WEIGHT: 83.8 lbs.
METRIC HEIGHT: 1.2 m
METRIC WEIGHT: 38.0 kg

POSSIBLE MOVES: Tackle, Foresight, Quick Attack, Double Team, Sonic Boom, Detect, Supersonic, Uproar, Pursuit, Ancient Power, Hypnosis, Wing Attack, Screech, U-turn, Air Slash, Bug Buzz

YANMA   **YANMEGA**

YANMEGA

Ogre Darner Pokémon

TYPE: BUG-FLYING

It prefers to battle by biting apart foes' heads instantly while flying by at high speed.

This six-legged Pokémon is easily capable of transporting an adult in flight. The wings on its tail help it stay balanced.

HOW TO SAY IT: yan-MEG-ah
IMPERIAL HEIGHT: 6'03"
IMPERIAL WEIGHT: 113.5 lbs.
METRIC HEIGHT: 1.9 m
METRIC WEIGHT: 51.5 kg

POSSIBLE MOVES: Bug Buzz, Air Slash, Night Slash, Bug Bite, Tackle, Foresight, Quick Attack, Double Team, Sonic Boom, Detect, Supersonic, Uproar, Pursuit, Ancient Power, Feint, Slash, Screech, U-turn

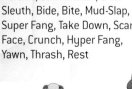

YANMA   YANMEGA

TYPE: NORMAL

Its stomach takes up most of its long torso. It's a big eater, so the amount Trainers have to spend on its food is no laughing matter.

Although it will eat anything, it prefers fresh living things, so it marches down streets in search of prey.

YUNGOOS

Loitering Pokémon

HOW TO SAY IT: YUNG-goose
IMPERIAL HEIGHT: 1'04"
IMPERIAL WEIGHT: 13.2 lbs.
METRIC HEIGHT: 0.4 m
METRIC WEIGHT: 6.0 kg

POSSIBLE MOVES: Tackle, Leer, Pursuit, Sand Attack, Odor Sleuth, Bide, Bite, Mud-Slap, Super Fang, Take Down, Scary Face, Crunch, Hyper Fang, Yawn, Thrash, Rest

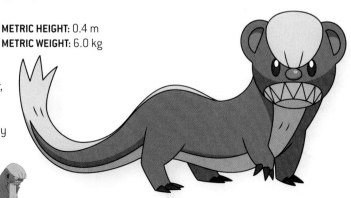

YUNGOOS   GUMSHOOS

YVELTAL

Destruction Pokémon

LEGENDARY POKÉMON

TYPE: DARK-FLYING

When this legendary Pokémon's wings and tail feathers spread wide and glow red, it absorbs the life force of living creatures.

When its life comes to an end, it absorbs the life energy of every living thing and turns into a cocoon once more.

HOW TO SAY IT: ee-VELL-tall
METRIC HEIGHT: 5.8 m
IMPERIAL HEIGHT: 19'00"
METRIC WEIGHT: 203.0 kg
IMPERIAL WEIGHT: 447.5 lbs.

POSSIBLE MOVES: Hurricane, Razor Wind, Taunt, Roost, Double Team, Air Slash, Snarl, Oblivion Wing, Disable, Dark Pulse, Foul Play, Phantom Force, Psychic, Dragon Rush, Focus Blast, Sucker Punch, Hyper Beam, Sky Attack

DOES NOT EVOLVE

REGION: GALAR

ZACIAN
Warrior Pokémon

TYPE: FAIRY-STEEL

Now armed with a weapon it used in ancient times, this Pokémon needs only a single strike to fell even Gigantamax Pokémon.

Able to cut down anything with a single strike, it became known as the Fairy King's Sword, and it inspired awe in friend and foe alike.

HOW TO SAY IT: ZAH-shee-uhn
IMPERIAL HEIGHT: 9'02"
IMPERIAL WEIGHT: 782.6 lbs.
METRIC HEIGHT: 2.8 m
METRIC WEIGHT: 355.0 kg

POSSIBLE MOVES: Bite, Close Combat, Crunch, Giga Impact, Howl, Iron Head, Laser Focus, Metal Claw, Moonblast, Quick Attack, Quick Guard, Sacred Sword, Slash, Swords Dance

CROWNED SWORD

HERO OF MANY BATTLES

DOES NOT EVOLVE

ZAMAZENTA
Warrior Pokémon

REGION: GALAR

TYPE: FIGHTING-STEEL

Its ability to deflect any attack led to it being known as the Fighting Master's Shield. It was feared and respected by all.

Now that it's equipped with its shield, it can shrug off impressive blows, including the attacks of Dynamax Pokémon.

HOW TO SAY IT: ZAH-mah-ZEN-tuh
IMPERIAL HEIGHT: 9'06"
METRIC HEIGHT: 2.9 m
IMPERIAL WEIGHT: 1730.6 lbs.
METRIC WEIGHT: 785.0 kg

POSSIBLE MOVES: Bite, Close Combat, Crunch, Giga Impact, Howl, Iron Defense, Iron Head, Laser Focus, Metal Burst, Metal Claw, Moonblast, Quick Attack, Slash, Wide Guard

CROWNED SHIELD

HERO OF MANY BATTLES

DOES NOT EVOLVE

ZANGOOSE
Cat Ferret Pokémon

TYPE: NORMAL

Memories of battling its archrival Seviper are etched into every cell of Zangoose's body. This Pokémon adroitly dodges attacks with incredible agility.

Zangoose usually stays on all fours, but when angered, it gets up on its hind legs and extends its claws. This Pokémon shares a bitter rivalry with Seviper that dates back over generations.

HOW TO SAY IT: ZANG-goose
IMPERIAL HEIGHT: 4'03"
IMPERIAL WEIGHT: 88.8 lbs.
METRIC HEIGHT: 1.3 m
METRIC WEIGHT: 40.3 kg

POSSIBLE MOVES: Scratch, Leer, Quick Attack, Fury Cutter, Pursuit, Slash, Embargo, Crush Claw, Revenge, False Swipe, Detect, X-Scissor, Taunt, Swords Dance, Close Combat, Hone Claws

DOES NOT EVOLVE

ZAPDOS
Electric Pokémon

LEGENDARY POKÉMON

TYPE: ELECTRIC-FLYING

This legendary bird Pokémon is said to appear when the sky turns dark and lightning showers down.

HOW TO SAY IT: ZAP-dose
IMPERIAL HEIGHT: 5'03"
IMPERIAL WEIGHT: 116.0 lbs.
METRIC HEIGHT: 1.6 m
METRIC WEIGHT: 52.6 kg

POSSIBLE MOVES: Roost, Zap Cannon, Drill Peck, Peck, Thunder Shock, Thunder Wave, Detect, Pluck, Ancient Power, Charge, Agility, Discharge, Rain Dance, Light Screen, Thunder, Magnetic Flux

DOES NOT EVOLVE

ZEBSTRIKA
Thunderbolt Pokémon

TYPE: ELECTRIC

When this ill-tempered Pokémon runs wild, it shoots lightning from its mane in all directions.

They have lightning-like movements. When Zebstrika run at full speed, the sound of thunder reverberates.

HOW TO SAY IT: zehb-STRY-kuh
IMPERIAL HEIGHT: 5'03"
IMPERIAL WEIGHT: 175.3 lbs.
METRIC HEIGHT: 1.6 m
METRIC WEIGHT: 79.5 kg

POSSIBLE MOVES: Quick Attack, Tail Whip, Charge, Thunder Wave, Shock Wave, Flame Charge, Pursuit, Spark, Stomp, Discharge, Agility, Wild Charge, Thrash, Ion Deluge

BLITZLE → ZEBSTRIKA

REGION: UNOVA

ZEKROM

Deep Black Pokémon

TYPE: DRAGON-ELECTRIC

This legendary Pokémon can scorch the world with lightning. It assists those who want to build an ideal world.

Concealing itself in lightning clouds, it flies throughout the Unova region. It creates electricity in its tail.

HOW TO SAY IT: ZECK-rahm
IMPERIAL HEIGHT: 9'06"
IMPERIAL WEIGHT: 760.6 lbs.
METRIC HEIGHT: 2.9 m
METRIC WEIGHT: 345.0 kg

POSSIBLE MOVES: Thunder Fang, Dragon Rage, Imprison, Ancient Power, Thunderbolt, Dragon Breath, Slash, Zen Headbutt, Fusion Bolt, Dragon Claw, Noble Roar, Crunch, Thunder, Outrage, Hyper Voice, Bolt Strike

OVERDRIVE FORM

DOES NOT EVOLVE

ZERAORA
Thunderclap Pokémon

REGION: ALOLA

MYTHICAL
POKÉMON

TYPE: ELECTRIC

It electrifies its claws and tears its opponents apart with them. Even if they dodge its attack, they'll be electrocuted by the flying sparks.

It approaches its enemies at the speed of lightning, then tears them limb from limb with its sharp claws.

HOW TO SAY IT: ZEH-rah-OH-rah
IMPERIAL HEIGHT: 4'11"
IMPERIAL WEIGHT: 98.1 lbs.
METRIC HEIGHT: 1.5 m
METRIC WEIGHT: 44.5 kg

POSSIBLE MOVES: Fake Out, Power-Up Punch, Quick Attack, Scratch, Snarl, Spark, Fury Swipes, Quick Guard, Slash, Volt Switch, Charge, Thunder Punch, Hone Claws, Discharge, Wild Charge, Agility, Plasma Fists, Close Combat

DOES NOT EVOLVE

ZIGZAGOON
Tiny Raccoon Pokémon

TYPE: NORMAL

It marks its territory by rubbing its bristly fur on trees. This variety of Zigzagoon is friendlier and calmer than the kind native to Galar.

Zigzagoon that adapted to regions outside Galar acquired this appearance. If you've lost something, this Pokémon can likely find it.

HOW TO SAY IT: ZIG-zag-GOON **METRIC HEIGHT:** 0.4 m
IMPERIAL HEIGHT: 1'04" **METRIC WEIGHT:** 17.5 kg
IMPERIAL WEIGHT: 38.6 lbs.

POSSIBLE MOVES: Baby-Doll Eyes, Belly Drum, Covet, Double-Edge, Flail, Fling, Growl, Headbutt, Pin Missile, Rest, Sand Attack, Tackle, Tail Whip, Take Down

ZIGZAGOON   **LINOONE**

GALARIAN ZIGZAGOON
Tiny Raccoon Pokémon

TYPE: DARK-NORMAL

Its restlessness has it constantly running around. If it sees another Pokémon, it will purposely run into them in order to start a fight.

Thought to be the oldest form of Zigzagoon, it moves in zigzags and wreaks havoc upon its surroundings.

HOW TO SAY IT: ZIG-zag-GOON
IMPERIAL HEIGHT: 1'04"
IMPERIAL WEIGHT: 38.6 lbs.
METRIC HEIGHT: 0.4 m
METRIC WEIGHT: 17.5 kg

POSSIBLE MOVES: Baby-Doll Eyes, Counter, Double-Edge, Headbutt, Leer, Lick, Pin Missile, Rest, Sand Attack, Scary Face, Snarl, Tackle, Take Down, Taunt

GALARIAN ZIGZAGOON   **GALARIAN LINOONE**   **OBSTAGOON**

ZOROARK

Illusion Fox Pokémon

TYPE: DARK

This Pokémon cares deeply about others of its kind, and it will conjure terrifying illusions to keep its den and pack safe.

Seeking to ease the burden of their solitude, lonely Trainers tell Zoroark to show illusions to them.

HOW TO SAY IT: ZORE-oh-ark
IMPERIAL HEIGHT: 5'03"
IMPERIAL WEIGHT: 178.8 lbs.
METRIC HEIGHT: 1.6 m
METRIC WEIGHT: 81.1 kg

POSSIBLE MOVES: Night Daze, Imprison, U-turn, Scratch, Leer, Pursuit, Hone Claws, Fury Swipes, Feint Attack, Scary Face, Taunt, Foul Play, Night Slash, Torment, Agility, Embargo, Punishment, Nasty Plot

ZORUA   ZOROARK

ZORUA

Tricky Fox Pokémon

TYPE: DARK

Zorua is a timid Pokémon. This disposition seems to be what led to the development of Zorua's ability to take on the forms of other creatures.

Zorua sometimes transforms into a person and goes into cities to search for food. When Zorua does this, it usually takes on the form of a child.

HOW TO SAY IT: ZORE-oo-ah
IMPERIAL HEIGHT: 2'04"
IMPERIAL WEIGHT: 27.6 lbs.
METRIC HEIGHT: 0.7 m
METRIC WEIGHT: 12.5 kg

POSSIBLE MOVES: Scratch, Leer, Pursuit, Fake Tears, Fury Swipes, Feint Attack, Scary Face, Taunt, Foul Play, Torment, Agility, Embargo, Punishment, Nasty Plot, Imprison, Night Daze

ZORUA   ZOROARK

ZUBAT
Bat Pokémon

TYPE: POISON-FLYING

Emits ultrasonic cries while it flies. They act as a sonar used to check for objects in its way.

HOW TO SAY IT: ZOO-bat
IMPERIAL HEIGHT: 2'07"
IMPERIAL WEIGHT: 16.5 lbs.
METRIC HEIGHT: 0.8 m
METRIC WEIGHT: 7.5 kg

POSSIBLE MOVES: Absorb, Supersonic, Astonish, Bite, Wing Attack, Confuse Ray, Air Cutter, Swift, Poison Fang, Mean Look, Leech Life, Haze, Venoshock, Air Slash, Quick Guard

ZUBAT   GOLBAT   CROBAT

ZWEILOUS
Hostile Pokémon

TYPE: DARK-DRAGON

While hunting for prey, Zweilous wanders its territory, its two heads often bickering over which way to go.

Their two heads will fight each other over a single piece of food. Zweilous are covered in scars even without battling others.

HOW TO SAY IT: ZVY-lus
IMPERIAL HEIGHT: 4'07"
IMPERIAL WEIGHT: 110.2 lbs.
METRIC HEIGHT: 1.4 m
METRIC WEIGHT: 50.0 kg

POSSIBLE MOVES: Assurance, Bite, Body Slam, Crunch, Double Hit, Dragon Breath, Dragon Pulse, Dragon Rush, Focus Energy, Headbutt, Hyper Voice, Nasty Plot, Outrage, Roar, Scary Face, Slam, Tackle, Work Up

DEINO   ZWEILOUS   HYDREIGON

ZYGARDE

Order Pokémon

LEGENDARY POKÉMON

TYPE: DRAGON-GROUND

HOW TO SAY IT: ZY-gard

POSSIBLE MOVES: Glare, Bulldoze, Dragon Breath, Bite, Safeguard, Dig, Bind, Land's Wrath, Sandstorm, Haze, Crunch, Earthquake, Camouflage, Dragon Pulse, Coil, Outrage

ZYGARDE CORE

ZYGARDE 10%

This is Zygarde when about 10% of its pieces have been assembled. It leaps at its opponent's chest and sinks its sharp fangs into them.

Born when around 10% of Zygarde's cells have been gathered from all over, this form is skilled in close-range combat.

IMPERIAL HEIGHT: 3'11"
IMPERIAL WEIGHT: 73.9 lbs.

METRIC HEIGHT: 1.2 m
METRIC WEIGHT: 33.5 kg

ZYGARDE 50%

This is Zygarde's form when about half of its pieces have been assembled. It plays the role of monitoring the ecosystem.

Some say it can change to an even more powerful form when battling those who threaten the ecosystem.

IMPERIAL HEIGHT: 16'05"
IMPERIAL WEIGHT: 672.4 lbs.

METRIC HEIGHT: 5.0 m
METRIC WEIGHT: 305.0 kg

ZYGARDE COMPLETE

This is Zygarde's perfected form. From the orifice on its chest, it radiates high-powered energy that eliminates everything.

Born when all of Zygarde's cells have been gathered together, it uses force to neutralize those who harm the ecosystem.

IMPERIAL HEIGHT: 14'09"
IMPERIAL WEIGHT: 1,344.8 lbs.

METRIC HEIGHT: 4.5 m
METRIC WEIGHT: 610.0 kg

DOES NOT EVOLVE